HANNAH LUCINDA SMIT[...]                              [...]ey,
where she has covered confl[...]                   [...]o-
versial president Recep T[...]                      [...]he
country, she has also repo[...]                     [...]he
frontlines of the battle against Isis in Iraq, and joined the mass
movement of migrants on their journey to Europe in 2015.

'A comprehensive and nuanced account of Erdoğan's rule and the way he has ridden the tides of politics. For anyone interested in Turkey it is a must, but it also roams widely through the study of power and populism, full of revealing detail . . . Smith has a subtle intelligence; she deftly weaves the blowback from the collapse of Syria into her contemporary story . . . She writes very well, with an engaging mix of personal anecdote, acute observation, interviews and well-informed research; there's no fat on this book and never a dull page'

*The Times*

'Does a brilliant job of revealing what has been going on in Turkey . . . Smith adheres to the journalist's dictum that to find out what is really happening requires asking the right people. Written in a lively and inviting style, her book records journeys throughout Turkey and its borders in search of those who can help to explain, or at least illuminate, Erdoğan's years in power'  *TLS*

'Offers a lucid explanation of how, since 2001, one man has dominated the Turkish political stage . . . The Western media tends to take a very one-dimensional view of [Erdoğan] . . . Yet this book reminds us that no one has done more to help Turkey's Kurds, bringing employment and huge investment into the southeast . . . It is refreshing that Smith has used a wide-angle lens to capture her subject with accuracy and fairness'  Diana Darke, *TLS Books of the Year*

'A fine book showing an aptitude to look way beyond the surface, and an eye for telling details which comes from her being an accomplished journalist based in Turkey'  *Independent*

'One should begin by applauding Smith's courage and determination in remaining in both Syria and Turkey during their upheavals and keeping her cool as a journalist . . . Could not be timelier . . . Excels in explaining elements of recent Turkish history'  *New Statesman*

# ERDOĞAN RISING

A Warning to Europe

HANNAH LUCINDA SMITH

WILLIAM
COLLINS

William Collins
An imprint of HarperCollins*Publishers*
1 London Bridge Street
London SE1 9GF

WilliamCollinsBooks.com

First published in Great Britain in 2019 by William Collins
This William Collins paperback edition published in 2020

1

ISBN 978-0-00-830888-9

Maps by Martin Brown
Typeset in Garamond 3 LT Std by
Palimpsest Book Production Ltd, Falkirk, Stirlingshire

Printed and bound in Great Britain by
CPI Group (UK) Ltd, Croydon CRO 4YY

For my dad, who planted so many seeds

# CONTENTS

# MAPS

# CAST OF CHARACTERS

*Clique*

**Recep Tayyip Erdoğan**    president of Turkey, former prime minister and mayor of Istanbul

**Berat Albayrak**    Erdoğan's son-in-law, current economy minister

**Hüseyin Besli**    Erdoğan's speechwriter

**Ahmet Davutoğlu**    foreign minister, later Turkish prime minister

**Necmettin Erbakan**    leader of the National Salvation Party, Erdoğan's first party

**Abdullah Gül**    Erdoğan's early ally, former president

**İbrahim Kalın**    Erdoğan's spokesman

**Hilâl Kaplan**    pro-Erdoğan journalist

**Erol Olçok**    spin doctor

## Opposition

**Mustafa Kemal Atatürk**    founder of the Turkish Republic

**Selahattin Demirtaş**    Kurdish political leader

**Muharrem İnce**    Erdoğan's 2018 presidential rival

**Kemal Kılıçdaroğlu**    leader of the opposition

## Enemies

**Fethullah Gülen**    Islamist cleric and accused coup plotter

**Abdullah Öcalan**    leader of the PKK, Kurdish militant group

# ACRONYMS

**AKP** *Adalet ve Kalkınma Partisi*: Justice and Development Party, Erdoğan's group, centre-right Islamist

**CHP** *Cumhuriyet Halk Partisi*: Republican People's Party, Atatürk's group and main opposition, led by Kemal Kılıçdaroğlu, left-leaning secularist

**FSA** Free Syrian Army: mainstream armed opposition to Syria's President Bashar al-Assad. Originally nationalist, later infiltrated and overtaken by Islamist elements. Supported at various times by Turkey, Qatar, Saudi Arabia, US, UK and other European countries

**HDP** *Halkların Demokratik Partisi*: People's Democratic Party, main Kurdish group, led by Selahattin Demirtaş

**Isis** Islamic State of Iraq and Syria: extreme Islamist group comprised mainly of foreign fighters who travelled into Syria via Turkey. Initially tolerated by the FSA, later turned against them and seized huge tracts of rebel-held Syria

**JAN** *Jabhat al-Nusra*: the Support Front, Al-Qaeda's franchise in Syria. Comprised mainly of Syrian Islamists, largely fought alongside the FSA. Listed as a terror group by the US in December 2012

**MSP** *Milli Selâmet Partisi*: National Salvation Party, main Islamist group in 1970s and Erdoğan's first party, led by Necmettin Erbakan, anti-Western Islamist. Closed following the 1980 coup

**PKK** *Partiye Karkerên Kurdistanê*: Kurdistan Workers' Party, Kurdish militia founded by Abdullah Öcalan in 1978, fighting insurgency in south-eastern Turkey since 1984. Banned in Turkey, EU and United States

**RP** *Refah Partisi*: Welfare Party, Erbakan's new group and main Islamist party in 1980s and 1990s. Closed following the 1997 coup

**YPG** *Yekîneyên Parastina Gel*: People's Protection Units, Syrian wing of the PKK. Founded in 2004 but rose to prominence during the Syrian conflict. Classed as terror group in Turkey; allied with US in fight against Isis

# TIMELINE

1923   Atatürk founds the Turkish Republic

1938   Atatürk dies

1950   Turkey's first democratic elections

1960   First coup of the republic

1971   Second coup of the republic

1980   Third coup of the republic

1994   Erdoğan becomes mayor of Istanbul

1997   'Postmodern coup' brings down Necmettin Erbakan, Turkey's first Islamist prime minister

1998   Erdoğan sent to prison for reciting Islamist poem at a rally

2002   November: AKP voted in for the first time

2003   March: Erdoğan becomes prime minister

2007   Abdullah Gül becomes president

2011   Syrian uprising begins

2013 March: Turkey begins peace process with the PKK
     May/June: Gezi park protests in Turkey
     December: Corruption scandal rocks the AKP, crackdown on
     Fethullah Gülen begins

2014 August: Erdoğan steps down as prime minister and becomes
     Turkey's first directly elected president

2015 Refugee crisis brings more than a million people from Turkey
     to the European Union
     July: Turkey–PKK ceasefire collapses

2016 March: Turkey and EU sign 6 billion euro refugee deal
     July: Rogue generals launch coup attempt against Erdoğan

2017 April: Erdoğan wins constitutional referendum to change
     Turkey from parliamentary to presidential system

2018 June: Erdoğan wins presidential elections, triggering constitu-
     tional reforms and installing him in the palace until 2023

Yet the school of Turkish politics was so ignoble that not even the best could graduate from it unaffected.

T. E. Lawrence, *Seven Pillars of Wisdom*

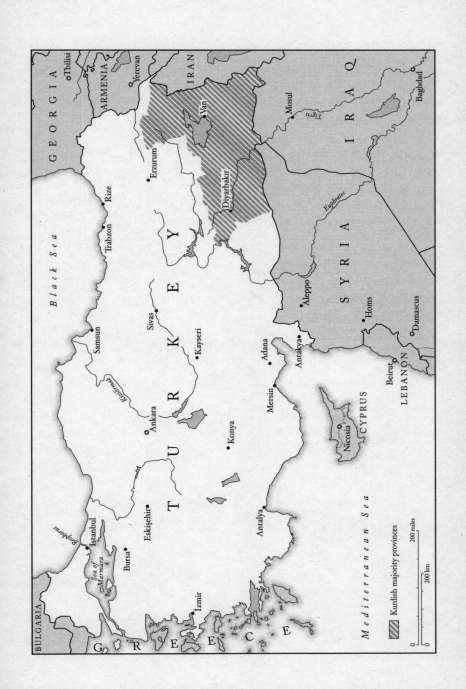

Kurdish majority provinces

# INTRODUCTION

*July 2016*

It is less than forty-eight hours since rogue soldiers tried to kill him and here Erdoğan is, back on stage. The sun is setting and the call to prayer is sounding, and the president is wiping a tear from his eye.

'Erol was an old friend of mine,' he starts, then breaks. 'I cannot speak any more. God is great.'

Erol Olçok: Erdoğan's ad man, his trusted spin doctor, his loyal friend. One of the first to race to the Bosphorus bridge, his corpse now before us in a coffin.

Nothing will be as it was before, for Olçok's family, for Erdoğan, or for Turkey. Two nights ago, as Istanbul's glitterati sat drinking on the banks of the Bosphorus, tanks filled the bridge and war planes split the skies. The army was revolting against Erdoğan – but soon Erdoğan's own infantry was on the streets, with Erol Olçok at the first line. Bare-chested young men stood side by side with headscarved women in front of machine-gun fire on this midsummer night; others lay down on tarmac in front of rolling tanks. And as fortunes turned against the putschist generals, Erdoğan's angry, shirtless, sweaty men removed their belts to whip the coup's surrendering foot soldiers.

Their twisted faces were lit with the perfect aura of an early summer's morning in Istanbul: a glorious backdrop of dawn over the city that spans two continents. The images flew around social media within minutes. They were beautiful, and they were horrifying.

The coup has been crushed but the toll is huge. Two hundred and sixty-five people have died over the bloody span of this night, more than half of them civilians who came out to resist in Erdoğan's name. Erol Olçok was shot dead alongside his sixteen-year-old son, Abdullah, as soldiers fired into the protesters on the bridge. Thousands more have been injured. There are still sporadic bursts of fighting as suspected plotters resist arrest; Istanbul's airspace reverberates with the roar of patrolling F-16 fighter jets. The streets have been hauntingly quiet all weekend, as Turks stay inside, watch the news and pray.

Among the dead: a local mayor shot point blank in the stomach as he tried to speak with the soldiers; the older brother of one of Erdoğan's aides; a famous columnist with the pro-government newspaper *Yeni Şafak*. A crack team of special forces soldiers had burst into the Mediterranean resort where Erdoğan was holidaying, ready to kill him if necessary and missing him only by minutes.

Erdoğan has already bounced back, his close brush with death seemingly leaving no dent. He has returned to Istanbul, banished the soldiers back to their barracks, and called the coup attempt a 'gift from God' that will allow him to finally cleanse the state of those trying to destroy it. Six thousand people have been detained by the time he addresses the thousands-strong crowd at Erol Olçok's funeral, at a mosque on the Asian side of Istanbul. The imam implores God as he leads the prayers for the slain man and his son: 'Protect us from the wickedness of the educated!'

A weight is descending on Turkey. Each night Taksim Square fills with huge crowds of Erdoğan's supporters, turning out to make sure his enemies don't come back. Within days a state of emergency is declared, and every day thousands more suspected collaborators are arrested. The alleged ringleaders are paraded on state television with black eyes and bandages around their heads.

Privately, friends tell me they are worried. *Goodbye to the Republic*, writes one by text message. *Goodbye to democracy*.

The heart of my Istanbul neighbourhood, which usually bustles at all hours with street sellers, taxi drivers and prostitutes, is near-silent the morning after the coup; the pavements empty, the traffic thinned down to a few lonely cars. The only people I bump into as I walk around the deserted streets are the women who always stand on the main thoroughfare on a Saturday, selling black-and-white postcards to the shoppers. Usually they ask for five liras for this low-resolution print of Atatürk, father to the Turkish nation. Today, a middle-aged woman with blonde perm presses one silently into my hand.

'Man, this is nothing but a country of cults,' says my friend Yusuf a few days later, dazed and still trying to make sense of what is unfolding. 'It's Jerusalem in the Year Zero.'

In the years that have passed since July 2016, as I have filled newspaper column inches with stories of Erdoğan's swelling crackdown on his opponents, his skewed election wins and questionable wars, I have been asked the same question time and again: 'Why doesn't the West just cut Erdoğan off? Make him a pariah, and leave him and Turkey to go their own way?'

The morality is complex but the answer is simple: we can't turn our backs on Turkey because Turkey and Erdoğan matter. Forget old clichés about East-meets-West – it is far more important than that. Here is a country that buffers Europe on one side, the Middle East on another, and the old Soviet Union on a third – and which absorbs the impacts of chaos and upheaval in each of those regions. During the Soviet era, it took in refugees from the eastern bloc looking to escape the despotism of communism. When that empire collapsed, it became a place where the poor ex-Soviets went for work, and the rich showed up to party. Now, with the Middle East sinking into ever-greater turmoil, it is the world's biggest refugee-hosting nation, with five million from Syria, Iraq, Afghanistan and others.

Turkey is a member of the G20, and is recognised as one of the world's largest economies. It has the second biggest army in NATO, the Western military alliance which, with the rising expansionist ambitions of Russian President Vladimir Putin, is finding itself sucked into a new Cold War. More than six million Turks live abroad, the street ambassadors of a country that trades and negotiates with almost every other nation on earth. This is not a far-off hermit-state, isolated from the rest of the world. It is a major player, vital to global security and prosperity.

For millennia, the ground on which modern Turkey stands has been coveted and fought over because it stands at the nexus of trade routes and civilisations. To see it for yourself, spend an hour people-watching under the soaring ceiling of the new Istanbul airport, the biggest of Erdoğan's increasingly outlandish vanity construction projects. It was opened in April 2019, and the Turkish government says that more than 200 million people will pass through its halls by the year 2022, making it the biggest and busiest in the world – twice as many passengers as Atlanta Airport, two and a half times as many as Heathrow. Cruise through its duty-free shopping area and you will spot Gulf Arab women wrapped in black fabric with only their eyes showing alongside sunburnt and flustered Brits in ill-advised tank-tops and shorts. There will be dreadlocked backpackers, preened Russian princesses, and, if you time it right, Islamic pilgrims swathed in white sheets making their way to Mecca. There will be people with wide Asiatic faces, and statuesque African women swathed in fabulous prints. Turkey sits at the centre of all of this.

It sits, too, at the centre of the journeys that the people on the wrong side of globalisation are making – the illicit trafficking routes that stretch from the Middle East and Africa, through Turkey and the Aegean Sea to Europe. In Istanbul's backstreet tea shops another kind of travel market is flourishing, no less buoyant than that in the ticket halls of the new Istanbul airport. Here, shady men in leather jackets cut deadly deals with desperate people. Survival does not come guaranteed with a smuggler's ticket to Europe, but it will cost you more than a budget flight from the shiny new airport.

So let's think about what might happen if Erdoğan were to turn Turkey's back on the West entirely, or if the country were to descend into full-on chaos. That surge of people in 2015, travelling from Turkey's shores to Greece in search of a new life in Europe? That was nothing. There are millions more in the developing world still desperate to make that journey, and a collapsed Turkey could be their back door. What if, even worse, there were to be a major conflict or economic collapse in Turkey itself? Not only would thousands, perhaps millions, of Turks join the flow to Europe, but shrewd leaders like Russia's Vladimir Putin would be quick to capitalise on the chaos to expand his territories and influence, just as he has done in Syria.

Erdoğan is no fool. He knows how important he is and he plays on it, often seeming to push his Western allies' buttons just to see what will happen. He may sometimes look like a man deranged, but he is also a smart political operator who was refining his brand of populism a decade and a half before Donald Trump cottoned on. If Western countries want to contain and control Erdoğan – as they will have to if they are to keep Turkey stable and engaged in the world – then first they need to understand him. More than that, they need to understand why so many Turks adore him.

What is there to adore? On the face of it, not very much. Recep Tayyip Erdoğan lives in a thousand-room palace complex, Aksaray (White Palace), that he built almost immediately on becoming president. He and his followers have a taste for outlandish historical dressing-up. In a photo call with Palestinian President Mahmoud Abbas, he posed on the staircase of Aksaray with soldiers decked out in costumes from the various eras of the Ottoman Empire. Despite his constant harping on about his working-class roots, and his apparent championing of the underdog against the elites, his wife and daughters dress in haute couture from the famous fashion houses of Europe.

The party Erdoğan leads, the Justice and Development Party (*Adalet ve Kalkınma Partisi*, or AKP), is the most successful in Turkey's democratic history, even though it has never won more than 50 per cent of the vote. Erdoğan himself has stood at the helm of Turkish politics longer than any other leader in the country's history. Since first becoming prime minister in 2003 he has quashed the power of the military, rewritten the country's constitution, remoulded its foreign relations and mastered divide-and-rule politics better than any other current world leader.

Erdoğan's grip on power might often appear shaky – he only just clinches victory each time he takes his country to the ballot box. But it is this constant sense of threat, this dread that he could be ousted and everything go back to the way it was before he came, that galvanises his supporters. He is not an Assad or a Putin, who use their faked and overwhelming electoral victories to cling on in their palaces. Erdoğan's continuing dominance over Turkey rests as heavily on those who despise him as it does on those who idolise him. In order to be loved more, he must show his fanbase that there are those who are ready to overthrow him – and could feasibly do so. So, too, must they sense the constant threat in order to feel the wave of overwhelming ecstasy when he comes out on top after yet another crisis – and there have been many of those.

Turkey is still officially a candidate for EU membership, yet in my time covering this country as a newspaper correspondent I have been detained by the police twice, tear-gassed more times than I can remember, and had a Turkish tank turn its turret on me as I tried to speak with Syrians fleeing an onslaught of violence behind the closed border. From my front door I have watched the country I call home nosedive down the rankings for democracy, press freedom and human rights. Like every other journalist in Turkey I am constantly reconfiguring the limits of what I can say. Can I laugh? Criticise? Question? The threat of imprisonment or deportation always lingers in the air for the country's international press corps, but for Turkish journalists it is real. Some sixty-eight are currently behind bars, the highest number of any country in the world. Add to them the tens of thousands of academics, opposition activists, serving politicians and alleged coup plotters who are also languishing in jail, waiting for trials that are likely to take years to come to court, and you start to get a sense of the kind of country Turkey has become – although a tourist searching for a cheap holiday might still look at the weak lira and the turquoise seas and happily bring their family here for a fortnight. While the package-deal masses race to the all-inclusive resorts and adventurous weekenders explore Istanbul's atmospheric backstreets, Turks are watching their savings crumble, food prices soar and their children frantically search for any way out of the country.

To write – and to live – under Erdoğan's tightening authoritarianism is to cohabit with a voice in your head that asks *Are you sure you want to say that?* every time you press send on an article or crack a joke with a stranger. It is to see your tendency for social smoking soar into a daily, furtive habit that you indulge by the window late at night, and then to look in the mirror in the morning and realise that the faint worry line between your eyebrows is setting into a deep crevice. Dictatorship screws with your sex life; it makes you go through an internal checklist on every person you meet – what are they wearing? Where are they from? Who do they work for and how far can I trust them? I hear my neighbours rowing more often these days, witness more fights breaking out on Istanbul's streets. The Turks who love the way things are going like to rub it in everyone else's face. The Turks who hate it usually spill everything to the Westerners they meet – some of the few safe sounding boards they have left. Conversations that start with 'How long have you lived in Turkey?' usually come round to 'Why on earth do you still stay?' The stress of wondering if your phone is tapped and your flat being watched slows down your brain, becomes a tiring distraction, while at some point, you realise that all your conversations with friends come back to politics, and that although there is plenty of material for cynical, satirical humour none of it makes you feel much better once you're done laughing. To live in this system is to watch people you know be seduced by power and money, and happily throw away their moral compass as they pursue them. It is to suck up to people you despise because in order to survive you have to – and then to start despising yourself.

All of this creeps up on you, and by the time you realise what you are looking at it is already too late. It was only after the coup attempt that I saw clearly what had been happening all along – the descent of Turkey's shaking democracy into one-man rule, the dawn of the state of Erdoğan. While I was focusing on the minutiae of daily news, on the war in Syria and the refugee crisis in Europe, his dominance had grown so entrenched that he had become inseparable from the state, and the state indivisible from the nation. Now, the answer to the eternal question posed by every journalist in Turkey is that it is fine to laugh and question and criticise – so long as you leave Erdoğan out of it. But in a country so monopolised, that leaves very little room for any discussion at all.

I have seen Turkey and Erdoğan through seven elections, dozens of terror attacks, a coup attempt, a civil war, foreign misadventures, slanging matches with Europe, mass street protests, a refugee influx and a massive purge of the public sector. And each time, when I have thought, *this must be it, this will finish him*, he has come out on top even stronger.

I have to give it to him – Turkey's president has handed me some great material. Often, I have wished I could hand it back.

Erdoğan is the original postmodern populist. In power for seventeen years, his latest election win in June 2018 means he will stay until at least 2023. Already there is a generation of Turks who can remember little or nothing before the Erdoğan era, and his detractors have much to worry about. They fret over his creeping Islamisation of Turkey, once the staunchest of secular states. They point to his fierce crackdown on Kurdish rebels in the east of his country, where hundreds of thousands have been killed or displaced, and his cosiness with armed rebel groups of questionable ideology in Syria. Europe, which once saw Erdoğan as its darling, now deals with him increasingly as if he were an obnoxious teenager. The inhabitants of the Greek islands within spitting distance of the Turkish coast hold their collective breath and brace each time he threatens to open his borders to allow hundreds of thousands of migrants to flow across the Aegean in cheap plastic boats.

I have spent six years watching Erdoğan, speaking to his followers, and sniffing the winds. I think about him every day and write about him on most days, even though we have never met. But I never set out to be an Erdoğan-watcher, or even to be a Turkey correspondent.

In early 2013 I moved from London to Antakya, a tiny town on Turkey's southern border with Syria, to pursue a career as a freelance war correspondent. The war next door had turned Antakya into a busy hive of spooks, arms dealers, refugees and journalists. The Syrian rebels had captured two nearby border crossings from President Bashar al-Assad's forces, and I spent a year crossing back and forth through them into Syria to report on the spiralling slaughter. But as Syria turned darker and colleagues started to go missing at the hands of criminal gangs and Islamist militias, the journalists dropped away from Antakya. Along with most of the Syria reporter crowd I moved north, to Istanbul, where not so much was happening.

The huge Gezi Park protests, which in the spring of 2013 had briefly morphed from small environmentalist demonstrations into the most serious street opposition Erdoğan had ever faced, had now petered out into leftist forums scattered across Istanbul's upmarket districts. They were happy protests – anyone could stand on a soapbox and, instead of clapping (too bawdy and overwhelming), the audience would wiggle their raised hands in appreciation. I doubt they caused Erdoğan too much anguish. For a year or so after Gezi, small-scale street demonstrations became the city's number one participation sport – with protagonists boiled down to a hard core who just seemed to enjoy getting tear-gassed. One student ringleader I interviewed talked about upcoming protests as 'clashes with the cops', as if that were the main point of the event. The demonstrations became so common and predictable they were more of a nuisance than news. Several times over the course of that year, tear gas seeped into my bedroom as I tried to sleep.

I was bored and sad. I had left Syria, a story I had moved countries for and invested so much energy in. I yearned for the day I could go back and start reporting from there again. I was still dating a Syrian man down in Antakya, and I spent half of my time there with him. Strange as it feels to remember it now, there just wasn't much of a story up in Istanbul.

But one day I fell in love. Travelling back from Antakya to Istanbul on the cheap late-night flight, I looked out of the window as the plane came in to land in a huge swoop across the city. On either side of the black scar of the Bosphorus, millions of pinprick lights marked out the shape of the shoreline, the traffic-clogged roads, the bridges and the palaces. From above, this scruffy city glistens, and I was glad to be back: it's a feeling I still get every time the seatbelt sign comes on over Istanbul. It had taken me six months to realise that my banishment from Syria had landed me in the most beautiful, melancholy, fascinating city in the world. Gradually I stopped going down to Antakya, and my relationship with the Syrian fell away.

So, by chance rather than by my own good judgement, I was one of the few reporters based in Turkey full time when the news started flowing – the bombings, the diplomatic spats with Europe, and the overwhelming interest in Erdoğan. As the months progressed, I realised that even the most parochial, insignificant Turkish story could make a headline if Erdoğan were somehow involved. One I particularly remember is a story about his wife, Emine, and a speech she had made suggesting that the Ottoman sultans' harem, the place where scores of potential sexual partners were kept, could be considered a bastion of feminism. The Western press went nuts – even though there is a serious line of academic debate that would concur with Emine. The interest in Erdoğan, as well as the growing chaos in Turkey, soon landed me regular work filing reports for *The Times*.

I found myself fascinated by him, too. The first time I saw Erdoğan in the flesh was not for a story – it was just because I happened to be in the area and was interested. In May 2013, while I was still living in Antakya, a double car-bombing hit Reyhanlı, another small Turkish border town hosting thousands of Syrian refugees. The attack was the first spill-over from the Syrian conflict, and the toll was horrific: fifty-two people killed and the heart of the town ripped out. Pieces of seared flesh were later found in the town's sewers, so intense was the force of the blasts. Some Syrians headed back across the border into the war zone, fearing they might soon feel the brunt of the locals' anger if they stayed. A week later, Erdoğan went to Reyhanlı to speak to the people. As it was only half an hour down the road from Antakya, I decided to go.

Compared to what I would see in later years, the crowd then was small and calm and Erdoğan's speech was measured. But that day I noticed certain things I would go on to see again and again: how hundreds of people appeared to have been bussed in from every corner of the country, how party volunteers were handing out flags and baseball caps which, when televised, gave the appearance of a sea of red, and how the people who had showed up seemed to care far more about being close to Erdoğan than about what had happened in Reyhanlı.

How different that low-key event was to the time I saw him four years later, on a chilly May Sunday in 2017. It was a month after he had snatched narrow victory in a constitutional referendum to switch legislative power from the parliament to the president, and the AKP was holding its party congress in Ankara's main basketball arena. By the time I took my seat at 8 a.m., the entire place was packed and rowdy with young men chanting for their hero. Erdoğan was due to take the stage around noon, to reclaim his place at the head of the party. He had nominally stepped down when he resigned as prime minister and was elected president three years earlier – the head of state was supposed to be politically unaffiliated according to the old, now-discarded constitution. In reality he had never loosened his grip over the party. He continued to campaign for the AKP in parliamentary elections, and had publicly ousted a prime minister who had dared to stray too far from his line.

As a political spectacle, the congress was incredible. There were men in the crowd who had arrived dressed as Ottoman sultans, sitting alongside Kurdish women holding banners proclaiming they were from Şırnak, an eastern town that had recently been decimated by fighting between Turkish security forces and Kurdish militants. 'Everything for the homeland!' they whooped, ululating as Middle Easterners do at weddings – a bizarre celebration of their home town having been smashed to rubble. Music boomed non-stop from the speakers – a limited repeat playlist of Ottoman marching music, and the referendum campaign song titled 'Yes, of course'. The one that got the loudest singalong was the *dombra*, a paean to Erdoğan and an unashamedly cringing anthem. 'He is the voice of the oppressed, he is the lush voice of a silent world. Recep Tayyip Erdoğan!' the lyrics begin, continuing on a similar theme through four verses.

Erdoğan entered the building as scheduled, accompanied by his wife and son-in-law, the then-energy minister Berat Albayrak, who most believe he is priming as heir. Tubs of red carnations had been strategically placed around the edges of the stands and Erdoğan threw them out to his adoring crowd as he did a victory lap. The grey men on the stage must have felt rather outshone as they reeled through their dry lists of candidates for various posts within the party. For top job Erdoğan was standing uncontested, and that was the only item on the agenda that really mattered.

Turkey is different from the other countries falling under the sway of strongmen. It boasts not one, but two – perhaps even three or four – coexisting personality cults.

· There is Erdoğan's, a cult in the ascendant I have seen evolve before my eyes. There is the cult of Abdullah Öcalan, the grand-fatherly-cum-psychopathic leader of the PKK (*Partiya Karkerên Kurdistanê*, the Kurdistan Workers' Party – the Kurdish militia fighting against the state in eastern Turkey), who has been banged up in an island prison since 1999, yet still commands a huge following among the Kurds and their diaspora. As well as the Turkish PKK there are affiliated militias fighting in his name in Syria, Iraq and

Iran. His appeal stretches to Western leftists who are so enchanted by his ideas on women's equality and government without the state that they are willing to overlook the atrocities that his gunmen and women commit. As the latest peace process broke down in the summer of 2015, I went to interview Öcalan's brother in the south-eastern mountains of Turkey, having been told I would find him an intelligent, sensible kind of guy who would give me an honest account of his notorious sibling. Mehmet Öcalan's home-grown figs were delicious, but the interview quickly veered into the bizarre. He tried to convince me that his brother knew, and by extension controlled, exactly what was going on in the Middle East day by day from his solitary prison cell, thanks to his psychic powers. Throughout, he referred to him as 'Serok' (Kurdish for 'leader') – never Abdullah or 'my brother'.

There was, and perhaps still is, the cult of Fethullah Gülen, a wizened Islamic cleric who has been commanding a network of secretive followers since the 1960s. He has been living in exile on a secluded and heavily guarded ranch in Pennsylvania, USA since the 1990s, but until recently his devotees occupied high ranks within the Turkish bureaucracy, police and judiciary. They used their positions to bully and punish anyone who opposed them, most notably secularists who were uneasy with the idea of a secret Islamic cult wielding so much power in their country. Erdoğan and Gülen were allies, of sorts, until they fell out spectacularly in 2013 and began a personal war played out through the state. Erdoğan accuses Gülen of organising the attempted coup of 2016. At present, a Turk's life can be ruined by the mere suggestion that they have at any time and in any way been affiliated with the movement.

And then there is the cult of Mustafa Kemal Atatürk, founder of the Turkish republic and possibly the only man capable of raising a serious challenge to Erdoğan despite the fact that he has been dead for eighty-one years. Atatürk – or at least the Atatürk who is still very much alive in the imagination of today's Turks – stood for almost everything Erdoğan despises, and vice versa. He was an unbending advocate for secularism, non-aggression in dealings with other states, and a Turkey that is allied to Europe and the West.

Atatürk has always been a Turkish hero, but increasingly he is also the figure Erdoğan's opponents rally around. During the 2017 constitutional referendum campaign the streets of my Istanbul neighbourhood – a secular bastion that voted 81 per cent against Erdoğan's plans to gather power in his own hands – turned into an open-air gallery of Atatürk-inspired artwork. The 'İzmir March', an anthem to militarism and Mustafa Kemal, was the unofficial theme tune of the 'No' campaign. It is common, both inside Turkey and without, to hear Erdoğan's detractors bemoan how he is unravelling Atatürk's legacy.

Maybe it said more about the state of the opposition than it ever did about the enduring strength of Atatürk. There is no question that this cult continues, but its cracks are beginning to show. Over the course of Erdoğan's reign, those who have in the past quietly loathed Atatürk and all he stands for have found they can finally speak out. They are primarily the religious poor, dispossessed by Atatürk's unbending secularism, though they also include liberals who wince at the thought of unbridled adoration in any direction. But those same liberals who once supported the downgrading of Atatürk's legacy are now recoiling at Erdoğan's transformation from man to deity by his followers. And so, Turkey has become a fascinating Petri dish – a perfect place to observe one cult of personality in the ascendant, alongside another in slow decline.

Over six years I have travelled to every corner of this huge, diverse, often baffling and always fascinating country, and have also reported on the chaos it borders in Iraq, Syria and south-eastern Europe. Along the way I have spoken to politicians, criminals, policemen, taxi drivers, warlords, flag-sellers, refugees . . . My notebooks are so stuffed with characters that the material could keep me writing for years. In Erdoğan, I have found the most compelling protagonist a writer could wish for.

But it wasn't the coup attempt that spurred me to write this book, despite all its Hollywood drama and the front pages it garnered. That night in July 2016 was just the prologue, the scene-setter for the real tragedy that then unfolded. I started writing this book a year on, after the grandiose celebrations held on the first anniversary of the coup attempt revealed fully the depth of the personality cult that Erdoğan had assembled. By the time I had finished the first manuscript eleven months later, he had sealed power through the presidential elections that will keep him in his palace until 2023 – two decades at the top of Turkey.

This story is bookended by those two events, but at its core is the entire period in which I have taken a front-row seat at Turkey's descent. When I arrived here in early 2013, thinking that I would stay for a few weeks to report on Syria before going back to my life in London, Erdoğan was just tipping over from being a flawed but largely tolerated democrat to a relentless autocratic populist. Within two years he had turned into a hate figure that the whole world had heard of – and then he led his country into its most turbulent era in decades. In the space of eighteen months in 2015 and 2016, Turkey suffered a refugee crisis, a wave of terror attacks, a fresh eruption of violence in its Kurdish region, and a coup attempt. Since then, even with some kind of daily stability and normality restored for most Turks, Erdoğan has consolidated his position further and stamped down harder on his opposition.

Spotting the narrative's threads has not been easy: his path has not always been steady or clear. Multiple plot lines unfold simultaneously, linears converge and loop back on themselves. Events outside Turkey wash over its borders, feeding forces that are brewing inside the country while Erdoğan holds up his own skewed version of the world to his people like a fun-fair mirror. I worked forwards and backwards through shelves of my notebooks from Turkey and Syria as I wrote, trying to work out what I'd witnessed. I reread old diaries and rang up old friends, trawled through newspaper cuttings from the past twenty-five years and plundered the historical archives at *The Times*.

I spoke to historians and political scientists and drew up huge lists of diplomats, Erdoğan's insiders, lobbyists, advisers and opponents and contacted them all, asking them to speak either on the record or privately. Most of them ignored me, some of them refused. The ones that agreed usually did so on condition of anonymity, and each has shaded their own part of this portrait of Erdoğan and Turkey. Some names have been changed, usually in order to protect people who are still inside Syria or who have families there. In other cases I have referred to interviewees by first names only, or by the position they held. It is a mark of the current state of the country that I cannot thank or acknowledge by name most of the people who have helped me write this book; in the future, in better times, I hope I will be able to do so.

There is a vague chronology to this story, but Turkey never makes sense on a single timeline. To understand the present you need to link it to the past, and to unravel Erdoğan and his followers you must also acquaint yourself with all the other bit-part players who share his stage. Remembering recent history has become an act of rebellion in Erdoğan's Turkey; memories are being erased and events rewritten as he fashions the country to his liking. By 2023, when the next elections are scheduled, the memories of the old parliamentary system will have faded and no one much under forty will have ever voted in an election in which he or his party did not, somehow, claim victory.

So this book is my attempt to document what I have seen, before it is erased from Turkey's official story in the way that history's winners always rub out the bits they do not like. It starts a year on from the coup attempt, in a country that has started to believe its own lies and the middle of a crowd high on the rush of its leader's ascent.

# I

# TWO TURKEYS, TWO TRIBES

*July 2017*
*Coup anniversary*

S tout old grandmas, svelte young women, mustachioed uncles and thick-set hard men: they are all moving together like a single being, and all waving Turkish flags high above their heads. I'm in the middle of a river of red. When I break away and climb up onto the footbridge over the highway they look like microdots in a pixellated image. I squint, and their fluttering crimson flags merge into one pulsating mass.

Serkan watches them stream past with a humorous, anticipatory eye.

'BUYURUUUUUUUN!' he shouts – the call of the Turkish hawker, which imperfectly translates to: 'Please buy from me!'

A family stops to eye his wares, which he has spread on the pavement – a rough stall laden with cheaply made T-shirts, caps and bandanas on which are printed the serious face of a man with a heavy brow and a clipped moustache, usually depicted beneath an array of sycophantic headings:

OUR COMMANDER IN CHIEF!

OUR PRESIDENT!

TURKEY STANDS UPRIGHT WITH YOU!

Serkan – his own mannequin – dons the full set, a cap above his round and ruddy-cheeked face, one of his T-shirts stretched over his middle-age paunch, and his accessories of armbands and a scarf. He wears it all with aplomb, his friendly grin at odds with the stern printed image of Recep Tayyip Erdoğan on display.

'It's just business,' he confides once his customers have moved on. 'I'll sell at any political rally, but right now the Erdoğan merchandise sells the best.'

A few metres further down the pavement the next seller, Savaş, expands.

'Maybe it's because the people who buy the Erdoğan stuff are younger,' he ventures. 'But I sell about six or seven times more at the Erdoğan rallies than I do at the others.'

He is right. Turkey's youth, its largest and most frustrated demographic, is over-represented in the crowd packing through an unremarkable Istanbul neighbourhood this July evening. There are families here too, and ballsy young women in headscarves hustling along in tight groups. One of them waves a printed placard: WE HAVE ERDOĞAN, THEY DON'T! But the more I keep moving with the mass of people, the more I might fool myself that I'm on my way to a football match.

Tonight these streets are theirs – the Erdoğan fanatics – celebrating the first anniversary of the failed coup, which, in the year since the guns fell silent, has opened the way for Erdoğan to grab even more power. For this crowd, that is a reason to party. We are heading for one of the icons of Istanbul, the graceful bridge arching over the Bosphorus Strait that, when the sun sets, sparkles with thousands of colour-shifting fairy lights. One of my favourite indulgences is to cross this bridge in a speeding public minibus late at night, boozy and sentimental. Look to the right as you cross from Europe to Asia and you see the southern end of the strait open out suddenly into the Sea of Marmara, backlit by the silhouettes of Istanbul's Ottoman centre in the distance. To your left you see a decadent spread of rococo palaces along the river banks, alongside the turrets of the Kuleli military high school, *alma mater* of generations of ambitious young officers, and the minarets of the monumental, neo-Ottoman Çamlıca Mosque, Erdoğan's tribute to himself. However rowdy the bus is in the early hours, it always falls silent on the approach to this mesmerising vista.

Within weeks of the coup attempt the bridge was renamed and rebranded – now it is the 15th July Martyrs' Bridge, a monument to Erdoğan's finest hour. The road signs have been rewritten, and new announcements recorded for the bus routes. On this anniversary night it is the epicentre of the commemorations; the roads leading onto it have been lined with loudspeakers blasting out patriotic music to spur on the thousands of people milling around.

Erdoğan is the star of this show. First, he unveils a memorial to the martyrs. Stuck up on a grassy hill at the east side of the bridge, it resembles a space-age luminescent moon: huge, bright white and incongruous. Inscribed inside it are the names of the civilians who died. The Islamic funeral prayer is broadcast from here loudly, twenty-four hours a day, though, as one of my cynical friends points out, it is impossible to hear it over the roar of the traffic.

Next come the speeches from the stage set up at the apex of the bridge. The immediate audience is VIP only, but big screens have been arranged in the area just outside the eastern entrance for the tens of thousands who are here in order to be in close proximity to their leader. The event is also being streamed live on every Turkish TV channel. As Erdoğan takes his seat, a range of dignitaries take turns to pay homage.

'Thank you to our martyrs, and thank you to our commander in chief!' shrieks the announcer. 'Recep. Tayyip. ERDOĞAAAAAAAAAN!'

Devout men in skullcaps spread flattened cardboard boxes on the road and kneel in the direction of Mecca. Everyone else falls silent as the announcer rolls through the names of the dead. Then Tayyip himself takes to the podium to deliver a speech full of invective against the traitors and the meddling foreign powers, packed with promises to chop off the heads of those responsible. He is then chauffeured to his private jet, which will fly him and his retinue to the capital, Ankara, where they will do it all over again.

Those who do not belong to Erdoğan's fan club escape to Turkey's liberal coastal towns, avoid the TV and newspapers, and drink cocktails on the shores of the Mediterranean until it is over. Yet their president finds them. Shortly before midnight, anyone using a mobile phone gets Erdoğan's recorded message on the other end of the line: 'As your president, I congratulate your July fifteenth democracy and national unity day. I wish God's mercy on our martyrs and health for our veterans,' he says in his distinctive, drawn-out tones. I get six calls within an hour from friends who just want to test it out, not quite believing that even Tayyip would pull such a stunt.

Events like the coup anniversary have become Turkey's rock concerts – especially since the actual concerts dried up. I had tickets to see Skunk Anansie, a band I was obsessed with as a teenager, with an old school friend in Istanbul a few days after the coup. But the band cancelled the gig soon after the news broke of the 15 July massacres. Attendance at football matches – a working-class passion in Turkey – has also fallen since the Passolig, an electronic ticketing system designed to stamp out hooliganism, was introduced in 2014. Turkish politicians, though, always seem to find reasons to get on stage to bellow to their flag wavers.

At least the street sellers still have events where they can hawk their merchandise.

'I used to sell at the football matches,' says Mehmet, a small, gnarled old man with a thick grey moustache and a clear disdain for this evening's show. 'You know – fake team shirts, scarves, that kind of thing. Then they started cracking down on us. The Zabıta' – a unique Turkish crossbreed of trading-standards-officer-meets-traffic-warden – 'started issuing fines, and now the teams' lawyers walk around and check out our stalls. If they see you selling anything with logos, they sue you.'

'When did the crackdown begin?' I ask.

'When Erdoğan came to power!' he laughs as he replies.

Even here, at Erdoğan's own event, Mehmet is being screwed:

official event marshals are riding around in pick-up trucks laden with Turkish flags and baseball caps bearing the official coup commemoration logo, cheap mementoes they are handing out for free. I pick some up to add to my burgeoning collection of Turkish political tat, and continue on towards the bridge.

Just before the arch takes flight the crowds grow so thick I lose the will to keep pushing through. Instead I stop, look around, and take in the febrile buzz. A friend and fellow journalist has texted me, warning that the riled-up crowd has been chanting abuse at the CNN news crew. I thought that, with my notebook firmly in my rucksack, I would blend in. I was wrong.

'Excuse me, are you a journalist?' asks a slight young woman in black abaya and headscarf who emerges from nowhere, catching me by my elbow, and off guard.

Yes, I reply, I am.

'Which channel?'

Her eyes are hard and suspicious, not friendly as those of nosy Turks usually are. I tell her I work for a newspaper, not for TV, but she doesn't believe me.

'Really?'

My companion for the evening was caught in a mob attack during the coup in Egypt four years ago, and is alert to the warning signs. Other people are beginning to look around, so I shake the woman off and we push deeper into the crowd. When I stop again, I notice a young man with terrible teeth, dark brown and shunted into his mouth at weird angles, gazing up at the screen and grinning.

'Tayyip!' he yells as live pictures of his hero, just a few hundred metres down the road, flash up. 'TAYYIIIIIIIIIP!'

He is so enraptured he doesn't notice me staring.

## The Justice March

One week earlier: it's the other tribe's turn. On a humid Sunday afternoon scores of Turks in white T-shirts descend onto a corniche on the Asian bank of the Bosphorus. There is no Erdoğan merchandise on sale here.

Kemal Kılıçdaroğlu, the leader of the opposition, has just walked here from Ankara – a 280-mile, three-week trek in the blistering heat, accompanied by hundreds of police officers. Along the way he has gathered thousands of supporters shouting 'HAK! HUKUK! ADALET!' (Rights! Law! Justice!) as they weave through Istanbul's poor outer suburbs. One side of the highway leading into the city has been shut down for the marchers. Vans travelling up the other side beep their horns in solidarity. From the balconies of crumbling concrete apartment blocks, women swathed in black burkas shake their fists and scream in fury. Others hold up their hands in a four-fingered salute with the thumb tucked under – the sign of the Egyptian Muslim Brotherhood, adopted by Erdoğan's fan club.

Kılıçdaroğlu walks the final mile alone – a small, defiant figure surrounded by rings of black-clad cops. No one thought he would get this far. When he began walking, spurred by the arrest of one of his party members, he was mocked. Now he is about to step on stage in front of hundreds of thousands – perhaps millions – of people who support him, and who despise Erdoğan.

But Kılıçdaroğlu's face wouldn't look quite right on a T-shirt. He is grey, diminutive, pushing seventy. A career bureaucrat. A man who has spent his seven years at the head of the Republican People's Party, or CHP (*Cumhuriyet Halk Partisi*), Turkey's secularist party, eclipsed by six-foot ex-footballer Erdoğan. So instead of Kılıçdaroğlu's face the street sellers' wares bear the face of a blue-eyed blond with sharp cheekbones and a debonair dash: Mustafa Kemal Atatürk, who not only founded Kılıçdaroğlu's party, but also the Turkish republic. He was a polymath, a womaniser and a thirsty drinker, a war hero, a visionary and a statesman. And he is a hero – to this half of the country. He has been dead for eighty-one years, and he is still Erdoğan's biggest rival.

Here is the Atatürk legend. He was born simple Mustafa, son of a former civil servant and a housewife, in 1881 in Thessaloniki, now in modern Greece but at that time one of the richest and most diverse cities in the Ottoman Empire. He followed the familiar path for a bright boy from a modest background. First, he attended military school, where he studied Western philosophy alongside the bedrocks of literacy and numeracy, and was bestowed with the second name Kemal, meaning perfection, by a maths teacher. After finishing school he became an army officer.

He was serving an empire in decline. The Ottomans had once ruled a great stretch of the globe spanning Europe, Asia and Africa, but by the beginning of the twentieth century the peripheries were breaking away. The army Kemal joined was growing increasingly disloyal to the sultan, and by the onset of the First World War had all but overthrown him. Kemal was a lower-level player in the revolt, and a passionate advocate of reform. His experiences serving on fronts in the Balkans, North Africa and the Levant convinced him that such a huge, unwieldy, multi-ethnic empire could no longer survive and that it must be trimmed back to a Turkish nation state.

The Great War was the Ottoman Empire's inglorious finale. By then it was being run de facto by the Young Turks, a cadre of military officers including Kemal. Meanwhile the sultan, Mehmet V, sat sulking in his palace in Istanbul, fully aware that almost all his power had drained away, even though by name he was still head of an empire.

Kemal was dismayed when his fellow officers decided to enter the war on the side of the Germans, but he fought with distinction. He secured his reputation as a war hero at the Battle of Gallipoli in 1915, when troops from Britain, France, Australia and New Zealand launched a huge naval attack on the Dardanelles, the last maritime bottleneck before Istanbul. Against all odds, the Turks led by Kemal beat them back in a final show of force – and then the empire crumpled entirely.

The Ottomans' decision to ally with the Germans proved terminal. On 13 November 1918, just two days after the end of the war, British, French, Greek and Italian forces moved into Istanbul. Soon after, the Greeks seized a large swath of the Aegean coast and Thrace, the funnel of land leading from Istanbul into Europe. Meanwhile, the French had moved into the cities of the south-east, close to the current border with Syria, as well as the coal-rich regions of the north.

A new sultan, Mehmet VI, did little to prevent the unpicking of his empire. In 1920 he signed the Treaty of Sèvres, which recognised the various foreign mandates in his own lands. The fight appeared to have gone out of the Ottomans – but it had not gone out of Mustafa Kemal. Almost as soon as the armistice was signed he began hatching plans to reverse the damage. Slipping Istanbul, he headed for Samsun, a city on the Black Sea coast in northern Turkey, and began building a national resistance movement. Despite opposition from the sultan, who ordered him to cease his activities, by early 1920 Mustafa Kemal had built a massive following and established an alternative parliament in Ankara, a small city on the Anatolian plain. From there, he launched the Turkish war of independence, seizing back the Anatolian territories, the coast and then, finally, Istanbul. The last British warship departed the old imperial capital on 17 November 1922. Aboard was Mehmet, the last sultan, expelled in disgrace by the new parliament set up by Mustafa Kemal. Mehmet returned six years later, in a coffin, having lived out his remaining years on the Italian Riviera.

Five days after Mehmet was discharged, the sultanate was dissolved. His cousin, Abdulmecid, was appointed caliph – head of the world's Muslims – but his tenure was similarly short. Less than two years later, the caliphate was also abolished. The 600-year-old Ottoman Empire was over.

Mustafa Kemal had led a movement that saved Turkish pride and reclaimed great swaths of its territories. From the ruins of the Ottoman Empire he established a modern republic: in 1923 the Treaty of Lausanne was signed, recognising Turkey as a sovereign state. For most men, this might have been enough. But it was here that Mustafa Kemal's most remarkable work began. As the first president of the republic, from its founding in 1923 to his death in 1938, he set himself an enormous task: to pick up his people, shake out their old habits and mindsets, and reshape them as citizens for the twentieth century. Among his more famous reforms was to scrap the Ottoman alphabet, written in the same script as Arabic, and replace this with Latin letters. He introduced secularism into the constitution and banished God to the private sphere, and had everyone choose a surname in the Western tradition, leading to a plethora of colourful monikers in present-day Turkey. It is not unusual to meet a Mr 'Oztürk' ('pure Turk'), 'Yıldırım' ('lightning') or 'Imamoğlu' ('son of an imam'). Mustafa Kemal's own choice, 'Atatürk', means 'Father of the Turks'. And he advocated passionately for the equal rights of women.

For the people who wave his flag, Atatürk is the man who saved Turkey from the fate of some of its unfortunate neighbours. 'If it wasn't for Atatürk, we would be like the Arabs!' is a common refrain. If that sounds bigoted to a Westerner's ears, then some time spent in the Middle East might bring you round. Travelling and working as a woman in the Arab world can be infuriating at best, scary at worst. I have been heckled, grabbed, groped, patronised and scorned during my time working in Arab countries – simply because I am a woman – though I would like to pay tribute here to my scores of male colleagues and friends in that part of the world who do not fit the stereotype, and who have often saved me from those situations. In Turkey, women seem simply to sigh inwardly at embarrassingly clichéd chat-up lines, and learn how to deal with machismo displays of jealousy and the constantly hungry stares from men. What they don't sigh at but have to bear is the appallingly high, and apparently rising, rate of domestic violence and killings of women at the hands of their male relatives. Yet in the secular neighbourhoods of Turkey's western cities at least, women can live almost as freely as they do in the West. I can go running, Lycra-clad, in the morning, and hit bars and clubs wearing mini-dresses at night in Istanbul. Atatürk's admirers would credit that to him – whether that is true or not.

Atatürk's fan club is secular (at least politically if not always privately), relatively wealthy, educated, well-coiffed and decidedly less spiky to deal with. In short, they are almost the mirror image of the Turks who turn out for Erdoğan. During Kılıçdaroğlu's long walk, a joke goes around that his supporters who can't be bothered to walk alongside him are sending their drivers instead. The people who turn out to what has become known as 'the justice rally' look like professors, writers and engineers. There are large groups of middle-aged women who arrive on chartered coaches from faraway cities, cackling between themselves at crude jokes as they walk to the parade ground. I watch sweet old retired couples in matching JUSTICE T-shirts walking hand in hand along the corniche. These people belong to the same Turkey as the old ladies with fur coats and small dogs who live in my 1960s apartment block, clinging to their crystal tumblers of whisky, their cigarettes and all the former glamour from those heady days. There is no horror-show dental work on display here.

'Aaaaaah, we're among the beautiful people!' says Yusuf, a Turkish photographer who is firmly of this world, even though it pains him to admit it. When I really want to needle him I call him a 'White Turk', the lazy label for this half of the country. It refers to the elites, the secularists, 'those people who sit by the Bosphorus sipping on their whiskies', as one of Erdoğan's staunchest allies once put it, with a visceral sneer of disgust. The president is proud to represent the other half of Turkey – the poor, the religious, the marginalised. 'Your brother Tayyip is a Black Turk!' he once roared in a speech to his faithful. Whenever I call Yusuf a White Turk, he rolls his eyes and huffs a little. But he never denies it.

The walk down the corniche to the Maltepe parade ground, where Kılıçdaroğlu will take the stage, has the air of a genteel Sunday stroll. The white-clad masses lick ice creams and pause for tea in the kitsch waterside cafés. There is a happy, easy hum of conversation – I pick up snippets of holiday stories, and of updates on how the children are doing at university. There is less venom here than at Erdoğan's rallies – but also less sense of drive and direction. These people lost control of Turkey fifteen years ago, but they still wear the easy nonchalance of power. Meanwhile Erdoğan's supporters are still full of the scrappy aggression of the underdog. Old habits are hard to give up.

Kılıçdaroğlu, the bureaucratic grey man, has always made an easy target for ridicule. During his rallies Erdoğan plays videos showing the state of Turkey's hospitals in the 1990s, when Kılıçdaroğlu was head of the state health department. Admittedly they were terrible back then, full of filthy wards and mind-numbingly long queues. The crowd boos whenever Kılıçdaroğlu's face pops up on the screen. And as Kılıçdaroğlu begins his walk, Prime Minister Binali Yıldırım – a Erdoğan loyalist to the bone – mocks him.

'Why don't you use our high-speed trains?' he baits, highlighting the sleek new rail link, one of the government's vote-winning projects.

But by the time Kılıçdaroğlu nears Istanbul Erdoğan is spooked. As thousands of Justice March supporters file past the neo-Soviet-style billboards for the upcoming coup commemorations it becomes embarrassing for Erdoğan: this inadequate rival, stealing his thunder? And so he starts accusing him of tacitly supporting both Gülen, the alleged ringleader of the coup attempt, and the PKK – a known terrorist organisation – through this endeavour.

'Politics in the parliament has become impossible, so I'm taking it onto the streets. They can't cope with my free spirit,' a suntanned and fit-looking Kılıçdaroğlu tells me, back in his Ankara office five days after he has finished the march. With so few trusting the ballot box, these rally turnouts have become the new battleground.

Each time the politicians call their legions to the streets, fierce debate breaks out over the numbers. The CHP claims two million attended Kılıçdaroğlu's Justice Rally; the office of the Istanbul governor (a government appointee) counters, saying the real figure was 175,000.

Meanwhile, the government's claims for its own rallies – generally held in the purpose-built Yenikapı parade ground on the European side of Istanbul – always stretch into the millions. At the post-coup 'Unity Rally', they claim five million. At a pre-referendum campaign meeting, despite the large gaps in the crowd, they say one million. When I write in my report for *The Times* that the figure appears to have been inflated, pro-government journalists howl in protest. One accuses me of being a Zionist trying to destroy Erdoğan. The headline in the rabidly loyal newspaper *Sabah* screams that 'millions' turned out on the bridge for the coup anniversary. But even the *Sabah* journalist loses faith by the first paragraph, revising the figures down to 'hundreds of thousands'.

For perhaps the first time ever, Istanbul's Office of the Chamber of Topographical Engineers finds itself in the position of political referee. It weighs in with a statement on the justice-rally numbers, couched in rather different language to the usual Turkish rhetoric:

> The rally area of Maltepe is approximately 275,000 square meters. Participants were also located in an area that was closed to traffic, which is around 100,000 square meters. So citizens took part in the rally over a space covering 375,000 square meters . . . In estimating the participant number, it is usually accepted technically that three to six people are located per meter square, so it can be stated that at least 1.5 million joined the 'Justice Rally'. Experts say that considering the fullness of the rally area, this number could even be as high as 2 million.

My own back-of-a-fag-packet calculations concur: the areas of the Maltepe and Yenikapı parade grounds are roughly similar, while the part of the bridge where Erdoğan's coup commemoration was held is not large enough to hold more than 200,000.

'They don't inflate the numbers, they just make them up!' Yusuf says, our calculations hieroglyphing pages of my notebook.

Mehmet the street hawker doesn't need mathematics.

'I spend my life in crowds and I know the size when I look at them!' he says. 'There were at least three million at the Justice Rally. They were lying when they said a hundred and seventy-five thousand.'

So, yes, Kılıçdaroğlu has boosted his image beyond anyone's expectations. Yet over his shoulder looms the man who really called out the party faithful: Mustafa Kemal Atatürk.

## The rivals

If you have ever read Daphne du Maurier you might recognise Erdoğan's relationship with the blue-eyed blond. Just as the unnamed narrator of *Rebecca* obsesses over her husband's dead first wife, it is easy to imagine how the thin-skinned Erdoğan, desperate to establish his own place in history, spends hours fretting over the continuing popularity of his biggest rival.

You could forget that Atatürk is no longer with us. He is so present in Turkey that you might expect him to pop up at a rally, or be interviewed on TV. Like the Queen, his face is so familiar it becomes difficult to see it subjectively. Right now, he is the only person who might wield more power than Erdoğan. He is definitely the only one whose picture you will see more often as you travel around Turkey. Erdoğan's face, always twenty years younger in photos than in real life, looms large from the banners strung between apartment blocks in conservative neighbourhoods. But it is Atatürk who hogs Turkey's limelight.

It helps that he was photogenic – a natty dresser who instinctively understood the power of the camera at the exact moment the camera was becoming ubiquitous. Each stage of Atatürk's career – officer, rebel, war hero, visionary – together with his transformation from conventional Ottoman gentleman to twentieth-century statesman and style icon, is represented in a series of classic images.

Anıtkabir, Atatürk's mausoleum in Ankara, can probably be classed as his fanbase HQ, but you will find miniature shrines around every corner and underneath almost every shop awning. In his earliest portraits and photographs he looks like any other stiff-backed Ottoman officer. But in later images Atatürk swims, dances and flirts with the lens, dressed in finely tailored clothes and smoking monogrammed cigarettes. There is the famous silhouette of him stalking the front lines at the Battle of Gallipoli, deep in thought with a finger on his chin and a fez on his head. There is another of him in black tie and tails dancing with his adopted daughter, sleek in her sleeveless evening gown. There is the one where he stares directly into the lens, his cigarette in one hand and the other in his pocket, a Mona Lisa smile on his lips. There he is in a nerdish knitted tank top, teaching the newly introduced Latin alphabet to a group of enthralled children. The list goes on . . .

I like to try to guess the character of any individual Turk through the picture they display. Whenever I see a military Atatürk pinned up behind a counter I imagine the owner to be a patriot who looks back on his own military service with pride and warmth. If they have opted for a besuited and coiffed Kemal, I wager them to be pro-Western intellectuals. If, as in one *meyhane* (a traditional rakı-and-fish restaurant) close to my flat, the walls are plastered with various portraits from the start of his varied career to its end, I guess them to be full-blooded Atatürk fanatics.

My own favourite is the picture pulsing with such life and humour that the first time I saw it, hung behind the cash register of an Istanbul bakery, I yelped in delight. It is a colour photo of Atatürk on a child's swing, aboard a pleasure steamer on a trip to Antalya. It was taken three years before his death, and he is not a well man. His sunken bright eyes and his receding blond hair, his pallor and stout middle betray his love of drink; he would die from cirrhosis of the liver aged fifty-seven. Yet he is grinning so widely you can almost imagine him whooping as he flies. A second, less famous frame taken minutes before or after this one shows him standing on the swing with a young child peeping between his legs. This, I thought, is a personality cult I could get with – and a personality cult is what it is. Insulting Atatürk or defiling his image can still land you with a prison sentence, or at the very least the probability of a beating from the nearest Atatürk devotee. Back in 2007, under Erdoğan's government, a court decided that all of YouTube should be blocked because it carried a few videos deemed insulting to Atatürk. The ban stayed in place for two and a half years.

Internet censorship is still widespread, although these days insulting Erdoğan is far more likely to bring down a court order. Meanwhile, though, Atatürk's genuine appeal burns strong. It is not unusual to see young Turks use an image of Atatürk as their Facebook profile picture, or tattoo his signature down their arm. You can buy T-shirts, mugs, bumper stickers and keyrings emblazoned with his face. My own collection boasts a wine carafe, an egg timer and a compact mirror. In almost every town you can find small museums dedicated to him in some way, staffed by volunteers and visited by Turks who earnestly take selfies with the Atatürk waxworks. During Gezi, the 2013 summer of riots sparked by plans to concrete over the epony-mous park in Istanbul, the young protesters quickly realised that if they added an Atatürk image to the anti-Erdoğan slogans they spray-painted on the walls, the authorities would not paint them over. The council workers charged with this unenviable task decided to walk the tightrope between the two camps by painting out the slogans while fastidiously leaving the Atatürks. Though Erdoğan might dislike it, Atatürk's cult endures. And so, Erdoğan has nurtured his own.

Shortly before the parliamentary elections of November 2015 – a contest in which Erdoğan, by that time president, was not even running – I visited his home district of Kasımpaşa, a port neighbourhood in central Istanbul. In a backstreet shoe shop, I found Fatma Özçelik, a lively 59-year-old who had known Tayyip from childhood.

'Ooooh, he was so handsome!' she told me. 'So tall. So handsome! Yes, he's a bit aggressive on screen. But what can you do?'

I asked who she would be voting for.

'Tayyip!' she replied.

But Erdoğan isn't on the ballot, I said. Did she mean she would be voting for the AKP?

'Nope!' she insisted. 'Don't like any of them! I'm telling you, the guys ruling the AKP now are terrible. They're blaming Tayyip for all their shit.'

I pressed on. But would she be giving her vote to Ahmet Davutoğlu, the prime minister (later purged by his boss for being too independent of spirit), knowing that it would actually be an endorsement of Erdoğan?

'Nope! I don't like that Davutoğlu, I don't trust him. I don't like any of them – only Tayyip! They can't replace him. It can't be the AKP without him.'

She would not countenance any other option, and I never did get to the bottom of whether she would be voting or not.

Around the corner I dropped in on Ahmet Güler, perhaps the most famous barber in Istanbul, with the country's most famous customer. A small TV screen in a corner of his shop played live footage of Erdoğan speaking at a rally in the Kurdish city of Diyarbakır. Both Ahmet and the cloaked and shaving-foamed customer in his chair had the same clipped moustaches as their hero.

'We should all be proud of Erdoğan, he's a son of Kasımpaşa!' he told me. 'He's still one of us. I know him well and I don't feel he's changed at all.'

He paused, thought a little, and then added a brutally honest and very Turkish appendix:

'Well, OK – he's tired and old, so he's getting bags under his eyes. But otherwise, I have only positive things to say!'

How does he do it, this grumpy old man in an ill-fitting suit? It is a question I have often asked myself as I travel around Turkey talking to his faithful. Usually I get the sense of a demographic who feel their time, and their man, has come. For decades Turkey's poor, conservative voters found they could participate in democracy, as long as they did not threaten the order. When the politicians they elected looked as though they might actually change things in the way their supporters had been yearning for, the army – self-appointed guardians of Atatürk's secularity – stepped in to overrule them.

Yet that is only half the story. Alongside the women banned from universities and the public sector because they wear the headscarf, and the men who long yearned for a politician who prays and abstains from booze just as they do, there are others who you would never expect to support Erdoğan – yet they do. Over lunch on a waterside terrace one afternoon, a blonde, wine-drinking academic who grew up

in the UK spoke openly about the things that irk her about Erdoğan.
Single, secular and childless, she said she felt personally offended when
the president had described women like her as incomplete, his latest
in a series of bullish statements alienating anyone less pious than he
is. Ultimately, though, she – like his other supporters – let him off
the hook. When I asked her why the most powerful man in Turkey
appeared so sensitive, so petulant and so undiplomatic, she threw back
her glamorous coiffed head and laughed: 'Because he's a Pisces.'

What is the root of his appeal in these unexpected quarters? One
secular, Western-educated journalist told me that she has two great
political heroes – Erdoğan and Margaret Thatcher. She sees the same
traits in both of them – a tireless work ethic, and a single-minded
belief that their way of doing things is the right way, and screw all
the haters. She also admires the way that both were self-made, people
who had started from modest backgrounds and clawed their way to
the top. Others, even if they do not admire him, can appreciate the
way Erdoğan has broken the grip that the Kemalists, the devotees of
Atatürk, kept on the country for decades.

It is easy, now that they are the underdogs, to romanticise Turkey's
secularists, and to imagine that all would be right with the country
if only they could seize back power. But those who remember the
secular glory days know they could be as despotic as any religious
regime. The dogmatic banning of headscarved women from higher
education and from working in the public sector after the coup of
1980 confined millions to a life of child raising and housework –
ironic, given Atatürk's outspoken feminism. Atatürk pushed his own
bizarre law banning the fez, the iconic, tasselled, brimless red felt
hat ubiquitous in the later Ottoman Empire. This decision sparked
a 'Hat Revolution' on the part of stubborn fez-wearers in the conservative eastern city of Erzurum that was crushed by Atatürk's military,
thirteen of the ringleaders being executed.

Though Atatürk may not have wished for it, the self-appointed
keepers of his legacy – who for decades dominated the courts, the
universities and, most notably, the army – stamped down on anyone

who stood in the way of their mission. And if you find yourself in eastern Turkey and talk to the Kurds, you're unlikely to find many Atatürk fans – for it was he who ordered their cities bombed when they revolted against his Turkish national project. Even today, in the Kurdish regions, the Atatürk statues seem a little bigger, a little more brash: visual slaps to the descendants of those who died at the hands of their own government. The plaques engraved with one of his most famous sayings – 'How happy is the one who says, I am a Turk' – seem to be there simply to mock the Kurds. The first Turkish president to apologise for what happened in the 1930s? Erdoğan. It's odd, now that Erdoğan is waging his own war against Kurdish radicalism.

'You see the look the Erdoğan people have in their eyes now? That conviction that they know the ultimate truth? Well, that is exactly the same look as the Kemalists used to have,' said one Turk who remembered very well. Half of his family, a bunch of outspoken leftist intellectuals, were imprisoned following the 1980 coup.

Here is another way of looking at Erdoğan's success: lucky timing. Erdoğan is not the first politician with ambitions to take Turkey in a new direction, he is just the latest in a line of leaders who have professed their piety, and their opposition to the old order. The support base has always been there. Atatürk never fully, or even mostly, achieved his ambition of making Turkey a truly secular country. And Erdoğan's demographic is growing more rapidly than Atatürk's – put crudely, the poor and the religious tend to have more children. Meanwhile, the opposition screams foul at Erdoğan's plans to grant citizenship to around one in ten of the three million Syrians who have settled in Turkey after fleeing their own country's civil war. They are convinced he is only doing so to reap their votes in the future.

But what differentiates Erdoğan from his ideological predecessors is how he managed to gather support from those outside his base – social liberals, supporters of globalisation and free trade, opponents of military tutelage – before going on to crush those very same people. The irony was not lost on Amnesty International, who – as Erdoğan intensified his post-coup jailing of opposition journalists in 2016 –

wrote an open letter reminding him that they had once stepped in on his behalf when, in 1999, he was imprisoned for reading a religious poem at a rally.

Since Atatürk died in 1938, Turkey has been like a round-bottomed toy that rocks precariously to one side or the other but always returns upright. The opposing pull of the country's two major forces have always brought it back to a central position – though Erdoğan's charisma, political skill and good timing might now have upset the balance.

Even amid a purge that has stripped tens of thousands of their freedom and livelihoods, those who are not charmed by Erdoğan can still fall prey to his powers of persuasion. Once, as I was chatting to a man who was telling me how his company had recalled 200,000 T-shirts because they feared the design might offend the president, we came on to the subject of Europe – Erdoğan's pet hate at the time.

'But Europe lies!' said the man, certainly no Erdoğan fan. 'We have three million Syrian refugees and Europe gives us nothing!'

This was one of Erdoğan's claims – that almost none of the money promised to Turkey by the European Union under a deal to stop asylum seekers surging across the Aegean had materialised. But it was rubbish. Over a period of eighteen months the EU had signed off on projects worth almost three billion euros, exactly what it had promised, with another three billion ready to hand over. European money was pouring into the Turkish health and education systems, refugee camps, asylum detention centres – and that was just one branch of funding. Billions were also being handed over in accession grants, the money given to countries that might one day be EU members to help them bring their standards up to European level. But Erdoğan had managed to convince his people that Turkey was being screwed by Brussels. Erdoğan's lies are not a web, they are a paste that he slathers on so thick that nothing of the truth underneath is left showing. His motivations for doing so are clear.

'Look,' he is telling his fellow Turks. 'You may not like me, but

I am saving our honour against those who would seek to destroy it.'

It is a well-tested method. Part of Atatürk's appeal, after all, lies in the fact that he rescued Turkey from nefarious foreign powers almost a century ago. Maybe these two cults share more similarities than either would care to admit.

'He is Dictator in order that it may be impossible ever again that there should be in Turkey a Dictator,' wrote H.C. Armstrong, a British officer and contemporary biographer of Atatürk in 1932, as the founder's reforms moved ahead in top gear. Today it is Erdoğan's turn to change his country, and to overpower anyone who stands in his way, so that it may never go back to the old order. And that is just the way his tribe likes it.

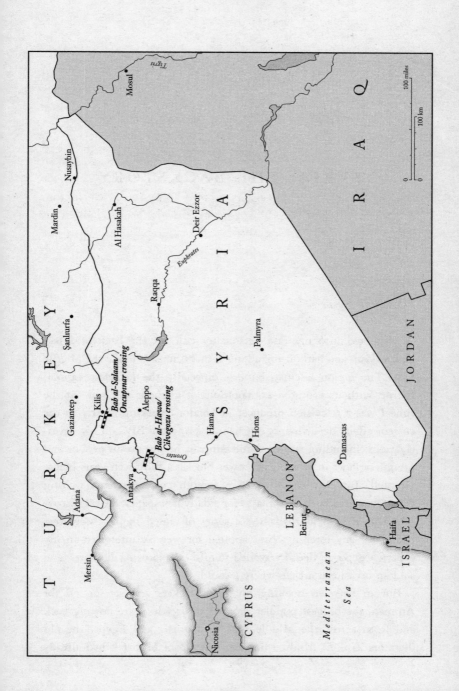

# 2

# SYRIA: THE BACKSTORY

*April 2011*
*Damascus, Syria*

I wandered into my first personality cult off the back of a bad break-up and harbouring a long-term curiousity to see the Middle East. The region fascinated me – especially the Lebanese capital, Beirut, with its evocative connotations of glamour and war. At the time I was a television producer in London, working mostly in the current affairs departments of Channel 4 and the BBC on big investigations, including stories about rampant heroin use in prisons and fire safety flaws in refurbished tower blocks, a full seven years before Grenfell. But I yearned to be a foreign correspondent, writing dispatches from turbulent places for a daily newspaper. Soon I discovered that British journalism is a series of closed shops; the editors hiring for any foreign jobs I applied for weren't interested in my experience. So, in lieu, I travelled to off-beat places for holidays, and sold an occasional article where I could.

But in between booking my plane tickets and setting off for Amman, the biggest popular protests in decades were flowing back and forth across the Middle East. In Tunisia and Egypt, the old dictators Zine El Abidine Ben Ali and Hosni Mubarak had already been bundled from their palaces by popular grassroots movements. In Libya, the armed rebellion against Colonel Muammar al-Gaddafi was soon to win the backing of NATO airstrikes.

In Syria, small demonstrations in the southern provincial city of Deraa, close to the Jordanian border, had been swelling for a fortnight by the time I entered the country. Syria's president, Bashar al-Assad, initially seemed immune to the unrest spreading elsewhere in his region, partly because he kept his own country so closed. To get a fourteen-day Syrian tourist visa I had enlisted a friend at a small company to fake a letter of employment for me, claiming that I was his secretary. Had I written on my visa application that I was a journalist, there was no way I would have been allowed in by the time I arrived at the border – an American traveller I met in my hostel in Amman had just been turned back at the frontier. By now, a fragmented opposition movement was rising against Assad, and there was a growing security crackdown in response. It was happening mostly in places like Deraa, and the poor outer suburbs of the cities where scores of rural migrants had arrived over recent years, forced from their farms by drought. But young educated activists in Syria's urban centres – Damascus, Aleppo and Homs – were picking up on the chance to finally challenge the dictator they hated. Via Facebook, they organised 'Days of Rage' after each week's Friday prayers.

All I could see of this from my shared taxi – a Chevrolet so old it was retro that boomeranged along the 125-mile road between Amman and Damascus – was Syrian army tanks blocking the exit to Deraa. The driver looked ahead and said nothing, while the two old couples travelling with me fell into silent contemplation. The TV in my room at the once-glamorous Orient Hotel, a faded grandma located in what had become a red light district in central Damascus, broadcast the official version of events on Syrian state television. From the huge and sagging bed I watched protests in front of the presidential palace a kilometre away, as the area filled with supporters shouting how much they loved Bashar. Sensing my chance to hit on a story, I set about trying to contact opposition activists.

In the meantime, I wandered the old heart of Damascus, a maze of narrow alleyways between thick stone walls, laced with sweet whiffs of jasmine and shisha smoke. Here I found trinket shops dedicated to souvenirs decorated with Bashar al-Assad's image – lighters, coffee mugs, car bumper stickers. Bunting bearing his face, identical on each little fluttering flag, criss-crossed the rafters of the souk. One morning I walked through the main drag with a new friend, a sweet Syrian girl in a tight white headscarf who had approached me minutes earlier as I stared awestruck at the nearby Umayyad Mosque. She grasped my arm and pointed to him.

'*Beheb Bashar* – I love Bashar,' she said, with the earnest gaze of a recent cult convert. 'Do you love Bashar, too?'

What could I say? The president is weak-chinned, long-necked and speaks with a lisp. And, already, he was a murderer. As she and I walked through that souk on a fresh April day, Assad's thugs were opening fire on demonstrators in Deraa, eighty miles down the road, picking them off from the rooftops with the indifference of schoolboys playing video games. I hummed a non-committal murmur, which seemed enough to satisfy her.

After a series of protracted emails, phone calls that came from a different number each time, missed meetings and finally some good luck, I eventually found an opposition activist called Roua. She was one of the young Damascenes – there were so few of them at the time it's incredible they managed to find each other – who was trying to organise the Day of Rage that Friday. So far, the activists hadn't scored much success – mere handfuls of people were showing up to their protests, and most were immediately arrested. Their ranks, such as they were, had been fully infiltrated by Syrian intelligence.

When Roua came to meet me, on a sultry Tuesday night in a bustling restaurant in the Christian quarter of the old city, she was wearing a paper dental mask over her nose and mouth, and didn't take it off in the whole time we spent together. She claimed she was hiding some work done recently on her teeth.

'We are speaking to each other using Skype,' she told me in perfect English. With her hennaed hair and hippyish clothes she wouldn't have looked out of place at Glastonbury. 'We use false names, and actually we wouldn't even know each other if we passed on the street.'

Her parting sentence confirmed my suspicions: she was terrified that if she showed her face, someone might notice that she had been meeting with a foreigner and start putting two and two together.

'The walls have ears,' she said, tapping her knuckles on the age-worn stone of the restaurant's wall as she rose. I never managed to meet her or speak to her again; her phone numbers rang out, my emails to her went unanswered.

All that fear and paranoia had birthed a society of sycophants. Everywhere I went in Damascus in that month when the uprising was just sprouting I found pictures of Bashar al-Assad. Bashar in military uniform, pasted onto a kebab shop's heated glass cabinet. Bashar administering eye drops to a baby, pinned up on the door of a stationery shop. Bashar in dark glasses, superimposed onto the rear window of a sleek black Mercedes.

Syrians who wished to go one step further put up posters of the Shia troika – Bashar with Hassan Nasrallah, the pugnacious leader of the Lebanese Shia militia Hizbollah, and Mahmoud Ahmedinejad, the president of Iran at that time. For real favour-winning bonus points, they would also stick up a picture of Hafez al-Assad, Bashar's father and first president of the dynasty – over a decade dead, but never too far away. Some young Syrians I met, befriended and went drinking with warned me to be careful on Fridays.

'Stay in your hotel,' said Faris, a plump and cheerful guy from an upper-class Sunni family. 'Don't go to the mosques or the old city. Wait until Friday prayers are fully over.'

One of the others, a gay man called Ahmed, said he was sick of Bashar, but deeply apprehensive about the opposition. 'We don't know who they are,' he warned me. 'They might be Islamists, anybody.'

I left Damascus and its small sparks of revolution in the spring of 2011 and returned to London to pitch the story. I got a couple of commissions from marginal magazines, but nothing more: the uprising in Libya was revving up and would dominate the news from the region until Gaddafi's bloody end at the hands of a mob in October of that year.

Meanwhile, the protests were growing in the Syrian cities. Homs, a multicultural university town close to the Lebanese border, was one of the epicentres, with thousands of people turning out around the old clocktower in the centre of the city chanting: 'The people want the fall of the regime!' With no international media able to operate freely in Syria the news of the demonstrations leaked out through shaky mobile phone footage. And as the protests spiralled out of the government's control, the security forces started posting snipers on the rooftops to fire into the crowds. The increasingly emboldened activists were rounded up by the score and thrown into the regime's feared prisons.

Then, in the autumn of 2011, videos started appearing on YouTube showing groups of armed men in mismatched camouflage waving a three-starred flag – similar to but distinct from Syria's official two-starred flag. The three stars quickly became the symbol of the opposition and the rebels announced themselves as the Free Syrian Army (FSA). Soon after, scores of Syrian military officers started defecting to join the FSA and the protests turned into full-blown conflict. Assad's army placed the centre of Homs under siege, and the death toll began to soar. Suddenly Syria was the story.

I had witnessed the opening acts and was desperate to go back and report there again. So over the next two years I saved up, made some more contacts in the newspaper industry and bought a flak jacket, and in February 2013 travelled to the Turkish borderlands with a few phone numbers and a plan to cross the frontier and go into rebel-held Aleppo. Thousands of Syrians were flooding into Turkey every day to escape the fighting between the FSA and Assad's forces in the northern provinces of Idlib and Aleppo. Going the other way and entering the war zone was as easy as showing your passport to a Turkish border guard.

*February 2013*
*Free Syria*

The Syrian rebels had captured two main border crossings with Turkey, Bab al-Salaam (the Peace Door) and Bab al-Hawa (the Windy Door), and the Turkish government kept them open allowing rebels, refugees and journalists to cross in and out of rebel-held Syria. What had once been sleepy frontier outposts frequented by intrepid backpackers and cross-border traders were now funnels for weapons, aid and desperate people. My Syrian fixer, who had picked me up the night before and run through the basic logistics of the route into the war zone, left me at the first Turkish checkpoint at Bab al-Salaam, telling me that he would pick me up on the other side. With no passport, he had to travel into Syria via one of the smuggling routes a few hundred metres along the border. It was discombobulating enough to be left alone among the crowds of grimy kids tugging at my leg to sell me water, amid lines of cars, packed in every spare space with blankets, nappies and clothes. But that was nothing next to what I found on the other side of the frontier, past the scrums of shouting Syrians waving their documents at exasperated Turkish bureaucrats, the looted duty-free store, and finally the huge scrappy flags of the FSA that had been hastily sewn together and hoisted over their captured frontier. WELCOME TO FREE SYRIA, read the sign.

Free Syria looked like a set from *Mad Max*. Armed men, many with their faces covered, roamed through city streets pancaked by Assad's airstrikes. Mortars had slammed into the top floors of the housing blocks, leaving masonry dangling like melted cheese, but families still lived on the lower floors and on the street traders sold trinkets, children's jewellery, scarves and wristbands decorated with the FSA's three-starred flag. Hawkers at the side of the road sold the

illegal brew that they dispensed from plastic
nich screwed up car engines in months.

el-held suburbs of Aleppo city in February 2013 I found
of idealistic young activists I had tracked down in Damascus
at they had been overwhelmed by the men with guns. Now, the
so-called 'liberated areas' were battlegrounds for warlords who wanted
to extract their share of bounty from the chaos. A thousand new little
fiefdoms had sprouted in the space Assad left behind, each with an
egocentric man drunk on hubris at the top and a score of lackeys
beneath him. Former merchants, construction workers and imams
had become self-styled leaders, their men either looting with abandon
or, increasingly, imposing their own draconian ideas about Islam on
the suffering population.

At night, the city went dark – at least, the rebel-held part did.
The electricity was cut off there and most people relied on generators
powered by the moonshine fuel from the roadsides. The tarry smoke
caught in my nostrils as I sat inside a scruffy makeshift media centre,
once a family home and still dotted with keepsakes on the cracked
and dusty shelves. Outside, young rebels took over the streets at night
to fire mortar rounds into government territory, just a couple of
kilometres away and still fully lit and functioning. That inevitably
drew return fire, and curses from everyone desperate for a full night's
sleep.

Stark daylight revealed huge piles of rubbish moulded into hillocks
at the side of the Aleppo streets. Leishmaniasis, a flesh-eating disease
spread by the sand flies living in the garbage, was tearing through
the population, especially children. At a clinic set up by a local charity
I watched distraught toddlers receive daily injections into their gaping
sores. As we approached the city's checkpoints, run by armed groups
of increasingly hazy affiliation, my drivers and fixers would switch
the music on their stereos to *nasheed*, a cappella chants about violence
and loss beloved by the jihadis. On the road back to the Turkish
frontier we passed through whole villages that had been recently
flattened and abandoned.

The revolutionary promise of two years before had sunk beneath a malodorous tide of tragedy; front lines were crystallising across Aleppo city, and hundreds of thousands of people had fled their homes as the regime's air force launched relentless raids on rebel territory. The death toll was in the tens of thousands, and the war's descent into extremism had started. Syria was already well on the way to giving the world a grim litany of new cultural reference points – barrel bombing, chemical attacks, heart-eating rebels, and Isis.

Crossing back over the border into Turkey at the end of any assignment in Syria was like stepping from a sepia film into full colour. Kilis, the first Turkish town after the Syrian frontier, is only forty miles from Aleppo as the crow flies. It is the beigest of any Turkish city, its tiny Ottoman heart smothered by rings and rings of new tower blocks housing masses of rural peasants. It would not feature in any Turkish guidebook, but compared to Aleppo it was paradise. Each time I came back I ripped off the black shawl I had used to cover my clothes, and drank in the colours hitting my eyes. After the privations of Aleppo, hot water, privacy, electricity and undisturbed sleep in a Turkish fleapit felt like a night at the Savoy.

*Summer 2013*
*Rebel-held Aleppo*

The most powerful rebel faction in Aleppo city in the summer of 2013 was the Liwa al-Tawhid, an Islamist militia led by Abdulkader al-Saleh, a diminutive former spice importer. He had assumed the *nom de guerre* of Hajji Marea, Hajji being the title bestowed on Muslims who have completed the pilgrimage to Mecca, and Marea being the spit-and-sawdust town north of the city he came from. The urbane and wealthy population of Aleppo had been none too pleased to find Hajji Marea and his brigade of bumpkins entering the city the previous summer and quickly carving it up, with the Tawhid and other rebel brigades controlling the poor, conservative districts to the east and the regime clinging to the wealthy west. There, the residents might have known their president was a tyrant, but many of them preferred to stick with the devil they knew rather than take their chances on the unknown, ragtag rebels.

The Tawhid had built a slick PR operation, which I encountered within minutes of arriving in Aleppo on my first morning as a war reporter. We had driven directly to Ard al-Hamra, one of the chaotic neighbourhoods that made up almost all of eastern Aleppo. A Scud missile fired by Assad's forces had hit it in the inky hours before sunrise, and the street in front of me – a little parade of honey-coloured houses – had been flattened. Children were running about on top of the rubble looking for salvageable and saleable remnants. The survivors had already been extracted, and so too had the identifiable bits of the dead. Severed body parts and smashed furnishings were all that was left under the dust. It was all so familiar from the news reports I had been watching over the past two years – crumbled houses, crying women, scowling men with guns slung over their shoulders – only now it was here in front of me in full HD. I was so transfixed that it took me a few seconds to realise that the hysterical children across the street were shouting at me, beckoning furiously and pointing at the space above my head. When I looked up, I saw that a huge chunk of stone, the corner of a dainty Juliet balcony, had cracked away from the building above me and was about to topple onto my head. I moved away and gave them a weak smile and a wave of thanks.

Seconds later a lorry with its rear shutters rolled up backed screaming around the corner, and the people who had been milling about crowded around it. Here was the humanitarian face of the Tawhid rebels, who ruled by the gun but wanted the world's media to show a different face. In front of my camera and that of a young media activist called Farouk, they started throwing out blankets and food packages to the waiting gaggle who surged forward to scrap over the goodies. Over the following months I would watch all the other armed rebel groups do the same, in a series of increasingly odd charity stunts that their media relations officers would then try to sell to foreign journalists and our fixers as worthy international news stories. Al-Qaeda set up a subsidised bus service. Others opened bakeries with money from unnamed Saudi or Kuwaiti donors, handing out bread to the poor but refusing to allow the male volunteers to serve women. Even Isis got in on the act, in the first months after it sprouted like a poisonous weed amid the misery and before it got down to ruling through fear alone. In August 2013 it organised a children's fun day in Aleppo, where armed men in balaclavas watched over a group of six-year-olds embroiled in an ice cream-eating competition. As the day's finale, a group of Isis fighters competed in a tug-of-war against a team from Al-Qaeda, treating their enthralled audience to the darkly comic spectacle of overweight and bearded men in thobes and sandals sweating as they grappled with the rope. Isis won – a nice metaphor for what happened a few months later. The two extremist groups – identical sartorially and ideologically – turned their guns on each other.

The fixer I travelled into Aleppo with on that first assignment was a fat and slightly stupid guy called Mohammed who, like many others at that time, was making a wedge of cash off foreign reporters while doing little more than airing the Tawhid's propaganda. Although Syrian by origin he had a distinct Iraqi accent, and had grown up in Baghdad. His father, a devout man from the conservative northern Syrian town of Jisr al-Shugur, was a member of the Muslim Brotherhood – a network of pious believers who preferred to live in the shadows until the onset of the Arab Spring beckoned them into the open.

The Brotherhood is feared and loathed by the Middle East's old authoritarian regimes because it provides a vision for an alternative system of government that appeals directly to the oppressed, using the world's most powerful religious ideology as its glue. Distrusted but tolerated in the West, the Brotherhood was public enemy number one in the Arab world's secular regimes, like Mubarak's Egypt and Ben Ali's Tunisia. In Syria, it was so hated that schoolchildren had to spew vitriol against it each morning as part of their ritual oath-giving

to Assad's Ba'athist state. In 1980, membership of the organisation
was made punishable by death, and the Brothers retaliated with a
series of increasingly violent protests and guerrilla attacks. Finally,
in February 1982, President Hafez al-Assad sent his army to the city
of Hama, epicentre of the Brotherhood's uprising, where, over twenty-seven days, it besieged and bombarded the entire population. Up
to 25,000 people were killed, but with media access restricted and no
way for people inside the city to communicate with the outside world,
it went virtually unreported. Everyone inside Syria heard about what
happened, but their fear of what the regime might still do brought
down a self-imposed *omertà*. Back then there was no independent
media operating inside Syria and no internet to help the news leak
out. The insurgency was crushed, whole city centres were destroyed.
The remaining Brotherhood members were imprisoned or fled, and
in Syria no one spoke of it again.

In the aftermath of Hama, many of Syria's surviving Brotherhood
members fell into the arms of a willing patron, the one Middle Eastern
strongman who saw that there might be a use for them – Saddam
Hussein.

The Iraqi president, though also a Sunni Muslim and a sectarian
ruler, did not build an alliance with the Syrian Brotherhood out of
religious conviction – later he would carry out his own crackdown
on the Iraqi wing of the movement. But in the 1970s and early
1980s, Saddam's main enemy was the Shia goliath Iran, to which
Assad's Syria was allied. By cuddling up to the Syrian Brotherhood,
Saddam could undermine Damascus, his neighbour to the west, and
in turn also Tehran, his neighbour to the east.

Saddam had funded and trained the Syrian Brotherhood prior to
1982, and then opened his country to those who fled after the group's
revolt against Assad failed. Syrian Brotherhood families were given
homes in Baghdad and lavished with generous benefits, just as the
rest of Iraq was slipping into a gruelling poverty inflicted on them
by their leader's increasingly erratic behaviour. The war with Iran,

which began in 1980, was to drag on for eight years. Two years after it ended, Saddam invaded Kuwait and brought international sanctions hammering down on the heads of his people. By some estimates, half a million Iraqi children died in the 1990s through the direct or indirect impacts of the sanctions, which placed an almost total trade embargo on the country.

My fixer Mohammed recalled that time quite differently. 'Baghdad was amazing, so many parties,' he said dreamily. The good times for the Brotherhood families only came to an end in 2003, when the US-led 'Coalition of the Willing' invaded Iraq and toppled Saddam. Ten years on, Mohammed still sneered in disgust when he thought about the capture, trial and execution of a man who, whatever the errors of the West in toppling him, was one of the most brutal dictators in modern history.

Whenever Mohammed spoke of Saddam, it was with a finality that implied there was no other reasonable point of view. 'Saddam was a very great man,' he would say – and there was no way of persuading him how ironic it was that he was now embroiled in an uprising that was, purportedly, all about freedom from another dictator. Quite how or why he and his brother had come back to Syria from Iraq in 2011 would always remain a fuzzy enigma. Looking back, I'm sure that those old family ties were the reason why Mohammed was in Aleppo, a city with which he had few links, and why he was so keen to take me straight to the headquarters of the Tawhid Brigade, the Brotherhood's armed proxy in the city. Three decades had passed since Assad the father had crushed and banished the Syrian Brothers. Now, in the Syrian revolution, they saw their chance to take revenge on the son.

The Tawhid was described by its apologists as a moderate Islamist group, which, in comparison to Al-Qaeda and Isis, it was. But moderate is a relative term. The more time I spent around the Tawhid, the more irritated I became at the strict code of Islamic behaviour they forced on me, a foreign atheist journalist who had come to tell their story. On the streets of Aleppo, a multi-faith city in a multi-faith country, they commanded that I wear the headscarf. They said it was to 'show respect for the people'. It wasn't; instead, it was all about respect for the Tawhid. Usually, when I entered ordinary people's homes in Aleppo, the first thing they did was tell me I could remove the headscarf if I wanted to.

One day in May, as I was waiting inside the Tawhid's base in a baking hot car with an agonising migraine for an interview that never materialised, and growing gradually more furious at being ordered to wear an uncomfortable symbol of someone else's faith, I ripped the headscarf from my head. 'Fuck this,' I muttered to myself.

I will never forget the looks I got from the surly fighters hanging around the base. Several times I heard them whisper between themselves 'sahafiya' – 'journalist'. To their credit, no one approached me and told me to put the headscarf back on, but I could feel the intense hostility.

Even more troubling was Hajji Marea's willingness to accept the presence of Jabhat al-Nusra, Al-Qaeda's Syrian franchise, in Aleppo and to fight alongside them on the front lines against Assad. Nusra's base was next door to the Tawhid's, and they had kept their hostages – including foreign journalists and aid workers – in the basement of a building the two shared. James Foley, the American reporter later passed on to Isis and murdered on camera, is believed to have been held in that basement while he was in Nusra's hands – and while Hajji Marea was receiving the rest of us for interviews in a room just metres away. We never did find out if Hajji Marea knew the extent of what Nusra was doing – he was killed in a regime airstrike in November 2013. Most of the Syrians I knew changed their Facebook profile to a picture of him on news of his death.

In August 2013 I visited the Tawhid's base for the last time, and found the road outside had been freshly tarmacked and a promenade of elegant white flagpoles erected, leading up to the heavily guarded entrance.

'We call it the UN,' laughed Mahmoud, the suave, funny and far more intelligent fixer I had found after firing Mohammed. Mahmoud was no fan of the Tawhid.

I was disgusted at the arrogance too – this tacky show, this waste of desperately needed funds, just metres from water mains burst by artillery and schools and homes obliterated in the fighting.

But in Syria I also saw what happens to the trimmings of a personality cult when it crumbles. Across the rebel-held north in 2013 I came across the same banners depicting Bashar al-Assad that I had seen in that Damascus souk two years earlier, only now with his eyes scratched out and obscenities scrawled across his face. I found what was left of a bust of his father, Hafez, the architect of this terrifying regime, in the lobby of a hydroelectric dam that had been taken over by Jabhat al-Nusra. Somehow, they had managed to almost completely incinerate it. Another statue of Hafez in a nearby town had a leather sandal rammed into its mouth – the ultimate Arab insult.

And when I returned to Aleppo in the spring of 2014, after a bleak winter in which Isis overran the rebels in the east of the city and Assad's forces started dropping barrels filled with explosives from helicopters, I found the Tawhid had been bombed out of their base. The old eye hospital, already tattered when they occupied it, was now just ruined columns jutting out of rubble. Those flagpoles were a row of twisted stalks, and with Hajji Marea dead his undisciplined mob had forgotten their once-eternal fealty to their leader and had been absorbed by rival factions. It's what happens to them all, in the end.

## Turkey's cults

Maybe it was because I wasn't looking for them, but I didn't pick up on the first hints of Turkey's personality cults until I had been there for several months. Although I was living in Antakya I was barely connected to Turkey at first. I worked inside Syria, hung out with Syrian refugees in Turkey during my downtime, and devoted most of my attention to the war over the border. Turkey was the place I came back to at the end of assignments in the war zone, to drink beers and wear sleeveless tops and enjoy the unlimited electricity and hot water on tap. I sat in shisha cafés in the Turkish border towns as I wrote my articles about what was happening on the other side of the frontier and whatever was going on politically in Turkey was just background noise – unless it overlapped with what was happening in Syria.

I knew of Atatürk, of course. Every Turkish guidebook mentions him, and warns tourists not to speak ill of him in public. I also remembered a passage in a book I had read as a teenager, written in the 1930s by a Turkish woman who had been so proud when her leader travelled to Europe wearing a suit and trilby hat like every other modern leader. Apart from anything else there is no way to avoid Atatürk in Antakya; a crude rendering of his face is cast in lights on the dramatic mountains that loom behind the town, visible from every street and rooftop terrace. The first time I saw the stylised line drawing of his face that is rendered in paint or metal signage in every public office in Turkey, I was struck by how much he bears a likeness to the British pop star Sting.

Erdoğan and the AKP I knew of mainly because they rose to power when I was in my first year of university in Manchester. One of my classes focused on contemporary European politics – a hopeful, expansive subject at that time. The theme de jour was the endless possibilities for EU enlargement, and the imminent accession of the central European states that had once been Soviet satellites. In my seminar that day we had discussed the Turkish elections and their implications for Europe. Amid all the doom of that year – the slow cranking up to the war in Iraq, the worsening quagmire in Afghanistan – it seemed to be a glint of hope. The Turkish secularists who were howling at the rise of these seemingly benign Islamists were the ones who looked like fundamentalists.

The Gezi Park protests, which started when I had been living in Turkey for three months, were the first major news story I took note of. They made small waves down in Antakya, where the local population of Turkish Alawites – members of the same sect of Shia Islam as Bashar al-Assad – held thinly attended protests in the main square. Maybe my views on Gezi at that time were coloured by the Syrians surrounding me: they mostly viewed Erdoğan as their champion – no other world leader was opposing Assad and welcoming refugees so consistently – and they distrusted the Turkish Alawites for their kinship with Assad's hated regime in Syria. The tear gas used by the Turkish police to put down the demonstrations in Taksim seemed minor compared to the live rounds fired by Syrian security forces on protesters there.

But, after Gezi, I started noticing how Erdoğan was becoming much more than a prime minister. When new football stadiums opened, he would play in the inaugural matches – and always, without fail, score a goal. He appeared on an evening chat show and sang a lilting Turkish song in a tuneless voice, to enthusiastic applause. Barely a day went by when a television channel did not broadcast one of his speeches or visits. After he gave up the job of prime minister and won the presidential elections in 2014, his picture started appearing everywhere. And when the AKP won in parliamentary elections a year later, my Syrian boyfriend's father phoned from Saudi Arabia, where he was living. He had never even visited Turkey.

'Erdoğan! Erdoğan! Erdoğan!' he sang in delight.

That was where my fascination with Erdoğan and the people who idolise him started – the moment when I became obsessed with untangling the appeal of the Turkish president.

# 3

# BUILDING BRAND ERDOĞAN

The president likes to wear sunglasses. It is part of a look that, over the years, he has honed to a crossover between Islamist and mafia don.

There is the clipped moustache that has been there from the start – an essential element of any pious man's image. Back in the 1990s it was a glossy chestnut brown, set off by his bouffant hair. Over the years, as both have got shorter and greyer on their original wearer, the moustache has spread through Erdoğan's inner circle like a catwalk trend. As the 2017 referendum approached, a *Daily Mail* journalist totted up that twenty-seven of the thirty cabinet members were sporting the *badem biyik* – or 'almond moustache'. Of the three with no moustache, one was a woman.

There are the oversized suit jackets, cross-hatched and most often in a dark powder blue. They originally made an appearance around the time of the presidential elections in August 2014 – when Erdoğan first won the post – and have since become so iconic that when a friend decided to dress up as the president for a raucous post-referendum dinner party all he had to do was don one of these suits and grow a week's worth of moustache. In 2015, as the fashion spread in Erdoğan's circle, one of Turkey's leading designers bestowed it with a name: the 'prestogal' jacket.

'President Erdoğan is the man who brought the checkered fashion to Turkey. Nobody influences our president; he does not follow the world, but rather he creates his own fashion,' Levon Kordonciyan, the designer, told the state news agency, Anadolu.

And then there are those shades, aviator-style with thin gold rims. Erdoğan dons them at rallies and walkabouts, the lenses so dark that his eyes are inscrutable. When he walks en masse with his entourage, all of them dressed in black and wearing shades to match him, you get the sense that the mob boss has arrived. It's the same with the screaming convoys the high-level politicians move about in – first police on motorcycles, then the swarm of blacked-out cars travelling in packs half a kilometre long down the highways. They have grown more common everywhere since Erdoğan became president – and his own entourage is by far the biggest – but you see them most often in Ankara. Whole intersections must be slickly closed and reopened to allow the government motorcades to pass through, jamming another stick in the spokes of the capital's dreadful traffic.

It is impossible to guess to what level such privileges go down. Erdoğan travels like that, for sure, as do the high-ranking members of his cabinet. In August 2016, a month after the coup attempt, prime minister Binali Yıldırım's press team called me and a couple of dozen other foreign journalists to an Ottoman palace on the Asian bank of the Bosphorus. A jolly Yıldırım ordered us to tuck into the opulent Turkish breakfast, served in the gardens – young cheeses with succulent figs, delicate tea and hot, crunchy pastries – while burly men in black T-shirts, olive-grey combat trousers, shades and earpieces scanned the scene in every direction with assault rifles ready. After a two-hour discussion and a sincere vow from the diminutive, grandfatherly Yıldırım that we should do this more often, we watched as he was whisked away in a helicopter in a flourish of political showmanship.

Other ministers travel in more low-key style. But in September 2016, down in Diyarbakır, de facto capital of the Kurdish south-east, I happened to be in the city's premier breakfast spot as the city

governor, newly appointed from Ankara, came in. The Hasanpaşa
Han is an Ottoman-era caravanserai, a two-level eating and shopping
centre around an open central courtyard that was built in the sixteenth
century. Back then the traders traversing the Silk Route would spend
the night inside its black basalt walls, resting their horses in the
straw-strewn central space and dining and sleeping in the warren of
surrounding rooms.

Today, there are stalls at ground level selling trinkets, colourful
silk scarves and rugs printed with images of Kurdish heroes. For a
time you might have found PKK leader Abdullah Öcalan's face among
them. Now the rug sellers stick to uncontroversial figures, mostly
Kurdish singers and poets; none go so far as to sell any bearing
pictures of Erdoğan, as I have seen in other parts of the country.
Through tiny arched doorways steep stone steps lead up through the
blackness of the han's thick outer walls like secret warrens in a medieval castle, before they spill out to the mezzanine of the second level.
Here, breakfast is served – Diyarbakır style. Endless small plates of
cheeses, olive oil, jams, spicy pastes, sliced tomatoes and cucumber,
honey, kaymak (a kind of Turkish clotted cream), tahini, fried eggs,
spicy sausage sizzling in butter are heaped onto tables along with
endless bread and tea, refilled as soon as it is finished.

I was there with my translator and her friend, who had run a café
in the grounds of Surp Giragos, the largest Armenian church in
Anatolia, until fighting between local PKK militants and the Turkish
security forces enveloped it. He closed up and left his café in December
2015 and had not been back in the ten months since, but a colleague
who had been able to get into the curfew zone to check on the church
had taken photos for him. It was not so much the loss of his business
that made his hand tremble with grief and rage, but what had been
done to Surp Giragos. He held up his phone to show me photos of
the camp kitchen that the soldiers had set up under the soaring gothic
arches of the nave and the Atatürk portrait they pinned up in place
of the icons.

It was at that moment that a gaggle of close protection guards, the same guys in olive and black who had accompanied Yıldırım, filed in and fanned out on both levels of the han. The bubbling conversation hushed as if someone had turned down the dial, then the governor walked in and took his place at a breakfast table. Slowly the chatter returned, but we stopped talking about the church and the war that had ravaged the districts just behind these thick old walls and stuck to banal small talk for the rest of the morning.

But the portraits in the public corridors of Aksaray, Erdoğan's thousand-room palace, show the other side of the man at the top of the clique that rules Turkey. He is still in suits and dark glasses but now in the world's misery spots rather than the halls of power, kissing the hands of old women in headscarves or surrounded by adoring African children.

The president's loyal insiders – and often even his opponents – insist that such personal warmth is genuine. One lower-level bureaucrat working in the presidency tells me that in meetings, Erdoğan makes sure everyone has a glass of tea in front of them before he starts. An adviser insists that he berates Turks to have at least three children only because he cares about them as he would his own family. The head of the foreign investment board, who was personally appointed by Erdoğan, says people see the president as their father.

Turks who have met Erdoğan in person say time and again: he is funny. But his instinct to bring an iron fist down on those who oppose him politically is a bona fide part of his personality, too.

'What I know from his life and his family is that he is not concerned on a macro level,' a former aide told me. 'He may cry and help a person but if you tell him that there are thousands of people gathered there, he sends somebody to bust them. A thousand people is something political. The other is something humane.'

Foreign diplomats paint a similar picture. For sure Erdoğan can be charming, and they agree his personal warmth is real. But they also say he can be obstructive and caustic, especially when he feels he is not getting his way or being treated with respect.

'I don't find him particularly funny, but he definitely has a presence,' said one. 'He was quite warm. He was always patting me on the back. To be this successful you must have something and he absolutely does. He has a very magnetic personality, which does not really come out. He always seems very angry and harsh in his public speaking. But he does not seem like that in private.'

Another, who had personally felt the force of the president's fury several times during his posting, said there are two Erdoğans: 'the diplomatic, polished guy who wants to make friends and is trying to act to his capabilities in order to influence others. This is the nice Erdoğan. Then there is the tough, awful Erdoğan. And you never know which one is going to show up.'

Outside the country, Erdoğan's mercurial and often bullish personality wins him more detractors than fans. But inside Turkey – which is, at its heart, an Eastern country even if it often assumes the veneer of the West – it is seen as his biggest attribute.

'One of his strongest points is that he is genuine in both doing right and wrong,' a former adviser tells me. 'He is very transparent, and that's a good thing in Turkey. He does not conceal anything. He speaks his mind, and this is why he makes so many mistakes. He sometimes says absurd things. But he is not a European politician in that sense. He is more like a guide figure, like a politician of the Ottoman times.'

## The speechwriter

The photo Hüseyin Besli has chosen for the wall of his Istanbul office is a classic of the genre. Erdoğan is smiling, shaded and waving, dressed in a black greatcoat and surrounded by his entourage. It is the new Tayyip in the new Turkey – a place where he is firmly in charge. But with his Marlboro reds, diamond-patterned sweater and tired and sagging grey face, Besli himself looks like a relic of the old – more like an ageing shopkeeper or a minor bureaucrat than the architect of a revolution. His shoulders hunch forward and his smile is resigned. The way he sucks his cigarettes through his own moustache – a little longer than Erdoğan's and just as grey – suggests a deep sadness. Maybe he is just lost in his thoughts.

We meet in his writing room, a neat, wood-panelled attic in an old Balkan-style house, nestled in the heart of a bubbling district in Asian Istanbul. The streets of Çengelköy are narrow and cobbled, lined with family-run grocers. The district sits on the banks of the Bosphorus, at a point where the land juts out to gift it a panoramic view of the first of the three suspension bridges with the outlines of the mosques of Istanbul's Ottoman centre in the hazy blue background. The din of a Monday evening rush hour leaks in through the huge window by Besli's desk as I settle into one of his comfy leather chairs. Revving motorcycles and shouting shopkeepers blend with the wail of the sundown call to prayer. His floor-to-ceiling shelves are packed with books on religion and politics. There is a sticker of the Muslim Brotherhood's Rabia hand, a four-fingered salute with the thumb tucked under, pasted onto the window, and that Erdoğan portrait is the first thing you're confronted with as you walk in the door.

Besli chain smokes and occasionally apologises as he breaks off to answer his phone. He says he is sure that I won't represent his words properly, because the foreign journalists never do.

'Then why did you agree to speak with me?' I ask.

'Because I am polite,' he laughs.

But I suspect he also craves some recognition for the years he spent moulding the image of the most powerful man in Turkey.

It was in 1974, when Besli was in his mid-twenties, that a tall and striking young man walked into one of his meetings. The National Salvation Party (*Milli Selâmet Partisi* or MSP) was one of the few overtly Islamist organisations in Turkey at that time, and Besli was head of its youth branch. The country had just undergone its second military coup, and a mushrooming street war between leftist and nationalist youth gangs had sent the murder rate soaring. The rival factions were shooting and stabbing each other to death on the streets and in the university campuses. The MSP stayed outside the violence and the factionalism, meeting to pray, plan and organise. It was a tactic that bore fruit.

Throughout the 1970s, the MSP won places in two coalition governments despite never winning more than 12 per cent of the vote, largely
thanks to the hopeless fracturing of the non-Islamist parties.

In 1974 Erdoğan, aged twenty-one, was leader of the MSP's local
branch in Beyoğlu, his home borough in inner Istanbul. Besli, a couple
of years older, remembers him as a charismatic guy who could already
work a room. 'I don't remember where I first heard Erdoğan speak, but
I remember that he was great, even back then,' he says. 'He could make
himself heard. When he spoke, people felt sympathy with him.'

Within two years, Besli's term in office had ended and Erdoğan was
elected his successor. They were the young bloods in a party led by
the middle-aged and nerdish professor Necmettin Erbakan, who was
pursuing an agenda beloved of Islamists since the late Ottoman era.
Erbakan insisted that Turkey's ills could be blamed on foreign meddling
and Western influence, and that the cure was to turn it back towards
Islam and build relations with the Muslim world. The nefarious secular
elites who ruled the republic had done her a disservice by taking her
into NATO and cosying up to Europe; what was needed was a revival
of strong Islamic morals, population growth and rapid industrialisation
to bring Turkey's living standards up to those of the West.

The establishment was rattled. The army stepped in, launching
the third coup of the republic in 1980.

The MSP, like all the other parties, was shut down by the generals.
But young Erdoğan's rise continued. In 1985 he became Istanbul
chair of the Welfare Party (*Refah Partisi*, or RP – which replaced the
MSP), and then stood unsuccessfully as their candidate for the mayorship of Beyoğlu in 1989. In 1991 he ran for parliament for the first
time – and although he won, had to hand his seat to another parliamentary candidate due to the party's preferential voting system. None
of these setbacks discouraged him. That same year Besli began working
as Erdoğan's speechwriter, assembling the strategy that finally
propelled him to the Istanbul mayor's office in 1994. Erdoğan has
never conceded victory at the ballot box since.

'Our struggle was not so much about power, it was about a cause,'

Besli says, when I ask him what drove them to continue even when so much was stacked against them. 'When you have a cause, you don't give up just because you're not in power. And when you're a man of fate, you tell yourself that you have to struggle and the result will not be defined by you. You do what is necessary and leave the rest to Allah.'

We are twenty minutes into our conversation, yet it is the first time God has been mentioned. I can't tell whether it is deliberate; however, when I later ask Besli what their biggest hurdle has been, he admits it was the fear and scepticism of Turkey's secularist voters. He refers to them as the generation raised by the republic, brainwashed into rejecting their faith and their Eastern traditions in favour of a false affinity with the West. But he also says that a key part of his strategy with Erdoğan was to keep religion away from their image, so that they could broaden their appeal beyond the narrow, pious support base the MSP had commanded. When Erdoğan entered the mayor's office, he signed a paper promising that no one would lose their jobs because of their political affiliations or be forced to adhere to Islamic rules. On the job, he won respect for his party's technocratic efficiency.

Erdoğan's early conciliations in the mayor's office quickly gave way to a more combative tone. During a rally in the eastern town of Siirt in 1997 he read out a poem that blended nakedly Islamist metaphors with militaristic nationalism: 'The mosques are our barracks, / The minarets our bayonets, / And the faithful our soldiers.' The judicial system – dominated by Kemalists – seized the opportunity to take Erdoğan back down to where they believed he belonged. The mayor of Istanbul was sentenced to ten months in prison for inciting religious hatred. And he had already left the Refah Party, which was closed down anyway only eleven months later. But jail time proved the best image boost Erdoğan could have dreamed of.

## Jail time

In 1999 the future Turkish president joined Johnny Cash and Tupac Shakur, and released an album from prison.

*Bu şarkı burada bitmez* (This Song Does Not End Here) – is a 35-minute compilation of Erdoğan reading poetry over a soundtrack of lilting Turkish melodies. Produced by Ulus Music, a label specialising in 'introducing to the world the richness, colour and variety of Turkish music and same time making sure that the whole world can take advantage of our cultural preciousness', the album remains widely available on CD and cassette on Turkish second-hand trading websites.

By the time the glamorous 43-year-old mayor of Istanbul broke with Refah and was sent to jail, he had already started an aggressive spin campaign to reinvent himself as Turkey's number one Islamist. In the eleven months between his conviction and the start of his jail term, Erdoğan called his first major press conference. As mayor of Istanbul Erdoğan had almost always refused to speak with foreign journalists. Now, he needed the media to reboot his image for the world stage. So he invited a group of correspondents based in the city for a slap-up lunch at an upmarket restaurant serving hearty Ottoman-style food.

'Why are you meeting with us now?' asked one of the more cynical correspondents.

Erdoğan turned in surprise to his assistant, a pleasant young man who had always relayed his boss's rejection of interview requests with an apologetic air. 'Why didn't you tell me these journalists have been wanting to meet with me?' he berated the unfortunate bureaucrat.

It was, says one of the correspondents who was at the lunch, a transparent attempt to save face. 'A charm offensive,' was how another described it.

As the court case against Erdoğan dragged on, Istanbul city council turned its website into a protest page featuring messages of support and a link to the full text of his defence statement. By the time his appeal failed and he was finally sent to prison in March 1999, he had built a reputation as a free-speech crusader with a legion of loyal personal supporters. Before he was jailed he was allowed to attend Friday prayers at the Fatih Mosque in Istanbul for a final time. Huge crowds came to pray alongside him, and formed a convoy to escort him to Pınarhisar jail, north-west of Istanbul. When he was released in July 1999, having served only 119 days of his ten-month sentence, thousands turned out again to greet him.

## The ad man

Erdoğan was not the only Islamist mayor to have been imprisoned in Turkey at that time. In 1996 Şükrü Karatepe, the mayor of Kayseri in central Anatolia and also from the Refah Party, had told a rally that his 'heart was bleeding' because he had been obliged to attend a ceremony honouring Atatürk. Convicted of insulting the eternal leader in April 1998, a week after Erdoğan's conviction for inciting religious hatred, he had a one-year sentence slapped on him and was sent straight to prison with no time for appeal. But Karatepe did not have a marketing genius behind him – and he was forgotten as soon as his cell door slammed shut.

Erdoğan, meanwhile, was working with the best in the business.

'Even when Erdoğan was forbidden from engaging in politics we were engaged in communication campaigns. There was a political ban on him but we were trying to do as much as the law allowed,' says Cevat Olçok, the bearded and sharp-suited director of Arter, Turkey's first political marketing agency. I am sitting across from him at a huge desk in the agency's minimalist-industrial-style Istanbul offices in April 2018. The clean lines of the shelves behind him are ruined by Ottoman-style knick-knacks, books and framed pictures of Erdoğan. Pride of place, though, goes to the photos of his brother, Erol, and nephew, Abdullah, both killed on the Bosphorus bridge by coup soldiers on 15 July.

Erol Olçok, who founded Arter with Cevat, first worked with Erdoğan as a spin doctor in the Istanbul mayoral election campaign of 1994. He was raised in a poor and religious family in the Anatolian town of Çorum and, like Erdoğan, had graduated from religious high school. But instead of entering the clergy like most of his peers he went to art college – the first from his village to take advantage of higher education.

'I will never forget the day I first passed the Bosphorus,' Erol later said of his first day in the city in 1982.

In 1986 he graduated with a degree in art history and started working in advertising. It was a relatively new and rapidly expanding sector; prime minister Turgut Özal, the first elected leader after the 1980 military coup, was opening up Turkey's economy and Turks were becoming consumers in the Western style. After working with a number of commercial agencies Erol started Arter in 1993, and a year later was contracted by Erdoğan. Such was the bond that developed between them that, having won the Istanbul mayoral elections, Erdoğan appointed Erol Olçok his press adviser.

'Erdoğan never stopped marketing himself,' says Cevat Olçok. 'We were making greetings cards from him for religious holidays and important dates for the country. When he had the political ban, his motto was "this song does not finish here". We designed the poster for everybody in Turkey. There was a huge demand for it. It was in every city in Turkey.'

Arter's iconic poster was the namesake of the later album of poetry: a picture of Erdoğan in profile, speaking from behind a podium with a Turkish flag in the background. At the top, his name. At the bottom, that slogan – a statement. And other than that, nothing else: no party logo, no symbol and no explanation. None was needed. Erdoğan had become a brand.

## The rebels

As Erdoğan was serving his jail term, a separate group of young renegades was calling for change from within the Refah Party. These rebels, like Erdoğan, had grown frustrated with Necmettin Erbakan's way of doing politics. From cosmopolitan, professional backgrounds, they included Bülent Arınç, a suave lawyer of Cretan heritage, and Abdullah Gül, a former economist at the Islamic Development Bank.

Gül stood as candidate for the leadership of Refah in 1997, hoping to reform the party from within. He was narrowly beaten – but a few months later the party was closed down anyway.

'We had many successes with Refah. But later on, the political landscape changed and we started to make mistakes,' Gül tells me in the huge drawing room of his Istanbul palace. 'There was a convention and I became the candidate. I was talking about democracy, I was talking about fundamental rights, about human rights and saying that if the rhetoric is not good in politics we have to adopt the correct policies. The party was very authoritarian at the time. There was no chance for me yet I was about to win. It was a shock. The party was then closed by the constitutional court without justification . . . I was trying to save the party.'

As had happened so many times over the decades, Refah reformed under a new name, the *Saadet Partisi* (Felicity Party). But the new guard led by Gül did not join them – instead they split and formed a new grouping. They started their public relations drive with a rally in Kayseri, Gül's home city, and followed it up with a tour of Turkey. And they had attracted a star – Erdoğan, recently released from prison and with a soaring reputation. Gül had lobbied the European Parliament to oppose Erdoğan's jail sentence and personally approached him to join his new party once he was released. The soft-spoken technocrat says he had no issue with handing over the top position in the party he had founded to the most charismatic Islamist Turkey had ever produced. The demand for him to do so came, he says, from within the ranks.

'We all decided to make Erdoğan chairman. His popularity was higher,' Gül says.

The Arter team came as part of the Erdoğan package – and so they got to work on the new party's branding.

'We worked on the name, the logo and corporate identity,' says Cevat Olçok. 'Erol was the leader in all these things. We made additions to the party's manifesto, and we worked on the name. There were many ideas for that: one of them was the *Genç Partisi* [Young Party]. They did not like it. Then there was *Beyaz Partisi* [White Party] and from that it became *Ak* [meaning pure]. It became AK Partisi because Turkey needed a clean page. All the political establishments were tired, and the society was not getting what it wanted. But the people in this party were clean and wise – this is why we proposed AK Partisi.'

As Arter revved up the spin, speechwriter Hüseyin Besli was working out who the Turkish people actually were – and how the newly hatched AK Party might win their votes. Such polls are unremarkable in most developed democracies, but in Turkey the entrenched system had ensured that power always lay in the hands of the secular elite. They would vote one way and the religious masses would vote another and, ultimately, the army and other facets of state would decide how the country should be run. There had seemed little point in any political party trying to effect change. But that's what Erdoğan's team did and continues to do – obsessively.

'We did comparative studies of the Turkish people, and of the dynamics of the previous coups and the reasons why they had happened,' Besli says. 'We found out what people's reactions to the coups were, and then we considered all the information we had gathered. We wanted to avoid anything that might lead to such events in the future. Today, Erdoğan says we are not the ones who founded the AKP – it was the people. Our main motto was to be the voice of the voiceless. We really understood what people wanted.'

Abdullah Gül credits the expanding television coverage of parliament and political debates in the mid-1990s for Refah's, and then the AKP's, growing success.

'Before politics happened in meetings. Politicians were talking with people and then coming here' – to Istanbul and Ankara – 'and living and doing things differently,' Gül says. 'When TVs started to show parliament, people started to monitor their representatives. In the village they were supporting someone, and then seeing what they were doing in parliament. We were addressing their feelings. We were being live broadcasted. The first live broadcast started in the 1990s. It was one of the contributions to Turkish democracy. Before, political allegiance was just a tradition that was passed on. Now it is more transparent. Refah got rooted in the country in the 1990s. People listened on TV. They saw that we were addressing their feelings. This is how everything was restructured.'

Turkey's economy was also creaking by the time the AKP launched in 2001; the currency was slipping into hyper-inflation and unemployment rocketing towards 10 per cent. All the existing parties were tarnished with corruption, incompetence or both. The logo Erdoğan and his team eventually plumped for to represent their new party was the light bulb – a symbol of hope in dark times. And to fit with the letters A, K and P, they came up with a full and generic name – the *Adalet ve Kalkınma Partisi* (Justice and Development Party).

Soon, the AKP was the most talked-about party in Turkey. A secularist newspaper columnist said it should be pronounced as its letters – A-K-P – rather than as 'Ak Party', as the marketers had intended. It is still a point of contention today – and a great way of determining a Turk's feelings about the party. Every time I say 'A-K-P', Cevat Olçok pulls me up.

'Ak Partisi!' he snaps, without irony.

'When it started, the goal was to make AK Partisi . . . a brand in Turkey and the world,' he continues. 'This was said at the foundation. AK Partisi: a world party. Seventeen years have passed. You will see AK Parti everywhere in Turkey, and always with a corporate identity.'

In November 2002, only fifteen months after it was officially launched, the AKP won an outright majority of seats in the parliament. The Organisation for Security and Cooperation in Europe (OSCE), one of the major international election monitors, was glowing in its opening assessment of the poll. It wrote in its final report:

The 3 November elections for the Turkish Grand National Assembly (TGNA) demonstrated the vibrancy of Turkey's democracy. A large number of parties campaigned actively throughout the country, offering the electorate a broad and varied choice. The sweeping victory of opposition parties showed the power of the Turkish electorate to institute governmental change.

But the OSCE also noted some serious flaws in the system. The AKP had won just 34 per cent of the vote but taken almost two-thirds of the seats in parliament. The only other party to take up seats was the CHP – a result of Turkey's arcane election rules, which state that only parties that tally more than 10 per cent of the vote can enter parliament. The votes of those that fall below the threshold are distributed between those who have reached it.

Erdoğan, though chairman of the victorious party, could not take up one of its seats – his criminal conviction barred him from taking public office. Abdullah Gül became prime minister, but the AKP immediately began gathering cross-party support for the law barring Erdoğan to be changed. Gül served for just five months before stepping aside for Erdoğan in March 2003. Some within the party were unimpressed.

'No one was expecting me to resign, even *Tayyip Bey* [a Turkish honorific, roughly Mr Tayyip],' says Gül. 'Everything was going very well. There was a lot of pressure, but I did not think it would be ethical for me to stay. [Erdoğan] was chairman of the party. It was an ethical matter. I thought it would be better for me to leave [the prime minister's position].'

By April 2018, when I meet Cevat Olçok, Arter has stuck with the AKP and vice versa for seventeen years, through ten election campaigns and countless other publicity drives – and now the loss of their founder and visionary, Erol Olçok. Under him, they took their AKP formula international, working on political campaigns in northern Cyprus, Iraq, Georgia, Egypt, Malaysia, Albania, Macedonia, Libya, Tunisia and Ukraine. They also take on other work in the commercial sector.

But for Erdoğan, their number one client, Arter has always gone above and beyond the role of spin agency: Erol Olçok even stage-managed the grandiose society weddings of the president's children. It was he who commissioned the song about Erdoğan for the 2014 presidential elections – and convinced his boss of its merit.

'The mathematics of our campaign was like this. Our hero was Erdoğan,' Erol Olçok later said. 'Then Mr Erdoğan called me to his side. He said, "Is it too late to say this song is very personal and it would not be right to use it?" I said to him: "Mr Prime Minister, this song has nothing to do with you. This song is for the people who wish to express their love for you. This is their statement."'

Set to the rhythm and tune of the *dombra*, a pounding Turkic-style war song, the lyrics still echo around the Erdoğan rallies I go to five years on: *He is the voice of the oppressed, the lush voice of a silent world! Recep Tayyip Erdoğan* . . .

'Erdoğan is a genius in regards to political communications and so was Erol,' says Cevat Olçok. 'They knew . . . how to touch people and understand their feelings. They were a match.

'Erdoğan and his party came to get rid of the old order. They widened Turkey's perspectives and horizons. He gave us self-confidence. Now we have much bigger dreams. We will build our own electric car. We are building our own fighter jets and tactical helicopters. We are the seventeenth biggest economy in the world. We were the most expanding country in this year's G20. Erdoğan is realising Turkey's dreams. This is why he is a great brand.'

# 4

## ERDOĞAN AND FRIENDS

### The diaspora

Ufuk Seçgin is a Turk without Turkish citizenship and, at heart, a liberal. In Germany, where he was born, grew up and went to university, he supports the left-leaning Social Democrat Party. In Britain, where he has a second citizenship and runs his business, he is a Remainer. But in Turkey – in his DNA – he is a solid supporter of Erdoğan and the AKP. It is about more than just clever marketing.

'You should have been in Turkey in the 1990s. Compare that with now, it's day and night!' Seçgin tells me in his crisp German-accented English. 'Going to hospital was high risk, basically. I can remember how we were buying medicine from pharmacies in Germany and sending them because either they were not available in Turkey or they were so expensive they couldn't buy them. And food banks, water cuts – there was no clean drinking water. Like fuel stations you would have water stations in the city. People would go with their empty containers and fill them, every day. Electricity just a few hours a day. You see that and then you see this, what's going on now. And you say, well, this was definitely a success of the Ak Party.'

As a child born to Turkish migrant parents in Hamburg in the

1970s, Seçgin could at first only claim Turkish citizenship. His German identity documents listed him as a 'son of a *Gastarbeiter*', the name for the Turks who flocked to Germany as economic migrants in the post-war boom. They were not allowed to become German nationals. Then, in the election campaign of 1998, the Social Democrat Party pledged to lift the rule that meant only people born of German parents could claim citizenship. Seçgin, a business student with big plans, saw a new spread of opportunities open up with the promise of EU citizenship. But though the SDP won the election they were shunted back on their promise by pressure from the right wing. The amendment to the citizenship law that was eventually passed allowed the children of Turkish migrants to become German citizens – but only if they renounced their Turkish nationality. Migrants from anywhere else were allowed to keep both.

'That was because they wanted to avoid people running on both cars,' says Seçgin. 'It's black or white. You're German or you're Turkish. Where are your priorities, that type of thing.

'I still remember, I went into one of my local meetings with what was then the head of the foreign commission in the German parliament, a so-called veteran of politics. He had been forty years an MP in our region. I asked him why are you doing it this way, and gave him a list of citizenship rules from other countries. He started to give me stupid answers and I pushed further, and further. And the answer he gave me was: "What if Turkey enters a war against Germany? Who would you fight for?"'

Seçgin took German citizenship, and renounced his Turkish, in 2004. The Turkish government provides German-Turks in the same position as he is with a blue card, which allows them to live and work in Turkey as if they were citizens but without the right to vote. Nonetheless, they are invested. Seçgin was studying for an MBA at Cardiff University when the AKP was first elected in 2002. He was already a keen supporter. His flatmate – another German-Turk who, unlike Seçgin, weaved a booze-filled, Casanova-like path through British university life – joined the party online as he saw the votes coming in.

'I said: "Anything Erdoğan or the Ak Party says is completely the opposite of what you believe. So why on earth are you joining?" And he said: "I'm going to be a businessman, and the earlier I join AKP the better for me in the future."'

Both Turkey and Germany have since yanked at Ufuk Seçgin, trying to make him decide whom he loves more, but really all he wants is to be a successful Muslim businessman in a globalised world. Like many Turks he feels fed up with the EU and the endless merry-go-round of Turkey's attempts to join it. He once supported Turkey's membership bid, but now feels it would be better outside it. At the same time, in the UK he is facing the impacts of a Brexit he didn't vote for, and which doesn't appeal to him. He will no longer be able to hire talent from the continent with the same ease as he hires British workers, or to work across borders so easily.

Now, in the AKP and Erdoğan, Seçgin sees a party and a leader with some problems. He says there are few signs of a succession plan, no new generation of leaders being nurtured, and he feels the arrests of journalists in the wake of the coup attempt have gone too far. He worries that the Turkish economy, once so buoyant, may soon start to shrivel. But in uncertain times across the span of his world, Erdoğan is one of the few certainties Seçgin can cling to. The president has brought wealth, stability and honour to Turks like him – and to those looking in from the outside, Erdoğan's flamboyance masks many of his flaws.

'I don't see, who has got that charisma? Someone like Erdoğan doesn't come along every ten years. He comes along every thirty years or whatever,' Seçgin says. 'Even his opponents say he is really charismatic, knows his stuff. He has put Turkey back on the map.'

## The new Muslim middle class

Seçgin is part of a wave of pious businessmen who have made it big in Erdoğan's Turkey. Halalbooking.com, the business he co-founded in 2009, is an online holiday booking service aimed at observant

Muslims. It is a fast-growing market; Halalbooking.com is currently valued at $60–70 million.

In May 2017 – the start of his most successful season to date – I accompany Seçgin on a tour of the halal resorts of Antalya alongside two dozen businessmen and women, all of them European Muslims. Thirty-six-year-old Songül, a stylish German-Turk from the city of Bremen, donned the Islamic headscarf and started practising her religion by the book six years ago after the birth of her two daughters. It was only then that she realised the dearth of lifestyle brands aimed at middle-class Muslims – and so she became one of the pioneers. Songül started her online bookings business in 2016, and still had only one competitor in the online halal tourism sector in Germany a year on.

'It was a boutique industry before, all very expensive,' says Songül. 'You would either hire a private villa or go to exclusive resorts where it costs around four thousand euros for a family holiday for one week.'

Over four days, Seçgin leads us on a tour of the new wave in pious holidaymaking – the mass-market halal hotels. The Bera, the first to be awarded halal status in Turkey, is our first stop. The sweet smell of hookah smoke wafts through the cavernous lobby, and a wide panorama of Istanbul's Bosphorus Bridge with a mosque in the foreground hangs behind reception. The Bera is owned by a conglomerate with ties to Erdoğan: when he was mayor of Istanbul, the municipality sold it a piece of prime real estate in the heart of the city for a fraction of its true value. The television screens are showing ATV, a pro-Erdoğan channel, and *Yeni Şafak* and *Sabah*, its newspaper equivalents, are propped up in a rack by the door. On leaving, I am handed a gift: an encyclopaedia of Ottoman history.

Otherwise, The Bera is just like any other package resort: filled with hyped-up small children and parents who look as if they've been craving this holiday since they flew home from the last. I ask a couple from Preston who are slumped in the lobby's comfy chairs as their two tiny girls scoot around whether they thought twice about a holiday in Turkey after the coup attempt and terrorist attacks.

'We've not really heard about those,' the mother tells me, clearly wishing I would move on so she can relax. 'We just came here last year and we liked it, so we decided to come again.'

The food at the buffet is halal – but otherwise no different to any other resort. In my comfortable, clean room I find not a Gideon Bible and a minibar stocked with beer and wine but a Quran and a *Qibla*, an arrow stuck to the ceiling to show the direction of Mecca. At reception in the women's spa and beach area I am frisked by a (female) security guard and stripped of my phone and camera before being gestured through smoked-glass doors. Through the changing rooms and treatment suites, the path leads out onto a fifty-metre stretch of beach surrounded by billowing curtains of fabric hung between flag-poles thirty metres high. You cannot see out to the sea – the view is blocked by the sails, although the water can still lap in underneath. The women wear reasonably conservative bikinis on this boxed-off beach, even after being freed of the male gaze. I ask one if it bothers her that she cannot contemplate the horizon as she sunbathes.

'But if it was open, the men could look at us as they come past on boats and jet-skis,' she replies.

In the lobby that evening, as we relax with tea and flavoured tobacco, I ask Seçgin how the drop in visitor numbers to Turkey since last year's coup attempt has affected his business. He looks at me as if I were crazy.

'Drop?' he replies. 'Last year we doubled our business, and this year we doubled again!'

By 2017, Turkey has risen to become the world's third most popular destination for halal travellers, a four-place rise on the year before (only Malaysia and the UAE score higher). In a global halal tourism market now worth $151 billion annually, Turkey dominates the beach-holiday sector. The country accounts for a disproportionate amount of the hotels listed on Halalbooking.com, not out of a conscious effort on Seçgin's part but simply because Turkey is the place with the best-developed concept of what an all-inclusive halal holiday means. This, after all, is an evolution of the model the Turks have been fine-tuning on booze-soaked European tourists since the 1980s.

'Turkey is the centre of package resorts,' Seçgin continues. 'At the lower end there are the mass-market resorts. And at the high end in the halal market there's the Angels Resort, where the rooms start at three hundred and fifty euros a night. I have one customer from Ukraine this year – he booked six weeks there and spent thirty-one thousand euros!'

But this is Turkey. And here, the sacred always comes with a side serving of the profane.

The original pioneer of the country's now-booming Islamic leisure sector is the unlikely Fadıl Akgündüz, who goes by the nickname 'Jet' and is a conman of such confidence that every time he is released from prison he starts plotting his next swindle. Most recently, he served fifteen months for a libel conviction after he claimed that the governor of an Aegean province had tried to assassinate him in a car crash. Before that, he defrauded hundreds with dodgy timeshare deals, and back in the late 1990s he collected millions of pounds from investors, many of them Turks in the European diaspora, for a construction project in Ankara that never materialised. Before that, though, he launched his first and only successful project: Turkey's first halal holiday resort.

The Caprice Hotel in the Aegean seaside town of Didim is a monstrosity of glass and plastic façades that looks, at a distance, like the stern of a sinking cruise ship. Inside, it is pure neo-Baroque. The domed ceiling of its lobby is painted with tulip motifs in the style of the old mosques of Istanbul. Its floor is inlaid with gold mosaics. Like any other hotel catering to the mass tourism market, it has an all-you-can-eat buffet every mealtime, a huge swimming complex and spas, and a path leading straight to the beach. There are also à la carte restaurants serving Chinese and Italian food, and a designer boutique offering some of Turkey's top brands. Turkish stars perform in the hotel's entertainment centre every week. The well-heeled tourists who stay here would have no reason to leave its gaudy confines, apart from acute claustrophobia. And if they are devout Muslims – as almost all of them are – they can relax safe in the knowledge that they will never miss prayer time.

Jet Fadıl Akgündüz opened the resort in 1996 with the strapline: 'A modern vacation complex, where the call to prayer is heard five times a day.' The idea of a hotel catering to the Islamic market was unheard of in Turkey at that time. It was the era when the Refah Party's Necmettin Erbakan was prime minister and Erdoğan the mayor of Istanbul – but Erdoğan's jailing and the toppling of Erbakan's government in the 'postmodern' military coup of 1997 would remind everyone that the Kemalists were still in charge. Local residents in this largely secular part of Turkey were dismayed when Akgündüz bought what had once been a resort for debauched European tourists and turned it into a haven for the devout – but his business boomed. Muslims with money to spend had previously had to share their hotels with customers who followed totally different lifestyles: drinking alcohol, sunbathing in bikinis in mixed-gender areas, and disregarding the patterns of the Islamic day. Now, they could spend their leisure time in an environment just like that of their homes. In halal hotels, the swimming pool and spa areas are segregated by gender, there is no trace of alcohol anywhere, and prayer rooms are provided so that guests can slip straight from the poolside to the prayer mat.

Slowly, other Turkish businessmen caught on to the potential and by the time the AKP took power in 2002 there were five halal hotels in Turkey. By 2014 the sector had mushroomed to 152 halal resorts, spas and boutique hotels across the country, including a halal ski resort and a cruise ship. Part of that growth can be explained by the overall rise in wealth in Turkey over the same period, which lifted the poorest – and generally most pious – section of the society from a subsistence-level existence to a level affording them disposable income. The average annual income in Turkey in 1998, two years after the Caprice opened, was $8,567 and the average rent costs in the *gecekondu* – literally, 'built in the night' – districts ate up half of a family's income. By 2014 the average wage was $19,610 and rent or mortgage repayments now only took up a quarter of their pay. A new middle class has risen, buoyed by a growing class of businessmen from the conservative cities of central Anatolia. And they want in on all the things the elites have been enjoying for decades.

There is also the Erdoğan factor.

'There is more Islamic political influence now,' says Seçgin. 'Muslim people are standing up and saying: "Hang on, I also work hard, I have more money, I want to take part in all these great things that everyone else is doing, the upper ten to fifteen per cent of the society." The industry was starting to develop before Erdoğan, and until recently there hadn't been a single policy by the tourism ministry in support of this industry. Nothing. So, you might argue that without Erdoğan the industry would probably have developed anyway. But my fear is that for political and ideological reasons, some people in Turkey may have tried to prevent this sector from thriving. By Erdoğan and the AK Party being in power, their passiveness, they have helped the industry to thrive. They didn't support us at all, but they also didn't do anything to prevent or hinder us. And that's already a good thing, because under different governments, I can imagine some would have tried to stop this industry from going further.'

The Turkish Standards Institute started providing halal hotel certification in June 2014. Until then Turkey had lagged behind in the sector compared to other Islamic countries such as Malaysia and the United Arab Emirates; even the UK's tourism board, Visit Britain, held halal tourism conferences before Turkey. But without much official help, the sector has taken root and flowered amid the fleshpots of the Aegean and Mediterranean coastlines. Some of the halal resorts are spanking new and purpose-built. Others are older hotels that were once stuffed with hard-drinking Russians and Europeans but which have now been converted – stripped of their bars, fitted with prayer rooms, their swimming pools and beaches divided into men's and women's sections.

As the halal tourism market evolved, so too did the business plan of its original entrepreneur, Jet Fadıl Akgündüz. As more mass-market resorts opened, he upgraded the Caprice to a five-star luxury resort and changed the 'Hotel' in its name to 'Palace'.

'Thank you, Caprice Palace, for providing so much for the ladies!' gushes the dubbed star of the hotel's tacky and stilted promotion video, as an unseen male narrator guides her through the seemingly endless facilities. 'My god! What beauty is this? What spaciousness? What tranquillity? Caprice Palace . . . I wouldn't have believed that a palace like this existed in the world!'

Akgündüz was also working on other projects: a second Caprice in Istanbul, a residential complex in Ankara, a football club packed with celebrity players and a plan to manufacture Turkey's first indigenous cars in the impoverished eastern province of Siirt, his birthplace. None of them came to fruition, and scores of investors were left empty-handed and furious. Akgündüz fled the country in 1998 to avoid criminal charges, but only four years later, after the 2002 elections (in which the AKP took power for the first time), he returned to Turkey after standing for and winning a seat in Siirt as an independent candidate. His political career was short-lived; the high election council immediately cancelled his parliamentary membership, meaning that he was also stripped of the immunity from prosecution that he had briefly enjoyed as an elected deputy. He was sent to the Istanbul courthouse and then to the prison in his private limousine with the number plate 34 JET 25.

A year later Akgündüz was freed, and spent the next decade skipping town before serving another jail term and then hatching another plan. In 2014 he announced that he had bought an island in the Maldives, which he would turn into 'an island for the Muslims'. He began to dress in robes and turban in the style of an Ottoman dignitary, and claimed to be investing $170 million in his new project. Some of Turkey's most prominent pious Muslims gave it their backing by issuing a *fatwa* (an Islamic legal decree) stating that such a project was permissible in the eyes of Allah. When investors in this latest scheme discovered that it was a swindle, too, one of the preachers who had given it his stamp of approval was confronted by a journalist. 'I didn't say buy a place. I just said it's permissible under the *fatwa*,' he insisted. 'If you didn't listen and did a stupid thing, so did I. I lost my apartments, too.'

In 2015 a court order was issued for the original Caprice to be confiscated in order to help pay the compensation claims levied against Akgündüz's still-unfinished Istanbul project. The local police raided the Caprice Palace Didim and began loading the furniture, minibar fridges and computers onto trucks in front of 600 startled guests. At the last minute the hotel's lawyers managed to cut a deal, and the fittings were returned – but three months later Akgündüz was arrested on embezzlement charges. He served sixteen months, and then immediately began talking about his next project.

'The east will come to life, Turkey will be developed!' he proclaimed to journalists waiting at the prison gate on the day of his release in March 2017.

## The Gülenists

Akgündüz remains a free man – for now. The original owner of the similarly high-end halal Angels Resort in Marmaris, Turkish businessman and newspaper owner Akın İpek, has not been so lucky.

İpek shot into the stratosphere of the Turkish business elite during the first decade of the millennium – the early AKP era. It was a time when certain connections promised considerable bounty, both political and economic. İpek, like many others, was an open supporter of Fethullah Gülen – the cleric turned cult leader who built his small Turkish congregation into a worldwide movement. Born in 1941 in the eastern province of Erzurum, Gülen trained as an imam and joined the Diyanet, the state's religious agency, which was set up under the republic's first constitution in 1924. The Diyanet employs all of Turkey's clerics and posts them to mosques around the country. Gülen graduated in 1958 and was dispatched to coastal İzmir, where he quickly began working to extend his reach outside the mosque. According to the movement's biography, he began speaking in tea houses and at town meetings. 'The subject matter of his speeches, whether formal or informal, was not restricted explicitly to religious questions; he also talked about education, science, Darwinism, about the economy and social justice,' the biography claims.

Having built his local following, Gülen retired from the Diyanet in 1981 and started preaching freelance both in Turkey and abroad. He also began opening schools and charitable foundations.

In the conservative city of Kayseri, one businessman remembered how a charismatic imam came to town in 1986 and started delivering lectures to huge crowds. 'His speeches were so good, all the women in Kayseri's high society soon started wearing the headscarf. We all liked his speeches and meetings so much that we started collecting money for the movement. I gave one cheque to them. There was a doctor, he wasn't interested in religion but the *hoca* [teacher] even converted him. After a while I began to see that they are conmen, but lots of people didn't care. All the state contracts were given to Gülenist businesses when the AKP came to power. One of my friends said to me, "I got rich because of them, they are buying everything from me." People wanted to believe in what the Gülenists were saying because there was so much state pressure on religion. And here was a Muslim organisation that was working in every area except the political space.'

In February 1997, the Turkish army launched what became known as its postmodern coup. Tanks rolled through Ankara and Istanbul, setting off a series of events that would eventually force Fethullah Gülen into exile. The generals had been stirred into action after Necmettin Erbakan, leader of Erdoğan's Refah Party, became prime minister in 1996 – Turkey's first full-blooded Islamist premier. After the generals issued a memo from their boardroom, and Erbakan's governing coalition partners rounded on him, he stepped down. For the next years political Islam was again forced into the shadows in Turkey; Refah was shut down, Erbakan's political career was finished, and the AKP's shoots started growing in the dark.

Gülen moved to the United States in 1999 and has remained there ever since, now living in a vast secluded ranch in Pennsylvania and rarely venturing out. But he has never stopped preaching. Gülen's videos draw millions of views and both adulation and hilarity on YouTube (one has been superimposed with cartoon watermelons to make it look as though the imam is chopping them with his flailing hands as he rants).

Although he was little known outside Turkey, Gülen's following had grown so huge by 2013 that he was propelled to the number one spot in *Time* magazine's annual 100 Most Influential People in the World list. His devotees, loyal, worldly and highly organised, had voted en masse to get him there. The magazine's blurb betrays the bemusement the editors must have felt at finding the votes flooding in for this unknown man. But there is also a prescient hint of what was to come:

Fethullah Gülen is among the world's most intriguing religious leaders. From a secluded retreat in Pennsylvania, he preaches a message of tolerance that has won him admirers around the world. Schools founded by Gülen's followers thrive in an estimated 140 countries. Doctors who respond to his wishes work without pay in disaster-afflicted countries.

Gülen, however, is also a man of mystery. His influence in his native Turkey is immense, exercised by graduates of his schools who have reached key posts in the government, judiciary and police. This makes him seem like a shadowy puppeteer, and he is scorned by almost as many Turks as love him.

The political rise and fall of the Gülenists is the murkiest and most controversial part of the Erdoğan story. But the first thing to say is that the core of Erdoğan's allegations against the group are true – that as bizarre and conspiratorial as it sounds, Gülen's followers really did become a shadowy cabal who spent decades inching their way up through the Turkish state.

Here is a taste of how the Gülenists operated. In September 2015, as the relationship between Erdoğan and Gülen was imploding, an email dropped into my inbox from Hawthorn Advisors, a London public relations and 'reputation management' agency, publicising a study written by a group of British barristers. It was titled *A report on the rule of law and respect for human rights in Turkey since December 2013*, and had been commissioned by the Journalists' and Writers' Foundation – a well-known Gülenist front group. Established in 1994, the JWF operated from an office in Istanbul's pious Üsküdar district and was, according to Joshua Hendrick, a US academic who immersed himself among the Gülenists in the 2000s, 'the primary public face of the movement'.

'They have a very strategic and long history, in Turkey and the world, of peddling favour from influential people, including elected officials, journalists and other leaders,' Hendrick told me.

They had certainly picked the report's authors well. Two of the four were serving British politicians, Sir Edward Garnier in the House of Commons and Lord Woolf in the House of Lords. Garnier's Register of Interests entry for the work reveals that the JWF paid him £115,994 for his 100 hours spent on the project. Six months after the report was published, Garnier stood up in the Commons during a debate on the EU–Turkey migrant deal to raise the 'serial and appalling human rights and rule of law abuses by the Turkish government'.

'While these abuses continue,' he said, 'there should be no question of opening any chapters [on Turkey's EU membership] at all, even though we need Turkey as a member of NATO and its agreement to help with the migration problem.'

Although he mentioned in his statement to the House that he had worked on the report, he did not reveal who had commissioned it. In his response to me in August 2016, when I reported the story in

*The Times*, Garnier insisted that he and the other authors 'are not supporters or adherents of [the Gülen movement] but wrote the report as independent English lawyers based on the evidence we had reviewed'.

There is no doubt that he knew who he was working for, though – the original press release sent to me by the Hawthorn PR agency had included a blurb about the Gülen movement at the end: 'The Gülen movement is a civil society network of individuals and religious, humanitarian, and educational institutions that subscribe to Islamic scholar Fethullah Gülen's advocacy of interfaith dialogue, community service, and universal education.'

It is easy to see how a British politician might be sucked in. Outside Turkey the Gülenists sell themselves as purveyors of modern, pluralist Islam, a pitch that is directly and deliberately tuned to Western ears. Using that narrative they have built up a large following within the Turkish émigré community and organised endless outreach programmes and round tables in the West. In the UK, where much Gülenist capital has fled since Erdoğan's crackdown started, they still run a lobby group, The Dialogue Society, which has hosted Cherie Blair and former Liberty director Shami Chakrabati among its guest speakers, as well as an educational trust that offers free weekend tuition to pupils in the state school system. You have to dig fairly deep into their websites before you see that these organisations are linked to the Gülen movement.

Inside Turkey, the Gülenists were best known for running high-achieving private schools for the children of rich families and subsidised university dormitories for those of the poor. 'Everyone was aware of Gülenists but they were not seen as particularly threatening,' said one Western diplomat based in Turkey in the early AKP era. 'They were seen as a kind of irrelevance, a rather eccentric secret society that raised money, did good things and ran schools in Turkey and other parts of the Islamic world. It felt like a normal part of the Turkish society. We did not, as diplomats, focus on things that we probably should have done more. It did have the civic elements, particularly in Anatolia. It felt almost like Germany or old UK, like the Rotary Clubs. It almost fell into that bracket rather than a serious political thing.'

Overseas the Gülenists ran Turkish language and cultural institutes. Their members, having come up through the elite Gülenist schools or been handpicked in the university dorms, were the brightest, the best educated and the most fluent foreign-language speakers – the perfect cultural ambassadors for Turkey abroad. While some members were directed by the higher ranks of the movement to take jobs in the Turkish state and security services (and often handed stolen test papers in advance to ensure they would get the plum positions), others went abroad and opened more schools overseas. Poorer, developing nations – particularly the Muslim parts of Africa, the Balkans and central Asia – were delighted to have such polished and pious people coming to provide education. An opaque group called 'Citizens Against Special Interest Lobbying in Public Schools' has released a document online titled 'Every continent but Antarctica', listing 101 countries where Gülenist schools were allegedly operating, from Afghanistan to Zambia.

'I remember that after the Berlin wall came down and the Soviet Union disintegrated, there were hopes from Turkish nationalists and even centre-right parties to bring in their brothers through Central Asia under the Turkish umbrella, sort of a near abroad for Turkey,' says a US lobbyist who has previously worked for the AKP government. 'They were going to go as far east as the Chinese border. Those hopes were quickly dashed because seventy years of communism takes its toll – their plans did not work out. But there was still a soft power idea more modestly expressed. The Gülenists were seen as a useful tool. And the Gülenists wanted to do it. It was a win-win situation, and it only became a liability later. It's funny because for years it was a Turkish foreign policy priority to get these schools up and running. Now the priority is to close them down.'

In those early AKP years Erdoğan was happy to piggyback on the Gülenists' established networks. His party was electorally strong but institutionally weak, and facing a hostile state and military dominated by the Kemalists. There were few AKP people working within the bureaucracy – this was, after all, the party that had risen from the fringes, and was only now making its way to the centre. The army wanted to bring Erdoğan down. Much of the judiciary wanted to bring him down. The only way he – and his party – could survive was to build alliances.

'After the AKP came to power in 2002, I, like many others, was hearing informal reporting that the Gülenists were being recruited more and more in some government departments, especially in the police and the judiciary,' says one former parliamentary deputy. 'I tried to collect some information on such informal reporting, but I couldn't get much reliable results. In one case I talked to an ex-Minister of Interior who had recently left that position, asking if it were true that large numbers of Gülenists were being recruited to the police. He said yes, to some extent it was true, but rhetorically asked "what could I do when those people performed much better than others in the entrance tests and examinations?"'

## The liberals

Erdoğan's alliance with the Gülenists was only one among many. The AKP was also reaching out to liberal, anti-army activist groups, and to members of the secular opposition who had grown tired of their stale old parties. Many joined up with the AKP right at the start in 2001. Süleyman Sarıbaş, a lawyer who had been a deputy in Turgut Özal's Anavatan Party (Motherland Party, or ANAP) since 1983, signed up shortly before the elections of November 2002. Erdoğan personally approached him to join the party. Sarıbaş agreed, despite some misgivings about Erdoğan's character.

'I regarded Erdoğan as a civilian, but he never completely retained Western values,' Sarıbaş says. 'He was emotional and easily scared. Timid. His lifestyle was something between an urban lifestyle and the provincial rural lifestyle. He was very much in the middle. I will give you one example. He would pull out his Swiss army knife from his pocket and clean his teeth with it. He is a villager in that sense. But he has been raised in Istanbul and he is very urban at the same time. In the period I met him, he was being judged. He had court cases against him. He was afraid about being arrested. After he became the chairperson of the AKP there was a court case against him about his property. He seemed to have too much property and it was not clear how he had managed to own it all. He said that it was the gold belonging to his children that he had exchanged. At about five p.m. we went to see the prosecutor and he wanted to put him under arrest. They were about to close the court. The judge arrived a little bit late on that day. We waited for half an hour for the judge to arrive. Erdoğan was white at the fear of being arrested.'

Sarıbaş joined the AKP because it seemed, in 2002, to offer a reformist agenda. Within three years he had left it again, part of the party's first mass wave of resignations. He was one of thirteen deputies who quit between February and April 2005, throwing the AKP into its first real crisis. Erdoğan was already showing himself to be 'fretful and ill-tempered', according to an AFP report on the mass exit of members. On resigning, Sarıbaş said that the party was not truly committed to EU-focused reform, and that its inner workings were corrupt and authoritarian. Musa Kart, a cartoonist at *Cumhuriyet*, a secularist newspaper, depicted the prime minister as a cat tangled in a ball of yarn as the crisis in his party grew. Erdoğan sued him for $3,500. He also called the defectors 'the rotten apples in the bag'.

The mass of remaining deputies seemed willing to overlook any growing disquiet about Erdoğan's character. The AKP survived its 2005 crisis, and two years later scored a huge victory over its old enemy, the army – and over the CHP, the largest opposition bloc in parliament. In May that year, the generals threatened a coup over the nomination of AKP founder Abdullah Gül as president. The constitutional court took up the thread and started a case to close down the AKP. Gül is a moderate Islamist and a pro-European. The army's problem with having him as president? His wife wears the Islamic headscarf.

Erdoğan called their bluff and called a snap election. The AKP won overwhelmingly, affirming the people's support for the democratically elected government over the self-appointed secularist saviours. Tens of CHP deputies and hundreds of rank-and-file members left their party and joined the AKP.

'The AKP between 2002 and 2007 seemed to be following a reformist political line,' says Haluk Özdalga, a CHP deputy who was among those who crossed the floor. 'We had extensive consultations with party people, and a majority supported the idea of going over to the AKP. In Ankara, which is my political district, a couple of hundred CHP members followed with us, and they gradually got various elected positions within the AKP organisations. This flow of members from the CHP to the AKP continued until approximately 2011. I consider myself as a social democrat, and at that time the AKP stood ideologically closer to me than the CHP. That may sound a little unusual for those not knowing the CHP and the AKP of that time. Many social democratic politicians in Europe at that time felt the same way. The AKP appeared to be structurally a more democratic party, not dominated by a single person.'

Another of the nine who joined in 2007 was Ertuğrul Günay, a CHP veteran who had left the party in 2004 and was in parliament as an independent. Günay believed he saw in the AKP the promise of a new type of Turkish politics. Erdoğan appointed him minister of culture.

'It was directly from Erdoğan that I received a proposal to join the AKP,' Günay says. 'After a few meetings, and after consulting my friends, I accepted. During its first term in government the party was promising on the issues of democracy, social welfare and pluralism. CHP as the only opposition party in the parliament followed a much more conservative line about the issues of EU and pluralism – I know many "leftists" from the CHP who thought that the EU would divide Turkey. I had hoped that with the AKP, a new social movement in Turkey would form itself, leading to the rise of a progressive politics that would be at peace with the values of the people.'

Erdoğan at that time was a man willing to take criticism, to listen to others, and to learn: 'well-intentioned and sincere about democracy', according to Günay. One diplomat said that in his early years as prime minister Erdoğan would arrive at meetings with a stack of notecards on the issues to be discussed. Another said that he was 'one amongst many important people in the system . . . more equal than anybody else but there were other players who argued with him, whether Abdullah Gül, Abdüllatif Şener [another AKP founder, who left the party in 2007], or Ali Babacan [economy minister]. These other voices were from smart individuals, who had come into government with a lot more experience on a world stage than Erdoğan. He relied on them. He trusted them and respected their advice and judgement.'

In the rest of the world, too, this charismatic rising star of Turkish politics was making a good impression. The AKP won its first elections in November 2002, just as the US and its coalition of the willing were gearing up to declare war on Iraq. They desperately needed allies in the Middle East – and a moderate Islamist, westward-looking Turkey fitted the bill perfectly. Erdoğan visited Washington in December 2002, while he was still legally blocked from serving in parliament, but when it was clear that the law would be changed and he would become prime minister. According to Faruk Loğoğlu, the Turkish ambassador to the US at the time, Erdoğan was 'given the red-carpet treatment . . . received by George W. Bush in the White House, not in the Oval Office but in the Atlantic Room. He could not go into the Oval Office because he was not a prime minister but it was important for American interests at the time. It was not a secret that he was going to become a member of parliament. It was not something that the US discovered on its own. It was an open secret.

'Turkey was the lead for the US in the fight against Islamic radicalism. It was like fighting two birds with one stone: Turkey could fight radical Islam, and be part of the Sunni axis containing Iran.'

Turkey watchers within the US State Department knew that Erdoğan would be unlikely to live up to these high expectations.

When he became prime minister on 15 March 2003, parliament having voted to overturn the law that blocked him from office (a move supported by the CHP), he inherited a problem. Two weeks earlier, the Turkish parliament had voted against joining the US-led war on Iraq. It was a surprise to everyone – AKP ministers had appeared open to joining the coalition. But the deputies' votes reflected the overwhelming opposition to the war among the Turkish population. They had chosen to satisfy their people rather than kowtow to their powerful US ally. Over the coming years, Erdoğan would repeatedly make the same calculation knowing that, without the support of his people, he was nothing. And the US generals would never forget the Turkish betrayal.

'We oversold this idea of the democratic Muslim thing because it seemed to combine everything, from the Muslim Brotherhood to membership of the EU,' said one US diplomat. 'Diplomacy is a competitive business. You are the coach at a beauty contest and you want all the attention. There is first place, a very distant second, then almost an irrelevant third place and then everybody else. Therefore, you try to get presidential visits. The first visit of the Obama administration was to Turkey. In a rational world, Turkey is an easy sell. It is still today. But it brings so much baggage in what it does. And even more baggage in our warped perceptions of what a "loyal" NATO ally should be.'

While Erdoğan built his reputation as a democratiser overseas, back at home the Gülen network was quietly using the leeway afforded it by its alliance with the AKP to stretch out further into the police, judiciary, bureaucracy and army. It was fast turning into an anti-democratic, secretive and powerful force within the Turkish state and society. As journalists, academics and opposition politicians began digging into the murky network and asking questions about what their true intentions were, the Gülenists used their connections and positions to punish and silence them. One foreign journalist based in Turkey in the early AKP era told me how he discovered that his home phone and internet had been tapped by the group when the non-Gülenist police, who by this time were launching investigations into their own colleagues, called him in and presented him with reams of transcripts. Separately, an official from the prime ministry told me a nearly identical story.

Most notoriously, it was Gülenist prosecutors and judges who, with Erdoğan's blessing, brought a series of court cases that collectively decimated the power of the military. Between 2008 and 2013, hundreds of officers, journalists and politicians were found guilty of coup plotting and handed hefty prison sentences. The trials proved a turning point. On the one hand, the Gülenists had helped Erdoğan neutralise his biggest foes: the army and the Kemalists. On the other, they had shown him how much power they could wield – and so Erdoğan's fear of the military was gradually replaced with a fear of Fethullah Gülen.

'Erdoğan felt more liberated because of his increasing neutering of other institutions but also more threatened by the Gülenists,' said a diplomat posted in Turkey as the relationship between the two men began to crumble. 'As a reaction, there was a series of events from 2009 until the attempted coup in 2016. Erdoğan started striking the opposition, particularly aiming at the Gülenists.'

## The scandal

The one-time allies began circling each other in the ring. In 2013 Erdoğan, still the prime minister, announced that he would be running in the coming year's presidential elections. Meanwhile Gülen was rumoured to be planning his return to Turkey from the US, where he had lived in self-imposed exile since 1999.

Erdoğan had also overseen a détente with the PKK through a peace plan engineered in the mid-2000s, and it riled Gülen. The PKK, with its core ideology of godless leftism, made a natural enemy for the devout Gülenists. In south-eastern Turkey and the Kurdish region of northern Iraq, the movement moved onto the PKK's turf by opening their study centres and schools. As far as Gülen and his people were concerned, it was piety – not political dialogue – that would defeat the PKK. In a piece for the movement's website, university researcher Adem Palabıyık wrote:

Attendance at Friday prayers, the spread of the headscarf, Quran courses and the emergence of a young generation that is familiar with Islam is the last thing that [the PKK] would like to see because members of such a generation would not go to the mountains; instead, they would attend Friday prayers and they would fast in Ramadan. Moreover, they would not kill others, they would not be hostile to their state and they would have an Islamic code of ethics.

Both knew there was not enough room in Turkish politics for two charismatic and pious men. The smouldering Erdoğan–Gülen alliance combusted in December 2013, when a Turkish police investigation revealed a huge corruption scandal with all the ingredients of a Hollywood thriller. At its heart was a series of gold deals between Turkey and Iran that had helped Tehran evade US sanctions. A Turkish-Iranian gold dealer called Reza Zarrab had oiled the trans-actions with bribes to people in high places in Turkey – Rolex watches, primarily, and cash stuffed in shoe boxes. Turkey's state-owned Halkbank was implicated, as were the sons of Erdoğan and four of his ministers.

Turkey still crackled with the scent of uprising at the time: only seven months had passed since Gezi. As the intrigue grew, Istanbul exploded again into a riot of Molotov cocktails and tear gas. Graffiti covered the streets: *Thieves everywhere*, it read. I have never been tear-gassed so badly as I was during those protests of December 2013, nor seen demonstrators in Istanbul so intent on causing maximum damage. On İstiklal, the mile-long pedestrianised shopping street that runs through the heart of the city centre, they used fireworks as weapons and tore up cobblestones from the side streets to lob at the police – I saw one unfortunate onlooker take a glancing blow to the back of his head. Others used shop frontages and roadworks signs to build flaming necklaces of barricades along the street. When the police mounted their fight-back, it was savage. First they sent water cannon down İstiklal to douse the fires, then they used tear gas and smoke grenades, and then in the fug of panic and smog they fired rubber bullets into the crowd and down the narrow side streets where everyone was escaping.

I barged into a bar with around twenty others in a scrambled attempt to avoid being hit. Thinking I had made it to safety, I started to relax and even thought about getting a beer as the chaos rumbled on outside. Then a fresh tear-gas canister landed right outside the window and its fumes leaked in through the side of the panes. Like everyone else I tried to escape the acrid cloud by running up to the next floor, but soon the entire place was filled with gas. Choking and almost vomiting, I dashed back out into the narrow street where the police were still firing rounds of rubber bullets and ran blindly, somehow making it to the other end and out onto the wide Tarlabaşı boulevard, haunt of Kurdish mobsters and transsexual prostitutes. Finally back in fresh air, I collapsed onto the kerb and heaved deep breaths as a kind shop owner passed me some water and gave me milk to splash on my burning face. The only good thing about tear gas is that its effects wear off almost as soon as you get away from it, leaving you feeling ridiculous for being so sure that you were about to drown in your own fluids only moments earlier.

That night, it looked as if the government might fall, but everyone knew the scandal was not all it seemed. There was little doubt among the Turks on the streets that Gülenist police chiefs had organised the investigation, as true as its substance might be. Even at the height of the protests, those taking part knew what might happen.

'We fear that we may be seen as acting with the Gülenists,' one young woman who had joined the protests told me. 'Actually, we want the people of Turkey to have the power.'

Within days Erdoğan had accused Gülen of orchestrating the investigation in a bid to topple his government. Hundreds of high-ranking police officers were sacked, the case files were closed, and Erdoğan clung on to power by his fingernails. His party would never be the same again. In the days following the scandal, eight AKP deputies who raised their voices in protest at the way it had been handled by the government resigned from the party under threat of expulsion.

Haluk Özdalga, who had crossed the floor from the CHP to the AKP in 2007, was one of them. 'At that time [in December 2013], I had already begun considering to part ways with the AKP . . . I spoke out almost as soon as the graft case became public, even before the government made its position clear on the issue. There was credible evidence of graft against four ministers, so they must resign and be given a fair trial, and we all get to know if they are innocent or guilty. The party, after some deliberations, instead decided to avoid a legal process, and took a politically motivated vote in the parliament to sweep the case under the carpet.'

Once he had re-entrenched his power, Erdoğan moved into all-out assault mode against the Gülenists. First, he ordered their network of private schools, which had been some of the most high-performing in Turkey, to be closed. Then the courts started targeting businessmen with links to the movement. One of the first was Akın İpek. His conglomerate, Koza İpek, was the umbrella for twenty-two companies spanning media, education, mining, tourism and air travel. In its stable was not only the halal Angels Resort in Marmaris, but also the *Bugün* newspaper and Kanaltürk television channel – both of them opposition voices.

In September 2015 the Turkish government opened an investigation into İpek and his links with the Gülenists. There were certainly strong signs that he had been involved with the movement, although he denied ever having bankrolled it in return for leg-ups for his businesses. Up until late 2012, İpek had still been granted private audiences with Erdoğan, although they had been growing increasingly frosty – in the last, according to İpek, the fuming prime minister read out a critical *Bugün* column to his face. Now, İpek found himself the first victim of the war. The private university he had set up was closed down, and his brother and several other relatives were arrested while İpek himself fled into exile in London. In November 2015, three days before parliamentary elections, the courts seized his company and its $7 billion worth of assets. In the pro-government press İpek was accused of plotting alongside Gülen to unseat Erdoğan, and in one particularly unconvincing piece of joining the Freemasons in London. After a convoluted chain of emails with a man who appeared to be İpek's assistant, I finally managed to get him to answer some written questions in March 2016.

'In my whole life, I have never even committed a traffic offence,' İpek told me. 'We are a loving family who only helped poor people. The reason the government is attacking me is that I refuse to be part of the pro-government media. This is not about the Gülen movement. [The government] created two choices: you are with them, or against them.'

The next big name to fall was the *Zaman* newspaper – the unofficial mouthpiece of the Gülen movement, and the biggest-selling title on Turkey's newsstands. It had been a consistent voice of support to Erdoğan, even featuring his advisers as guest column writers, until the December 2013 graft scandal when it turned into a consistent voice of opposition.

In March 2016 the courts ordered the takeover of Feza, *Zaman*'s parent company. Police officers entered the newsroom, detained the editor and chief columnist, and then looked over the remaining journalists' shoulders as they typed their stories. The editorial board was sacked and replaced with caretakers who tossed away those stories anyway, and instead filled the paper with pro-government pieces apparently written in the newsroom of government-supporting *Sabah*. The last edition of *Zaman* sent to print, in the hours after the court ordered the takeover but before the police raid, featured a defiant front page declaring a 'shameful day for free press in Turkey'. A day later, the front page bore a photo of Erdoğan and a story about how he was to lay the final stone on Istanbul's controversial third bridge project, under the headline, EXCITEMENT BUILDS FOR HISTORIC BRIDGE.

'It is like the paper died on Friday night and was resurrected in a different body on Sunday morning,' *Zaman*'s foreign editor, Mustafa Edip Yılmaz, told me a week into the new regime. 'This feels like the worst time in the history of the Turkish republic for freedom of expression. I have never seen in my life violations as bad as they are today.'

The paper's new direction hit its bottom line immediately. Within a week, its circulation dropped from 650,000 a day to 6,000.

Since then, and particularly in the wake of the 2016 coup attempt, Turkey's media has been scythed. Almost two hundred media outlets – some of them Gülenist but others Kurdish, leftist or just critical – have been closed down by government decree. Aydın Doğan, a moderately independent media baron who owned CNN Türk, Hürriyet and the Doğan News Agency, finally gave up after years of government pressure and sold his titles to a pro-Erdoğan conglomerate in April 2018. All in, 319 journalists have been arrested since the 2016 coup attempt and more than 80 are currently behind bars – the highest number of any country in the world.

For fifteen months journalist Ahmet Şık was one of them. His book, *The Imam's Army*, revealed the Gülenists' infiltrations into the Turkish state and led to his first arrest in 2011. Back then, in the era before the alliance between Erdoğan and Gülen broke down, the Gülenist-dominated courts accused him of being a Kemalist trying to overthrow the government. Now, in the post-alliance era, a justice system declawed by Erdoğan is charging him with links to the Gülenists and the PKK. Şık was arrested in December 2016. In April 2018 he was convicted of 'assisting' banned terrorist groups, and handed a seven-and-a-half-year prison sentence, suspended pending appeal.

With Turkey's press castrated and the Gülenists in flight, it would take four years and an unlikely hero to bust open the truth about what had really happened in Turkey in December 2013.

When Adam Klasfeld opened the docket on his desk in March 2016, distant bells of recognition sounded in his head. This New York court reporter was used to covering cases that resonated outside the United States. In his decade working at the Southern District New York courthouse, one of the city's federal courts, he had watched villagers from the Ecuadorian Amazon try to sue one of the world's largest oil companies, while down in Maryland he had covered the enthralling progress of the military court martial against soldier-turned-WikiLeaker Chelsea Manning. He had visited Guantánamo, where he chipped away at the extent of the CIA's use of torture against terrorism suspects held there. The painstaking, often tedious work of his day job bore fruit in the satisfaction he got from knowing that he was often the first on to something big. The newspaper correspondents would turn up at the end of the major trials, just in time for the denouement, but he was always there from the start. Often, he would be the one to turn everyone's attention to the smoking gun that had just been revealed in the courtroom – the leaked document, the taped conversation, the killer testimony.

The case of Reza Zarrab was clearly going to be a juicy one – though not for the reasons Klasfeld first assumed.

'Back when it began, obviously the 2016 US presidential election campaign was going on [and] I was looking at it through a US-based lens,' Klasfeld tells me down the phone one evening in his rapid-fire New York accent. It is the second week of 2018, and the US east coast is being lashed by blizzards and winds that the media has branded 'bomb cyclones'. US President Donald Trump is battling his own storm: an explosive new book detailing the chaos at the heart of his administration. Klasfeld is huddled in a cubicle on the top floor of the courthouse, sipping his morning coffee from a novelty mug that reads *Someone at the Pentagon loves me*, and preparing for his next job covering a terrorism case.

'When it really started getting attention was when Trump's allies started being on retainer for Zarrab, including Rudy Giuliani, the former New York City mayor, including Michael Mukasey, a former US attorney general, a very influential Republican,' he says. 'But the gravity of the case was a very slow dawning, I think. I didn't realise just how important this case was for the millions of people in Turkey.'

Reza Zarrab: the gold dealer at the centre of the allegations of sanctions-busting, and the embarrassment who Erdoğan hoped had gone away.

Zarrab had continued his high-rolling life in Istanbul as Erdoğan's war against the Gülenists escalated after December 2013. He was often pictured dining in high-end restaurants with his Turkish pop star wife, with whom he had a daughter. They lived in a luxury villa on the shore of the Bosphorus, and kept seven yachts and a light aircraft. His friendship with Erdoğan endured. Zarrab had donated almost $5 million to a charity set up by Erdoğan's wife, Emine, and received an award for it as a mark of thanks. Erdoğan himself referred to Zarrab as 'a great philanthropist'. In Turkey, amid the growing crackdown on the Gülen-linked media, few journalists dared report on the now-closed corruption case lest they be labelled Gülenists themselves.

But in March 2016 Zarrab, for reasons unknown and hotly debated, decided to take his family to Disneyland in Orlando, Florida. He must have known it was a risky move – the case may have been closed in Turkey, but there was nothing stopping the US authorities detaining and charging him as soon as he landed in Miami. That is exactly what happened. He was arrested, and an indictment against him was prepared by Preet Bharara, an attorney known for his cases against Wall Street fraudsters in the courthouse that Adam Klasfeld covers. Also named as defendants in the document were four Halkbank executives and Mehmet Zafer Çağlayan, Turkey's economy minister at the time of the December 2013 corruption scandal and still a serving AKP member of parliament in March 2016.

Bharara's indictment made few bones about the links between Zarrab and Erdoğan's government. 'High ranking government officials in Iran and Turkey participated in and protected this scheme,' it reads. 'Some officials received bribes worth tens of millions of dollars paid from the proceeds of the scheme so that they would promote the scheme, protect the participants, and help to shield the scheme from the scrutiny of US regulators.'

Çağlayan, the former economy minister, was accused of taking bribes in cash and jewellery totalling tens of millions of dollars for his role in concealing Zarrab's transactions from the regulators. Back in Turkey, the pro-government press did a U-turn on fallen hero Zarrab, accusing him of links to Gülen. Erdoğan, though, took a special interest in his plight. While in New York in September 2016 he met with US Vice-President Joe Biden and lobbied for Zarrab's release. A month later, the Turkish justice minister Bekir Bozdağ – a close ally of Erdoğan's – flew to meet US attorney general Loretta E. Lynch to do the same. Phone calls from Erdoğan to President Barack Obama followed over the winter of 2016.

When Donald Trump won the White House in November 2016, Erdoğan believed that he could build a relationship with the new US president – they had so much in common, after all. Despite Trump's vitriol against Muslims and immigrants, the pro-Erdoğan press had nothing bad to say about him between the election and his inauguration. 'We can work with him,' one government official told me. Behind the scenes, Erdoğan and his people had started to lobby Trump and his people on the Zarrab case. It initially appeared to be bearing fruit. In March 2017, a year after Zarrab's arrest, Trump fired Preet Bharara, the attorney who had filed the indictment. In the same month, Zarrab hired a new legal team including Giuliani and Mukasey, both men with strong links to the Trump administration. There were reports that Erdoğan had even tried to offer a prisoner exchange deal with the US to secure Zarrab's return to Turkey.

But in October 2017, a month before the trial was due to start, Zarrab disappeared. The Turkish foreign ministry found itself unable to contact him at the federal prison where he had been held. The Turkish press speculated that he was being held hostage by the American government. In reality, Zarrab had struck a deal: he pleaded guilty to the charges against him, and agreed to turn witness against Mehmet Hakan Atilla, one of the Halkbank executives named in the indictment. Zarrab took the stand on 29 November 2017 to deliver an explosive testimony fingering Atilla and the other Halkbank executives, and claiming that Erdoğan and his former economy minister, Ali Babacan, had personally signed off on the scheme.

Klasfeld knew little of the building anticipation for the Zarrab case in Turkey when he started live-tweeting the trial, nor of its potential ramifications in Ankara. But within minutes, he was inundated with notifications of new followers.

'It was instantaneous, once I just made it known that I would be live-tweeting the case,' he says, still overawed by what happened next. 'That was retweeted by a lot of the Turkey watchers in the US who follow me. So that got some attention in Turkey and then it just happened. Within minutes. Thousands and thousands of people continuously started following.'

The names of Klasfeld's new audience were flecked with strange diacritics and often seemed unpronounceable. But otherwise, he found he had a lot in common with this growing group of Turks who were hanging on his every tweeted word from the courtroom. Many were highly educated and spoke great English. Some of them started translating his tweets into Turkish so that those who were not English speakers could follow too. Lots cracked Turkish witticisms – and where a lesser reporter might have stuck solely to the job at hand in the courtroom, Klasfeld fired some jokes back. He even learnt a few words of Turkish, and started opening each day's tweets with *Günaydın* [good morning] *from New York*.

'When I tweeted that I was going out to lunch, people would send me pictures of Turkish food and recommend that I eat it. I would get a lot of things like, "Visit Turkey! But just not yet",' he says. 'Imagine thousands of people arriving at your front doorstep who largely speak another language and are being very kind to you. You become a little interested, more than a little interested, especially if they're as fascinating as the Turkish people and Turkish country.'

And amid the growing warmth and humour of these exchanges, Klasfeld realised something: he had become the go-to reporter for a news-starved country that he had never even visited. With Turkey's pro-government media channels all bellowing that the trial was a

Gülenist plot, and the battered opposition media barely brave enough by this point to counter that claim, Turks were consuming Klasfeld's hard facts like a bone-dry sponge soaks up water.

'People wanted to know everything. They wanted to know how many audio recordings there were, what was on those recordings. I knew that it was a reckoning over the 2013 corruption scandal,' he says. 'I've never had quite the same experience, to have so many followers and so much interest in what I'm tweeting. I took this to be the hunger for information, that's what it was. My impression was that there is this tremendous hunger for information that relates to the Turkish government and relates to their future and their history.'

At four o'clock in the afternoon on New Year's Eve 2017 in New York – as the clock was striking midnight in Turkey – Klasfeld raised a glass of rakı with his American friends to toast his new friends on the other side of the world. Three days later, the jury found Atilla guilty on five of the six counts against him.

# 5

# SYRIA: THE WAR NEXT DOOR

It is hard to pin down the moment when Erdoğan's ambitions swelled beyond his borders. In the first years of his era, as he battled against the Kemalists and the army, he was too weak at home to contemplate intervention overseas. But the Arab Spring offered Erdoğan an opportunity to clinch a bigger global position, at the exact moment that the Gülenists' defeat of the army enabled him to do so. Erdoğan's response to the cataclysm that has rocked his neighbourhood has turned him into one of the most divisive leaders in the world today – a champion of the oppressed to some and a byword for Islamist authoritarianism to others. The roots stretch back to the very start of his era, when the Turkish parliament voted against joining the US 'Coalition of the Willing' in Iraq in 2003. That was the beginning of a rift between Erdoğan's Turkey and America's generals that would never fully heal, even in the years when political relations were good. Eventually, it would crack open into a raw wound that has dragged Turkey's relations with Washington down to their lowest point in decades and repeatedly brought the two NATO allies to the brink of armed standoff.

## Ahmet Davutoğlu: the ideologue

In the years after that 2003 vote, Erdoğan and Ahmet Davutoğlu, a foreign policy adviser who would later become foreign minister, quietly set to work building new relations in old Ottoman lands. Turkey had long neglected its Muslim neighbours, focusing instead on strengthening ties with Israel and Europe. But Erdoğan and Davutoğlu forged friendships with Muslim-majority nations from the Balkans to the Arab Middle East and large parts of Africa, opening their diplomatic pitches with expressions of their shared faith and history and sealing them with investments, visa-free travel and soft-power outreach, primarily through the Gülenist networks.

Davutoğlu, like Erdoğan, was a pious man from the provinces. But unlike his street-fighter boss, he was an academic who had taken his Ph.D. in political science from the prestigious Bosphorus University before teaching in Malaysia and Turkey. He had joined the AKP as an adviser before being promoted to the top of the foreign ministry, where he became the engineer of the party's world plans. He based the AKP's foreign policy project on his 2001 book, *Strategic Depth*, in which he argued that Turkey should pursue proactive foreign outreach in the old Ottoman territories, with the aim of becoming the world's Muslim superpower.

'Davutoğlu had the full sophisticated foreign policy strategy,' says one foreign diplomat. 'He had his ideology around Ottoman power and strength. He was more of a democrat [than Erdoğan]. His desire was not for an authoritarian Ottoman empire. But it was for a highly powerful Turkey exerting this power through democratic means rather than through authoritarian means.'

Domestic observers schooled in the old way of Turkish foreign politics were less forgiving in their assessment of Davutoğlu and his new direction. 'In contrast to Erdoğan, Davutoğlu is a hardened ideologue entrenched by his academic side,' said Faruk Loğoğlu, Turkey's ambassador to the US when the AKP first won the parliament in 2002. 'He lived in the world of his own constructs, all of them rooted in an Islamist ideology and governed by theoretical absurdities . . . You could judge that his mind does not work very well by the fact that when you meet him he talks incessantly, without stopping; it is not a product of a thoughtful mind. Davutoğlu's ideological commitment to the Muslim Brotherhood and to Sunni access was reflected in both domestic and foreign policy.'

Davutoğlu's ideas appealed to Erdoğan because they promised to propel him to the top tier of the world's Sunni Muslim leaders. The AKP's early democratising reforms, driven by a roaring economy, had turned Turkey into the richest and most open Muslim-majority state in the region. In the West, leaders started to talk of Turkey as a model for Islamic democracy. Davutoğlu summed up his foreign policy with two catchphrases: 'zero problems with the neighbours' and 'less enemies, more friends'. And at that time Erdoğan had no better friend than another apparent reformer – the young Syrian president, Bashar al-Assad.

## Assad's Syria

Assad had inherited Syria from his father, Hafez, in 2000, when he was just thirty-four years old. He seemed to be in power reluctantly; after all, he had not been brought up to expect it. It had been Bashar's older brother, Basel, who was groomed for the job while Bashar, the shy second son, planned to lead a life out of the spotlight. He studied hard, largely shunned the luxurious trappings of his position, and went to London to enjoy a life of relative obscurity as a trainee eye doctor.

But in 1994 Basel was killed in a car crash. Bashar, now the heir apparent, was forced to abandon his medical studies and returned to Damascus to begin his political apprenticeship. When Hafez died six years later in June 2000, Bashar stood uncontested for the presidency: Syrians could vote yes or no for Bashar, but they weren't offered any alternative. And with the *mukhbarat* – the feared Syrian secret police – eyeing voters as they dropped their slips into the ballot box, few were inclined to vote no. Bashar was sworn in with a 97 per cent mandate.

Soon after, he married his beautiful and stylish British-raised fiancée. Asma al-Assad, from a powerful Sunni family from the central city of Homs, had attended a Church of England primary school, studied computer science at King's College London and worked as an investment banker at JP Morgan. Bashar, with his educated wife by his side, also seemed to be in tune with what Syria's upcoming generation wanted. He was technologically savvy; one of the first things he did when he came to power was allow access to the internet – albeit heavily restricted and monitored – and he became head of the Syrian Computer Society. He was a nerd who seemed to eschew the ostentatious trappings of wealth that had so beguiled the Middle East's other dictators, such as Libya's Muammar Gaddafi with his snakeskin shoes and satin robes. Bashar took pride in the fact that he drove himself and his family around the streets of the capital, Damascus, in an unarmoured car and without bodyguards.

In Bashar's early years as president, Syrians dared to believe that their country might be changing. He gave lip service to allowing other political parties into parliament, though they would never have been given a chance to form a government. He permitted civil societies and discussion groups to open in the public sphere. Many political prisoners were released, Damascus got a stock exchange, and Syrians were at last given access to mobile phones. The first two years of Bashar's tenure came to be known as the Damascus Spring – artists, intellectuals, campaigners and ordinary citizens breathed a collective sigh of relief as their regime's iron grip on the country seemed to relax.

It didn't last. In 2002 the Damascus Spring screeched to a devastating halt. The thinkers and dissidents who had taken advantage of the past two years' new freedoms were rounded up and thrown into prison. The fledgling civil society sector was cut down. Syrians realised that their new communication tools simply gave the regime more options for spying on them, and the fear and loathing swelled until the spring of 2011, when the nascent wave of Arab revolution washed into Syria and Bashar al-Assad's people rose up against him. His reaction was quick and brutal – within six months, the protests had morphed into all-out civil war.

Erdoğan and his wife, Emine, had holidayed with the Assads in the fashionable Turkish resort of Bodrum in 2008, just three summers before the revolt. After their getaway, Erdoğan started referring to Assad as his 'brother', and trade ties between the two countries flourished. But with the onset of the Arab Spring uprisings in late 2010, Erdoğan saw that he could grab an even bigger role for himself in the region. Old secular dictators were being overthrown, and Islamist parties were increasingly dominating the opposition. Erdoğan had visited Egypt in the wake of its revolution, taking the stage in front of an ecstatic crowd chanting 'Turkey and Egypt are one hand'. He went on to Tunisia and Libya, where similar scenes awaited him. All three countries voted in new leaders with strong links to the Muslim Brotherhood.

Erdoğan was initially more hesitant to back the Syrian opposition – Assad was his neighbour and professed friend, not a faraway pariah like Mubarak or Gaddafi. But in the US there was growing determination that the Syrian strongman should go. And so it turned to its regular Muslim ally, Turkey, for support.

'From mid-2011 Washington put increasing pressure on governments around the world to break with Assad and to call for his ouster,' says a US diplomat based in Turkey at the time. 'Ankara was reluctant. Some, including Davutoğlu, still believed that Assad could be weaned away from Iran and toward reform. Davutoğlu and Erdoğan made a couple of efforts, including at least one trip to Damascus, and got some promises to change that Assad did not keep. After several such go-rounds, the Turks realised that the effort was pointless, broke with Assad, and joined US calls for him to step down. One very senior Turk told me that Ankara thought it would be joining onto a US strategy for getting rid of Assad and was later dismayed to learn we had none.'

Inside Turkey, the opposition was disquieted when Erdoğan and Davutoğlu did an about-turn on Assad. The CHP, with its secular zeal, was horrified at the thought that the Syrian president, brutal as he was, might be overthrown and replaced with an Islamist government. The party's stance was at least partly swayed by the large Alevi bloc in its voter base; the Turkish Alevis, followers of a branch of Shia Islam, are loosely linked to Assad's own Alawite sect, and are similarly terrified by the prospect of a fundamentalist Sunni resurgence in the Middle East.

The CHP sent a delegation to meet Assad in October 2011, a month after Erdoğan cut ties. Faruk Loğoğlu, who had by then retired from the diplomatic service and rejoined his party, was part of it: 'Assad told us his version of the events. At the beginning Turkey and Syria enjoyed a very good and positive relationship. The Turkish side was offering advice to the Syrian banking sector, and counselling Assad as to how he could soften his presence in the lives of the people. Assad did not mind this brotherly approach from our elders. But then a point in time came in which this advice and counsels offered were not from one equal to another but more of a command. Assad did not mind the tone but it was not appropriate to the head of a state. He told us that what broke the camel's back was the Turkish government's insistence that he incorporate the Muslim Brotherhood into the Syrian government.'

Abdullah Gül, president of Turkey at the time the Syrian crisis erupted, also counselled both his government and the US to be cautious. 'I told the Americans that the rhetoric was too high. If there was not going to be force, it was a dangerous thing. Later on, we discovered that they were not going to put force,' Gül said.

## 2011–2013
### Syria's descent

As the bloodshed escalated in north-western Syria in late 2011, Turkey opened its borders to fleeing civilians and provided a safe fallback position for both the political and armed opposition. Erdoğan and Davutoğlu were now building their Syria policy on the reckoning that Assad could be toppled quickly as Mubarak, Ben Ali and Gaddafi had been in Egypt, Tunisia and Libya, and so they openly supported his opponents. Unease swelled inside Erdoğan's government.

'Until 2011 Syria had very good relations with Turkey,' says Ertuğrul Günay. 'We held joint meetings of the cabinet. We had established joint tourism destinations. Afterwards I suppose Erdoğan thought that Assad would fall quickly, and he wanted to have a say in the new [Syrian] administration. As a member of his cabinet I had tried to explain to him that this would not be possible. He believed the Syrian question would be resolved in six months.'

Others say that, in retrospect, Erdoğan's turn against Assad in 2011 marked a bigger moment, when the prime minister began pursuing an openly Islamist agenda both in foreign policy and at home.

'Erdoğan is ideologically in line with the Muslim Brotherhood, representing the Turkish version of it. He wants Turkey to be in leading position among the Islamic countries, especially within Turkey's historical hinterland,' says former AKP deputy Haluk Özdalga. 'The Muslim Brotherhood agenda is the best way to understand the foreign policy the AKP has been conducting. Only under the light of such an agenda would Ankara's international policy, full of zigzags, otherwise difficult to explain, make sense in its whole – just look at the policies followed in relation to Syria, Egypt, Sudan, Qatar, UAE, Iraq, Saudi Arabia, Libya, Palestine, et cetera, and even vis-à-vis the West. The crisis in Syria has turned out to be long and defining in many respects for the AKP and Erdoğan.'

Had the rebels managed to unseat Assad in the early years of the war, Syria would almost certainly have been taken over by a Brotherhood-led government and become another Arab state in which Erdoğan could wield huge influence. But that is not how it panned out. After the rebels stormed into Aleppo in the summer of 2012 – aided by the sanctuary and training they were receiving in Turkey and the weapons supplies coming through the border – the uprising turned into a bloody war of attrition. The front lines barely moved for three years, while Assad used his air power to punish the civilian population with endless airstrikes. Donors from the Gulf began co-opting rebel groups, offering them huge wads of cash on the condition that they change their name to something Islam-inspired, fight in the name of Allah and implement Sharia law. Soon, Islamic fundamentalists from outside Syria also moved in to plant their flag in the rubble. Many Syrians welcomed them at first, not so much for their religious ideas as for their strict code of law and order – a welcome break from the anarchy of rebel rule.

On each trip I made back into the war zone over the spring and summer of 2013, I saw that the war's paradigm had shifted a little more. The fundamentalists had always been there to varying degrees, although in the early days it was fairly easy to avoid them. But signs of their presence and growing influence were piling up. Young rebel fighters who had once overloaded on hair gel and pulled on tight jeans and knock-off designer T-shirts now started growing their hair straggly-long and shaving their top lips clean while leaving their beards intact, a homage to the Prophet Muhammad. One stinking hot August day I spotted a badly transliterated piece of teenage graffiti on an Aleppo backstreet: *Ben Laden*, scrawled in red spray paint on an un-rendered wall. The hardliners fought harder, played smarter and paid more, and the troops voted with their feet. I interviewed an Al-Qaeda fighter who had once worked in the alcohol department of the duty-free store at Aleppo airport but had now decided that Islamism was the best path, and, somehow, managed to convince another that I was not an atheist by reciting the Lord's Prayer, the lines swimming back to me across two decades from primary school assemblies.

'I'm not saying you should be a Muslim, but you have to believe in God!' he'd beseeched me. 'Because you're a nice person, and I don't want you to burn in hellfire.'

The irony was that, as the extremists grew in power, so newspaper readers back in the West cared less about what Assad was inflicting on his people and more about the threat that these black-clad young men might soon pose to their own lives and societies. And that, in turn, powered Al-Qaeda all the more, because it could claim, with increasing validity, that no one in the West cared when Muslims were dying. One teenager I had got to know in Aleppo, a seventeen-year-old called Molham who spent at least fifteen minutes each morning styling his hair and stopped to do top-ups in car mirrors throughout the day, knocked me speechless as we were eating shawarma.

'Hannah, I'm going to join Al-Qaeda,' he said. 'All my friends are dying and they are the only ones doing anything about it.'

I stared back at him, my mouth full of chicken and mayonnaise. He flashed a wad of hundred-dollar bills that he said the group had given him as his joining-up fee. Once I had gulped down my food, I offered him the only pallid discouragement I could think of: 'Please don't.'

Some of the more hardcore rebels took to wearing suicide belts full time, in what I initially took as a swaggering statement of fashion more than intent. But then I interviewed the father of a fighter who had gone the whole hog and detonated his belt at a regime check-point. The father could not wipe the smile from his face as he talked about his first-born, dead for less than a week.

'Are you upset?' I asked him.

'Of course not!' the father replied. 'He took at least ten of Assad's men with him. He's a martyr.'

I asked whether the family had held a funeral for him. The father's expression shifted from pleasure to one of the pain reserved for an idiot.

'Of course not,' he said. 'Nothing to bury. He was kebab meat.'

## Isis rises

Then, Syria got even darker.

'There is a new group,' my fixer Mohammed told me as I prepared for my next trip into Aleppo in April 2013. 'It has come from Iraq and it is called Isis.'

It was hard to weigh the danger at first – Syria's sands were always shifting in those months, sometimes swallowing rebel groups and sometimes spitting out new ones. I asked all my contacts whether Isis would talk. *Difficult*, I was told, *they don't like journalists*. But eventually, I was taken to meet a skinny young man called Abu Mahjin, who was dressed in shalwar kameez and showed only kohl-lined eyes through his balaclava. He had brought his Kalashnikov along even though I had requested no weapons in the room. His condition was that I cover my head and wear an abaya, and so we sat opposite each other, both looking ridiculous – a mujahid in make-up and a sweaty white woman wearing a tent. The scene grew more surreal when the woman whose house we were doing the interview in brought in two bowls of vanilla ice cream and set them in front of us, an impeccable Syrian host to the last. He couldn't eat his without removing his face mask and I didn't want to offend him by eating mine, so they melted as he told me how he believed Syria's chaos had been foretold in the prophecies.

'The Prophet said that we should follow jihad in Syria because that is where the angels will bestow their wings on Islam,' Abu Mahjin said. 'Our aim is to implement Sharia law in Syria and uphold the principles of the Islamic State. If that was not the aim then we wouldn't have come from far afield to fight here; we would have left the Syrians to fight by themselves. The Syrian people don't decide on this – it is the Prophet Muhammad who decided it.'

Isis had spread its tentacles across northern Syria well before it officially announced its existence. It had spies in every rebel-held town, reporting back on who was doing what. It had fighters from various Islamist rebel militias ready to swear their allegiance as soon as it was formally founded. In Manbij, the small town north of Aleppo where I had met Abu Mahjin, a local FSA leader told me how he was trying to mediate between Isis, which had recently set up a large headquarters there, and the town's native rebel groups. His efforts were proving futile. That same morning, a crowd had pulled the local imam from the pulpit as he recited Friday prayers in Manbij's main mosque, demanding that he be replaced with one of Isis's hardline foreign preachers. The extremists had already arrested several of the town's most corrupt FSA leaders, a popular move with anyone who had suffered their campaigns of extortion. On the morning I interviewed Abu Mahjin, I sat in a parked car and watched as a teenage motorbike gang circled Manbij's town square, the pillion passengers standing and holding aloft black flags of Isis.

Crucially, Isis had a captive and suffering population that had grown cynical at the secular West, which preached one thing at meetings in New York and Geneva but did quite another in practice. Since the start of the uprising, almost every Western country and international institution had pleaded with Assad to stop slaughtering his own people. But the UN's resolutions were repeatedly blocked by Russia, and what difference would they have made if they had been passed? The UN could send weapons inspectors and ceasefire monitors, but it couldn't send in an army to fight back. The Syrian president had powerful friends in Moscow and Tehran, and that was what made his country different to Egypt, Libya and Tunisia. He could be sanctioned and he could be deplored, but for two years he carried on smashing dissent with missiles and bombs, growing ever more certain that no one would stop him. The US, UK and France joined with Turkey and Qatar to clandestinely train and equip selected rebels in southern Turkey and Jordan, but baulked at offering open and fully fledged support and airstrikes as they had in Libya. Every rebel leader I interviewed in Syria ordered that I publish his demands for heavy weaponry; one went so far as to take me to his makeshift ammunitions factory in the basement car park of an apartment block in rural Aleppo, combustible piles of explosives presided over by chain-smoking workers, which he then used as a backdrop for his tirade against Western inaction. Among Syria's battered civilians I watched a growing tiredness, a swelling cynicism about the Western rhetoric on human rights that they had once believed was sincere. Almost unfailingly, everyone I interviewed was polite and kind – and horribly, searingly honest when they told me they were happy to welcome the fundamentalists, because what other choice did they have now it was clear that the West would not live up to its promises? I felt shame as I tried to explain the nuances of democratic party politics in Britain, the scar that the Iraq war had left on our collective psyche and the reasons why our politicians would not go against their people even when it was the right thing to do. My interviewees could trump all of my explanations with a single sentence: *But we are dying here.* And I had no comeback to that. Because what does nuance and party politics and parliamentary process and even democracy in a faraway land matter when bombs are falling on your head and your own president is trying to kill your children?

*May 2013*
*Erdoğan goes to Washington*

The wider world had not yet heard of Isis when Erdoğan went to Washington in May 2013 for talks with President Obama. His state visit was trimmed with honours aimed at preserving the relationship that Obama had spent his first tenure in the White House tending to. After assuming office in 2009, Obama had included Turkey on the itinerary of his first overseas trip, making it the first Muslim-majority country he visited as president. In Ankara, he had addressed the parliament. Obama's overtures to Turkey and its prime minister meant that he was able to act as mediator when Erdoğan weighed into a row between the Muslim world and Denmark over the publication in a Danish newspaper of cartoons depicting the Prophet Muhammad.

In May 2013, Erdoğan, together with his foreign minister Davutoğlu and Hakan Fidan, head of the Turkish intelligence services, was greeted in Washington with full state honours and the rare gesture of dinner with Obama in the White House. Syria was only one item on a long agenda that also spanned trade, Palestine and Iran's growing influence across the Middle East. But Erdoğan was hoping he could use the visit to persuade Obama to bump up support for the Syrian rebels so they could finally battle to Damascus and finish off Assad. There was mounting evidence that the Syrian regime was deploying chemical weapons against civilians – in that same month, I had visited Saraqeb, a town in Idlib province, where doctors showed me videos and medical reports of an airstrike that had left victims foaming at the mouth and retching. The double car-bombing in Reyhanlı five days before the visit, which Erdoğan blamed on Assad's intelligence services, had now brought the war next door crashing across Turkey's border. In Turkey, newspapers billed the meeting as 'historic', and as Erdoğan boarded his jet in Ankara he told reporters that it would 'determine a new roadmap toward the Syrian crisis'. Analysts predicted that he would try to persuade Obama to lift the US veto on arming the rebels or even help establish a no-fly zone in northern Syria.

But Obama had other concerns. By now Western intelligence agencies were tracking the march of Isis's black flag across northern Syria and briefings had reached the US president. Obama, lukewarm from the start about offering full backing to the insurgents, was perturbed by news that scores of committed, violent jihadis were travelling almost openly through Turkey and across the leaky border into Syria. Elsewhere, Obama was watching another Arab Spring uprising that the US had supported morph into a bloody blowback. In Libya, less than a year after a NATO intervention had dislodged Gaddafi, the US consul in the city of Benghazi was murdered by Islamist militants. Exactly one month before Erdoğan arrived in Washington, two pressure bombs planted by brothers of Kyrgyz origin and radicalised by the wars in Iraq and Afghanistan had exploded at the Boston Marathon, killing three. So, by the time the two presidents met, their views on Syria were already diverging – though the reporters gathered in the White House Rose Garden may not have realised it as they listened to the warm joint press conference that followed their opening meeting.

But that evening, over dinner in the White House, the two men and their entourages engaged in diplomatic battle. Erdoğan explained that the Syrian war, now dragging on into its second year, was beginning to cause huge problems for Turkey, thanks not only to the refugees it was hosting but also to the security problems it was throwing up. Erdoğan expected that the US, as a NATO ally and the country that had first corralled Turkey into supporting Assad's overthrow, would take his side. He was wrong. Obama instead told Erdoğan that he had to cut off the extremists' route into Syria and stop Turkey's support for the more hardline armed rebel factions, and broke the news that the US would not be throwing any more support behind the rebels while the fundamentalists were there.

Erdoğan felt he had been betrayed by Obama – and, according to party insiders, began wondering whether there was a plot to overthrow him brewing in Washington. On his return to Turkey, a sudden challenge rising from the streets would, in his mind, prove him correct.

*May–June 2013*
*Gezi uprising*

Twelve days after Erdoğan met with Obama, a small group of environmentalists started a sit-in in Istanbul's Gezi Park. The scrubby patch of grass in the middle of Taksim Square, a huge plaza in the heart of Istanbul, was litter-strewn and dangerous after dark, but in the midst of the city's sprawl it was a small haven where office workers sat to eat their lunch and gay men cruised for lovers. When it was announced that the park was to be concreted over and turned into a shopping centre built in the style of an Ottoman barracks, it lit the touch paper on a discontent that had long been simmering unspoken among Turkey's youth. After the police evicted the environmentalists and burned down their tents, others came to show their solidarity. Within days, the dreadlocked hippies among the trees had been joined by tens of thousands of protesters who occupied Taksim, calling for Erdoğan to resign.

Erdoğan, still smarting from Obama's riposte over Syria, accused the demonstrators of acting on the orders of nefarious foreign powers, and sent the riot police in en masse. Aerial photographs of Taksim on the fiercest days of the protests show the whole huge plaza blanketed in tear gas. The crackdown drew condemnations from Europe and the US, deepening the paranoia that from now on would never leave Erdoğan. Meanwhile, his rhetoric against the Gezi protesters was at odds with other senior members of his party, including Abdullah Gül, the president, who urged a softer response from the state.

Two months later, with Gezi still rumbling, Erdoğan suffered another blow. Egypt's Muslim Brotherhood government – the same that had been anointed by Erdoğan during his visit there in 2011 – was overthrown by a military coup following two years of mismanagement and rising fundamentalism. The Egyptian people, once so happy to be shut of a secular dictator, now came on the streets to cheer the overthrow of the Islamist who had replaced him. Erdoğan had not only lost an ally in the region. He was also watching his own model of government, the Islamic democracy on which the West had poured such flattery only two years earlier, being dismantled and discredited.

A month later again, in August 2013, Bashar al-Assad used chemical weapons against his own people, not for the first time but on a scale that was now impossible to ignore. Pictures of rows of dead children shrouded in sheets in the Damascus suburb of Ghouta, and of others foaming at the mouth as they gasped for breath, stunned a world that was yet to grow desensitised to Syria's slaughter. Fourteen hundred were dead from sarin gas, a nerve agent that kills by slow asphyxiation, and everyone expected a game-changing retaliation. US President Barack Obama had said the use of chemical weapons would be his red line. Analysts later argued that it had been an offhand remark, but that didn't matter to the Syrians, who had been suffering for more than two years and had hung on to those words. The US, UK and France seemed to be moving into position to launch strikes on Damascus, and the Syrians living as refugees in Turkey were overjoyed.

'I'll be riding back home on top of a French tank!' laughed my friend, Aboud, who had defected from Assad's army and escaped to

Turkey a year earlier. Within minutes of meeting him on the first day I arrived in the borderlands in 2013, I realised that his shaved head and imposing stature belied a huge heart and a great sense of humour. The Syrians had forcibly conscripted him and put him in the special forces, believing it to be the best place for him. In Turkey, he was translating for journalists, doing humanitarian work for the growing numbers of refugees and, with me, talking over beers about the day he would return home.

His hopes soon fell apart. After the UK parliament voted against taking action, the US and France backed down, too. The red line had been crossed, yet nothing was done. That was the turning point – the moment when Syria morphed into war without end.

## The West changes course in Syria

There was an understanding in Ankara that defeating Isis must now be the first priority for the West. But there was also a growing chasm between the US and Turkey over the future of Bashar al-Assad. While deposing the Syrian dictator had all but fallen off the agenda in Washington, in Ankara it was still seen as the necessary bedrock for future stability in the region. Meanwhile, the Pentagon was increasingly taking the lead on Syria policy instead of the White House – and the generals cared only about defeating Isis, not about maintaining the relationship between the US and Turkey.

'I had the sense that the Turks were looking for American leadership on how to deal with Isis. However, this was not the only thing they were concerned about,' says a US official involved in negotiations to build an anti-Isis coalition in 2014. 'Turkey wanted to support the steps to bolster the capabilities of the Iraqi security apparatus to fight against Isis and other enemies. They seemed to be in favour of the steps in Syria to destroy Isis. But [they were also asking] what is the strategy for Assad? What will be the strategy when Isis gets defeated? What comes next? They continued to insist on an answer. Our answer in 2014 was to focus on defeating Isis. The Turks were willing to buy that. But they wanted to know the strategy in regards to Syria. It was never resolved, and it is still at the core of the problem in the relationship. In 2014 there was no one at a senior level in CENTCOM' – US Central Command, overseeing the military operations against Isis – 'interested in or willing to work on the US–Turkey relationship. They see Turkey as the problem. They would prefer not to deal with it at all.'

Behind the scenes, there were also growing tensions between the two men who had moulded Turkey's Syria policy. In October 2014, when Erdoğan was voted in as president, he promoted his foreign secretary, Davutoğlu, to prime minister. Davutoğlu was determined to keep control over the Syria file. Erdoğan had other ideas.

'When Davutoğlu was made prime minister, and especially as the Isis stuff unfolded, there was, almost immediately, tension between him and Erdoğan,' says a former Western diplomat. 'What foreigners could see was that Davutoğlu was becoming less and less involved in foreign affairs by the day. One time he had come back from some factory tours and he seemed delighted to get back into a conversation with [then US Secretary of State] John Kerry [but] it was clear that he was not entirely speaking for the government . . . It was bound up in this broader phenomenon of Erdoğan dominating the landscape. Erdoğan and the people around him did not want Davutoğlu playing that role any more . . . [and] Erdoğan was showing very little flexibility or interest in working together in ways to solve these problems. He was not adding to the problems, but he was not very cooperative. Erdoğan was saying what Turkey needed and what the US should do. It comes back to his confidence or arrogance. It was different from the Erdoğan that I had experienced before, who would actually have a conversation about what to do. Before, there would be a genuine give and take.'

As the politicians squabbled and the war metastasised, Syrians began pouring into Turkey – not only because some of the worst fighting was close to the frontier, or because Ankara had kept the border crossings open, but because Turkey was by far the best host. Instead of forcing refugees to live in decrepit camps, as was happening in Lebanon, Jordan and Iraq, Turkey allowed them to rent apartments and live freely. For the poorest, it provided high-quality camps, many with homes made of shipping containers rather than canvas. And, although it didn't officially recognise Syrians as refugees due to a technicality in the Geneva Convention, after April 2013 it provided them with 'Temporary Protection' status, which gave them access to free healthcare, and allowed them to send their children to school and be hired for jobs Turks did not want.

Ankara's generosity meant that Syrians were soon also arriving from third countries. Many of the 300,000 Syrians who had initially fled to Egypt relocated to Turkey after the 2013 coup as the once-welcoming mood turned against them. Others who had been living and working in the Gulf before the conflict broke out found that their residence permits were being cancelled, so they too went to Turkey. Increasingly, those who had been escaping into Lebanon and Jordan from fighting in the south of Syria moved straight on to Turkey if they could afford it. The numbers soared. In 2013, there were 225,000 Syrians in Turkey; a year later, there were more than six times that number. The number has risen every year since, and there are now between three and four million Syrians living in Turkey. Many of them see Erdoğan as their champion – the only leader who has stuck by them as the rest of the world has broken its promises or lost interest. But although the West had turned its back on the Syrians, it would not be able to ignore them for long.

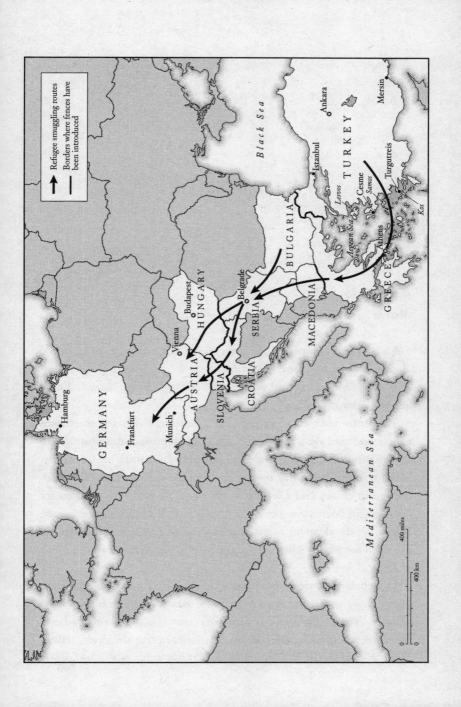

# 6

# THE EXODUS

Abu Laith flung open his arms with a camp flourish and planted a kiss on both my cheeks.

'You get more beautiful every time I see you!' he exclaimed. 'Come on, I'm taking you out.'

The worst guys are often the most charming. This was the fourth time I had met Abu Laith, one of a crop of businessmen cashing in on the people-smuggling industry that was flourishing in the underbelly of Turkey's holiday resorts in early 2015. Short and blue-eyed, dressed in chinos and a loud summer shirt, he could have passed for a tourist in Mersin, a gaudy city on Turkey's Mediterranean coast. But as we drove along the seafront to the fish restaurant he kept an eye open for places where he might peddle his business in the black of night.

His choice locations were spots on the city's northern outskirts, where fancy waterfront apartments gave way to older, less salubrious suburbs. There was a tree-shaded park between the main road and the water where he would take his customers in late afternoon, telling them to pose as families throwing a birthday party as the sun set. A few miles further on there was a small, seasonal beach town, a few hotels gathered around a stretch of sand and deserted in wintertime.

'In the summer this place is amazing,' Abu Laith said. 'There are lots of people and parties. Coves all along the coastline. But in the winter all the work in this area is related to smuggling.'

Moonless skies were the best, he said – less likelihood of being spotted. In the blackness his customers abandoned their fake celebrations and climbed into eight-metre motorboats that took them out past Turkey's sea border into international waters, where they would meet up with others and transfer into bigger vessels that could take hundreds of people at a time. Then they would set a course west for Italy, with an estimated journey time of a week. The captains of the boats – usually Syrians from the port cities of Latakia and Tartus – would also claim asylum once they hit European shores. The bigger boats were ancient eighty-metre fishing vessels bought from Egyptian traders and often destroyed by the Italian authorities once they had sailed their final voyage.

Abu Laith told me proudly of a wheeze he had cooked up in the hotter months: hire one of Mersin's party boats, stage a wedding party, and drift just far enough out into international waters that the passengers could transfer to the main vessel. That was a luxury service, organised for people with tens of thousands of euros to spare. At the very top end of the market, would-be asylum seekers could buy fake or stolen European documents and travel by plane from Istanbul to London, Paris or Berlin.

But in Mersin Abu Laith catered to the mass market, not the big spenders. Only 300 miles from the Syrian border, it hosted a large population of refugees and was big enough to absorb the illicit industry. Passengers could buy lifejackets in the city's numerous sailing shops before they embarked. Hotel owners could be persuaded to turn a blind eye to the unusual numbers of Syrians staying in their establishments in the off-season. All of the town's smuggling middlemen said that money was crossing the palms of Turkish officials to keep the whole thing running.

But the smugglers had got too cocky. In December 2014, a ship with no captain, stuffed with nine hundred desperate, hungry, dehydrated people, had almost crashed into the Italian shore. After the survivors revealed the details of their route, the Turkish authorities began clamping down in Mersin.

In the meantime, new opportunities were opening, Abu Laith said. The Greek islands dotted around Turkey's Aegean coast, 600 miles west of Mersin, are often so close you feel as if you could wave to someone standing on the foreign shore. The complicated operation and long journey the smugglers had picked out from Mersin to Italy would not be necessary there — Abu Laith could send his customers over to Europe in rubber dinghies in a couple of hours. He could give one of the men on board a crash course in using the motor, insist on one small bag only per passenger to create as much space as possible, and then point them in the right direction. No need for boat deals with Egyptians, no need for sea captains from Syria. All his smuggling needs could be bought in the nearest outdoor shop.

Abu Laith was one of the Syrian war's great opportunists. He had a handy self-exoneration for every shady deal, every new misery he brought upon his countrymen. Before the conflict he had run a money-changing business in Azaz, a Syrian town next to the Turkish border long known as a hotspot for cigarette and drug smuggling. When the war kicked off and anti-Assad rebels captured Azaz and its nearby border crossing with Turkey he restyled himself as a gunrunner, carrying weapons across the frontier.

'I wanted the revolution against Assad to succeed!' he said.

Next, when foreign jihadis started heaping into Syria, he set himself up as a relocation agent, smoothing their journey across the border and ensuring they were provided with living quarters and weapons. 'I thought they were coming to help the revolution!' he said.

And now, with his ravaged homeland haemorrhaging refugees and its neighbours roiling under the influx, he had reinvented himself again, this time as a people-smuggler's agent touting for customers and dealing with the payments and logistics. He was relatively small fry, the bottom of the feeding chain, working for the big guys above, the mafiosi who carved up the Turkish coast between them, reaped the profits and never dirtied their hands or names with the grunt work. The Kurds controlled Mersin, he said, and the Russians Bodrum and Antalya. They were already making millions each month from their trade. Meanwhile, for each passenger who paid 6,500 euros for their journey to Italy, Abu Laith got a cut of 1,500 euros. With an average of seven or eight customers each month it was a tidy income. But he wasn't doing it for the money, he insisted.

'I want to help Syrians find a better life in Europe. This is a humanitarian project,' he said. 'Don't blame the smugglers, blame your governments. Why are they not accepting asylum applications through their embassies? Europe is a partner of the mafia.'

Over the course of the next year I followed the mass exodus of more than a million people from the shores of Turkey into Europe, as they travelled on rickety boats in the hands of men like Abu Laith and then took long, silent night treks through the mountains and valleys of the Balkans. It turned into one of the defining stories of my career: a huge humanitarian crisis on one level, a massive and fascinating crime investigation on another, and moreover the trigger for events that would rock the European Union, and Turkey's relationship with it, to the core. But during my first encounter with Abu Laith in the winter of 2014 he had mentioned the growing people-smuggling industry as an aside; we had actually met to speak about Isis and the war in northern Syria.

My interest was piqued when he mentioned how he was earning a living. I was also picking up snippets from Syrian friends of a slowly swelling exodus from Turkey, like a dripping tap that has finally filled a sink and is about to overflow. The Syrians I met in my first months in Antakya were mostly educated and urban young Damascenes who had skipped their military service or been sent out by their families. They had quickly found decent apartments and NGO jobs in the Turkish borderlands in 2013, but were now talking about how they would take a boat to Europe. They swapped information on the best country to get to, where they could get passports quickest and integrate the best: Sweden was favoured at that time, Germany a close second. These middle-class, law-abiding Syrians could easily reach out to the organised criminals running the industry. Men like Abu Laith set up Arabic-language WhatsApp groups and Facebook pages where they outlined prices, information and contacts. They had innocuous names: one was called 'Syrians in Mersin', another 'Information for asylum in Europe'.

Though the Syrians were largely safe in Turkey, Isis's rout of the rebels in northern Syria in 2014 had crushed their hopes of returning to their homeland any time soon. Meanwhile, Turkey's generosity took them only so far. The middle classes who arrived earliest, when the refugee population was still in the hundreds of thousands, settled quickest and snapped up the best jobs. Others who came later found most of the NGO jobs taken and the cheap apartments occupied. For those at the other end, the very poorest who flooded into Turkey in huge waves every time there was an outbreak of raw violence in Syria, Ankara built a network of high-quality camps to house around 300,000, a tenth of the total refugee population. But life was tough for those in the middle. Some lived in farm outbuildings or shanty towns in deserted corners of the border cities. In the early mornings, huge crowds of young Syrian men lined the main roads to the countryside to wait for farmers who would pick them up for cash-in-hand day work. Others rented the cheapest apartments and packed as many families into them as they could. When my then boyfriend heard that the flat above his in Antakya had come free we decided to take a look at it. Within two seconds of opening the front door we realised that several women and their children had been living there: children's drawings were tacked up on the cupboards, mattresses propped against the walls of every room, and, because they couldn't afford curtains, white paper had been placed over the windows. They had kept so quiet in all the months they lived there that we never once heard them.

Mustafa Kemal Atatürk,
founder of the Republic

Atatürk's funeral in Ankara,
November 1938

Recep Tayyip Erdoğan, British Prime Minister Theresa May and US President Donald Trump participate in a meeting on counter-terrorism during the G20 Leaders' Summit in Hamburg, Germany

Turkish preacher Fethullah Gülen speaks to members of the media from his home

Russian President Vladimir Putin listens as Erdoğan speaks during a business meeting at the Grand Kremlin Palace

Ahmet Davutoğlu, AKP adviser, foreign minister and prime minister, ousted in a party coup in May 2016

Muharrem İnce, presidential candidate of the Republican People's Party (CHP), Turkey's main opposition party

Rebel fighters guarding a Sharia court in Aleppo, Syria, May 2013

Turkish soldiers hold back Syrian Kurds who are trying to cross the border into Kobanî during the Isis attack, September 2014

Kurdish woman in a neighbourhood of Cizre, south-eastern Turkey, destroyed in fighting between the PKK and Turkish security forces, March 2016

Kurds watch Kobanî burn across the Turkey–Syria border, September 2014

An explosion after a US airstrike hits Kobanî, Syria

Cizre with neighbourhoods destroyed in fighting between PKK and
Turkish security forces in the foreground, March 2016

Bostancı Street, Cizre, destroyed in the fighting, March 2016

Rebels with the Free Syrian Army announce the formation of their brigade
in front of opposition media activists, Idlib province, 2012

## The activists

The rise of Isis in northern Syria also meant banishment for Aleppo's activists, the young, educated men and women who had been working for what they called 'the revolution', back when there was still a revolution to speak of. These students and young professionals opposed Assad but were too urbane to join a rebel faction. Instead they set up media centres, providing much of the early footage of what was happening in their city, and then worked with foreign journalists as translators and fixers. The more secular among them sensed the danger straight away as the war in their city took a dark Islamist turn. While they tried to maintain smooth working relations with the masked men taking over Aleppo, they knew it was a matter of when, not if, the group would turn against them. Meanwhile the rebel brigades had tolerated the presence of Al-Qaeda but were warily eyeing Isis, even though they never said it publicly at first.

Some, though, placed a naïve trust in these strangers flocking to their city. 'They're good Islamic boys!' one of my fixers, Soheib, told me one evening in August 2013 as we sat in the Aleppo apartment he and his friends had taken over as a base for journalists. On the floor below was the office of an FSA faction; on the floor below that a makeshift clinic. The streets outside were usually deserted – the apartment block was just a few hundred metres from the front line with Assad's forces and most of the residents had left. The proximity gave it a strange kind of protection, since it was too close to their own side for the regime's jets to bombard it.

But nowhere was safe from Isis and its informants. Over that sticky-hot summer, bearded men in pick-up trucks started prowling the street outside the media centre. One day, as I sat in a sleeveless top smoking cigarettes with my Syrian friends, there came a loud hammering on the front door. Mahmoud, an English student in Homs when the uprising started, was in charge of the centre and had grasped imme-diately how dangerous Isis was. He had fitted a huge steel security gate over the door days earlier. Now, he peered through the peephole and saw an Isis fighter, a local guy he had known before the war who had originally joined the FSA and then been lured to the extremists. He had come over for a chat – and to check up on what Mahmoud and his team were doing. My friends bundled me into a back room with an order not to smoke, and for the next hour I sat in silence trying to pick out words from the conversation across the hallway.

In the years since I have often wondered how I survived, when so many other foreign journalists were kidnapped and handed to Isis that summer. My friendship with Mahmoud and Aymann, a nuclear physics student and also an activist at the centre, was surely a large part of it – they remain the most honest and loyal people I met in Aleppo, and by concealing me that day they risked their own lives. They were also firm with me when I pushed to do stories that were, in retrospect, suicidal. I had wanted to visit a camp for foreign fighters in the countryside between Aleppo and the Turkish border in the spring of 2013, back when the reports of Europeans flocking to join the Islamist factions were nothing more than numerous but unconfirmed rumours. They stopped me. Those same foreign fighters were later revealed to have been instrumental in the kidnappings of journalists.

Being a woman also helped, since I could easily conceal myself with a headscarf and abaya. In my disguise, complete with sunglasses to conceal my eyes, I managed to drift through a Friday demonstration organised by Al-Qaeda and into the city's Sharia court, where the extremists handed down punishments according to their interpretation of the Qur'an. Women became faceless, ghostly beings in Aleppo as Al-Qaeda and then Isis tightened their grip, floating through the streets with faces covered and heads lowered, studiously ignored by the men they encountered. For a female journalist it was a gift – even though my height and European habit of striding along with quick steps must have looked odd among the diminutive and slow-paced Syrians. But inside I boiled, desperately sorry for the Syrian women and girls I met behind closed doors, who would rip off their coverings and vent fury at the men who were forcing this on them. One day, as I walked through Aleppo's empty, crumbling side streets with a group of young Syrian activists, a woman rounded the corner with her two young children. She had flipped up the black sheet that covered her face and was tilting her head back towards the sun with her eyes half closed. When she caught sight of us she quickly brought the sheet down over her face again, and bustled past us in silence.

My fixer Soheib's optimism about Isis was born of his apparent obliviousness of death in all its forms. He was brave to the point of crazy, at odds with the gelled side-parting and pencil moustache that made him look like a middle-aged accountant. Because of that I was never fully comfortable going out to report with him. He would gesture towards checkpoints manned by Al-Qaeda fighters and suggest, in all seriousness, that I ask to interview them. When we went to the front lines, dead zones running through the heart of the city where rebel fighters occupied one building and the regime men another, so close we could hear them lighting their cigarettes, he would bound up ruined steps onto rooftops and stand there shouting for me to come and join him. One day we went to the crossing point at Bustan al-Qasr, the only place left in cloven Aleppo where it was possible to pass between the rebel and regime sides of the city. On the rebel side the road was blocked off a hundred metres up from the crossing by a makeshift barricade, two burnt-out buses flipped onto their sides and piled one on top of the other. It was a crude shield against government snipers, but the people of Aleppo, their reflexes weakened by a year of random violence, still flocked to the market stalls between the buses and the crossing point. A dark brown bloodstain on the pavement marked where a Canadian-Syrian medical student called Sam treated the snipers' victims. They opened fire every day, Sam had told me, more on Fridays. Sometimes it seemed they were playing games – they would shoot only at children on one day, at pregnant women on another. As he tired of my questions, he started interrogating me.

'Why do you come here?' Sam asked. 'What is it that you're looking for?'

Soheib and I pushed on further, right up to the sandbags that marked the final metres of rebel territory. My guts started to flip, not only from the knowledge that there were sniper rifles trained on us but also from the fear of being so close to Assad's soldiers, just on the other side of the crossing. They would love to get their hands on a British journalist, I thought, to parade me on Syrian television as a spy and then throw me into one of their prisons. With my thoughts elsewhere I hardly noticed the growing danger we were in from the rebels manning this side of the crossing. One had caught Soheib's arm and was demanding to see his papers. Another had spotted my camera. Soheib had assured me before we set off that it was a friendly brigade manning this checkpoint, that we would encounter no problems. But Aleppo's war was so fluid in those months, it stank so heavily of testosterone that fiefdoms could change hands within hours. The men peering at us weren't Islamists, I was sure, but they were scruffy and I could smell their lack of discipline.

Our saviour came from an unlikely place: at that moment, one of Assad's snipers opened fire. The *crack-crack-crack* rang down the street and the crowd parted in panic. Soheib and I took our chance and melted away with them, scrambling for a market hall opposite Sam's clinic that had lost all its windows and taken several mortar rounds to its walls. The half-minute it took me to run to the hall and clamber through its window seemed to last an hour: I wasn't wearing my flak jacket, and I felt the softness of my flesh and spine as bullets flew past me down the street. Once inside my relief turned to sweat that poured profusely down my face, and I collapsed shaking against a wall. Soheib had other ideas. He hopped back through the ruined window onto the street as the sniper kept firing.

'What are you doing? Come back out here!' he shouted. 'Come and take photos of this!'

'Are you fucking insane?' I shouted back, as he stood on the deserted street waving his arms.

I started to believe that Soheib was charmed, a cat with nine lives who would walk away unscathed from everything Aleppo threw at him. I was wrong, of course. It wasn't his gung-ho nonchalance in the line of fire that did for him, but his geekiness and blind faith in the fundamental goodness of the Isis men. Soheib kept lists of everything – new rebel groupings, how many fighters they had, where their money was coming from and what areas they controlled. He saved those documents and thousands of photos and videos on his laptop, which he took with him everywhere and shared freely with the journalists he worked with. And when Isis called to tell him they had arrested his brother in Azaz, he went to their headquarters there with his laptop and lists.

We never saw him again. Both I and another British journalist who worked with him received Skype messages from him on the same day a few weeks later, before either of us knew he had disappeared. I twigged straight away that something was wrong: the message I received was a single word: 'Hello.' Soheib never started a conversation like that – he would always address me as 'Miss Hannah', and craft a polite, slightly old-fashioned introduction.

Mahmoud told me what had happened when he himself fled to Turkey weeks later, the steel door and the machine gun he kept in the footwell of his car no longer enough to protect him. Aymann was also arrested but scored a lucky escape when he was placed in the charge of an old acquaintance who had joined up with Isis, and who took pity on him. The extremists had turned on the activists, just as we all knew they would, and on the Aleppo rebels who had misguidedly tolerated the Isis presence in their midst. By January 2014, almost all of rebel-held Aleppo was under Isis control and any activists, fixers or translators who had stayed were rounded up, accused of spying for Western governments.

Two years later I met with another old Aleppo activist, a graffiti artist I had watched paint revolutionary slogans and smiley faces on the rubble in 2013. He had been held in the same Isis prison as Soheib. Finally, I got the last piece of his story: an Isis court had found Soheib guilty of sedition, and his punishment was a bullet to the head.

*Summer 2015*
*The refugee highway*

There were times in Aleppo when I could kid myself that I really understood the torment of the people I was writing about. I would stay in their homes and sit with them as Assad's jets howled over, our conversation ebbing and flowing as they came and went. Sometimes, as they approached, someone would turn the lights out and everyone would stop talking, as if we could hide in the silence and darkness. As the din subsided we would unclamp our tensed muscles and smile at each other, trying to cover our fear as we anticipated the next one. At first there were patterns to where the bombs struck – hospitals, schools and crowded markets were the most dangerous places to be. But once the regime, whether for sadistic or logistical reasons, switched to using barrel bombs instead, death became horribly random. When Mahmoud and I returned to Aleppo in April 2014, after the rebels had pushed Isis back to the city's eastern borders, we drove in silence through deserted neighbourhoods that had been turned into concrete skeletons, the remains of apartment blocks jutting like broken teeth from a ruined mouth. In the quarters that were still inhabited, everyone on the streets turned their eyes to the sky. Barrel bombing happened in evil slow motion, much more agonising than the quick *whoosh-blast-death* of the jets. The grace with which the barrels tumbled from the helicopters, arcing towards the ground like swooping birds and then morphing into huge mushrooms of smoke and dust, gave you the feeling that you could escape them if only you ran fast enough.

Each time I left Aleppo I felt overwhelming relief and a fierce stab of guilt as I said goodbye to the people who had to stay. No way could I ever know what this was like for them – not even close. A few days in that city was enough to make me chain smoke and fixate on my own mortality, desperate to wash the stink of the generator diesel out of my hair and the dust off my skin. So what was it doing to these people who stayed there for years, and to the kids born into a world where buildings exploded at random around them?

But my Aleppo dissonance was nothing next to the night in May 2015 when I stood on the deck of a small pleasure boat and watched a huddle of people pray as their sagging dinghy started to take in water. It was only a month since Abu Laith had talked about shifting his route north to the Aegean coast, and all the other middlemen had hit on the same idea. The long and expensive route to Italy dried up along with the local smuggling economy in Mersin, so the smugglers started organising short hops across the Aegean to Greece in rubber boats designed for children's playtime. The retail price of a route into Europe dropped overnight from more than 6,000 euros per person to around 1,000, and the trickle of people taking the journey turned into a flood.

I was working alongside a British television news crew when we spotted the slowly sinking boat. We had decided that the best way to witness this new Aegean smuggling operation in action was to persuade a Turkish captain to take us out just beyond a bay that we knew to be a smuggling hotspot, drop anchor, and wait. We faked a party as the sun went down, blasting out cheesy music and dancing on the deck. As the last wisps of light faded, we saw pinpricks of light sparking up in a wooded hill that dropped straight down into the sea 500 metres away from us – the picturesque backdrop to a beachfront honeymoon resort. The lights were people picking their way down to the shore having been dropped off by the smugglers in the middle of a mountain road, told where to go and ordered to keep their mouths shut. By 2 a.m., in the pitch-black silence and waiting for the flotilla of small dinghies to arrive, most of us had fallen asleep.

I woke up at 3 a.m. to an urgent whisper from the news crew's reporter. He had spotted the first boat, drifting just a few metres away from us. We turned on a camera light and started shouting out questions – and saw for ourselves the reality of this journey, sold by the smugglers as a short and easy hop across to the Greek island of Kos.

The dinghy was four metres long, and every spare inch of it was filled. The women and children sat in the middle, and the men on the lip around the edge. It was probably meant for eight people but there were at least twenty on board, and it was starting to sag beneath the waterline. One man tried to mop up the water inside the boat with a towel, wringing it out over the side every few seconds. They were only a few hundred metres from the Turkish shore, and they were already sinking.

The reporter asked them whether we should call the coastguard as they passed us ten metres away.

'Stay with us, please,' shouted out one of the men, a Syrian who spoke perfect English. 'Don't call the coastguard, just follow us.'

'What are you running from?' I called out to him.

'War,' he replied. 'Just war.'

'And what are you looking for?' I yelled as the boat pulled off towards Greek waters.

'Freedom,' came his response.

## The shores

Turgutreis, the closest town to the smuggling point, is a tourist resort on the Bodrum peninsula, home to a gaggle of British expats and seasonal workers who throng there in summer. Signs of its burgeoning night sport were scattered everywhere by May 2015 – young Arab men with small backpacks hanging out in the main square by daytime, deflated and abandoned dinghies in the quieter coves and often, in the early mornings, the sight of the coastguard bringing in the people they had rescued or captured.

'I come to the same sun lounger every morning,' said Ann Davidson, a retired British nurse with pink hair who had lived in Turgutreis on and off for two decades. 'And a few weeks ago I started to see the coastguard going out more and more.'

When Ann first noticed huge groups of bedraggled people, including children, being brought in and herded into a lock-up at the end of the pier, her nursing instincts took over. She loaded the basket of her bicycle with water and biscuits and pedalled over to hand them out. As the coastguard and gendarmerie officers got to know her they started letting her into the cell, a bare cage with no seats but shaded from the sun at least. Talking with the people locked inside as she handed out her offerings, she began to realise the scale of what was happening in her adopted home town.

'They were all telling me how they had escaped from Syria and Iraq and were trying to get to Europe,' Ann said. 'And most of them had already tried several times and been caught. They said they would keep trying until they made it to Greece.'

One morning I walked down the Turgutreis pier with her to hand out refreshments and speak with the latest arrivals. The three dozen people sprawled behind the bars on the concrete looked exhausted, their fatigue turning to quiet amazement when they saw this middle-aged lady with candy-floss hair bustling in and handing out packaged cakes. A young Syrian man called Mohammed, his English polished to perfection over his career working as an interpreter in Dubai, started telling their story.

'This is the second time we've been caught, we also tried yesterday,' he said. 'We're not worried about what will happen. Yesterday we were held here for three hours, then they took us to the police station in Bodrum, took our fingerprints and photographs and released us. But this time we were only ten or fifteen minutes from Kos when we were caught.'

The group would try again tonight and keep trying until they reached Greece, Mohammed said. They had got to know each other, become friends – at least, the Syrians had. Half of the men in the lock-up were silent, staring men with darker complexions and rounder faces than the others. When I tried to speak with them all they would say was 'Burma, Burma.' One of the gendarmerie officers told me the authorities guessed they were actually Pakistani, but they had no papers to prove it either way. This nightly dance with the coastguard and the police would not and could not stop them: they would repeat their ritual until they finally passed over the invisible sea border to Greece. Each time, the smuggler would send four boats off in quick succession, and the coastguard might be able to catch one. They could not be the unlucky ones for ever. And Mohammed had nowhere to return to.

'When things started getting complicated in Syria the UAE stopped renewing my residency,' he said. 'So I took my wife and three kids back to Damascus – and then the apartment I had bought there with my savings from Dubai was bombed. I came to Turkey a year ago and opened a cake shop, but I was mugged of everything by a business partner. We do appreciate Turkey very much, but it's not easy to live here. I did my best but it didn't work. It's not easy to merge into the community here. The culture is similar but the Turkish people have started to feel angry about us being here. I told my wife that I'll use our last bit of money to get to Europe, and then I can bring them after me.'

One of Mohammed's children had stayed in Damascus with his parents. The other two were living in Mersin with his wife. He laughed in anticipation of the stories he would tell his grandchildren one day, in their future life in Europe.

'I am forty-one years old. I have lived the war and now I am living adventures at sea,' he said. 'I used to look at smugglers as criminals. But if they didn't exist we would just die in other ways.'

*The smuggling business*

Mohammed and the others had each paid 950 euros for their passage, a price that bought them as many attempts as they needed, and a measure of security. By now people-smuggling had become established, organised and competitive – the agents, dependent on word of mouth and good references, had realised they needed to professionalise. I went back to Mersin armed with scraps of information I had collected from Abu Laith, Mohammed and others like them, and started deciphering how the industry worked. At every level, smuggling's shadow economy was interwoven with Turkey's legitimate one. The smugglers' customers increasingly came into Turkey on official visas, stayed in tourist hotels, and paid their fees to the mob at the money exchange and transfer offices that litter every down-at-heel commercial district of every Turkish city.

Behind the grubby white Formica counter of the al-Sayeed money-changing office in Mersin, a young Syrian called Mahmoud sucked on a cigarette and told me about his business. He had started with just one office, which he set up when he fled to Turkey in 2012. As the wave of refugees increased, so did his trade: new arrivals found their way to him when they wanted to change the stacks of Syrian notes they had brought out – their life savings – for dollars or Turkish lira. He was making a decent living, nothing out of the ordinary for a small businessman – just enough to look after his family and put away some savings.

Then in 2014 Mersin's smuggling middlemen came to him. They needed an interlocutor, they said, someone who could act as the guarantor between them and their customers. He would take the payments from people who wanted to go to Europe, and for a fee hold it in trust for them until they reached the destination they had agreed with the smugglers' agents. On payment the customers were given two unique codes, known only to Mahmoud and themselves. They would give the first to the smuggler as they got on the boat as proof of their payment, and send the other back to him when they reached Europe. Once they texted the second one to him, he would hand the money to the smugglers and the deal was complete.

Mahmoud was already reaping the rewards. His single office in Mersin had grown into a chain of twelve in cities across Turkey, and he was opening others in Italy, the Republic of Cyprus and Bulgaria – all smugglers' entry points to the EU. Each month, he was holding payments for around four thousand people. His total fee for each customer was $180, $30 of it paid by them and the remaining $150 from the smuggler. That alone was bringing him an income of $720,000 a month. On top, he was dabbling in currency and gold speculation using the money he was holding. And Mahmoud was just the middleman of the middlemen.

'People are selling their house, gold, land, everything to get to

Europe,' he said. 'It's the middle classes mainly. I started doing this a year ago, just informally for friends at first. And then one person passed my contact on to another, and it grew from there.'

Of the six people working in his Mersin office, two were focused solely on the smuggling payments. The Turkish authorities, he told me, didn't bother him.

'The Turkish government doesn't know about it,' he said. 'We don't put any of our money in the banks, the intelligence would notice. And anyway, my business is not part of smuggling, it's just *for* smuggling. I'm saving this money for them as a humanitarian act.'

I struggled with that claim, and with the notion that the Turkish government had failed to notice what was happening. Over the next months I developed a fascination with these smoky, sparsely lit, shady money offices and visited dozens of them – in Istanbul, along the western coast, and down at the Syrian border. Throughout the whole of 2015, none of them ever said no when I walked in and told them I was a journalist and wanted to know how their businesses worked. All of them sat me down with a cup of tea and a cigarette, sometimes in a back room and sometimes just out on the shop floor, and told me as many details as I wanted to know.

Every second or third shop at one end of the main street of Şanlıurfa, a city close to the Syrian border, was a rough copy of Mahmoud's place in Mersin: a bare office with a desk, and a man sitting behind it with nothing but a laptop and a collection of mobile phones. Their windows were plastered with Arabic-language signs. There was no need for any in Turkish: almost all their customers were Syrian refugees from the cities of Raqqa and Deir Ezzor, which had been overrun by Isis. The terror group's Caliphate started just thirty-five miles down the road; Isis had captured both the Syrian frontier town of Tel Abyad and its border crossing with Turkey in January 2014. The border was still commutable: down at the Akçakale gate I stood in an abaya and headscarf and watched bearded men and burka-clad women show their passports to the Turkish guards and pass on through to the town, where the black flag was flying. There were even new clothes stores operating right on the Turkish side of the crossing, selling the Islamic garb needed to blend in over in Isis-land. Barbers who had escaped Tel Abyad when the men with the penchant for long beards had taken over had set themselves up again in Akçakale town, a few blocks back from the crossing, their customers now mostly Syrians who had had enough of living under Islamo-fascism and had come out the other way. Once in Turkey, they immediately indulged in everything they had been denied – a cigarette, a drink and a beard trim.

In those grimy Şanlıurfa offices I saw how capital was flowing across the border, too. The main business of these exchange offices was *hawala*, an informal method of transferring money across borders – in this case, across the frontier into Isis territory. If a Syrian in Turkey wanted to send money to relatives back home in Deir Ezzor or Raqqa they would visit one of the agents on Şanlıurfa's main street. There they would hand over the cash, and send the agent photographs of their ID documents and those of the receiver. The *hawala* agent then passed instructions to their counterpart inside Syria, who would hand the money to the specified person once they had produced that ID. The confirmations and photos of documents were all sent via WhatsApp, an encrypted messaging service the authorities could not spy on. The *hawala* agents on either side kept huge stacks of money and a record of the transactions they made, and evened up the discrepancies when they met a few times a year. Usually the agents were relatives, their blood ties a substitute for the legal guarantees built into formal money-transfer systems.

The *hawala* guys asked no questions about where the money was going. One, a brawny man called Ahmet whose arms were covered with scrappy homemade tattoos, admitted that his cousin in Raqqa was being taxed by Isis for each transaction he made – protection money, he said, to allow him to continue his business and help the people of the city to survive. With Syria's banking system frozen there was no other way to get money in to the people struggling to make ends meet in the war zone. Aid organisations often quietly use the *hawala* system to get money to their workers in areas held by rebel groups, although – unsurprisingly, given its usefulness for terrorists and money launderers – Western governments are keen to clamp down.

As the conflict bit harder and the value of the Syrian pound (or lira) started plummeting, formal money changers in Turkey stopped accepting it. The refugees coming out of the country with their life savings in Syrian cash had no choice but to go to the unofficial *hawala* offices to change it into dollars, where the rate they were offered was derisory. The agents, left with stacks of notes useless inside Turkey, soon arranged a new system to transfer the money back into Syria, where the Syrian lira was still holding up as the street currency. They sent the money to another middleman in Kilis, who arranged for it to be smuggled across the border by 'ants', children and young men who would traverse the illegal routes several times a day carrying backpacks stuffed with cash. Inside Syria, they would trade it with money changers for the dollars flowing into the country in sponsorship for armed groups and aid projects.

By 2015 the *hawala* agents were getting in on the business of holding money for the people-smugglers, too, the last link in a circular chain of misery. Syrians were selling everything in order to reach Europe through networks that were feeding money back to the very armed groups that had caused them to flee in the first place. The poorest, as always, were left behind in Turkey's camps, together with the women and children who were waiting in agony for their husbands and brothers to complete the dangerous journey to Europe, so that they could come safely on a family reunification visa afterwards. And by welcoming refugees at their borders but not offering any safe or legal route to get there, the governments of rich Europe provided a never-ending stream of custom for the smugglers.

On the second floor of a gritty Şanlıurfa shopping arcade, barely less hidden than the *hawala* places, Nabil Aldush ran another smuggling auxiliary – a document forgery office. Syrian passports, some of the weakest in the world, had become hot property since Angela Merkel announced in September 2015 that her country would accept any Syrians who made it over Germany's borders. Berlin was willingly breaking free of the Dublin Agreement, the EU rules on asylum signed in 1990 which state that refugees must make their claim in the first member state they arrive in. For those travelling the smugglers' route from Turkey, that had meant Italy, Greece or Bulgaria – poor countries unable to cope with a humanitarian emergency and definitely not places people would choose to stay. But now, if Syrians could make it all the way 1,500 miles north of the Greek islands to the German border, they could claim asylum there no matter what other EU countries they had travelled through.

Instantly, Germany rather than Sweden became the number one destination for the people trying to reach Europe. And for the scores of non-Syrians who had joined the exodus to Europe via Turkey – mainly Afghans, Pakistanis and Iraqis – a Syrian passport was a must-have. The smugglers told them they would be granted automatic refugee status in Germany if they could pass as Syrians – even though the authorities in Europe quickly wised up. Nabil had opened his office in late 2014, initially providing other kinds of forged documents to Syrians who had lost everything in the war: marriage contracts, driving licences and university certificates were some of his best sellers. A year on, passports had become his most lucrative trade. He had worked for the government back in Syria, and through a contact with the regime in Damascus he was buying genuine blank passports which he would print with the details and photographs of his customers. He charged $2,000 per passport.

'Six months ago the first Iraqis started coming,' Nabil said. 'They're frank – they say they want to go to Europe as Syrians. A lot of people ask me how they can get to Greece, but I tell them I just deal with documents, not with smuggling.'

Nabil took a certain pride in his work – he even kept an ultra-violet scanner in his office to prove that the holograms on his passports were genuine before he handed them over to his happy customers. He turned his nose up at what he called the 'Istanbul passports', the

obvious fakes; ten thousand of them had made their way onto the
market, he said, but he had never dealt in them. So legitimate was
his business, he claimed, that he was licensed by the Turkish government to do it – at least for his Syrian customers.

'They trust us, they know we just want to help Syrians,' he said.
'When the refugees go to the municipality and say they've come here
without any documents, they send them to us.'

As the trafficking business professionalised, its warp weaving in with
the weft of Turkey's legitimate economy, an even meaner subset of
criminals started operating in its shadows. The Syrians dreaming of
Europe made easy pickings for the conmen who now flocked to the
seediest districts of Istanbul, where they set up informal offices in
the tea houses.

'The smuggler told me to meet him by the tram stop,' a Syrian
called Rami told me, a few days after he had been relieved of his life
savings and left in huge debt to friends and relatives. 'When I got
there, I waited for thirty minutes and called him three times. I guess
he was observing me. When he came, he had an Aleppo accent and
told me not to trust anyone. I asked about using the money offices
for the payment and he told me no, they're thieves.'

The smuggler took Rami to a grungy hotel where his accomplice
showed him pictures of the European passports they could provide
him with. Rami had decided not to risk the sea route, instead
plumping for the high-end option of documents and a flight ticket
straight into the EU. The men told Rami they would provide him
with the passport of a European who resembled him, and that they
had contacts in Istanbul's airports who would ensure that no one
would look too closely. He would fly to the Emirates, and from there
to the UK. To ease his doubts they brought in another customer who
told him that his cousin had used their services days earlier and was
now in England. Convinced, Rami shook on the deal.

'I went around everyone I knew and collected money,' he said.
'They wanted $4,500 as a deposit, and the whole thing would cost

$15,000. I would send them the rest when I got to Europe. I paid them, and they said my flight would be booked for the next day. But when I went back to the hotel to meet them they were gone. Everything was gone.'

## The deal

The key to cutting off the smugglers lay not at sea, but on land. That was what the Turkish coastguard wanted to show me when he sneaked me aboard his patrol on a balmy September night. He was the skipper we had found off the Turgutreis bay four months earlier after the Syrian in the sinking dinghy had asked us to follow them to Greece. After a few panicked minutes of moral tussling we decided that we had to report what we had seen, and set off back to the port. The coastguard found us first, speeding up to us with sirens sounding in the gentle dawn sunlight. By law the owner of the boat needed a licence and a radar system to stay out in the bay all night, and he had neither. As the only journalist on board with a Turkish press card and some command of the language, I did the talking as he pulled alongside us.

'And what do you think of how the Turkish coastguard is handling this crisis?' he asked me after I had explained what we were doing.

'I think you're doing a good job in a very difficult situation,' I replied.

His demeanour changed, the stiff outer shell of officialdom dropping away as a smile crept across his face.

'Thank you,' he said. 'I'll come with you back to the port.'

Once we had docked he ticked us off for staying out on the water all night and took my details and telephone number. A few months later, he sent me a message asking if I would like to see what the trafficking trade looked like from his eyes.

A few hundred metres out from the coast he turned off the ship's lights, opened a packet of chocolate biscuits and handed me some night-vision goggles.

'Look out over there,' he told me, gesturing back towards the shore. At first there was just blackness, but within minutes I saw the first boats, picked out in sharp green lines. Soon I could see five of them scattered across the bay.

'Now this is my dilemma,' the coastguard said. 'If I go to stop one of them, what if another one sinks in the meantime? If I intercept one boat that is not sinking it will take me at least two hours to take all the people back to land and hand them over to the police. And if another boat sinks as I'm doing that, there is no one here to rescue the people.'

Once the boats were in the water it was too late, he said. The only way to stop the smugglers was for the gendarmerie to set up check-points along the coastal roads and catch them and their customers as they travelled to the launch points. He was sick of the blame being directed at him and his colleagues for the huge criminal and human-itarian crisis happening on his watch. Only days earlier, a photo from a nearby beach had torn across front pages around the world: a Turkish gendarmerie officer carrying the limp body of a three-year-old boy who had washed up on the shore. It sparked the first real wave of global rage about what was happening at the edge of Europe, even though it had all been going on for months. Volunteers of every stripe, from professional lawyers and medics to idealist leftists, flocked to the Greek islands to pitch in. Meanwhile, back in Turkey, Abu Laith was talking about how he was planning to send his twelve-year-old son on the boats to Greece and on to Sweden, to claim asylum quickly as a lone child and bring him on the parental visa afterwards. Such paternal cynicism happened. But there were scores of older teenagers I met along the route, sixteen- and seventeen-year-olds in parks in Belgrade or harbour fronts on Greek islands who simply knew that it was their responsibility as the eldest son to do something to save their families back in Syria. The brute truth was that it was hard, even at the height of the exodus, for anyone other than the young and fit to complete the trek from Turkey's shore to Germany's borders, via sinking boats, stuffed trains and military lines. Older family members would never make it like that. Many on the route were young people who saw what was going on in their homelands through clear eyes, and wanted no part in it. Ahmed, a seventeen-year-old Shia from Baghdad, had lost his whole immediate family in a car bombing four years earlier. Raised since then by an aunt, all he could think of was his chance to leave for a place where people didn't kill each other in the name of a God he didn't believe in.

'Will they accept me in Europe if they know I'm an atheist?' he asked me with scared eyes as we stood looking back over the sea to Turkey.

Though young men were over-represented on the smugglers' boats, there were plenty of girls and young women making the trek to Europe too. Many of the young Syrian women I met on the refugee route were Kurds, camping out in tents at the Macedonian border or crowding around a phone they were charging in a Greek café. A group of young Damascenes I met on Kos reminded me in every way of my group of Syrian friends in Antakya – same urbanity, same funny accent, same way of bursting into song and verbally jousting with each other non-stop. Among ten of them, only one was a woman, Leila, a 21-year-old student in a tight white hijab. They had all hung on to the Damascus life that my Antakya friends had left behind: Assad's Syria, relatively safe but scarily oppressive. They pushed me for my accounts of the unknown terror, rebel-held Syria, which they had heard so much about but never seen. One of the guys, a cheerful soul sipping a Mythos beer on this balmy evening, said that he supported Nusra, the Al-Qaeda-linked rebel faction in Syria, even after I had told him of all the bullshit they had peddled in Aleppo.

Leila clicked her teeth at her friend and slapped his leg.

'You need to listen to her, you fool,' she said, pointing at me. 'She's *seen* them.'

It would be comforting to think that it was the rising tide of death in the Aegean that finally forced Turkey and Europe to act against the people traffickers, and that the measures they took made it easier and safer for those legitimately seeking asylum to do so. By the end of 2015 more than a hundred people were known to have drowned in the sea and thousands more plucked out by the coastguard or volunteers on the Greek islands. The solution the leaders in Brussels finally hit on, a multi-billion-euro deal with Turkey to stamp out the smuggling industry and improve life for the Syrians Ankara was hosting, succeeded only in the sense that it staunched the flow of boats across the Aegean. But it also handed Erdoğan a major trump card.

The deal was signed in March 2016, and promised to hand six billion euros to Turkey in two tranches to provide better services for the three million Syrians living there. It also dangled the prospect of visa-free travel in the Schengen zone for Turkish citizens. In return, any person who travelled to Greece from Turkey's shores via the smugglers' boats would be sent back to Turkey. For each Syrian returned, one already living in Turkey would be resettled in Europe. On the sunny morning that the deal came into force I stood in the Turkish seaside town of Dikili with a scrum of other journalists, waiting for the first boat bringing in forcibly returned people – the final breakdown of an asylum policy Europe had operated for two decades. The boat was due to dock around lunchtime. But as around a hundred of us, television cameras, photojournalists and newspaper hacks, waited on the rocks next to the wire fence surrounding the port, workers came and hung up huge plastic sheets blocking the television cameras from capturing the big moment. In the end we caught a glimpse of a downcast huddle of men being ushered from the boat into a police bus, filed our stories, and then headed to the beach with beers.

The money the EU has handed to Turkey has been distributed among the camps, the Turkish health service, schools and other refugee aid projects. It has also funded detention centres where non-Syrians – mostly Afghans and Pakistanis – returned from Greece are held before being deported back to their countries. The flood of people travelling to the Greek islands has slowed to a trickle. But the measures Ankara has taken to cauterise trafficking have not much improved life for the Syrians who remain in Turkey. Most must now get a permission paper from the local government before they are allowed to travel out of the Turkish province where they are registered. Their residency documents must be renewed each year in a lengthy bout of paperwork, and in order to get them they must present a valid Syrian passport – a huge hurdle for those who left the country without documents, or who skipped military service and whose passports have expired. For a time, they too went to the passport forgers for their renewals, but the regime back in Damascus has now started issuing documents to defectors for huge fees in a bid to bring more cash into its coffers. The Syrian consulate in Istanbul, which has stayed open throughout the war despite Turkey cutting its diplomatic ties with Assad back in 2011, is constantly crowded with Syrians desperate to get their papers renewed, queuing from four in the morning down the gleaming pavements of the exclusive consular district. The process often takes six months and by the time the Syrians have their new passports they have already nearly expired again – men who have not done their military service get only two years' extension each time. Stuck in a never-ending loop between Ankara's bureaucracy and nonchalant contempt in Damascus, they are often never fully legal in Turkey, always in fear of being stopped by an unfriendly policeman.

Those caught without the right papers in Turkey have, on occasion, been forced back across the border into Syria – a breach of the UN convention on refugees. Meanwhile, from the middle of 2015, the Turkish security forces started sealing the frontier, building a huge wall along its length and militarising the area around it. There have been countless reports, some of them accompanied by horrifying mobile phone footage, of Turkish soldiers shooting at Syrians as they try to cross the border. Hundreds have been killed. Ankara flatly denies it, but a former Turkish commando who had served at one of the busiest border areas told me the instructions from their commanders had shifted over the course of 2015 and 2016. At first they were told to turn a blind eye, then they were told to keep the refugees back and to fire warning shots into the air if necessary. After that, they were ordered to shoot at their legs if they kept on coming. Finally, they were commanded to shoot to kill if they felt they were being threatened. There is no evidence of European collusion in Turkey's changing border policy, but it happened in sync with the bloc handing over billions to Ankara to stop migration to Europe. The EU has never criticised or even commented on the reports of the shootings.

Back in Ankara, Erdoğan has repeatedly used the deal as a way to lash out at Brussels. He has claimed that the bloc has not handed over the promised money, even though it is flowing to Turkey as scheduled. He has accused Europe of insincerity in its promise to grant visa-free travel to Turks – a part of the deal that has never been enacted due to Ankara's worsening human rights record since it was signed. He has even threatened to call the deal off and open his borders should Europe not give him what he wants, be it more money or more leeway to rule without reproach.

For most Syrians still in Turkey the biggest problem is insecurity – not knowing how long they will be allowed to stay and if they will ever be granted citizenship. Ankara has so far given passports to a select few Syrians, around 300,000 who are mostly educated professionals. But as opinion polls show that Turks are increasingly fed up with hosting millions of Syrians, so Erdoğan's rhetoric has turned. He now says the Syrians will eventually have to return to their homeland, that they cannot stay in Turkey for ever.

## The Syrians' saviour

Unpicking the story of Syria's revolution is like trying to untangle a knot of hair. In early 2011 no one wanted to tell a foreign journalist that they were involved in the uprising. By early 2013, everyone did. Two years on again, and everyone was just sick of telling the same old story to a world that had long grown bored of it.

So it wasn't until our conversation randomly tilted towards Damascus and the first protests of the revolution that I realised that Ahmed – a smiling, warm-hearted fixer from Aleppo who was taking me to meet Abu Laith, the smuggler – had been a member of the security forces that I had feared so deeply when I travelled into Assad's Syria on a tourist visa in 2011.

'Now everyone says they were there in the first protests, everyone tries to outdo each other with what they did for the revolution,' he said, as we drove along the smooth new highway to Mersin. Then his round face cracked into an irresistible smile. 'I *was* at the Day of Rage,' he laughed. 'Only I was on the other side.'

He had told me before how he had spent a couple of weeks fighting alongside the rebels in Aleppo before deciding that he could better use his skills by working as a fixer for the foreign journalists who were flocking to the city, but I had no idea about his narrow and lucky exit from the regime's army. Ahmed had been called up for his compulsory military service in July 2009. At the time he was vaguely annoyed – 'I had a good life in Aleppo,' he said – but he accepted it as inevitable. Every young man in Syria was obliged to spend a year and nine months in the army as soon as they turned eighteen, unless they had the money or the connections to bribe their way out of it. Some leeway was given to university students, who could delay their military service until they had graduated. Many stretched out their time at university for as long as they could, changing courses or signing up for another as soon as they had finished their first one. But Ahmed was a barber from a working-class family, and he had no get-out available. So he decided to make the best of his unavoidable circumstances. He excelled in his six months' training, and when that was finished he was selected to be one of the prime minister's bodyguards. It was an elite position, and he jumped at it. 'I didn't want to be one of those people who spends their whole military service in the barracks,' he said. 'I would have gone crazy if I couldn't go out every day.'

He pulled up a photo on his mobile phone, showing him back in his military service days. Dozens of other Syrian men had shown me similar photos, in which they usually looked far older, even when the shots had been taken years before. The service was so notoriously tough and brutal that it turned fresh-faced teenagers into gaunt shaven-headed young men with haunted eyes. They were forced to complete gruelling physical training every day on pitiful rations, sleeping in unheated barracks even in the freezing winter months and running for miles in boots that were often several sizes too small. The Sunnis suffered the worst; on top of the physical discomforts, they were humiliated by the Alawite officers. Praying was strictly forbidden, and anyone caught doing it would be beaten.

But in his photo Ahmed looked like a male model. He had a fashionable haircut, a designer suit and sunglasses, and he was leaning proprietorially against a gleaming Mercedes. This was the fortune of those who occupied the elite military positions – privilege, freedom, and carte blanche to behave how they liked.

'If I had wanted to be an asshole, I could have been,' said Ahmed. 'You could steal, or rape, or blackmail, and nothing would happen to you.'

By early 2011, he had been seconded to the personal protection team of the head of Damascus's political intelligence unit. In the days before the 15 March Day of Rage, preparations for the security service's response reached warp speed. There had already been one small demonstration in Damascus a month earlier; now, the regime knew that it had to prepare for more. 'We have twelve different intelligence forces in Syria and every single one knew what was being planned,' said Ahmed. 'I felt uneasy about it – I didn't believe that these protests could bring anything good.'

The Day of Rage protest started in the Souk al-Hamidiyah, the famous covered market in the old city. Ahmed was one of the dozens of officers assigned to it, far outnumbering the handful of protesters. Every officer wore plain clothes, mingling seamlessly with the demonstrators before moving in for the kill. As the protest moved into the old city along the ancient streets around the Umayyad Mosque, the security forces moved in from all directions. Ahmed and his colleagues arrested everybody – it didn't matter if they were taking part in the protests or not.

A few days later, his ambivalence about the slowly swelling protest movement turned to fear. President Bashar al-Assad gave a speech in which he promised that the security forces would not open fire. But the head of the political intelligence unit told his men something different.

'He told us that at the next protests, we were to fire on the protesters,' he said. 'Some of us spoke up – we said that the president had said that wouldn't happen. But he replied: "Shut up. This is what I'm telling you. And this is what you do." And then I realised that Bashar was saying one thing, but the security forces were doing something else.'

On 2 April, Ahmed attended his final protest in Damascus. Everyone in his unit had been issued with cattle prods that discharged 330 volts of electricity – enough to kill a person. The protest, near the political intelligence headquarters, was the largest yet in the capital. News of the spiralling violence in Deraa was spreading, and people who had spent years subdued by their fear of the regime were now galvanised by anger. It was not just the students and the young people who turned out to protest – this time there were older people too. 'I saw one old man next to me and I told him "Just run, just go",' said Ahmed. 'I knew what was going to happen.'

Within half an hour the security forces had turned on the protesters. Ahmed had deliberately spilled water over his cattle prod and broken it but others were fully invested in the mission they had been sent out on. Division Four – the elite and feared security force headed up by Bashar al-Assad's psychopathic brother, Maher – came out into the demonstration. Ahmed watched as they started laying into the protesters with crude maces – sticks of wood topped off with sharp metal. 'They were like animals,' he said. 'The old man I'd told to run had ignored me. I saw him getting beaten with one of those sticks.'

On 4 April 2011 – two days after that protest – he was released from military service and returned to Aleppo, charged with new hate for the regime and fear of the future, of what the things he had witnessed might turn into. Two weeks later, the regime stopped releasing men from their military service. For those still serving against their will, being forced ever more often to fire on the people they sympathised with, the ways out were closing down.

By the time I met him in 2014, Ahmed had fled Aleppo with the other activists and was living in Kilis in the Turkish borderlands. With his fluent English and rapidly improving Turkish, he was soon earning enough money to pay the rent on a newly built apartment and look after his wife and baby son in comfort. He was also developing a growing admiration for Erdoğan.

On the night of the 2016 coup attempt, he drove around the streets of his adopted town flying a Turkish flag out of the window. Soon after that, he was regularly posting pictures of the president on social media, alongside AK Party slogans and sycophantic dedications, so similar to those that Assad's loyalists devote to him. At first I couldn't figure out Ahmed's path from army defector, to revolutionary, to refugee, to Erdoğan supporter. But soon I came to see that he is not unusual – he is the norm. Many of the Syrians who loathe Assad as a dictator see Erdoğan as their protector and sole champion in an otherwise uncaring world. WhatsApp groups set up for the Syrians applying for Turkish citizenship are full of adoration for the president, and many of Turkey's pro-Erdoğan news services have launched Arabic-language versions to peddle their version of the truth to the refugees. And those Syrians who see the growing similarities between Erdoğan and Assad are wise enough to keep quiet.

'Syrians are frightened and the only positive signals they get are from Turkey,' one told me. 'When Erdoğan says there is a conspiracy, it makes sense for them.'

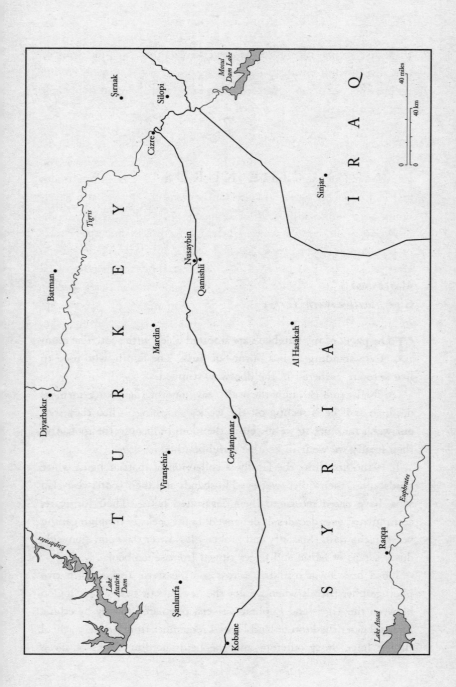

# 7

# THE KURDS

The pages of my notebook are smeared black with soot. The room I am standing in is a burnt-out husk. The family who used to live here are gathered in the doorway, stunned.

'A shell came through the wall,' says one of the young men, as deadpan as if he is reeling off the week's shopping. 'Then they shot our water tank up, so we stayed in the room built onto the roof. And then finally we went to another neighbourhood.'

It is the first time the family, a collection of matriarchs in white headscarves, their quiet, wet-eyed husbands and their sportswear-clad sons, have dared return to their devastated house. Their furniture, accumulated over decades, is destroyed. Light peeks in through gaping holes in the walls. Masonry and broken glass litter the floor, alongside dusty scraps of fabric and pages ripped from schoolbooks.

I had been on a road trip across south-eastern Turkey with two photographer friends when we got the news about Cizre. This region between the Tigris and Euphrates rivers, populated mostly by ethnic Kurds, boasts the kind of landscapes I remember from primary school Bibles: huge dusty outcrops and shepherds herding flocks of sheep through the mountains. We had visited Hasankeyf, an ancient cave town, and Mardin, a fortress city built high on a rock. We sipped wine brewed by local Assyrian monks as the sun set over the plain leading down to the Syrian border. And then one of us, I don't remember who, looked at the news and saw that the town of Cizre, an hour's drive to the east, had been reopened after almost three months under Turkish military curfew. We drove there at top speed, calling every government contact we could think of, and bargained our way through the army and police checkpoints with our press cards.

On the outskirts of Cizre, battered commercial neighbourhoods with every window smashed, we keep something of our holiday joie de vivre. But it vanishes as soon as we find the Yağarcık family staring goggle-eyed at the remains of their home.

The young men lead us to the roof where they had sheltered, up staircases treacherous with damage and debris. Up here, we find scraps of the battle, bullet and shell casings glinting in the early spring sunshine. This family never chose to be on the front line. Armed teenagers loyal to the PKK built barricades and laced the streets with explosives in a bid to keep police out of the neighbourhood. At first, there was little reaction from the state. Emboldened, Cizre's local government, run by a party with hazy links to the militants, declared autonomy and started a trend. The pattern was soon repeating itself across south-eastern Turkey.

The state's response, when it came, was brutal. In December 2015 Turkish tanks and special forces surrounded Cizre and other towns and ordered the civilians out. Artillery and air strikes pummelled the militants and anyone else who remained. A son points to the army base on the hillside, less than a mile away, where the Turkish tanks were stationed. It has a clear line of sight to the Yağarcıks' home, where they had been planning to hold weddings for three of their children this year.

The whole of this side of the street has suffered the same fate. Shells have punched holes through concrete, leaving buildings looking

like Swiss cheese. The PKK militants have scrawled their slogans on
the walls: *Biji Apo!* ('Long live uncle!', the nickname for Abdullah
Öcalan, the militia's leader and founder). Turkish soldiers later daubed
their response: *Piç* ('Bastard'), next to a crude rendering of the Turkish
star and crescent.

There is worse to come.

'This is the good part of the town,' a pair of young children tell
us with awful gaiety as we gawp at the remains of an office building
spilling out onto the ruined street. They point down the road to
another neighbourhood, called Cudi, which they say took the brunt
of the battle. As we turn off down the side street, down littered
pavements past the ruined frontage of a hotel I once stayed in, a
stunned old woman staggers towards us talking gibberish and pleading
with the sky. Dark blue armoured police cars prowl up and down the
street, sending the people on the pavements shrinking back towards
the twisted shop shutters. I wonder why no one is talking. Then the
cloying tang of decay hits the back of my throat.

A throng has gathered around a pile of rubble on Bostancı Street,
men scratching furiously at an opening in the ground. Swarms of
flies congregate around little hillocks in the dust. It used to be a
house, this mound of grey rubble.

'Journalists? Come down here!' shouts one man, and the crowd
parts to let us down into the basement. It is tar black, claustrophobic
and sinister, and I can taste the hot aroma of death. Men are sifting
through charred body parts and bones, silent as they dig and pass
their finds between them. But the crowd around the entrance is
appalled.

'We pulled out a boy no older than my son!' shouts one man,
pointing to a wide-eyed kid of about seven.

'Where is Europe? Where is America? Where is the world?' screams
another, an old man, crazed and spittle-flecked with rage. 'We know
why they keep silent – they are scared Erdoğan will send more refugees to Europe.'

Others start throwing us snippets of the rumours flying around

Cizre – of glimpsed sightings of paramilitary gangs pouring petrol over houses and torching them, of the numbers who have died in basements like these. One woman tells us there are sixty corpses down here. Another says there are twenty-seven, and that there are two more basements full of bodies on this street alone.

I flash back to a month earlier, when I managed to contact a group of people sheltering in a Cizre cellar. There was terror in the voice of the woman I spoke to over a fuggy mobile phone line. She told me of the shells raining down on the place and the four decomposing bodies lying down there with them – people who had died of their injuries.

'All the buildings around us have collapsed, there are massacres occurring. We have no medical supplies left and there is nothing we can do for the injured,' she said. They had been in there for four days. I was never able to reach her again.

'This is a war crime, a fucking war crime,' says Yusuf, a fellow journalist, dazed as he shoots photos of the horror. This is worse for him, a Turk faced with the brutality of his own. We leave Cizre before the sunset curfew comes down and drive back up the road to Mardin. Our glasses of Assyrian red wine leave a bitter taste this evening.

## Kurds and bears

'In Yüksekova we had been warned of the danger of Kurds and bears,' wrote Robin Fedder, *The Times*'s 'Traveller in Kurdistan', in November 1965. Fedder was journeying to Turkey's south-easternmost reaches, the mountainous province of Hakkari sandwiched between the Iranian and Iraqi frontiers. His trip was possible only with the authorisation of the district governor, and with the help of two local guides and six ponies who transferred Fedder and his voluminous luggage across the harsh landscape. The region had just been opened up to foreign travellers for the first time since 1925. A new road had been built through Hakkari, and it seemed like a fresh chapter was opening in this long-tortured place – the perfect moment for an intrepid correspondent.

Yet the Turks' old wariness of the Kurds, those tribal people with the fearsome warrior reputations, had not abated. The governor had insisted that one of the guides carry a gun. Had he himself ventured from his comfy office in urban Yüksekova up into the wilds of Hakkari he may have discovered, as Fedder did, that the guns the Kurdish men carried were 'merely status symbols'. Neither were the bears as scary as the legends had it: though Fedder spotted several, they all seemed to run away from him as quickly as possible.

It was only two years after the foundation of the Turkish republic, in 1925, that the Kurds revolted against the new order. They continue to do so today, the violence undulating according to popular sentiment and world events. The original Kurdish rebel was Sheikh Said, a tribal leader whose war was as much about winning superiority over the other Kurdish clans as about revolting against the Turkish state. Today, Abdullah Öcalan is the Kurdish cipher – a student of politics who graduated from the elite Ankara University into the stormy milieu of militant leftism. The PKK, the organisation he founded in 1978, blended Marxism-Leninism with Kurdish nationalism and quickly attracted scores of followers. At the same time, Öcalan took care to rub out his detractors and rivals, leaving the PKK as the jealous, sole vanguard of the Kurdish struggle. By the time he was arrested in Kenya in 1999, Öcalan was the PKK's undisputed leader and Turkey's public enemy number one. The PKK, which had quickly morphed from an intellectual movement into a violent one, was locked in a struggle with the state in south-eastern Turkey that had already left more than thirty thousand dead.

A fifth of Turkey's eighty million population are ethnic Kurds, with their own mother tongue and culture. Their politics is often tribal and insular; whatever rivalries and rows they may have between themselves, the outsider's criticism is met with furious resistance. I have discovered it myself on a number of occasions. Once I was branded a Turkish agent and a closet Islamic fundamentalist because I wrote articles documenting allegations of war crimes committed by a PKK-linked group in Syria. On another occasion, an erudite and friendly lawyer in Diyarbakır, Turkey's biggest Kurdish city, exploded into sudden rage when I brought up the nepotistic tendencies of Masoud Barzani, then president of Iraq's Kurdish region.

'You need to read the history and then come back to me!' the lawyer shouted. 'In the past the Kurdish system was a federation of clans. That's why people don't understand the situation in the Kurdish region!'

Five minutes later he had cooled down and was apologising profusely.

'We Kurds tend to have emotional reactions,' he smiled.

## Building Atatürk's nation

When the Turkish republic was declared in 1923, scores of ethnic and religious minorities were captured within its huge new borders, more than 1,600 miles of frontier cutting across the Middle East, the Caucasus and Europe. As well as the Kurds, there were Armenians and other Christian minorities who had sat out the bloody purges of 1915. There were Alevis, followers of a schism of Shia Islam considered heretical by many hardcore Sunnis. There were others who spoke Arabic, Laz and Kurdish dialects like Zaza as their mother tongues. Greek, Balkan, Roman and Asian blood goes into the mix of this nation that boasts native blue-eyed blondes as well as dark eyes and olive skin. Turkey was – and still is – a genetic and cultural kedgeree.

Atatürk and the builders of his new republic tried to paper over the fractures with a narrative of Turkishness that mixed truth with hearty doses of mythology and pseudo-science. The landscape of the new nation, ruined by years of war, needed urgent rebuilding – but so too did the minds of its citizens. In order to bring his people together and make them loyal to the new system, Atatürk needed a narrative of a Turkish history that could downplay the importance of the Ottoman Empire – not easy, since it had been the Anatolian paradigm for the past six centuries – and root the Turks firmly in the soil they now stood on. So, as the towns and cities were reconstructed in a blaze of high modernism, archaeologists, historians and linguists began hunting for Turkey's new past.

In 1930, on Atatürk's orders, a committee was founded to create the comprehensive history of the Turks. Most of its members were bureaucrats, not historians. They won their places on the committee because they were favourites of Atatürk, and had proved their dedication to the nationalist cause. Within months, the committee published its *Outline of Turkish History*, a tome which was in some parts a transcription of Atatürk's own streams of thought, and in others a mish-mash of translated foreign-language histories of the Turks – although only the cherry-picked bits. Overall, it was carefully constructed to tell a story of the Turks as a nomadic people of Aryan blood who had originated in central Asia and then migrated westwards in search of better climates for the growing of crops. They brought their genetics, culture and language with them. Islam was something that came later, and the Ottoman Empire an unfortunate glitch in the otherwise glorious march of Turkish progress. According to the *Outline*, not only was Turkish culture the greatest in the world, it was also the fountain from which all other cultures sprang. The *Outline* became the main history textbook for all schoolchildren aged between fifteen and eighteen.

Atatürk was also determined to reform the language to make it a tongue of pure Turkish, by purging it of its (many) foreign words. Turkish had previously been considered the rough street vernacular of the peasant, inferior to the poetic and often incomprehensible High Ottoman spoken by the elite. But Atatürk was dogged in his drive to 'bring out the genuine beauty of the Turkish language and to elevate it to the high rank it deserves among the world languages'. First, in 1928, he switched the alphabet from Arabic to Latin. Then he held drinking-table meetings to come up with new words to fill the numerous gaps in the now-stripped-back Turkish language, reportedly keeping a blackboard in his dining room so he could scribble down any 'Eureka' moments his guests might have over the entrées. Finally, in 1932, he launched the Turkish Language Society, tasked with sieving away the impurities and moulding what was left into the ideal language.

In a series of biannual summits attended by the world's most eminent linguists, the society hammered out a theory of Turkish language based on an obscure academic paper by Dr Hermann Kvergic, which Atatürk had stumbled across and then seized on. The Austrian Kvergic held that the origin of all languages was the primitive noises made by prehistoric man in response to patterns of nature, such as the sunrise. The bit that gripped Atatürk was Kvergic's note that these sounds formed the bedrock of the Turkish language – therefore handing it, in Atatürk's mind at least, grounds to claim itself as the wellspring. He melded this idea with the notions outlined in the *Outline* to claim that the Turks were a people who had travelled west, following the sun to their final home in Anatolia; this was named the 'Sun Language Theory'. And in conveniently circular fashion, the central claim that Turkish had evolved from the original language of prehistoric man meant that architects of the new Turkish could suck in foreign words when needed, since all foreign languages were ultimately descendants of the Sun Language anyway.

Archaeology followed history and linguistics. The Ottomans had opened their first archaeological collection in 1846 during an era of Western-inspired reforms, focusing heavily on the Hellenistic era of the ancient Greeks as proof of the empire's European links. The first projects of the republican era, though, looked for Turkey's deep past, something that could root the Turks firmly on the land inside their new borders. Focus shifted from the Hellenes to the Hittites, the Bronze Age people who populated much of what is now modern-day Turkey, Syria and Iraq around 1600 BC. That was well before the Seljuk Turks arrived in Anatolia from the east in the eleventh century; nevertheless, researchers were quick to spot evidence of Turkish influence. The Hittite language, which was slowly being decrypted, was claimed to be a precursor of modern Turkish. Scores of sun-shaped trinkets were found at one burial site, adding credence to the idea that the Hittites were the sun-worshipping forefathers of the Turks. Other renderings revealed swastika shapes woven into the designs

– more apparent evidence of the Hittites' Turkish roots, since the emblem had also been found on mosaics in central Asia. There were scores of digs on Hittite settlements around Ankara and through central Anatolia in the 1930s, and many of the Western archaeologists working on these sites were also keen to establish links between their finds and present-day Turkish culture. Eminent American archaeologist Erich Frederich Schmidt, of the Oriental Studies department of the University of Chicago, wrote in 1931:

> The fundamental features of Anatolian houses have not changed very much since these early, long-forgotten people built their houses at the Alishar site [in central Anatolia]. The present Anatolian houses, with their brick walls on stone foundations and their flat-topped roofs composed of beams, layers of branches and mud, may still illustrate the buildings of their predecessors some five thousand years ago.

Such was the pull of the legend that the Hittite sun was used as the emblem of Ankara from 1974 until 1995, when it was redesigned as a silhouette of a mosque with its lower parts fashioned into a star and crescent. Today, you can find it on the seal of the Turkish parliament and presidency.

Atatürk's obsession with finding a link between Turkish blood and Anatolian soil did not grow in a vacuum. The inter-war period was the age when empires were crumbling and nations encouraged to shape their own destinies. In his fourteen-point manifesto for world peace, drawn up in 1918 during the throes of the Great War's great hangover, US President Woodrow Wilson stated that nations should have the right to determine their own path. But the populations of the nations he explicitly named in his plan were all indigenous to the land they lived on. The Turks, on the other hand, had been scattered across a huge sweep of the world until the implosion of the Ottoman Empire at the end of the war drew them back to Anatolia. At the same time, millions of non-Turks who had lived in Anatolia for centuries had been slaughtered and expelled. No wonder Atatürk felt he had something to prove.

European Christendom, relieved that the Ottoman Empire was finished, had a vested interest in encouraging the success of Atatürk's Türkishness project. Sir Denison Ross, a distinguished linguist from London's School of Oriental Studies (later SOAS), talked with Atatürk about his theory for two hours at a 1936 linguistics conference, and came away saying that the Turkish president had held his own against all his academic attempts to tear holes in his ideas.

Behind the scenes, though, the thinkers were quickly losing faith in the Sun Language Theory – as, according to some versions of the history, was Atatürk himself. The introduction of the theory at the 1936 conference had been met with incredulity from many of the attending academics, despite Ross's generous recounting. Kvergic himself was surprised, when he visited Ankara, to learn of the ways his theory had been interpreted. By the time Atatürk died in 1938 the Sun Language Theory was almost completely discredited, and quietly died with him. But its legacy remains.

'What is remarkable is that a large proportion of these new words [created by Atatürk and his linguistics cadre], instead of being regarded as an abstract academic exercise, have been absorbed into the language,' recorded *The Times*'s correspondent in Ankara in 1961, twenty-three years after Atatürk's death. 'To such an extent has the language been changed that the speeches of Atatürk himself made in the 1920s are today almost incomprehensible to the modern generation.'

Today the science of genetics can offer fascinating insights into who the Turks actually are – and they are not the people depicted in the *Outline*. A 2011 study by two American geneticists found that the closest cousins of contemporary Turks are the Jordanians, and that they share more DNA with Britons than they do with central Asians. Another study by a Turkish researcher in 2006 found that central Asian genes make up only 22 per cent of twenty-first-century Turkish DNA.

Yet the idea of a Turkish bloodline, carried into the modern-day country from central Asia, has not died out: the most dogmatic of today's Turkish nationalists still believe they are part of a pure race that originated in the steppes of the east. I once sat with two Turks from the Black Sea town of Trabzon, a well-known nationalist hotbed. One was tall, blond and blue-eyed, and had TÜRK in the runic letters of the early Turkic languages tattooed across the back of his neck. The other had just come back from Syria, where he had lost the ends of all the fingers on his left hand in a mortar blast. Such was his belief in the integrity and superiority of the Turkish bloodline that he had volunteered to fight alongside a Syrian rebel militia made up of ethnic Turkmen, a minority who often speak Turkish as their first language. He was short and swarthy, and showed me reams of photos of himself in the war zone, channelling Rambo. In one, he was wearing camouflage, shades and a bandana, flashing the wolf hand-sign adopted by Turkish nationalists with one hand and brandishing a huge knife in the other. I caught glimpses of other photos of him petting kittens as he scrolled through his macho collection.

Over two hours and many strong teas in a smoky café next to the Bosphorus, the two told me their theories about the common genetics of all Turkic people stretching from western China to Aleppo, and how all should be united in a single state. I wondered whether they had ever stood together in front of a mirror . . .

Neither cared much about the broader Syrian conflict; both were horrified, in the classic way of the bigoted nationalist, at the number of refugees who had fled the war into Turkey, some three million by that time.

'Why are they all here and not fighting?' said the tall one.

'Fighting for whom?' I asked.

He didn't have an answer.

The war that the shorter man had gone to fight was one of Turkish honour, not Syrian revolution – although the Syrian Turkmen didn't see it the same way. He had returned from Syria not only minus his fingertips but also with his faith severely dented. The Turkmen were too religious, he said, and not quite Turkish enough for his taste.

They had a bad habit of scooping up food from communal dishes using flatbread in the Syrian fashion, and of lapsing into Arabic when they were talking between themselves. Still, he attributed that to their personal failure to stay faithful to their true Turkish roots rather than to the natural mixing and assimilation that the Turkmen had done over their ten centuries among Arabs.

But though the invaders from central Asia left little of their DNA in Anatolia, their impact on the culture – and language in particular – was colossal. Modern Turks share genetics with their neighbours to the west, but language with their neighbours to the east – an unusual phenomenon, since sets of genes and languages tend to stick together. Various forms of Turkic languages are found in Siberia, western China, the central Asian Stans and the Caucasus, while Azerbaijani is comprehensible (albeit comical) to Turks. Why the Turkic tongue caught on to such an extent in Anatolia even though the people who brought it did not spread their genetics is still not fully known. Maybe it is this lingering insecurity that has made language one of the most violent battlefields in modern Turkey.

## The forbidden language

Murat Akıncılar slaps a pile of books down on the table. They don't look much like revolutionary literature. Their covers are a blaze of primary colours: depictions of donkeys, lions and bears. The text inside is big and bold and, although I can't read Kurdish, it is clear that much of it is written in verse.

'We have collected all the children's stories, riddles, poems, songs and puzzles,' says Akıncılar, a linguistic researcher in the Turkish Kurds' de facto capital of Diyarbakır, as we flick through the glossy pages. 'Some are in Kurmanji [another of the Kurdish dialects spoken in eastern Turkey], some are in Zaza. We have spoken to eight hundred and fifty-four grandparents in fourteen provinces, thirty-two districts, two towns and seventy-six villages.'

It is the first collection of folklore in a language that has often had

to battle for its survival. Kurdish in its many forms is spoken across
a stretch of the Middle East that spans Turkey, Iraq, Iran and Syria,
as well as parts of Armenia and Azerbaijan. It shares its roots with
Persian, and has picked up influences from all the other languages it
lives alongside. In Turkey, it is the mother tongue of between fifteen
and twenty million people.

Yet for many years Kurds were discouraged or outright banned from
speaking their language. The first constitution of the independent and
internationally recognised Turkey, signed off in 1925, enshrined that
all Turks are equal before the law. It guaranteed freedom for any religion, sect, ritual or philosophic conviction – but it also gave strong
statements about who a Turk should be. 'The religion of the Turkish
State is Islam; the official language is Turkish,' it reads. Soon after,
we discover that while all citizens over the age of thirty can stand for
election to parliament, those who cannot read or write Turkish are
ineligible. The oath the president takes has him swearing 'to contend
with all my strength against every danger which may menace the
Turkish nation, to cherish and defend the glory and honour of Turkey'.

The sky-high illiteracy rates at the birth of the republic – estimated
by UNESCO to be almost 90 per cent in 1927 – offered an opportunity for the nation builders. Over the coming decades, the Turkish
state set up various compulsory literacy classes that taught the republic's citizens not only how to read and write, but also how to be good
Turks. There were also campaigns run by university students against
non-Turkish speakers (primarily non-Muslim minorities), and exhor-
tations from Atatürk himself.

'A person who says that he belongs to the Turkish nation, should,
primarily and absolutely, speak Turkish,' he said in one speech. 'If a
man who does not speak Turkish claims his loyalty to the Turkish
culture and community, it will not be correct to believe him.'

The Kurds, as the new republic's largest linguistic minority, found
themselves on the front line. That they were largely Sunni Muslims
also meant they couldn't swerve the Turkification project in the way
that non-Muslim minorities could. Meanwhile, the Sun Language

Theory proffered its own explanation for Kurdish, claiming that the Kurds were a Turkish tribe who had forgotten their native language because of their geographical isolation in the mountains and close proximity to Persian lands. When the Sun Language Theory was abandoned, its Kurdish aspects were replaced with even more preposterous ideas. In 1948, teacher Mehmet Şerif Fırat published *The Eastern Provinces and the History of Varto*, a cod history that repeated the claims that the Kurds were of Turkish origin. Thirteen years later, it received the seal of approval from the Ministry of Education, who republished it with a 'fake news' foreword stating that it was 'backed up with scientific evidence that cannot be refuted'.

Also in the 1940s, Fahrettin Kirzioğlu published *The Historical Turkish-ness of Kurds*, which claimed that the tribes of the east were simply 'mountain Turks'. It was a thesis that wafted in the winds of ultra-nationalism until 1980, when the army launched the third coup of the modern republic. In 1982, on the orders of the generals, it was adopted as state policy with a law that banned any language apart from Turkish. For the next nine years, Kurds could be arrested for even speaking their mother tongue or giving their child a name that included the letters X, W or Q (which exist in the Kurdish alphabet, but not in Turkish).

Over decades the Kurdish language went into retreat, particularly in the cities and among more educated circles. Part of this was down to the natural way that minority languages slip into the background as they become less useful for trade and as populations migrate and mingle. But as time went on, the crackdown also became more concerted. Little attention had been paid to clamping down on Kurdish in the first years of the republic. But by the post-coup 1980s, nationalist politicians and journalists worked up such a fury about Kurdish being included as a 'mother tongue' on the Turkish census that it was removed altogether.

It was in this atmosphere that Abdullah Öcalan, a leftist firebrand with only a perfunctory grasp of Kurdish himself, gathered a group of his comrades in a village hall close to the south-eastern town of

Lice. It was 1978, Öcalan was twenty-nine years old, and his life had already taken some radical twists. Born on the very edge of Turkey's Kurdish lands, he had initially planned to become a professional soldier. When his application to staff college was rejected, he instead became a minor bureaucrat and from there applied to university. He was offered a place at Ankara to study political science – but had already begun to delve into the world of militant leftist politics. In Istanbul, where he had worked as a clerk, he joined the Revolutionary Eastern Cultural Hearths, a Kurdish-slanted offshoot of a larger Marxist organisation. In 1972 he was jailed for seven months for handing out fliers for banned groups, and on his release became even more deeply entwined with his extra-curricular activities. His spell behind bars added an outlaw mystique to his natural charisma, and he began to build a personal following. After holding several small meetings in Ankara, he and his band of disciples decided to take their revolution to the south-east.

Öcalan soon proved to be a ruthless leader, as happy to slaughter his comrades as he was his rivals. Of the twenty-two people invited to the PKK's inaugural Lice meeting, seven were later killed on Öcalan's orders; a further five fled from the group after being accused of treachery, including Öcalan's own wife. The group made such swift work of launching their campaign of extortion and murder across the south-east that within a year Öcalan was being discussed in the parliament back in Ankara. In 1979 he fled into the open arms of Syria's Hafez al-Assad, a ruler who depended on the patronage of Soviet Russia and was quick to spot an opportunity to rile NATO member Turkey. From his comfortable new base in the Syrian capital Damascus, Öcalan exhorted tens of thousands of young Kurds back in Turkey to take up arms and die for his cause.

Over the next three decades an estimated forty thousand people, both Kurds and Turks, perished in the war between PKK and the state. The south-east, always the poorest part of Turkey, remained trapped in poverty, and tens of thousands of Kurds migrated to the cities of the west, where many became estranged from their culture

— ironic, since Öcalan's professed aim was to revive and champion Kurdish traditions. Scores of villages were destroyed in army operations, and the rural population poured into the cities. As hard as the PKK pushed, the Turkish state pushed back harder. It seemed as though south-eastern Turkey had sunk into a cycle of endless violence.

## Erdoğan's new era

I took my first trip to south-eastern Turkey in 2013. It was on a whim: I needed a break from Syria and was curious to see Turkey's Kurdish region. But as I was making my travel plans I realised that Newroz, the spring equinox celebrated by Kurds with huge pyres in the spirit of Bonfire Night (but with fewer safety precautions), was falling on the weekend I would be in Diyarbakır. Even better, the revelries would be the backdrop to the announcement of a new PKK ceasefire — the fruit of Erdoğan's years of hard bargaining with the group.

The parade ground on the edge of Diyarbakır is ringed by the kind of drab high-rises that make up much of the city's outer suburbs. They are not old and decrepit in the way that London's tower blocks are; instead, they are new and decrepit. Most were built in the last thirty years — it is shocking to see photos of Diyarbakır in the seventies, when its old core was all that existed, an intricate warren of alleyways surrounded by towering 3,000-year-old black basalt walls. Cheap paint peels from concrete in the onion rings of new suburbs surrounding the old city. Inhabitants still string up red peppers to dry in the sun on their tower block balconies, as they would in the gardens back in their villages.

Yet the crowd that poured into the parade ground on that hot Sunday afternoon was one of the most colourful I have ever seen. Almost everyone was decked out in red, green and yellow, the colours of the Kurdish flag, like tropical birds set loose in a concrete jungle. The women's dresses and headscarves were embellished with hundreds of sequins dazzling in the sunshine. High-pitched ululations, the tongue-wagging cry you usually hear at weddings, pierced the warm air. Young men linked hands to do the Kurds' traditional shoulder-shrugging, side-stepping dance. There were seas of flags emblazoned with the Kurdish sun – and, everywhere, images of Abdullah Öcalan.

Today, four decades after his murderous entrance into Kurdish politics and almost two decades since he was last seen in person, Öcalan has been deified almost to the extent of Atatürk. You can find his broad mustachioed face gazing down from banners across the Kurdish-inhabited regions of Turkey, Syria, Iraq and Iran alike. Unlike Atatürk, though, he only strikes two poses – one smiling, one not. In both, the eyes are dark and unreadable. Whenever I see a picture of Öcalan, I think of Big Brother. Invisible but omnipotent, Öcalan's physical absence only adds to his power.

Öcalan was arrested in 1999 after his long-term relationship with Hafez al-Assad broke down. For years Öcalan had trained his fighters in Palestinian camps, with logistical help from Assad. He also used Syria's Kurdish areas, abutting the Turkish border, as a place for his own fighters to regroup. It was inevitable that Turkey would eventually grow impatient with Assad's patronising of Öcalan and the PKK. In October 1998, Turkey moved its tanks to the border and threatened war with Syria should it refuse to give him up.

Assad immediately booted Öcalan out. For three months the PKK leader did a merry-go-round of countries he hoped might give him shelter but all of them, from Belarus to Italy, told him he wasn't welcome. Finally he hopped into Greece – another neighbour with a grudge against Turkey – and caught the ear of an official sympathetic to his cause. The Greek intelligence services hatched a plan to transfer Öcalan to South Africa, where he could claim asylum and remain out of Turkey's reach.

First, they took him to the Greek embassy in the Kenyan capital Nairobi, where they began preparing the next step of his escape. But there the plan went awry. The Kenyan authorities cottoned on to what was happening, and began questioning the Greek intelligence officers accompanying Öcalan. The Greeks, startled, ordered Öcalan to leave the embassy. He refused. After a brief diplomatic dust-up, the Kenyans offered Öcalan a plane to the country of his choosing. He was chauffeured to the airport in a Kenyan diplomatic car and led into a private jet – where he was handcuffed, blindfolded and gagged by Turkish agents who had been tipped off by the Kenyans. The US embassy in Nairobi had been bombed by Al-Qaeda just six months earlier. Kenya had no soft spot for foreign terrorists on the run.

Öcalan was taken back to Turkey and put on trial for treason on İmralı, an island fifty miles from the coast of Istanbul. In court he looked like a high school maths teacher behind bulletproof glass – greying and receding, with nerdish specs and an ill-fitting suit. Relatives of Turks who had died at the PKK's hands packed into the courtroom draped in Turkish flags and screamed abuse at him. Öcalan looked hangdog and withered – a different man to the warlord who had gloated at Ankara for twenty years.

In court, Turkey was expecting a tyrant's tirade. Instead, it got a rambling game of freedom bingo. Öcalan mentioned peace 78 times in his forty-page defence statement; democracy 144; democratic 269. He offered glowing praise of Britain, which he said had the 'best applied constitution in the world', though Britain doesn't actually have a constitution. He explained his own version of the history of Anatolia and Mesopotamia, in which the Turks from central Asia arrived in a region already heavily populated by Kurds. The Kurds, being more settled than the nomadic Turks, absorbed the newcomers, so that although the upper echelons of politics were controlled by Turks, society was Kurdish through and through. From the tenth century to the nineteenth, Turks and Kurds lived in harmony and brotherhood, only turning against one another as the Ottoman Empire began to decay.

Öcalan – cleverly – did not blame Atatürk for the misdeeds done in his name. The first president had imposed national unity because it was necessary to counter the divide-and-rule tactics of Turkey's enemies, Öcalan said, while Sheikh Said and the other leaders of the 1925 revolt were 'narrow-minded separatists'. Öcalan traced the republic's original sin against the Kurds back to İsmet İnönü – Atatürk's comrade, successor and fall guy. He claimed that İnönü, through his intellectual inferiority and weakness, had set the republic on the path to tyranny.

Öcalan's biggest shocker came on day one: he apologised, and offered to make peace. If found guilty he would face the noose, but said he could order his gunmen to lay down their weapons if his life were spared. He finally admitted to the charges that he had received training and weapons from Greece. The PKK continued its attacks as the trial went on and some of its supporters branded Öcalan a traitor. 'We feel betrayed, crushed. Öcalan no longer speaks for the Kurdish people. He has no role left for solving the Kurdish issue,' one told the *Economist*.

Regardless of his offer, Öcalan was found guilty of treason, separatism and murder and sentenced to death in June 1999. Twelve days into the new millennium, however, the Turkish government – a coalition led by secularist Bülent Ecevit – decided to give him a stay of execution. Öcalan, his ego revived, was grandiloquent in his response: 'If they execute me, the EU candidacy, the economy and peace will all go down,' he said. 'I am a synthesis of values, not just a person. I represent democracy.'

Ecevit was quick to outline the provisos: 'We have agreed that if the terrorist organisation and its supporters attempt to use this decision against the high interests of Turkey, the suspension will end and the execution process will immediately begin.'

The PKK, recognising the real threat to Öcalan's life, gave orders for its fighters to withdraw from Turkish territory. In a written statement its central committee said it was ready to negotiate with Ankara. It dropped the word 'Kurdistan' from names of its various political and armed wings, and said it would no longer be seeking Kurdish independence through armed struggle but would promote Kurdish rights through democratic forums. Not everyone was convinced: the Turkish press was cynical; the nationalists were still screaming for

Öcalan's execution and, inevitably, there was a split in the PKK. In the south-east, the conflict rumbled on.

When Erdoğan's AKP shot to power in 2002, one of its first goals was to take Turkey into the European Union – and for that to happen, things had to change in the south-east. But Erdoğan's enthusiasm to bring peace and new freedoms to the Kurds was not just lip service paid to give Turkey a leg-up into the EU: he and his party were genuinely different.

In August 2005, twenty-seven months into his prime ministership, Erdoğan went to Diyarbakır for the first time. He delivered his speech to a puny crowd, yet it was widely covered in the media and sparked cautious hope for millions. He pledged more democracy for the Kurds, more freedom to speak their language and practise their culture, and acknowledged that past Turkish governments had made severe errors. 'Denying mistakes that have been made in the past is not what strong states should do,' Erdoğan said. 'The Kurdish problem does not belong to a certain part of this society alone, but to all of it. It is also my problem.'

The old nationalist and secularist order were aghast. The opposition howled, with the loudest protests coming from Deniz Baykal, then head of Atatürk's CHP.

'Of all the leaders up to today, Erdoğan is the bravest,' Necdet İpekyüz, a Kurdish analyst with a political think tank in Diyarbakır, told me in September 2017. 'He said the same thing here as he did in Rize. All the others – Baykal, Çiller [former prime minister from a nationalist faction], Erbakan [former prime minister and leader of Refah, Erdoğan's original party] – they said one thing here and then something different in western Turkey.'

Erdoğan said the same thing everywhere – and acted on it. Seven months before his visit to Diyarbakır, the state had broken its silence on its treatment of Kurds for the first time. Lawyers brought a case against the Turkish security forces for the killing of a truck driver, Ahmet Kaymaz, and his twelve-year-old son, Uğur, in the south-eastern town of Kızıltepe in November 2004. The last time Uğur's mother saw Uğur alive, he was being pinned to the ground by Turkish policemen. He was later found with nine wounds to the back of his neck from bullets shot at point-blank range. The army said he had been killed during a firefight. The family's legal team disagreed. 'There is serious evidence suggesting that the murder of Ahmet Kaymaz and Uğur Kaymaz is an extrajudicial killing,' said Tahir Elçi, one of the lawyers.

These incidents were numerous and notorious. Everyone in Turkey's south-eastern regions was familiar with the sight of white pick-up trucks prowling the villages. Anyone pulled into one of those pick-ups disappeared into a black hole. In the same month as Kaymaz and his son died, a mass grave was discovered close to Diyarbakır. Eleven people who had been marched out of their village by soldiers in 1993, never to be seen again, were found shunted into this hole, their skeletons recognisable to their families because they were still dressed in the clothes they had been wearing the day they disappeared.

To report such things in Turkey had long been impossible. Much of the south-east region was off-limits for journalists. Those who did go there would struggle to find an editor willing to publish their stories. And the newspapers that did run the stories would almost certainly be closed down.

But now the leftist news title *BirGün* shattered the secrecy, publishing articles on the Kaymaz killings and the bodies found in the mass grave in early 2005. Erdoğan's government responded not by shutting down the newspaper, but by firing the deputy police chief of the province where the father and son had been killed and opening an investigation. In the same year, Turkish state television opened its first Kurdish-language television channel with the slogan: *We are under the same sky*.

Over the next thirteen years, the Turkish government, the intelligence services, Öcalan and PKK commanders began negotiating. The violence still ebbed and flowed in the south-east, the talks often staggered and suspicion lived on in both camps. Details of secret discussions between the Turkish government and the PKK in the Norwegian capital Oslo between 2008 and 2011 were leaked, most suspect by Gülenists working within the system and desperate to derail the peace process. The news caused uproar among Turkish nationalists, and Ankara temporarily called off the negotiations.

Meanwhile, prison turned out to be the best image boost Öcalan could have wished for. Frozen in time at the moment of his conviction and never seen again after he was led down to the cells in İmralı, where he has remained in solitary confinement, he managed to shape-shift from a squirming warlord trying to save his own skin into a kind of philosophical deity. Apart from the rebels who split from the mainstream PKK, the vast majority of his followers stuck with him. That his ensuing statements over the next decade came from a prison cell, to be read out by someone else, gave them a weight and clout that his long-winded and rambling defence statement did not. He was no longer a person of the real world, prone to gaffes, mistakes and rivals. He could insulate himself from whatever atrocities his terror group might carry out from then on. And he could claim to have joined the ranks of Mandela and Gandhi as a political prisoner of conscience.

It was this Öcalan 2.0 whose spirit, if not person, was there on the Diyarbakır parade ground in March 2013. A buzz whipped around the crowd as a speaker came on stage to read Öcalan's message, each sentence met with cheers:

Today we are waking up to a new Turkey, Middle East and future . . . We have come to a point where we say let the arms silence, and opinions and politics speak . . . I, myself, am declaring in the witnessing of millions of people that a new era is beginning, arms are silencing, politics are gaining momentum. It is time for our armed entities to withdraw from the Turkish border.

At the end, the huge Newroz bonfire was set alight, and the throngs began their whooping and dancing again. The aroma of a million knock-off cigarettes hung in the air, accompanying the woodsmoke. From the stage, where I had blagged my way into the press pen, the crowd looked like a field of whirling colours under a sky of azure blue. Back out in the midst of it I felt a mixture of two feelings I had never before put together: euphoria and pure terror. The ecstasy was clear on people's faces, but the mass was surging uncontrollably. Young men were pushing at the metal barriers around the stage, making them buckle almost to the ground. There were tiny children stuffed between the revellers – at one point I looked down to see the sweet face of a small girl smiling up at me from my feet, despite my nose being just an inch from the man in front. I was sure that, at any moment, something would set off a stampede. The organisers said a million people had come to hear the announcement. Everyone who was there – hundreds of thousands at least – seemed to be pushing to get to the front.

I fought my way out to where the pack was a little thinner and found a group of dancing young men. Given the elation that surrounded us and the grins that plastered their faces, I thought they would have been enthused about what had just happened. But amid the ululations and reedy music blasting at distorted levels from the boom boxes, they proffered a lukewarm response.

'He didn't say much, he was just trying to appease,' one said, pausing from his dance to light a cigarette.

His friend wiped drops of sweat from his hairline and chimed in. 'All he said is that the fighters should leave, nothing else. We have hope but we don't trust the Turkish government.' Then he smiled even broader, and broke into crystal-clear English. 'Welcome to Kurdistan!'

The ceasefire would last little more than two years.

# 8

## PEACE, INTERRUPTED

*October 2014*
*Kobanî, northern Syria*

It started going wrong at Kobanî, the small Syrian town that, for a month in the autumn of 2014, filled the world's television screens.

In September, Isis launched a huge offensive. At the time, the Islamic death cult was at the zenith of its power. In the space of three months it had stormed into Iraq, declared itself a caliphate, and massacred the Yazidis, an ancient polytheistic Kurdish sect living in the mountains near Mosul. Now it had set its sights on Kobanî, a Kurdish enclave in northern Syria. Isis had the town surrounded from every side except the north, where it abutted Turkey, and in the space of a couple of days, almost 200,000 terrified people streamed across the frontier. The fields were parched from the last fierce blasts of the summer sun, and it made an apocalyptic scene. Old women with tribal face tattoos stumbled across the scrub clutching jars of home-pickled olives they refused to leave behind for the hated enemy. Farmers tried to bring their livestock with them, and tough men cried as they realised they would not be allowed to take their animals across the border.

A small band of Kurdish fighters armed only with rockets and assault rifles stayed behind in the town to stave off the attack. They belonged to the *Yekîneyên Parastina Gel* (People's Defence Forces, or YPG) – a militia that, up to now, had played at the fringes of Syria's war. In this increasingly black conflict, where hope was fading fast and good guys were in short supply, the YPG looked like they could be the much-needed heroes. Their ideology was secular, leftists and ecologists and women fought alongside men in their ranks. They had already won the world's admiration a month earlier in Sinjar, where they saved tens of thousands of Yazidis by beating a path through Isis territory and opening a route to safety.

The YPG was a newish incarnation of a group that boasted a long relationship with Syria and the Assad family – the PKK. After the Newroz ceasefire announcement in March 2013, most of the PKK's veteran fighters had left Turkey. Some of them went to northern Iraq, where the group has a long-established stronghold in the remote Qandil mountains. Others hopped into Syria, across a border so artificial that in places it dissects towns, and so porous that people-smugglers could cut you a deal for a return journey for just $100. In Syria the PKK fighters joined the fledgling project started when Salih Muslim, a Kurdish politician from Qamishli who had been living in exile in northern Iraq, returned to Syria at the start of the uprising at the invitation of Bashar al-Assad.

Soon after Muslim and Assad met in Damascus in April 2011, Syrian government forces began withdrawing from the country's Kurdish-majority region, a large sweep of strategic territory, rich in oil and at the waypoint between Aleppo and Mosul. That allowed Assad to focus his military manpower on the fight against the rebels in other areas, safe in the knowledge that the country's two million Kurds were being kept in line by a friendly militia. There was also a second purpose to Assad's renewed warmth for the PKK – in the tried and tested way, it provided the perfect tool to needle Turkey, which had quickly thrown support to Syria's armed opposition.

I first encountered the YPG in November 2013, eight months

after Turkey's Newroz ceasefire, when I travelled to the Kurdish-populated north-eastern region of Syria. At that time the Kurds were battling against Isis but mostly against the mainstream Syrian rebels, and their leaders ardently denied their back-room deal with Assad even though it was clear to see. In Qamishli, Syria's main Kurdish town, regime soldiers manned checkpoints at the central roundabout and the nearby closed border crossing with Turkey, happily coexisting with the YPG troops manning checkpoints half a mile down the road. While the YPG's political wing controlled the state institutions in Kurdish areas, all the salaries of the workers were still paid by the Syrian government.

The YPG quickly built an image as the protector of Kurds amid Syria's Darwinian anarchy – much as the PKK had done for thirty years in Turkey. In many respects it was true. But, like the PKK, the YPG could be ruthless with rivals. One Syrian Kurdish doctor who had fled to Istanbul told me in intricate detail about the day in 2012 when YPG fighters dumped the corpses of a father and son who had opposed them outside the entrance to her hospital.

The YPG fighters I met on the front line near the town of Ras al-Ain, close to the Turkish border, were almost all veterans of the war in the mountains of Turkey. They spoke a brand of leftist Kurdish that even my translator, a native of Qamishli, had trouble deciphering. Sometimes they spoke Turkish among themselves and one, having spent time in Europe, was also fluent in French. All were well prac-tised in reciting the ideas of Öcalan.

'There is no difference between our fight before and our fight now in terms of ideology,' said Berwalat, a 29-year-old with sun-leathered skin and a strip of white lace woven through her long, plaited hair. It was her only nod to femininity; otherwise, she was dressed in an outfit that could as easily have been worn by a man. The rollneck of her red jumper sat up high against her chin, and her black leather jacket and khaki trousers were loose and shapeless. She told me she had joined the PKK when she was just twelve years old, and had dedicated her whole life to the cause. She recommended that women join the militia young, as she had, because it was better for them to carry a gun than to live as a slave in domesticity. She had not seen her own mother since 2005, she said. When I asked her if she would ever marry and have children, she creased double with laughter: the PKK bans sexual relations between its members. Men and women are not even allowed to give gifts to each other, lest it spark romantic feelings.

Now, in this new war and new phase in the PKK's history, Berwalat had a new enemy – the Syrian rebels, whom she referred to in blanket terms as Al-Qaeda. But neither had her old enemy gone away. 'The ideology of Al-Qaeda is stronger, and Turkey has the better technology,' she said in her soft, almost melodic voice, at odds with the battered old Kalashnikov laid out on the rug in front of her. 'But ultimately we can defeat them both.'

That still sounded ridiculous by the time Kobanî erupted less than a year later. The YPG's ranks were filled with hardened guerrillas, but they had no heavy weaponry. I found it difficult to take them seriously; they parroted the kind of leftist political theories that had gone out of fashion decades before most of them were born, and many had joined up when they were still children with malleable minds. But this bunch of slightly outlandish idealists was about to score a huge PR success, which would bring them US military backing and position them, for a time, as the war's biggest winners.

I was in Silopi, the last town in Turkey before the Iraqi border, as the battle for Kobanî geared up. It is a Wild West frontier of Kurdish smuggling and PKK fanaticism, each feeding off the other; a remote, deadbeat place, deep in territory that has long been neglected by the Turkish state. Silopi's potholed main street is lined with kebab houses and cheap motels catering to truckers on their way to the Habur border crossing, six miles down the road. The local men who hang out in the tea houses look as though they have little else to do.

I had witnessed the PKK's publicity machine in action here before; when Isis attacked the Yazidis in Iraq in August 2014, some of the first to flee managed to make their way over the border into Turkey and to a tiny hamlet next to Silopi called Nerwon. I scrambled down from Istanbul to cover the story and reached the camp as the first refugees were flooding in. The camp, on a sun-beaten patch of land and framed by a sweeping vista of the mountains over in northern Iraq, was disorganised and under-equipped – a huddle of half-finished dwellings and agricultural outhouses where the new arrivals squatted without water or electricity. It was August, and in the 45-degree heat even sitting in the shade was unbearable.

Everyone in Silopi knew where the Yazidis were staying, and they rallied to help their Kurdish brothers, bringing piles of blankets and huge vats of food in the backs of pick-up trucks, along with crates of bottled water taken straight from the deep freezer. Within a day, a bright banner hung at Nerwon's entrance: the flag of the PKK, emblazoned with the face of Abdullah Öcalan.

In the immediate absence of Turkish officials and international aid organisations in this far-flung corner of the country, the *Barış ve Demokrasi Partisi* (Peace and Democracy Party, or BDP – then the PKK's political wing and the local ruling party in Silopi) took charge. Officials picked the Yazidis up from Habur and brought them to the camp, arranged for the sick to be taken to doctors and roused the local people to donate carloads of food and clothing.

A BDP volunteer met me at the gate on the second day I went to the camp. 'Please write the truth about what is happening here,' he said before letting me in to speak to the Yazidis. 'Write that it is us, not the Turkish government, who is helping these people.'

Inside I met Dawd and Sivan, Yazidi friends in their early twenties who had graduated from Mosul University. One thing separated them: Dawd had a passport and had crossed into Turkey legally. Sivan didn't. He and his family had paid a human trafficker thousands of dollars to guide them over the heavily landmined illegal crossing route.

'We cannot stay in Iraq any more,' explained Sivan as we walked to the building where his family was staying. 'We can't live amongst Muslims after this.'

His aunt, Fatima, was a warm and kind-eyed woman who could not stop thinking about her pet birds. She had left them behind in her village as it was overrun by Isis fighters. 'I dreamt about them last night,' she said, smiling broadly. 'I could hear the noises they made.' Then she started sobbing, and one of Sivan's brothers fumbled to find her a tissue.

Over the following days Nerwon swelled. As more fleeing Yazidis crossed the border, rumours started circulating around the camp. 'We've heard the Turkish government are going to move us,' Dawd said one morning. 'They're going to take us to one of their official camps, and we don't want to go.'

The new camp being prepared by the Turkish government was in Midyat, a Christian town several hours' drive north-west of Silopi. Dawd had heard they would have to stay there twenty-four hours a day, and that their mobile phones – their only link with their friends and relatives still stuck inside Iraq – would be taken from them. These rumours blossomed every time the Turkish government opened camps for Kurdish refugees – and always they were unfounded.

Dawd and Sivan started planning, considering what their options could be. 'Maybe we should leave and go to Ankara,' Dawd said. 'We speak English, we're educated, we can find a job.' The initial appeal of their plan wore off when they remembered the reality of their situation: they had no work permits, no official leave to remain in Turkey and, in Sivan's case, no passport.

It wasn't hard to see why the Yazidis didn't want to leave Nerwon: the camp had quickly become a community. For over a week they had slept alongside each other, and eaten, cried and laughed together. The children had forged new friendships. In a tent that had been turned into a play area, I watched volunteers lead them in traditional Kurdish folk songs, praying for rain on the parched land. At the end of playtime the children ran to the doorway to find their shoes. As they did, they broke into a chant: 'Apo! Apo! Apo!'

Sivan smiled and shook his head. 'Yazidis had nothing to do with the PKK before this,' he said. 'Now so many of us love them.'

Now the streets of Silopi were alight: Kurds were again under attack in Kobanî, and this time they believed that Erdoğan was to blame. The riots were spectacular; it seemed as if the whole town, including women and small children, were coming out each night to build and burn barricades and lob Molotov cocktails at the cops. This was the night I realised why all the armoured police cars in the south-east are pitted with scars: it is where rocks and flaming bottles have bounced off them.

That kind of violence is exciting to cover, until it isn't. Invariably, it reaches a tipping point at which the rioters become completely invested in causing as much destruction as possible and the police get sick of people throwing burning stuff at them and decide to finish it by any means, as quickly as possible. Then, it becomes a zero-sum game in which you do not want to get trapped if you're not armed with something, because sure as hell the people who are armed will be aiming something at you. Each night, I tried to sense when we might be approaching the tipping point, and retreated back to my hotel.

Unfortunately, although the ambitiously named Grand was at the other end of town, Silopi was so small that the tear gas floated down to it eventually and seeped into my room. I had been waiting to cross the border into Iraq to follow a story there. But, as it became clear that Kobanî was going to become a huge news event, my editor dispatched me to go and cover it instead.

The next morning I hopped on one of the old intercity buses that criss-cross the length and breadth of Turkey, rickety carriages reeking of sweat, the drivers' stale cigarette smoke and the cheap sachet coffee the tea boy serves up every couple of hours. I have taken these buses so many times in Turkey's borderlands, starting when I first came as a hard-pressed freelancer with little money, and continuing even when my finances revived because I'd developed a grudging

kind of affection for them. They are uncomfortable and the attend-
ants have a bad habit of moving you from seat to seat like a
tiddlywink at every stop when you're a lone female traveller, because
it is unthinkable to have you sitting next to a man. Also, they can
be held up for half an hour or more at police roadblocks, as all the
passengers' documents and bags are checked. But I had never felt
unsafe on the border buses until this trip. Now, with Kobanî
exploding, something felt different as I travelled across south-eastern
Turkey; there was itchy static in the air.

Diyarbakır, where I stopped for the night to meet up with a translator
before travelling on to Kobanî, was no longer the friendly, laid-back
place where I had sat for long dinners with friends and listened to
Öcalan's words about peace. Nightly funerals were being held for
locals who had skipped across the border into Kobanî to join the
YPG in the fight against Isis. Each day, bigger crowds were coming
onto the streets to protest against what was happening to their Syrian
Kurdish brethren, to be met with the inevitable water cannon and
tear gas from the Turkish police.

'It was the way Isis cuts off heads; when he saw this he felt he had
to go and help the YPG,' said Mehmet Çelik of his son, Sertip, who
was being lowered into the ground of Diyarbakır cemetery swaddled
in white sheets. Mehmet's sorrow at his son's untimely death, at the
age of just twenty-seven, was drowned out by his indignation over
the injustice of it all. 'In Sertip's last phone call he said he was in
the centre of Kobanî and that all the villages around the town had
been taken by Isis. The biggest gun they had was a Dushka [a vehicle-
mounted machine gun], and they were being attacked with tanks.'

Kobanî, eighty miles south of Diyarbakır, was brimming with
stark desperation. The world's press had gathered on the Turkish side
of the frontier to await the town's inevitable fall to Isis. Even then,
it felt uncomfortable to pay so much attention to one battle when
Syria had been soaking in blood for three years. Some Syrians believe
Kobanî got so much coverage because it is a Kurdish town, and that

Kurds make more sympathetic victims than Arabs for Western audiences. That was certainly part of it but, above that, Kobanî was a battle made for television. From our viewpoint safe in Turkey the town was laid out like a diorama, spread over a hillside on the other side of the border fence. We could see where each mortar round hit. We could see Isis's positions outside the town, too, and watch their steady progress to the outer suburbs. We saw with our eyes as they raised their black flag over the hospital on the eastern edge of Kobanî. Later, as the Americans sent F-16s to strike the Isis positions and turn the battle's fortunes towards the Kurds, the huge thump of their bombs rolled right through the ground we were sitting on, sending the birds scattering from the trees.

It was hard not to join in with the local Kurds' cheers. Thousands had gathered with us, some watching with tears rolling down their faces and others determined to join in. Kobanî had been cleaved from Suruç, its Siamese twin town on the Turkish side of the border, by the European mapmakers who partitioned the Middle East after the First World War. The frontier between Turkey and Syria follows the old railway line between Baghdad and Berlin, slicing east–west through the heart of Kurdish lands with little heed for human history. The border means little to the families and communities who straddle it, and most think nothing of crossing back and forth on the illegal smuggling routes through the flat fields. Now, with Kobanî in flames, the Kurds living on the Turkish side were determined to cross over to help their kin. Young men and boys, some so childlike they could be mistaken for girls, made dashes for the border in full sight of the Turkish army and riot police, who had lined up to stop them crossing. Every few minutes there was a surge, with up to a hundred pulsing forward at once. Most didn't make it and were pushed back by the police, but each time a few more managed to cross, to the cheers and applause of those left behind. It was a strange thing to watch young men sprinting towards almost certain death.

'They are so brave,' said Aymann, my friend from Aleppo. He had come with me to the border because he knew how it felt to be besieged, and wanted to show his solidarity.

Persistent rumours held that Erdoğan was arming Isis in a bid to wipe out the Kurds in Syria. As the violent protests spread across Turkey, they took on an even fiercer anti-Erdoğan tone. Every Kurd I spoke to would eventually come onto the subject of how the Turkish president was puppet-master of their tragedy.

'This is a project of Turkey's!' said Mehmet Çelik in Diyarbakır, of the battle that had taken his son. It didn't matter to him that the Turkish authorities had brought his son's body back across the border and handed it to him to bury, nor that they were sending ambulances into Kobanî to bring out wounded YPG fighters and treat them in Turkish hospitals. The fact that Ankara was providing for the 200,000 Kobanî refugees who had flooded suddenly across its frontier with a brand new, high-quality refugee camp did not even register.

'For thirty years there has been this war between Turkey and the Kurds,' Mehmet continued. 'I myself was in prison for ten years, and my brother died while he was in jail.'

On the night of 7 October 2014, three weeks into the battle for Kobanî, Turkey's own tinderbox exploded. This time, as Kurds across the country came out to protest they were met by gangs of Turkish nationalists and Islamists. Thirty-one people were killed over three nights in pitched street battles fought with shotguns and swords. Öcalan had warned that an Isis victory in Kobanî would spell the end of the PKK peace process in Turkey, spurring many of his supporters onto the streets. Now, after fanning the flames, he dampened them down. In a statement from his prison cell he begged for calm, and Turkey's Kurds retreated. He had pushed the country to the brink, and then pulled it back.

The damage to Turkey's image had been done. Erdoğan, forced to walk a tightrope between his country's two most bitterly opposed camps, had made no public statements about all the things Turkey was doing to help the people of Kobanî. Instead, he pandered to his country's nationalists, at one point appearing to gloat about the imminent fall of the town. Officials insist that whatever Erdoğan said about Kobanî was taken out of context, and then spun by a shadowy pro-PKK perception machine to make it appear as if he were waging war on the Kurds by supporting Isis.

The truth about Turkey and Isis is complex. During my time living on the Syrian border in Antakya in the spring and summer of 2013 I witnessed scores of jihadists travelling openly through Turkey and into Syria. For more than a year the border was a revolving door. Refugees, journalists and aid workers also traversed freely and the Turkish government was praised for opening its border to Syrians fleeing the war, but criticised for allowing jihadists to cross it. Later, when it sealed the frontier with a huge concrete wall and instructed its border guards to shoot at anyone trying to cross it, it was criticised for trapping refugees inside Syria but praised for stopping the flow of jihadists. For the policy makers in Ankara the two went hand in hand, with no middle way and no win–win.

Throughout 2013 the cheap hotels in the border towns were full of silent, scowling men, with large beards and often dressed in Afghan style. We started to joke that passengers on the flights from Istanbul to the Syrian border could be clearly divided into two groups: journalists and jihadis. One Syrian who had set himself up as a 'jihadi chauffeur' would collect foreign jihadists at Istanbul's Atatürk airport, accompany them on the 24-hour bus journey down to the Syrian border, and then hand them over to the smugglers. They charged $50 to escort their clients through one of the long-established illicit routes used for decades to move guns, cigarettes and drugs, and so open they barely felt illegal – the smugglers unashamedly touted for business in the bus stations of the border towns. The intelligence services turned a blind eye to the extremists traversing the frontier for long enough that Isis mushroomed in northern Syria – and the Syrian chauffeur felt certain enough that he would not be arrested in Turkey that he allowed me to use his name and photograph in my article.

Turkey was openly supporting the broader opposition, including some deeply unsavoury elements of it. One café in Antakya, a place by the river with huge open windows bringing in the fresh air, was constantly packed with rebel commanders who spoke candidly to journalists about their meetings with Turkish officials in Ankara. Meanwhile the Syrian National Coalition (SNC), the opposition's government-in-exile, was operating from a five-star hotel in a chic-but-bleak district of highways and glass towers close to Atatürk airport. Funded by Qatar, the SNC had begun as a half-hearted stab at an inclusive political opposition and quickly became little more than the mouthpiece of the Syrian Muslim Brotherhood. Every so often, the SNC would call a press conference to remind journalists that Syria's revolution was a glorious and vigorous one fighting for democracy and the rights of all Syrians. But it grew further and further detached from the reality of what was happening inside the country until, one day in August 2013, it put out a press release about a battle I had just come back from covering. Menagh military air base was Assad's last redoubt in the countryside north of Aleppo, and the FSA had kept it under siege for ten months, as the government soldiers inside held out through air resupplies. There seemed no way for the rebels to break the deadlock, until Jaish al-Muhajireen, a brigade of foreign extremists led by Chechen rebel veteran Omar al-Shishani, came in to finish the job.

I had ducked into an abandoned farmhouse just outside the perimeter of the airfield, where one of the lonely few FSA groups taking part in the final battle in August 2013 had based themselves. Even though they were on the same side as Jaish al-Muhajireen, they were overwhelmed, outgunned, and in every way outpowered by the hardliners. The fighters I interviewed were freaked out that I was there; had one of al-Shishani's men stuck his head in, he would have been unimpressed to find a British female journalist. After an hour I made a swift and low-profile exit, and a few days later, as the final battle got underway one early morning, my fixer Mahmoud went back to the front line dressed in Afghan-style shalwar kameez. He managed to blend in for long enough to bring back footage confirming that this was a victory for the jihadists, not for the FSA. Nonetheless, back up in Istanbul the SNC lauded it as a dazzling victory for the mainstream rebels in the press release they sent out to all correspondents.

Nuance didn't feature in the good-versus-evil fairy tale of Kobanî. The YPG won in the end, and forged a firm friendship with the US that grew into formal joint operations in Syria that still continue today. The West had already lost heart in the Syrian revolution, and while the rebels turned radical and became further ridden by the infighting that had plagued them from the start, the Kurds seemed the best hope of a unified ground ally against Isis.

Despite the YPG's links to the PKK, Ankara had initially been willing to deal with the group. The stumbling block, according to Turkish foreign ministry officials working on the file, was the Kurds' reluctance to break their mutually advantageous détente with Assad.

'During the initial years of the Syrian civil war the AKP governments were in close contact and conducted negotiations with the Syrian Kurds and their leader, Salih Muslim,' says Haluk Özdalga. 'The main purpose was to convince them to join the opposition forces fighting to topple the Assad regime. Several times they flew Muslim back and forth to Turkey with government jets. However, the Syrian Kurds refused Ankara's proposals. Had they accepted, we would have been seeing an AKP willingly cooperating with the Syrian Kurds.'

Western diplomats working on the Turkey and Syria file say that whatever tensions were already brewing between Washington and Ankara before Kobanî, it was the Pentagon's ever-tightening relationship with the YPG after it that caused the greatest damage.

'We kept telling [Erdoğan] that the support [to the YPG] was temporary, tactical and transactional,' said one US diplomat working on the file. 'The Turks were complaining loudly, especially after the PKK ceasefire broke down in the summer of 2015. We were making calming calls with the PYD [the YPG's political wing]. They got it. But for Turkey this is existential.'

Erdoğan had also been bruised by another recent development on his doorstep; in Iraq, Kurdish fighters had taken over cities abandoned by the federal army in the summer of 2014 as Isis blitzkrieged across the country. The Kurds' new acquisitions included Kirkuk, an ethnically divided town sat on top of one of the biggest oil fields in the world. Among Kirkuk's minorities is a large population of ethnic Turkmen, who have strong ties to Ankara.

The Iraqi-Kurdish president, Masoud Barzani, was one of Erdoğan's strongest allies and closest personal friends in the region. Turkey had supported Barzani's project for semi-autonomy for the Kurds in northern Iraq since its inception in 1991. The Kurdistan Regional Government (KRG) shares a stretch of border with Turkey, and trade deals between the two have brought Turkish fashion brands into the malls of northern Iraq, and Kurdish oil to the port of Ceyhan, on Turkey's Mediterranean coast, through a pipeline that opened in 2014. But when Barzani's Kurdish army, known as the *Peshmerga*, seized Kirkuk in June 2014 and Barzani announced that he would hold an independence referendum, Erdoğan felt he had been stabbed in the back. Kirkuk's Turkmen fervently opposed the Kurds' grab for their city. Neither did Erdoğan much fancy the idea of a fully independent Kurdistan on his doorstep.

'His best buddy in the world, the one place where he had real influence and a guy he was a brother to,' says one diplomat. 'I cannot tell you the impact that this had on Erdoğan. When I saw him in September 2015, he went through the motions when he talked about the US sending weapons to the YPG. But when he got to what Barzani did he was shaking with anger. It had been a very lucrative and beneficial project for both sides. The only thing that Barzani could have done to screw that thing up, was exactly what he did. Barzani insulted the Turks and also the Arabs by including Kirkuk and its oil fields in the new independent Kurdistan. Erdoğan felt betrayed, and started to think that even the most cuddly "pro-you" Kurds can go for independence and you have to be careful about them.'

## Erdoğan's descent

Internationally, Kobanî was the moment Turkey's – and particularly Erdoğan's – reputation began to nosedive. Meanwhile, it triggered a chain of domestic events that upended the delicately balanced peace process. First, in June 2015, a bomb exploded at a Kurdish rally in Diyarbakır. Second, there was a suicide bombing in Suruç, the Turkish town directly across the border from Kobanî, in the cultural centre where I had sat for so many hours during the battle, interviewing refugees and local Kurdish politicians. Thirty-two leftist activists who had travelled from Istanbul to take part in a reconstruction project in Kobanî were killed, and a horrific video capturing the moment the explosion ripped through them circulated on social media. I recognised the garden, the gate. After the blast they were blackened, smeared with blood and strewn with limbs. Two days later, two Turkish policemen were shot dead in their homes in the nearby city of Şanlıurfa, in an attack that initially appeared to have been claimed by the PKK as 'revenge' for the Suruç bombing (the charges against the alleged perpetrators were quietly dismissed in court later, and no other suspects have yet been found). The 2013 peace process broke down, and almost immediately the war in south-eastern Turkey revved up again. One of the first victims was Tahir Elçi, the lawyer who had brought the Kaymaz cases against the Turkish government in 2005. Now serving as the head of Diyarbakır's bar association, he was shot dead in broad daylight in the city in November 2015, as he gave a press statement appealing for calm.

'If he was still alive, he would be so angry now,' Elçi's widow, Türkan, told me, less than two months after his death. Beautiful, dignified and still moved to tears when she spoke about him, she was horrified at the fresh violence now exploding in the city he loved. 'He was working for peace. Now I see no one doing that impartially, as he did.'

The descent of Erdoğan's image from peacemaker to warmonger happened so quickly that even he appeared shocked by it. Doubtless there are many Kurds – particularly those in the diaspora who trumpet the PKK but do not have to live with its endless insurgency – who have always had it in for him. They would feel the same about any Turkish leader, although an Islamist makes for an exceptionally good pantomime villain. But there were two moments when Erdoğan accelerated his own downfall.

The Gezi Park protests, and Erdoğan's rough handling of them, was the first, a mere two months after Öcalan announced the ceasefire at Newroz. Kurds played a major part in the Gezi demonstrations, even taking advantage of their newfound freedoms to wave banners bearing Öcalan's image and the red star logo of the PKK in Istanbul's Taksim Square – something that would have been unthinkable a few months before. The Gezi movement was a soup of unlikely alliances. Football hooligans stood with environmentalists, and staunch Kemalists stood with Kurds. It was the kind of broad consensus that Erdoğan himself had managed to craft in his early years. No wonder he got the jitters.

'Gezi was important in showing clearly how such spontaneous demonstrations, even though [they were] held within the democratic and legal frame, completely misfit into Erdoğan's agenda. Therefore, he reacted tough,' says Haluk Özdalga. 'One could discern he had a sense of urgency as he occasionally spoke about having to hurry up, that he didn't have much time. That a leader feels like that after having been in power for a decade may look puzzling, but for him the time to enact his true agenda had actually only just begun after waiting for so many years.'

Other senior AKP figures openly opposed the harsh crackdown on Gezi, among them Abdullah Gül, then president, who counselled a softer approach, and Kadir Topbaş, the mayor of Istanbul. Erdoğan ignored them all. Some have attributed that change in his once-open mentality to his physical health problems – Erdoğan discreetly endured treatment for early stage colon cancer at around the same time.

Ertuğrul Günay, culture minister at the time of the protests and an opponent of the redevelopment plans that sparked the unrest, put it more bluntly. 'Erdoğan saw the Gezi protests as the rehearsal of a possible insurgency against him,' he says.

The June 2015 parliamentary elections, in which the AKP lost its majority for the first time, was the second key moment. The success of the Kurdish-rooted *Halkların Demokratik Partisi*, the People's Democratic Party (HDP), which was partly down to the support that it leached from the AKP, clearly infuriated Erdoğan. There was no outright winner, and between June and the rerun of the elections in November that year the peace process broke down. Erdoğan began building an alliance with the hard-right (and staunchly anti-peace process) Nationalist Movement Party (MHP) – and the seeds of mistrust between him and the Kurds grew into unnavigable forests of hatred. Erdoğan, who had once spoken of peace in Diyarbakır, began adopting a stridently nationalist tone in his rhetoric about the PKK in order to keep his MHP allies onside.

'We want to speak again about peace but how can we continue? The government says it is fighting terrorism and has explained the new rules,' Kurdish leader Selahattin Demirtaş told me in the south-eastern city of Mardin in February 2016, as the fighting raged in Cizre ninety miles down the road. It was the day that the military curfew was meant to expire, but the violence continued in the town. Demirtaş spoke of the people trapped in the basements, claiming that the ambulances were attacked by the security forces every time they tried to reach them.

Nine months later, Demirtaş was arrested on charges of promoting the PKK. The first leader of a major party to openly oppose Erdoğan's plans to switch from a parliamentary to an executive presidential system, he believed that that was a major reason why he and his party, the HDP, were targeted. He remains in prison to this day.

'We were still hopeful for Turkish democracy, and because of this the AKP attacks us,' he had told me in Mardin. 'They are scared.'

## The dead

It is September 2016, a year since the war re-erupted. I count the graves in the Diyarbakır cemetery.

A whole section is decked out in red, yellow and green trinkets, the flowers fresh and the soil on top of the plots newly turned. There are thirty, forty, fifty . . . I stop as a group of gypsy girls approaches me. The oldest is sixteen, maximum. Her two little sisters are a lot younger, all of them dressed in age-flattening outfits of long, flowing skirts and loose headscarves. They sell water to mourners and keep the graves here tended for pennies.

'I want to be a guerrilla when I'm older!' says the smallest.

Her big sister rounds on her.

'Shut up!' she snaps. 'All these people died for nothing. It's stupid.'

I weave in and out among the grey marble, noting down the dates on the graves and the details that adorn them. Some are wrapped in the scarves their occupants died in. One has no headstone or marker, just a few wilting flowers on top. One of the dead was named Latife, like Atatürk's wife. Few were born before the turn of the millennium and most were fifteen and sixteen years old when they died.

'It started filling up after Kobanî,' says Farkin Amed, who has come to visit his son's grave. He tells me that, just a month ago, his younger son also 'left for the mountains' – the bucolic euphemism the Kurds use for joining the PKK, even though their wars are now mostly fought in the grimy squalor of the poorest city districts. His daughter has tried to go, too, but the PKK sent her back; she is only fourteen. He seems unbothered by the thought that she will likely try again and succeed within a year.

'At least my son died in honour, not in shame!' he says.

Farkin is forty-six but looks older – a malignant mix of sun, stress and sorrow has beaten the youth out of his face. His son, Mehmet, died in June 2012, one of six young Kurds who set themselves alight in the western city of Bursa to protest at the lack of progress towards a peace deal. Farkin clings to the belief that it was their self-immolation that finally pushed the parties to a cease-fire nine months later, in March 2013. But now it is September 2016, the peace process has been dead for a year, and his son's sacrifice has been in vain.

'I come three times a week,' says Farkin. 'First I water the graves of the new martyrs, then I come to my son. In some months recently there have been only three or four days with no funerals, especially during the curfew in Cizre.'

Two low-flying Turkish fighter jets scream over us. A police car prowls around the perimeter road. A burial is taking place on the other side of the cemetery, where the people who have died natural deaths are laid to rest. Two young men sit silently at a nearby grave draped in the flag of the BDP, the political party that had rallied for the Yazidis in Silopi two years earlier.

'I didn't put it there,' says Murat, the brother of the dead boy, eighteen-year-old Süleyman Güzel, who was killed in clashes in Diyarbakır earlier this year. Not even his family had known he was going out every night to build burning barricades with a scarf wrapped round his face and a gun in his back pocket.

'I don't know, he was a boy who never shared anything. He was like a closed box,' says Murat.

Süleyman had been a normal high school student until Kobanî, his brother says. Some of his friends went to fight in the town, and those who didn't joined the protests in Diyarbakır. The violence simmered down but their anger did not. After the PKK called off the ceasefire, they started blocking off their neighbourhoods and clashing nightly with the cops. Even when the tanks rolled in and the Kurdish youth fired back with rockets and assault rifles, Murat was reluctant to call it a civil war. The real fighters had gone to Kobanî, he said. The ones who died in Diyarbakır were just kids.

But a policeman I had met in the city while the fighting was at its heaviest told a different story. Diyarbakır in the worst days of its war, over the winter of 2015–16, looked like it had been hit by the apocalypse. The centre, the old neighbourhood of Sur, was under complete military curfew and a heavy snow had dumped on the city. Around the battle zone a network of metal police barricades weaved in and around the old city walls. There were sandbagged sniper positions and tent structures with chimneys for wood-burning stoves where the police drank tea and smoked. Baroque plumes of cigarette and wood smoke twirled together as they rose into the frigid night air.

The hotel where I always stay in Diyarbakır was now on the front line – to get to it I had to pass through the police checkpoints with a paper the receptionist had written out and rubber-stamped for me. Each night, as dusk fell, the soundtrack started, the staccato rhythm of each Diyarbakır night for the last eighty days banged out by the crackle of gunfire and the thump of explosions. I spent New Year's Eve in the city that year, locked into the hotel together with a few other journalists by the fighting and the heavy snowfall. We were the only guests, and we got blasted drunk and made a game out of deciphering the gunfire from the celebratory fireworks. As we stood swaying in the doorway and smoking cigarettes at three in the morning, a line of Turkish tanks filed past us down the silent street.

The PKK's youth militants had been pushed back to a small circle in the centre of Sur, but left webs of mines and improvised bombs behind. Ambulances screamed in and out of the curfew zone. Enes, the policeman, was tall, bearded and imposing, with a scar running through his left eyebrow. Most of his face was hidden by his balaclava, but as we started chatting he took it off to show a mop of boyish hair.

Enes was manning the last checkpoint before death alley – and he was bored. The special forces cops, with their camouflage uniforms and German-made weapons, were fighting the battle inside Sur. He, though, was a normal policeman with the misfortune to have been posted to Diyarbakır as the peace process broke down. He was a sitting target for the young PKK radicals who saw any cops as fair game. All he could think of was what he would do in five months' time, when he was due to be posted back to western Turkey.

I asked Enes whether he enjoyed his job. He laughed, and said he had joined up when he dropped out of university, pursuing an English literature degree, little guessing that he would end up on the front line of a civil war. His marriage to a policewoman had broken down. Here, he had fallen in love with a Kurdish girl, but neither her family nor his would accept the relationship.

'No one enjoys being a policeman in Turkey!' he said. 'But here it is worse. In any other area, when I finish my shift I am a normal person. Here, I'm always looking behind me.'

He had a very different view of the militants to Murat in the cemetery, who insisted his brother was just a kid playing at protest. There were about forty PKK fighters left inside Sur, Enes said, and the police were waiting for them to surrender. But the ones who remained there were the hardest of the hard core – the crack-shot snipers and expert bomb-makers. The young guys throwing Molotov cocktails had been weeded out long ago. The ones who were left were professionals, armed with rocket-propelled grenades, sniper rifles and land mines.

Eventually, inevitably, Turkey won in Diyarbakır. It took months and almost none of the militants came out alive. The whole area was left in ruins. Again and again, I saw the same thing repeated. Each time it was announced that a curfew had been lifted I raced to the town to report before too much of the clear-up began. It became so predictable that I struggled to find fresh ways to write about it for the newspaper, but each time I entered a newly devastated town, the wide eyes of the children and the sight of the elderly wandering around expanses of flattened masonry stunned me. Yet at the same time as this war was sweeping through the region, destroying almost everything it touched and displacing hundreds of thousands of people, Europe was handing billions of euros to Turkey in a sweetener to stop refugees flowing from its shores on the other side of the country.

A cloak of secrecy hangs over what really happened in south-eastern Turkey after the ceasefire broke down: who the militants were, who armed them, and how many civilians were caught in the crossfire. Time and again I managed to reach people who might give me an insight, like a doctor who was charged with carrying out the autopsies on the bodies brought out of Cizre. He told me that all were charred beyond recognition, and seemed willing to give a full interview – and then abruptly changed his mind and stopped answering my calls.

It was not only the Turkish government who tried to hide and fudge what was happening. So did the PKK leadership, who insisted that the youth militants were not under orders from them. By the time the ceasefire broke down the main Kurdish party was Selahattin Demirtaş's HDP, which had stormed to electoral success in June 2015 by appealing to liberal Turks as much as to Kurds. But it too was picked apart by the conflict. Demirtaş refused to criticise the violence while other members of his party openly praised the PKK militants. Some even went to the funerals of PKK suicide bombers who had slaughtered dozens of civilians in Ankara – and were promptly charged with terror offences. Even then, they were unrepentant.

'As the parliamentarian for this city, I have the responsibility to participate in most funerals,' Mehmet Ali Aslan, the deputy for the Kurdish town of Batman and one of those charged, told me. 'However the children died, we have a responsibility to their mothers.'

I pushed him on whether he would do the same if the bombers had carried out their act of terror for Al-Qaeda or Isis, rather than for the PKK. After dodging the question for more than ten minutes, he eventually conceded that he wouldn't.

The HDP released daily lists of the dead in the south-eastern towns, insisting that all were civilians. They were not.

Back in Silopi, one of the first towns to fall under curfew as the new whirlwind of violence hit, I tried to untangle the case of Necati Öden, an eighteen-year-old whose bloodied body appeared on Twitter with a soldier's boot in the background.

'That is how we found out he was dead,' said Öden's sister, Aysel, when I met her in January 2016, days after the military operations had finished. Bloated cow carcasses were still strewn around their neighbourhood; the underground water pipes exploded by roadside bombs. Families were returning to find that the militants had used their homes for shelter, and that the police had shot them – in situ – in their struggle to dislodge them.

Nine days after Necati's photo appeared online, his family were permitted to collect his body from the government mortuary and bury him in a small and hurried ceremony in his home town. The Turkish government said he had died as he fought alongside the PKK. His family, meanwhile, insist that he was not a militant, but was summarily killed by security forces as part of a campaign of collective punishment against the young men of Silopi.

'They had covered his whole body up to his face and would not let us open the sheet to see what happened to him,' said Aysel. 'They're not only killing the militants – they're killing the young men like my brother, too.'

The photo of Necati's body was thought to have been taken and first posted by a policeman who then deleted his account; after that, it was shared thousands of times. It became a rallying call for both sides – those who rejoiced that a dangerous terrorist had died, and those who claimed him as an innocent Kurdish civilian killed by the Turkish state.

The 36-day crackdown in Silopi, the first major operation of the war, left a fog of fear over the town. The PKK's graffiti still covered the walls in the neighbourhoods at the centre of the fighting, yet only one person I spoke to – a businessman who refused to give his name – would admit to knowing anything about the militants.

'Every single person in Silopi knows someone who is with the PKK or the youth,' he said. 'The people who fought here are sons of this town.'

This is the life Necati Öden appeared to have been leading. By day he worked on the minibuses ferrying foot passengers back and forth across the Habur border crossing with Iraq, six miles down the road from Silopi. As his family spoke about him they held out photos of a smiling young man wearing the fashionable clothes and haircut of any normal teenager.

I have taken those cross-border minibuses countless times as I have travelled in and out of Iraq. During Turkey's ceasefire years, as the PKK switched its attentions to other parts of the region, you could be sure that your driver would blast out pro-PKK music on his stereo. (One particular favourite in those times was a thumping tune with a chorus that endlessly repeated *biji biji YPG* – 'long live the YPG'. Its video shows the militia's gunmen on the front line and participating in huge North Korean-style military parades.) Meanwhile, Necati's Facebook page was a shrine to Kurdish militancy. A picture of a Kurdish fighter with the flag of the Syrian YPG was emblazoned across the top, and he described himself as a YPG sniper. Does that mean he was a member, or even had any contacts with the PKK? Not necessarily – it could have easily been teenage bravado. But Silopi is a place where smuggling, poverty and PKK militancy come together in a poisonous tangle. Those same minibuses are used to bring contraband cigarettes and tea, and probably much else, from Iraq into Turkey, the drivers stuffing their loot into custom-made spaces around their vehicles at the same time as they are carrying passengers. Other smuggling routes running through the mountains that cradle the Habur crossing are used for weapons and drugs. In both cases, the PKK takes huge cuts from the profits. For young men growing up in such places, life at all levels is intertwined with the PKK – it's not a black-and-white case of being in the militia or out.

After five months of escalating violence the police announced a total curfew in Silopi on 14 December 2015. The Öden family's neighbourhood, which had been laced with IEDs and explosive-filled trenches by the PKK's local youth militants, was at the deadly heart of the ensuing battle. 'Not even a cat could move outside without being shot at,' Aysel said.

Necati remained there as the rest of his family fled to a safer area – they were hazy about the reasons why, insisting that he had wanted to stay in the house because he wanted to protect it. Seventeen days later he was dead. His family say he was hunkering down in the house, and trying to find a way to leave the area. The Turkish government was unequivocal in its response.

'He was a PKK member,' said the government official whom I contacted about the case. Generally he was a chatty guy willing to talk through the nuances of any situation. Not this time: 'There is no further comment to make.'

Victory in Diyarbakır, Silopi, Cizre and the other towns of the southeast has not brought any rest for the Turks; still, the PKK fights on in the countryside, killing Turkish soldiers and policemen almost daily. It has also brought its terror campaign to western Turkey with a series of car bombings that have killed scores of people in Istanbul and Ankara. Meanwhile, the YPG has grown into a powerhouse in Syria, where it is no longer an outlying militia but the world's best hope against Isis. Kobanî, always more of a fairy tale than a news story, has already been twisted into a great myth. Those of us who were there saw that the YPG was on the verge of miserable defeat at Isis's hands until America steamed in with its game-changing airstrikes. Now, to hear the revisionists and propagandists speak of it, you would think the Kurds had managed to grab huge territories in Syria with Kalashnikovs and guts alone, rather than with the backing of the world's mightiest military.

Turkey's Kurds don't have such victories to brag of – only a new chapter to add to their litany of grievance and revenge. It will make for another festering wound when future PKK leaders want to radicalise a new generation. No one believes another peace process could begin any time soon.

On a bright Saturday afternoon in September 2017, I wander through Diyarbakır with my friend Xezal, a small, wide-smiling Kurdish woman with the gentle soul of an artist. The city is recovering. Thick crowds of shoppers throng the pavements and the kebab sellers are frying their delicacies on portable griddles. In the windows of the jewellery shops, the bright gold bangles and necklaces that Kurdish brides deck themselves out in for their wedding day dazzle behind the glass.

Xezal and I have spent three days shuttling between artists, activists and politicians in the city, building a story of how Erdoğan won and then lost the love of Turkey's Kurds. The heart of Diyarbakır has been decimated and the fledgling civil society that was beginning to blossom under the peace process has been crushed. Yet everyone, from an illiterate grandmother standing in the ruins of her home in Sur to a lawyer in his leather-trimmed office, tells us they had once hoped the pious man from Rize might be different.

'When the AKP came to power in 2002 most people were uneasy about their approach. But they said they were different and gave signs of change,' says Gule Ulusoy, an actor from Diyarbakır. 'There were Kurds, secularists, nationalists among them. We thought it could be a coalition. But now we realise that it was all a project of Erdoğan. He was just building power. At the start he was close to the Kurds. Now he has changed to being a nationalist. It is all for the benefit of him.'

Diyarbakır's municipality, a citadel of Demirtaş's HDP, has suffered great waves of closures and sackings since the breakdown of the peace process. In the wake of the coup attempt the crackdown has accelerated. The HDP mayor has been arrested and replaced with a government appointee. Kurdish and Armenian signs put up before 2015 have been removed. Xezal's husband, a teacher, has already lost his job. She works for the council's culture department and she fears that she could be next. We have spent the afternoon with Gule Ulusoy and a group of other actors who used to work for Diyarbakır's municipal theatre, once the hub of the city's colourful arts scene. Thirty-three of them were sacked at a stroke on New Year's Eve 2016 by the trustee appointed by the government to run things.

The trustee had claimed that the actors did not have the diplomas required to be working in a public sector job. The actors say they have been punished for putting on plays in the Kurdish language to sold-out audiences three times a week. It was only in the Erdoğan era that the ban on Kurdish had been lifted. Now, still under Erdoğan, it seems to be crashing down again, even if the government would never formally re-impose it.

Determined to continue, the sacked actors have rented a space in the basement of a decrepit shopping centre next to the main council building. The chain stores and more upmarket boutiques have long abandoned this place; all that are left are the bargain stores selling cheap plastic tat. It looks an unlikely place for high culture. But the actors have lucked out here – this basement space was once a theatre and the stage and seating are still intact. Their ticket sales just cover the rent.

'In legal terms the Kurdish language is not banned. But there are still people who claim it is an "unknown language",' says actor Ruknettin Gün. 'This is what happens when Islamist governments come to power – the first thing they do is to close down all the culture.'

An art gallery and a cultural centre in Diyarbakır have also been shuttered, as has the city theatre in nearby Batman. For a short while, a television network dedicated solely to broadcasting children's cartoons dubbed into Kurdish was taken off the air. The Diyarbakır Film Festival has been cancelled, and the archives of the Mesopotamian Cultural Centre destroyed. An independent cinema in Batman was closed by government decree, and then gutted in an unexplained fire. Several Kurdish-language institutes have been closed.

Meanwhile, a statue commemorating twelve-year-old Uğur Kaymaz and his father Ahmet has been removed from the spot where it had stood in Kızıltepe since 2009. Even the Kurds' ultra-Islamic party, HUDA-PAR, who once supported Erdoğan in almost everything he did, now accuse him of reverting to the old mindset of the Turkish nationalists.

'The AKP's position on the Kurdish issue has become like that of the Kemalists,' says HUDA-PAR's president, Şeymus Tanrıkulu. 'To say that they are totally Kemalist would not be true, but they support the Kemalist system. There are two columns to it: firstly Turkish nationalism, and secondly secularism. In our history many ethnic groups have been rejected by that system. Now, we see that the AKP's policy and approach has not changed anything. They said that the Kurdish language would be formalised in the constitution but nothing was done. Recently, they have started to move far away from these topics. They are using the language of the nationalists.'

Xezal and I walk across Diyarbakır's open plaza, where Sheikh Said's rebels were hanged by the Turkish state in 1925 and where the first Kobanî protests kicked off eighty-nine years later, towards the old walls that mark the perimeter of the city's latest tragedy. A black-and-white rendering of Atatürk peers out over the crowd of early evening shoppers from the top of one of the wall's watchtowers. I ask Xezal how today's Kurds feel about the founder of the republic.

She bursts out in a peal of laughter. 'I think we have started to like him more,' she says. 'Compared to Erdoğan, he was perfect.'

# 9

# THE COUP

*14 July 2016*
*One day before the coup*

People had been warning that it was coming — though rarely openly, and not in so many words.

'This is coup shit,' friends told me as we spoke about the tumult that was spreading across Turkey like cancer throughout 2015 and the first half of 2016 — the refugee crisis, the breakdown of the PKK peace process, and then the terror attacks. First there was the dustbin bomb in Diyarbakır in June 2015, then a month later the suicide bomber in Suruç. In October 2015 came the deadliest terror attack in the history of the Turkish republic — 109 people blown apart by two suicide bombers in the heart of Ankara during a peace rally. Then the carnage reached Istanbul. One bomber blew himself up next to a group of German tourists outside the Blue Mosque in January 2016, and another two months later next to an Israeli group on İstiklal, the grand boulevard running through the heart of the city. In June two men blasted their way into Atatürk airport with assault rifles and then detonated their explosive packs. All in, the terror attacks left more than two hundred dead in the space of thirteen months: to people whose lives are ruled by opaque forces, these things are never unlinked. Each of Turkey's previous coups had been preceded by similar chaos.

Two people were bold enough to say what everyone was thinking: Mehmet and Ahmet Altan, renowned journalists and brothers. When they appeared on the panel of a chat show on the evening of 14 July 2016, they spoke about the likelihood of the army again intervening in Turkish politics, as it had so many times before.

'Whatever the developments were that lead to military coups in Turkey, by making the same decisions, Erdoğan is paving the same path,' Ahmet Altan said.

'It is not certain when it will take its hand out of the bag and how it will take its hand out of the bag,' Mehmet added.

A day later they were proved right. But this time the coup would be different. The generals would come out the losers and by the end of Turkey's darkest night, Erdoğan's power would be galvanised further. And the Altan brothers, instead of being lauded for their foresight and plain speaking, would find themselves accused of sending subliminal messages to rally the coup-makers. They were both sentenced to life imprisonment. Though their convictions have since been overturned, Ahmet Altan remains behind bars.

## 15 July 2016
### The schizophrenic coup

The coup attempt of 15 July 2016 lasted a little over twelve hours and played out in real time on social media and live television. There could have been no better backdrop for the tanks and bullets than the bridge over the Bosphorus, nor a more obliging set of protagonists than the Turks who rushed out to defend Erdoğan against the soldiers. As the newspapers went to press on Friday night it seemed that the coup was succeeding: the generals had taken over state television and Erdoğan's whereabouts were unknown. But by the time the first editions were on the newsstands the next morning, the soldiers had been kicked back to their barracks and Erdoğan was

addressing crowds of his cheering supporters outside Istanbul's
Atatürk airport.

In the hours in between, the two sides of Turkey collided in a
sweaty tangle of rumours, gunfire and fear, as a putsch from a different
era met the resistance of 2016. Istanbul shops sold out of bottled
water and cigarettes while F-16 fighter jets broke the sound barrier
above them, shattering windows in apartment blocks and setting the
street dogs howling. The mosques sounded an eerie funeral prayer in
the witching hour as soldiers kicked in the doors of television news
studios and pulled the presenters off-air. While the devout rushed
into the streets wielding wooden planks and murmuring prayers, the
bohemians who had been drinking in Istanbul's hipster bars retreated
back into their homes. It was a coup planned via WhatsApp but
announced in a message on state television:

> Valuable citizens of the Republic of Turkey . . . The President and the
> government with heedlessness, heresy and betrayal are undermining funda-
> mental rights and freedoms based on the separation of powers. The
> indivisible unity of the nation and the state will eliminate the dangers
> faced by our Republic and ensure its survival.

By the time it was read out by a stunned blonde newsreader with a
gun just off-camera levelled at her head, almost everyone had already
switched to social media to find out what was really happening.

The real news was that, slowly, the balance was tipping away from
the coup plotters. General Ümit Güler, the commander of the First
Army, appeared live on the pro-Erdoğan channel A Haber and
announced that the coup was merely a revolt from a small group
within the ranks. The façade of a fait accompli started cracking. More
generals joined Güler, declaring their loyalty to Erdoğan and swearing
that the coup would be crushed. Then Erdoğan himself appeared,
quashing the rumours that he had fled by private jet to Germany.
Unlit, without make-up and appearing against a pale blue curtain
reminiscent of a photobooth backdrop, the president spoke to his

nation via Facetime, live from an undisclosed location. He looked old and terrified.

The studio cameras zoomed in on Erdoğan's image on the phone screen, held in the manicured hand of a CNN Türk news anchor, and every channel still operating independently switched to the live feed. Having spent a good part of his presidency railing against social media and bringing court cases against those who used it to ridicule him, Erdoğan was now using it to save his own skin. His aides had spent a frantic hour trying to set up a traditional television link before turning to the twenty-first-century option, a press man later told me.

'I urge the Turkish people to convene at public squares and airports. There is no power higher than the power of the people,' Erdoğan said. 'Let them do what they will at public squares and airports. The chain of command has been violated. This is a step by the lower ranks against their superiors.'

It was in that moment that Turkey's cities turned into war zones, when the rattle of gunfire began echoing through the streets and the enraged masses steamed into battle. They poured into Taksim Square, onto the Bosphorus bridge, and crowded to the airports and government buildings. The coup plotters, unnerved, ordered their men to fire on the people. In Ankara, they attacked the intelligence headquarters with helicopters and bombed the parliament with F-16 jets. But on the streets, the soldiers who had parked their tanks only six hours earlier, full of assurances from their seniors that they would be taking charge of the country, now began to lose faith. They started to surrender as dawn broke, spilling out and shedding their guns on the tarmac before they threw their hands in the air. Victorious and furious, swinging belts and fists, the civilians set about the men in uniform. The soldiers looked no older than teenagers, frightened young boys wondering what on earth had gone wrong.

## The aftermath

The death toll mounted through the morning hours, as bodies were cleared from the streets. The politicians held an emergency session in the bombed parliament. In Istanbul, Erdoğan addressed the crowds outside Atatürk airport.

'They have pointed the people's guns against the people,' he said. 'The president, whom fifty-two percent of the people brought to power, is in charge. This government, brought to power by the people, is in charge. They won't succeed as long as we stand against them by risking everything. I have a message for Pennsylvania: You have engaged in enough treason against this nation. If you dare, come back to your country.'

The coup was over, and the battle for its narrative began. Journalists questioned the scale of the arrests and the speed with which blame was pinned on Fethullah Gülen. Other vital information emerged – that the Turkish intelligence services had received a tip-off about the imminent revolt as early as 2.45 p.m. on 15 July, a full seven hours before the first tanks rolled onto the Bosphorus bridge. Why had they not taken action to stop it, and what happened in those hours? If the government was so sure the officers behind the revolt were Gülenists, how had they been able to stay in their positions until now?

Turkey requested the imam's extradition from the US less than twenty-four hours after the coup attempt began, even as the last rebellious soldiers were making their final stand in Ankara's Genelkurmay.

The European Union and the US issued statements urging Erdoğan to be restrained in retribution. Three days on from the coup, 7,500 people had been arrested and more than 9,000 dismissed from their public sector jobs. Four days on, the total number of people sacked or sitting in a prison cell had hit 50,000.

On the streets the crowds called for hangings. In Taksim they held aloft nooses and signs: İdam istiyoruz! (We want the death penalty!).

Erdoğan played their soundbite back to them as he spoke from stages across the city. 'I don't look at what Hans and George say. I look at what Ahmet, Mehmet, Hasan, Hüseyin, Ayşe, Fatma and Hatice say!' he told the delirious hordes.

'This stuff about the death penalty is rhetoric, I think,' one Western diplomat in Istanbul told me as the fervour grew. 'But we are watching Erdoğan closely. There is a danger he may become unhinged.'

## The winners

I mingle with the throng in Taksim one humid evening as the sun is setting. Erdoğan has told people to stay on the streets to guard against unknown and fugitive coup plotters coming back for a second strike. I spot the flags of Libya, Palestine, Saudi Arabia and the three-starred banner of the Syrian rebels, all mingled with the fluttering, ubiquitous Turkish star and crescents. There are other placards too: *Amrika* 0 – *Millet* 1 (America 0 – The nation – 1), reads one. Anger at Gülen, whom everybody now accepts organised the coup, has flash-morphed into anger at the US, whom everybody accepts is sheltering him.

Some of the men here are flashing the hand gesture of the ultra-nationalists – thumb clamped up to the outstretched ring and middle fingers and index and little finger extended skywards to make the shape of a wolf's head. Others let off huge coloured flares, and I fear a spark may catch the cheap synthetics of the flags and set the whole lot ablaze. There are chants of *Allahu Akhbar, Tebkir, Bismillah* – the war cries of the Islamists. I have heard them in protests across the Middle East, but never before in Turkey. All the fare gates are open on Istanbul's public transport system so that the masses from the suburbs can travel in to mix with the elites from the inner districts – there are women in burkas next to teenage girls with bare shoulders. Three years ago this square was the scene of the Gezi Park sit-ins, when leftists and Kurds and football hooligans came together in the first mass show of opposition to Erdoğan. Now, it is the gathering place of his faithful.

The local council has set up a stage here, flanked by two screens and speakers. They blast the usual rota of Ottoman marching music and AKP anthems, but then a video starts rolling onscreen – a glossy CGI-enhanced short film. The chanting dies down as the crowd in Taksim watches. In the film, a grey and faceless assailant is cutting the chain on a flagpole, sending the Turkish flag plummeting towards the ground. Across the country Turks watch in horror as it casts a shadow over buildings, fields and sea. Then they start running – students, housewives, Kurdish farmers and fishermen – as Erdoğan's sonorous voiceover reads the words of the national anthem. They throw themselves into the Bosphorus and start swimming, ants moving together as the camera takes in a swooping bird's-eye from above. Finally all converge on the flagpole and make a human pyramid around it – bodies in a pile, each climbing on top of the other to reach higher. The young man at the top grabs the loose end of the chain and pauses for a second before he leaps off the tower of people, sacrificing himself for the nation. The flag is raised again, and the crowd goes wild around me. Then the screen fades to an image of Erdoğan, smiling and with his hand on his heart.

The film, *Millet Eğilmez, Türkiye Yenilmez* (*The Nation Does Not Bend, Turkey Is Invincible*), was made by Erol Olçok's agency, Arter, for the AKP's local election campaign in March 2014. Back then, it was banned on the grounds that a Turkish flag cannot be used in a political party's advertisement.

The grey frontage of the Atatürk Cultural Centre, a modernist monolith that borders the north side of the square, looms up behind this ecstatic congregation in Taksim. The centre was built in the 1970s as an opera house and arts space, but within the space of only two decades its brutal lines already looked tired. Decommissioned in 2008, it was used as a base by the riot police during the Gezi protests. Until now, a picture of Atatürk has adorned the building's frontage, flanked by two Turkish flags, but this banner has now been removed, to be replaced with a portrait of Erdoğan. When news of the switch flashes across social media it causes uproar, so much so that a few days later Atatürk is rehung. But Erdoğan stays up alongside him.

Four days after the coup, İbrahim Kalın, Erdoğan's spokesman and one of his most trusted aides, invites a group of foreign journalists to the Ottoman-era Yıldız Palace for a press briefing. It feels like weeks since I last saw my friends. Dominique, a correspondent with the Associated Press, is eight and a half months pregnant and went on maternity leave three hours before the coup attempt started. With the solid good humour I got to know when we worked together in Iraq amid Isis's takeover and the 45-degree temperatures, she is now back at work and praying she won't go into labour. Everyone else just looks exhausted.

Kalın has brought us here to give us the blow-by-blow account of Erdoğan's escape from the coup-makers, and his quick recovery to overthrow the revolt. It's a gripping tale that will make the pages of all our newspapers tomorrow:

'Three helicopters were sent to Marmaris . . . a group of elite forces sent to kill the president and his family. Their orders were to bring him to Ankara, dead or alive. He left thirty minutes before they landed. Seven people were left at the hotel for security reasons; one was killed and another injured in the shootout. They were going room to room trying to find Erdoğan. When we found out about the attempt we mobilised our forces and agencies. The president made the calls on what should be done. When he saw the tanks and planes in Ankara he became aware of what was happening, and immediately decided to go to Istanbul. Once he landed safely at Atatürk airport, he coordinated everything from there.'

We scribble our notes as Kalın continues in his measured, perfect East Coast accent. This most loyal member of Erdoğan's inner circle wrote his Ph.D. at Georgetown University. Unlike his boss, he bears the polished finish of a Western intellectual. But he is still an Erdoğan man.

'It is important to remember what happened, to grasp it fully,' he tells us. 'You need to get the narrative right. We have seen some appear to be disappointed that the coup did not succeed. We have received strong international support, condemning the coup unequivocally. That is the way it should be. But when people start talking about how the law should be upheld, it sounds as if the coup didn't happen!'

By now, Western leaders are looking on with concern. Federica Mogherini, the EU's foreign policy chief, has reminded Erdoğan that Turkey is a signatory to the European Convention on Human Rights, which bans the death penalty. A group of European foreign ministers and US Secretary of State John Kelly express public alarm at the talk of executions.

There are also rumours that a state of emergency is about to be imposed. When one of our group asks Kalın if these are true, the otherwise placid intellectual explodes.

'This is like speaking to the US about the failure of its foreign policy the day after 9/11!' Kalın booms. 'We expelled this coup in the name of democracy. We got on the streets and shed our blood. You should all get your facts right!'

Three days later, parliament passes the state of emergency. It will last for three months, and allows the government to rule by decree. Those rulings can include shutting down businesses and other organisations, and sacking people from public sector jobs. Passports can be cancelled. Those arrested can be held for up to thirty days without charge, and in some cases detainees do not have the right to speak privately to their lawyer in case, for example, 'crypto messages' are passed back and forth. Those detained can have a ten-minute telephone conversation every fifteen days; their relatives must make an application if they want to visit them. The government has the right to impose curfews and ban rallies, and to censor any publication or broadcast it deems a threat to national security.

## One week on

The ground at Silivri is parched to bone white. At plastic tables around the scrappy strip of cheap cafés outside the prison gates, men and women sit pale and silent. Most hold their heads in their hands. All wear the drab, modest clothes of the rural poor.

I linger around the back of the stalls so that the gendarmerie officers milling about the entrance won't catch sight of me. They are nervous at first, these Turks who found themselves cast out of their own society in the space of one terrible evening, but they do begin to talk.

'He started his military service on Thursday and on Friday there was the coup,' says a woman from Diyarbakır. When she found out that her son had been arrested she got into her father's battered old car and drove the 850 miles west to Silivri, this fortress on the edge of Istanbul.

'He called me the next day,' she continues. 'He said an officer had sent his unit to the TRT headquarters, and then to Taksim Square. The next night he called again, and we've had two more calls from him since. The last call was from his lawyer's phone – he was in the court – and he asked for 10,000 liras [for his work]. I sent my son to defend the country. If he hadn't gone, they would have called him a traitor. But he went and he's still a traitor. I have to lie to my other family members about where I am, what has happened.'

In the car park behind the cafés, Şükriye and Şükrü Esoğlu stretch out on the sleeping mats they have pulled from their car boot. They too have driven here from Turkey's periphery: from Kilis, the town near the Syrian border that has taken in a great number of Syrian war refugees. Şükrü Esoğlu is a farm labourer on a day rate of 30 lira. They have no money for a hotel. They have heard nothing from their son, twenty-year-old Kadir.

'He had been in the military one month,' says Şükriye, who still has traces of henna on her hands from the party they threw for Kadir before he left for his compulsory military service. The rich can buy their way out of it – the sons of Erdoğan have never served. But for poor boys like Kadir, it is non-negotiable. His family spent 700 lira to rent a local band for his leaving party, and all his friends and relatives collected money for him, to help supplement his wages. Still, he had run short – after around twenty days in Istanbul he had called home to ask for some more. His parents could only spare 50 lira – around £12 – but they sent it to him anyway.

'Before he started his service he took a test to go in at a level above private, but he failed,' says Şükriye. 'But he wanted to be in the army – he wanted to serve in the east, to defend Turkey against the terrorists. I wanted him to serve in the west because it's safer. I was the one who thought Istanbul would be OK. He didn't know that he could be among terrorists – no, no, no, no! He was so happy to be serving his country. It is impossible that he could have been involved.'

The Esoğlus watched the opening acts of the coup on the television, thinking it was a security alert. Then they went to bed, only to be woken again by the *sala* prayer blasting from the mosques. They assumed it was an attack by Isis, over the border from Syria just a couple of miles down the road. Then they caught a few words about a coup, and ran to the streets to join their neighbours. They stayed out as the fear turned to anger and defiance, and then finally to jubilation as they realised the revolt had failed. It was only three days later that they got a call from their son's unit, telling them that he was in custody. Then the duty lawyer called to say that Kadir could be in prison for a long while.

This is the first time they have ever been to Istanbul. 'The lawyer said our boy was cheated, that he was told it was a military exercise,' says Şükriye. 'I have had a breakdown. I am using sedatives. I thought it would just be two or three days and then he would be out. But now my fear is getting bigger.'

In the gleaming hallways of the Çağlayan Justice Palace, Nazlı Tanburacı Altaç shuffles her papers and speaks in a low murmur, looking out for anyone who might be unhappy to see her talking to the press. Blonde, preened, in her twenties and sharply dressed, her world would never have collided with that of Şükrü and Şükriye Esoğlu had it not been for 15 July. As a young duty lawyer in this Istanbul courthouse – opened in 2011 and the biggest in Europe – it is her job to take on the cases that the more senior, better-paid advocates don't want to. But for these clients, she feels an extra sense of commitment.

'I've been here for forty-eight hours – everyone's busy,' Nazlı says. 'We asked to see the prosecutor and talk with him about the trial but he didn't respond because of his extreme workload.'

The courts are trying to process the ten and a half thousand now arrested and formally charged. But at the same time, the justice system itself is being purged. It was one of the strongholds of the Gülenists, the government says; so, one week on from the coup attempt, two thousand prosecutors and judges are among the tens of thousands already sacked from the bureaucracy.

Those who remain are working overtime. And a narrative is emerging from the jumble of testimonies given by the accused.

'Four of my clients are military school students,' Nazlı says. 'They're carefully chosen students who passed difficult physical and mental tests for higher level education. On the night of the coup they were in a camp in Yalova, a city close to Istanbul, and were taken to the bridge by their commanders at about eleven p.m.

'The prosecutor asked them: "Didn't you ask where were you going?" They said that they were told it was a drill, a military exercise. They did not know a thing about the coup. They had no electronic devices so no idea what was happening. They were wearing their full equipment and their guns – but that's normal on an exercise. They saw the new bridge' – the third over the Bosphorus, completed but not yet opened on the night of the coup – 'and they were surprised. Then they saw Ataşehir' – a high-rise district close to the centre of the Asian side of Istanbul – 'and one of them asked where they were going. The commander told them to calm down.

'They were taken to the bridge by a bus. Suddenly, at the bridge, the driver was shot and the bus crashed to a stop. After that they found themselves in the middle of the crossfire. One of them died in the bus – he was shot in the eye and died. My client told me: "It's the first time I saw a dead body. His blood went under my tongue."

'There were people throwing stones at them and shaking the bus. They realised there was something very wrong. After a little while, the crowd made a human corridor for them to take them to the side of the road. They rushed to emergency lane. They say they weren't assaulted or beaten, the crowd saved their lives. They were freed after their pleas. But prosecutors objected and now they're arrested again.

'Their families are having really hard times. Some of them can't hear anything about their sons for days. There are some families who haven't heard their voices for a week. Some of them call and ask me: "Could he be dead?"'

In the chaotic days and weeks immediately after the coup, some of Nazlı's clients are released, only to be promptly arrested again. Others disappear into the prisons and no one is able to reach them.

On the outside, the blood lust leaks into the graveyards. The bodies of the 105 putschist soldiers killed during the revolt are to be buried in a 'traitors' cemetery', a patch of ground on the edge of Istanbul that was being reserved for a new stray dog shelter. Major Mehmet Karabekir is the first to be interred. No prayers are said over his body as he is buried, and no headstone sunk into the freshly turned earth.

'The families of the high-level coup plotters are even thinking of changing their names,' says another lawyer, sitting outside the gates of Silivri. 'They ask how their relatives are looking – I just lie and say they're OK. When the government makes the public feel this way, some of them do not even want to collect the bodies of their relatives. People are deleting their WhatsApp conversations, their Facebook posts. It's fear. It started straight after that *sala* call to prayer on the coup night– I saw that people's mentalities are changing.'

## The crackdown

How do you spot a Gülenist? The government says there are ways. Even if they failed for years to notice them in the top ranks of their military and judiciary, they are sure about how to recognise them now. In the weeks following the coup attempt, conspiracy theories feed into news reports, which are then repeated by the politicians and become facts.

First, they claim that the imam in Pennsylvania has been issuing dollar bills to his followers, all of them bearing serial numbers that start with the letter F. The evidence? Eight days after the coup, a correspondent for the state mouthpiece Anadolu news agency reports that the police have found such bank notes on many of the Gülenist suspects they have arrested. Then the politicians take up the thread. Bekir Bozdağ, the justice minister, tells A Haber news: 'There is no doubt that this one-dollar bill has some important function within the Gülenist terror organisation. Prosecutors are asking as they investigate what these are. What does this mean? Why are they being carried? Does it signify a hierarchy to them? Is it some sort of ID that identifies them to one another?'

Other pro-government newspapers and sources also speculate. Notes with different serial letters have also allegedly been found – so each letter must refer to a rank. Gülen himself blessed the notes before distributing them to his followers, one columnist claims. Quickly, the dollar bill becomes grounds enough on its own for arrest, rather than a bit of coincidental evidence. One of the first to be picked up is NASA scientist Serkan Gölge, who is questioned by police acting on a tip-off a week after the coup attempt. The officers find a single dollar bill in a box in his brother's bedroom. In February 2018, after nineteen months in prison awaiting trial, he is found guilty on terrorism charges and sentenced to seven and a half years in prison.

But how many people have single dollar bills in their houses? I do – I keep a stack of them for when I'm travelling. It's small change in the world's most recognised currency. The bills are lying on top of my writing desk when my landlord comes to pick up my rent money two weeks after the coup. I had always thought of him as one of my allies in Istanbul, a flamboyantly camp guy who greets me with a kiss on each cheek every time we meet. But as he spots the notes he turns round and looks me in the eye.

'Aaaaah, Gülenist!' he says, and then tempers it with a cheerful chuckle.

I don't think he's serious, but I am spooked. That evening, in the first of many acts that, to an outside observer, might suggest I have lost my mind, I rip the notes into tiny pieces and flush them down the toilet.

Then there are the cheap mass-produced T-shirts from a Turkish chain store with the word HERO printed across the front. One of the coup suspects wears one during his first court hearing and *Sabah* newspaper decides it is a signal from Gülen: 'Hero' standing for *Hoca Efendi Razı Olsun* (may the teacher – Gülen – bless you). Erdoğan declares that the defendants must all wear brown overalls in the courtroom from now on. Out on the streets, the police start detaining ordinary Turks who are wearing the shirts. Within a few days, more than thirty people have been hauled in.

But despite such ham-fisted, so-called 'signals' the Gülenists are secretive, the government officials tell us. They are clever. They are cunning. They hide themselves, drink alcohol and, if they are women, go uncovered so they can pass as secularists. They have made such good work of concealing their true identities that anyone could belong to the movement.

Turks' hatred for the Gülenists is real: the Gülenists tried to take over the country for their own gain, then they turned the state's weapons against its citizens. They must be exposed and, if they are so adept at hiding themselves, everyone must be a suspect. Friends turn against each other, husbands inform on wives. There are several reports in the newspapers of divorce cases in which Gülenist sympathies are cited. A pregnant woman is attacked in Istanbul by a group who shout that she is wearing revealing clothes, so she must be a Gülenist. 'They wanted to lynch me,' she says.

For those under the state's microscope, the ones fired from their jobs or left behind when their partner is arrested, the accusations infect like leprosy. In the fashionable districts of Istanbul you might still walk the streets and not realise that a huge purge is leaching the heart out of this country. But I do. Almost every evening and weekend in the year after the coup, once I have filed my stories for the next day's paper, I travel out on the metrobus lines to the nondescript, unglamorous parts of the city.

There, I meet the outcasts. I don't know if they are Gülenists or not, but I do know that they are being judged and punished without trial. Almost every day in that first year of the purge, Turks working in the public sector turn to the country's legal circular, the Official Gazette, to see if their names have been added to the latest lists of dismissals.

'There were no warnings, no investigations,' a low-ranking civil servant called Ahmet who has spent his career working in a provincial city hall tells me. 'I swear I was the best person working in my office. My manager asked several times to have me back. I found my name in the Official Gazette and I was told to take my personal belongings from the office. No letter, no signature, nothing. They kicked me to the kerb. The reason they said is that I am working with terrorist groups – but they didn't even say which one, PKK or Gülenists. I had a lot of friends who are opponents of the AKP and I am an opponent too, of course.'

Ahmet's family and friends have turned their backs on him – only the ones who have also been purged still pick up the phone. To fill his empty days he runs through the reasons he might have been targeted, again and again and again. It cannot only be his opposition to the government, he is sure. The most likely explanation is that he once had an account with Bank Asya – a now-closed Gülenist business.

'I started a postgraduate degree in January 2014 at a state university, and they wanted me to have a Bank Asya account. I wish I had not started that course. I have lost my job, my passport, my friends, my relatives. I lost my future. I am hopeless. All I want is my passport so I can leave this country.'

Another public servant, Mehmet, walked into his office two weeks after the coup attempt to find the police waiting for him. His manager handed him an envelope containing a letter with a single sentence: 'You have been suspended due to the ongoing investigation.'

'I had to sign it, and I thought of not doing it,' Mehmet says. 'I had long known that irrational steps were being taken. I thought that this problem could not be solved by these people, so I signed it. Then I found out that there was a detention order in my name. We went down to my office along with the police. They searched the bookcase and the desk, and took the computer to investigate further. After that, we went to my house. They took my communication devices, and I was taken to a sports hall together with almost a hundred people.'

Twenty-six days later he was taken into the chaotic courthouse. He still had not been told what he was accused of. The prosecutor began reading out some of his social media posts. Still he did not say what the charges were.

'I asked in particular if there had been any official complaints about me, and what I was being accused of. The prosecutor replied briefly: "We're looking into it." I couldn't ask out loud why I had been detained for twenty-five days. I knew the answer: The conditions of the state of emergency, and of course, the court's workload.'

Mehmet was released from court, but ordered to sign in at an Istanbul police station twice a week. Days later, a decree published in the Official Gazette declared that he was formally dismissed from his job. Now he has discovered that he is accused of being a member of a terrorist organisation, and awaits trial. With 77,524 people having been formally charged in connection with the coup attempt as of April 2018 and almost twice that number detained, he will likely be waiting for years, if not decades. His appeal to the constitutional court has gone unanswered. The administrative court rejected it because of the state of emergency. Neither has the court of appeals replied. So, like 25,000 others caught up in the purge, he decided to take his case to the European Court of Human Rights, confident that he would at least get justice outside Turkey. The ECHR has said it can only take on cases once they have been exhausted in the domestic courts. And so Mehmet, like all the others, is stuck in a Kafka-esque loop between a justice system in meltdown, a toothless international court, and a president bent on revenge.

Some of the purged find unexpected ways of coping. Fatma, a woman with flawless English whom I meet with her bouncy ten-year-old daughter, says she started wearing the headscarf only after she and her husband were dismissed. The political connotations were not lost on her.

'Recently I started wearing the hijab – it was a hard decision. After my dismissal I started to study the Qur'an again. I'm from a secular family – it's very hard to explain this decision. They don't have religious roots, but they are culturally conservative, from Anatolia. They like Atatürk, my mum is uncovered, but she supports Erdoğan. But we all have prejudices in this country. People are more separatist now. Some support the hijab, others think it is politically abused. When I was first trying it, I tried different styles. I thought I looked too much like an AKP supporter. I wanted to shout that I am not an AKP supporter, I just believe in God. We have an Islamic government, but it is more difficult to practise your beliefs when you don't belong. My uncles don't know yet, but I think their reactions will be related to the government: "You became an Erdoğanist."'

She found her name on the suspension list at her workplace the Tuesday after the coup attempt – the same day I sat in Yıldız Palace listening to İbrahim Kalın telling us not to question the crackdown. Six weeks later she was fully dismissed.

'When I was dismissed only a few people called me. They were thinking two things: either that I must have some relationship with the Gülenists, or they didn't care about that but didn't want to lose their jobs. That doesn't surprise me, because people are very afraid of something. Former friends don't call. The people who are still in contact are in the same situation. This is very normal, because people will say, "Look! They have contacts!" They have made us like this. Us versus them – it is something they buy very easily.'

*

In early 2017 the European Union prepared an intelligence report about the coup and the subsequent purge. The report states that Gülenists were at the core of the coup attempt, but also that the Turkish government appears to have prepared a list of people it wanted to sack before the coup took place, and which also included civil activists who had been involved with Gezi Park. The events of 15 July have handed Erdoğan the chance to enact it. The report ends:

> AKP will try to derive benefit from the attempted coup and it may even strengthen as a result of that. In domestic politics AKP will settle scores with its one and only real rival and parallel with this in its international ties it tries to demonstrate that it is still strong in order to create a full presidential system.

Back in Turkey, millions might be thinking the same, but to suggest such a thing would be tantamount to treason. 'Thousands of people in prison, thousands fired, and thousands are not talking about these things,' one woman who lost her own job and whose husband had been arrested shortly after the coup tells me in July 2017. 'I can't believe my people, my Turkish people actually. I can understand Erdoğan because he is a dictator. But I can't understand why Turkish people are not talking. I read about the histories of Iran, Iraq, Syria. I never thought that Turkey could one day be like them.'

# ATATÜRK'S CHILDREN

There are two Mustafa Kemals. One the flesh-and-blood Mustafa
Kemal who now stands before you and who will pass away. The
other is you, all of you here who will go to the far corners of
our land to spread the ideals which must be defended with your
lives if necessary.

Mustafa Kemal Atatürk

*March 2017*
*Hatay province*

I had to come today, of all days.
'You don't have an Atatürk picture?' I ask Birsen Aldırma, as
she piles the lunch table with plates of hummus, meatballs, crudités
and yoghurt.

Her family members, gathered here with us, throw wide-eyed
glances at each other and then reply on Birsen's behalf.

'We have a big one! But it's being fixed,' says Feyzullah, the patriarch. 'Last week there was a storm, and it fell off the wall and smashed.
We've taken it to the glass shop. It'll be back tomorrow.'

But these might be the only people in Turkey who don't need to
see a portrait of Atatürk to feel close to him. Because the Aldırmas

and the Kuzulus, three generations of them squashed into Feyzullah's front room, have Atatürk's blood running through their veins.

Seventy-five-year-old Birsen is still bright-eyed and dark-haired. It seems impossible that she's the mother of 53-year-old Feyzullah, grey and tired, slumped in his armchair in the corner for most of the morning. He looks too old to be the father of 24-year-old Deniz and nineteen-year-old Derya, with their hennaed hair, trainers and piercings.

The girls' four cousins are a little older, respectable-looking family men and women in their early thirties. Şarap, Deniz and Derya's aunt (and Feyzullah's sister), is a portly but well-kept matron with fashionably cut short hair and a motherly way of squeezing my arm and smiling whenever she speaks to me. All of these nine people are the grandchildren, great-grandchildren and great-great-grandchildren of Abdurrahman Efendi, Atatürk's first cousin. They are the last fading flesh-and-blood echoes of a man who, a mere eight decades after his death, has almost become immortalised.

Only Birsen, who married into the family, can recall Abdurrahman. 'He was this gorgeous guy – charismatic!' she says.

None are old enough to remember Atatürk himself. Their proud bonds to the man they never met are built around a few scattered trinkets and anecdotes.

'When I was in primary school, I was always the one asked to read the poems about Atatürk,' says Şarap, a beaming smile splitting her face. 'I get very emotional when I think about that even now. The last time I visited his mausoleum, I cried!'

Feyzullah picks up as Şarap grows too emotional and falters. 'Thinking of Atatürk . . . it's like this kind of person comes along once in a hundred years,' he says. 'It's a great success what he achieved. Here we were in the heart of war. The world was boiling. And he saved our country, gave us freedom.'

They talk on, this warm, modest family. They were not what I expected when I boarded the flight from Istanbul back to Hatay, the southern province skirting the western end of the Syrian border and the region where I had lived for eight months when I first moved to

Turkey. Little had I known then that the relatives of the man whose face I was seeing everywhere were so close by. The Aldırmas and the Kuzulus live in İskenderun, a run-down port city facing the island of Cyprus across the water, and in Dörtyol, a town a few miles inland. Their apartments are small, tidy and cheerfully furnished in the typical style of the Turkish lower middle class: lace doilies over small side tables, and delicate, patterned coffee cups brought out only for guests. The walls are hung with framed vistas of Istanbul and Islamic incantations embroidered in Arabic script.

'This is what we prefer, we like to lead a modest life. We have never hidden behind the fact that we are his relatives. We never took advantage of it,' says Feyzullah, when I point out how different they are to the descendants of Mehmet VI, the last Ottoman sultan. After his banishment in 1923, they established themselves as part of the European jet set, holidaying in Monaco and, in 2010, opening a court case against Turkey to reclaim some of their lost riches. Now, they are also trying to weigh back into Turkish politics. In early 2017, with the post-coup euphoria just starting to wane, Erdoğan has called a referendum on Turkey's constitution, and whether it should be changed to one that hands him almost uncontested powers. Erdoğan's plan to switch Turkey's system from parliamentary democracy to executive presidency has been floating around since the turn of the decade, and gained momentum after he became president in 2014. If he manages to secure a majority of votes for his *Evet*, or Yes, camp, Erdoğan will be able to rule by decree and handpick the cabinet. The top ranks of the judiciary will be appointed directly by him and the parliament. The reforms will do away entirely with the system bequeathed by Atatürk.

In the final weeks before voting day, Sultan Mehmet's descendants have surfaced on state media voicing their support for Erdoğan's plans. In contrast, Atatürk's family rarely speak to the press; I'm the first foreign reporter to meet with them. I'm touched at the way they're dressed in their best clothes for this occasion, and how Birsen has spent hours preparing huge piles of delicious Hatay cuisine – the thing I miss most from my time living in this part of Turkey. The region's delicacies are famed across the country but difficult to find in their true form outside this province. Warmly spiced lentil soup, peppered beans and little parcels of meat wrapped in ground bulgur – the table is bejewelled with delicacies. Ağca, one of the cousins, has drawn out the family tree for me by hand and taken the day off work to join us. We chat a little about the ancient city of Antakya, my old home, and about the tens of thousands of Syrians who have now found sanctuary there. There is a family of them living next door, Feyzullah tells me. They are all empathetic; after all, the Aldırmas and the Kuzulus are the descendants of refugees themselves.

'Our family's journey started in Thessaloniki . . . from there we went to Istanbul, Bursa, then finally to here,' Feyzullah says. 'Dörtyol is where all the migrants went – it was the designated area. That's why most people here look like foreigners – they came from the Balkans.'

Atatürk's immediate family, including his mother, sister and cousin, Abdurrahman, were among the first Ottomans to find themselves uprooted as the empire crumbled. They left their home city of Salonica, now in northern Greece and known as Thessaloniki, during the Balkan war of 1912–13. The fledgling Christian nation states of Bulgaria, Greece, Serbia and Montenegro had united to boot the Ottomans out of their last bastions in Europe. The victory was celebrated in the capitals of Western Europe – but the toll was wrought on the Muslims of the Balkans, who were slaughtered and deported to Anatolia.

Over the coming decades, millions more would follow this initial and involuntary exodus, while the revenge exacted by the Turks against the minorities in Anatolia would send millions of Christian citizens of the Ottoman Empire fleeing in the other direction. It was the great tragedy of the Ottoman twilight – the bloody curdling of a once-mixed population. The ghosts still haunt Istanbul, a city once teeming with followers of all three Abrahamic religions but which today largely identifies itself as Muslim. Even so, lying in bed on a Sunday morning, I can still hear the sound of one lonely tolling church bell – a reminder of my neighbourhood's past as a district filled with Greek bourgeoisie. On a scruffy backstreet, where I would not venture were it not for my love of pork, is the city's last remaining Greek butcher. There is the air of a secret society within his cool, white-tiled walls; a conspiracy of guilty appreciation for his sausages and bacon.

Muslims from the European reaches of the empire fled or were banished back to the Turkish heartlands, where they could find safety and acceptance in their common religion. But by their features, pale-skinned and blue-eyed compared to the darker-skinned Anatolian Muslims, they were marked as outsiders. Later, they became weapons in Atatürk's war of Turkish independence.

'People from the Balkans were sent to Hatay because the region came under the control of the French and Armenians,' explains Ağca. 'The Turkish state wanted to use the Balkan refugees to populate this region.'

We talk on, past lunch and into the afternoon. Şarap shows me photos of their ancestors, and tells me stories about how people react to them when they learn of their famous connection. Today, they bring out their few keepsakes, including Atatürk's ceremonial sword, a gorgeous swoosh of engraved silver. The younger members of the family admit to using it in play fights as children. Apart from these last few prized possessions, they have given everything to museums, including the Cadillac Atatürk drove down here when he visited his cousin in the 1930s. He left it behind when the engine wouldn't start. It stayed outside the family's house until the 1960s, when the state-owned İşbank came and asked for it, along with a haul of old photos. They are now on display in Anıtkabir, Atatürk's mausoleum in Ankara.

'That was Atatürk's ethos,' says Feyzullah, 'to share all he had with his nation. He used to say, "Even the clothes I'm wearing belong to the people!"'

The family wish they had at least been mentioned on the plaque beside the Cadillac. 'They wrote "This is a gift from İşbank"!' says

Feyzullah, with a sad and incredulous shake of his head. 'We were going to donate the sword, too, but we changed our mind after that.'

All day, as I've listened to their stories and caressed their keepsakes, I've been sneaking glances at their faces, searching for resemblances to Turkey's most recognisable man. None of them have the giveaway laser-blue eyes, or the shock of fair hair. But in Deniz, a smart, funny university student, I sense something of the force of personality.

'Atatürk is being removed from everything, from school books, from coins,' she says suddenly, and I detect the first trace of tears in her eyes. 'Lately, in the university, everyone can say everything in the open. The people who want to praise him do, but others feel free to insult him. I don't understand why the lecturers don't say anything. This is the man who established the republic. I can't bear it.'

## Law 5816 – insulting Atatürk

The hundreds of Turks who have served time in prison for breaking Law 5816 might feel differently. Under that statute, anyone deemed to have insulted Atatürk, his image or memory faces up to three years behind bars. Anyone who encourages another to insult Atatürk may be prosecuted as if they had committed the crime themselves. If the insult was carried out publicly or in the press, the maximum sentence may be extended by half. And if the crime occurred at Atatürk's mausoleum, the perpetrator could be imprisoned for up to five years.

The law is not a quaint anachronism. Hundreds of people have spent thousands of days in jail because of it. Professors, poets, mayors and men of religion have fallen foul of the canon, some of them unwittingly, others in a protest of conscience. International human rights organisations and freedom of speech watchdogs have railed against it. But this law is not something Atatürk himself put in place. The notice declaring the new law was published in the Official Gazette on 31 July 1951 – thirteen years after Atatürk's death, and amid the first pushbacks against his reforms.

In May 1950 the Demokrat Partisi seized power from Atatürk's

CHP in Turkey's first free elections. Its leader and now prime minister, Adnan Menderes, claimed that the will of the people had been realised, and that the rule of the bureaucratic elites was over. Modern-day Turks would recognise the rhetoric – it is almost identical to the claims Erdoğan has repeated, and repeated again, since his AKP took power in 2002. There are other similarities between the two leaders: both sympathise with Turkey's religiously conservative masses – although Menderes was decidedly less personally pious than Erdoğan – and both sought to indulge them by loosening some of Atatürk's firm secularism.

The first law Menderes enacted when his party took power was to reintroduce the Arabic call to prayer. In 1932, Atatürk had passed a law decreeing that it should only be recited in Turkish, to the horror of the devout. So symbolic was this tussle in the greater struggle between secularism and religion in Turkey that it featured in the trailer for *Reis*, a cringeworthy cinematic hagiography of Erdoğan released in early 2017.

The film tells the story of Erdoğan's early life, back when he was just plain Tayyip from the tough streets of Istanbul. It casts him as a devout boy guided by his moral compass, unwilling to bend to peer pressure and winning both admirers and enemies because of it – a broadly accurate portrayal. But the trailer showing young Tayyip singing the Arabic call to prayer in defiance of the law? Erdoğan was born in 1953 – three years after Menderes reintroduced the Arabic recitals. By then there was nothing to defy.

Soon after, sensing a new wind of religious freedom, the Ticanis, members of a conservative Islamic order, began attacking Atatürk's statues. The sect had originated in the North African reaches of the Ottoman Empire in the eighteenth century, but grew radical and notorious with the birth of Atatürk's modern republic. They numbered several thousand, but were concentrated in Ankara. Since the Atatürk statue attacks were soon happening across the country, it seems impossible that all of them were carried out by Ticanis. Historian Jacob Landau suggests that the activity soon also caught on with student and youth protest movements. Nonetheless, the blame was levelled entirely at the men of religion.

Menderes faced a dilemma. He wanted to allow religious Turks a little breathing space, but he didn't want them going *that* far. It was Atatürk who had given Menderes his first job in politics, and there was still a lingering loyalty. Neither was he so personally invested in Islam as some members of his party – his wife was an opera singer, a purveyor of a very European art form. So he drew up a law making it a crime to attack Atatürk's memory.

It was a deeply controversial move. Much of the opposition came from the CHP – the party of which Atatürk is the 'Eternal Leader' – which thought the law undemocratic and unconstitutional. But Menderes also faced revolt from within his own ranks, with the more religious members of his party dismayed at the 'deification' of a mortal. One independent member of the house argued that the law would mean university professors could be prosecuted for their lectures – prophetic, since that is exactly what happened in later decades.

The bill was rejected by a sliver on its first vote, by 146 votes to 141, and sent back to the justice committee for redrafting. Word went round that the government was planning to retract the law – and then, the statue attacks escalated. On a single day, two Atatürk monuments in Ankara were defaced in broad daylight, right in front of an army base. The head of the Ticani sect was arrested, along with a dozen of his members, but the vandalism spree continued. Within a month, more than a hundred of the order's followers had been rounded up, and the investigations spread to the Nakşibendis, another conservative group. On 12 July 1951, the interior minister held a press conference vowing to 'liquidate the snake whose head needs to be crushed'. When the slightly amended bill came back to parliament twelve days later, it was approved by 232 votes to 50. Six members of the house abstained. Atatürk's honour was enshrined in law.

*Cumhuriyet* recorded the tumultuous scenes in parliament as the bill progressed. 'Deputies for and against the law made a lot of noise, banged on the desks, and some got into verbal fights,' wrote the newspaper's parliamentary correspondent.

Bedii Unustun, the MP for Çanakkale – the place where Atatürk led his soldiers to glorious victory in the Battle of Gallipoli – opposed the law with a poetic speech. 'Running the state as a dictatorship is like sailing a boat in a pool,' he said. 'Democracy is sailing in the open seas. This proposition is the government's way of locking open waters into a pool. The government is putting heavy burdens on its people in the disguise of Atatürk love . . . Its ship will lose its way and get smashed on the rocks.'

Most of what Unustun said was lost in the din of the shouting and banging. There was loud applause when the vote was passed. But some thought it didn't go far enough. Nadir Nadi, editor of *Cumhuriyet*, pondered in an opinion piece days before the law was passed:

> Imagine we caught all the Ticanis and changed the penalty for statue destroyers and Atatürk insulters to ten years. Will we be able to protect the revolution and the living memory (other than the stone and the brass) of Atatürk this way? If the proposed law passes as it is, will it stop people from abusing religion? Will the fundamentalists who are afraid of attacking statues refrain from attacking the revolution? Will overt and covert propaganda such as covering the women at home [with headscarves], bringing back the Arabic script, and overwriting the civil law and replacing it with Sharia stop with such measures?

Nadi supported the law, but also lobbied for similar punishments to be brought in for those who refused to obey Atatürk's dress-code reforms, or his introduction of the Latin alphabet.

Menderes eventually fell on his sword. As his tenure progressed, he grew bad-tempered, thin-skinned and corrupt, jailing journalists and rigging elections in a bid to cling to power. In 1960 the Turkish army – the ultimate guardians of Atatürk's legacy – stepped into politics for the first time, overthrowing Menderes and putting him on trial on a colourful array of charges including 'extravagance', fathering an illegitimate child, and embezzlement. The court found him and several other high-ranking figures within his party guilty of violating the constitution, and sentenced them to death by hanging. Menderes swung in September 1961. It was only three decades later, under the presidency of the whisky-loving but pious Turgut Özal, that his memory began to be rehabilitated.

Erdoğan has taken it a step further. Now, you will find boulevards, airports and parks named after Menderes. He is one of only three Turkish leaders, including Atatürk, whose graves have been turned into mausoleums (the other is Turgut Özal). And in 2013 the island in the Sea of Marmara where he was tried and hanged was renamed 'Democracy and Freedom Island'.

Yet it was Erdoğan's government that, in May 2007, enacted another parcel of legislation designed to keep Atatürk's reputation safe, this time in response to a very modern problem. In the age of the internet, the statue-smashers of the 1950s now make their feelings known in homemade films, in blog posts and on comment threads. Law 5651 allows websites to be blocked on a wide range of grounds including child abuse, indecency and copyright infringement. The law's original impetus, however, was the increasing criticism of Atatürk on the ungoverned space of the web. Over the next two years, more than 3,700 websites fell foul of the law, including MySpace, Google and several Kurdish news sites. But the big target was video-hosting site YouTube, which had refused Turkey's repeated requests to take down videos criticising Atatürk. In 2009 the Organisation for Security and Economic Co-operation in Europe tallied that 2,972 websites were blocked in Turkey for various alleged crimes against Atatürk – more than were blocked because they involved prostitution.

The ironclad limits of these laws leave little room for academic or even casual debate regarding Atatürk's life and work. Most Turks' knowledge of their founding father wanders little from the script of the 'Long Speech' – a thirty-six-and-a-half-hour blockbuster that Atatürk delivered to parliament over six days in 1927. In it, he outlined the history of the war of independence, and the principles of the new republic. He also delivered damning criticisms of everyone from the sultans and their court to the foreign occupying powers, while glossing over the Ottoman Empire's own misdeeds and errors in its final acts.

Above all the treachery and misfortune in this narrative sits Atatürk – part saviour, part prophet – who foresees and then orchestrates the Turkish nation's rebirth. This is the folklore narrative taught in schools, in universities, in films, and it has captured the official version of history even beyond Turkey's borders. Writing in *Turkish Studies*, an academic journal, in 2008 a Finnish historian totted up only six theses, in any language and published in any country, which examine the Long Speech with a critical eye. So is it any wonder that those Turks who aim to break the mould, to shake things up a bit, to question, are usually rounded on by the rest of their society?

Some of those who have done so recently include historian İpek Çalışlar, whose study of Atatürk's short-lived marriage landed her in court. The alleged offence? To have repeated an anecdote told to her by a relative of Atatürk's wife, Latife, about how the couple swapped clothes so that he could escape a group of rebellious soldiers who were plotting to kill him. 'In Turkey, we always have legal obstacles for writers. Like learning how to swim, you learn how to write without getting in trouble with the law,' Çalışlar told me.

Can Dündar, a well-known journalist writing for the pro-Atatürk *Cumhuriyet*, was repeatedly hauled into court for scenes in his 2006 documentary *Mustafa*, which showed Atatürk smoking and drinking heavily. One of Dündar's staunchest supporters was CHP veteran Ertuğrul Günay, who had joined the AKP in 2007 when it seemed like the party of liberal ideals.

'There is no habit of free and diverse thought in Turkey, neither on the left nor on the right,' he told me. 'Each side has their own taboos and subjects that they want to hold above all discussion. Political identifications are as dogmatic as religious identifications. Surely, Atatürk is very significant and precious for Turkey. But some

"leftists" who took the subject of Atatürk to be a taboo went as far
as demanding me to ban this film. This is in fact the greatest problem
that Turkey has. All sides of our political spectrum are in their essence
conservative. Our leftists are actually right wing, and therefore our
right wing is extreme right!'

Dündar's film was not even critical of the nation's founder. 'I wanted
to present Mustafa Kemal in a more intimate, affectionate light,' he
said at the time. 'All those statues, busts and flags have created a
chief devoid of human qualities.'

## The Atatürk impersonator

Jokes about Atatürk are glaringly absent from Turkish conversation
and culture. The few I have heard or read are incredibly lame and
demand a detailed knowledge of Turkish history. There is this one,
for example, that did the rounds following Menderes's execution:
Atatürk and Menderes meet in heaven, and the former asks the latter
how Turkey is doing. Menderes tells him of everything that has
happened, including his own unfortunate end. 'Well Adnan, that's
kismet [fate],' Atatürk says. 'No, not kismet – İsmet!' replies
Menderes.

İsmet İnönü was Atatürk's sidekick and prime minister, who took
over the CHP on his death. He is often blamed for keeping the party
locked in the past and enabling the rise of Menderes's DP. See? It's
hardly going to get them rolling in the aisles.

I did find one internet-age Atatürk joke that a few English-speaking
Turks might laugh at:

'What did Atatürk's father say to him when he did well?'

'Adda-Turk!'

Apart from this, the only Atatürk humour you will find are jokes
designed to offend Turks, usually penned on Greek or Armenian chat
rooms. What's the reason? If the career of Göksel Kaya is any indication, it's because Turks far prefer their Atatürk humour in the form
of high kitsch.

For thirty years, Kaya, an actor, has been playing one character. Each day he gets up, slicks back his hair, fluffs up his eyebrows, and dons a sharp suit and shiny shoes. His hair is bleached a radioactive yellow-blond and he wears shockingly blue contact lenses – although he insists that all his attributes are natural. He has studied the habits and mannerisms of his muse to the point where he now assumes them without thinking. OK, so he smokes Parliaments, a cheap brand, rather than handmade and monogrammed cigarettes. But he does so with the same flick of the wrist and self-conscious flair as Atatürk.

Sometimes Kaya plays his character on stage or in films. More often he just spends his days in character, walking the streets of his home city of İzmir – a bastion of Atatürk fanaticism on the Aegean coast, a stone's throw from the nearest Greek islands. It was where, as a soldier, the young Mustafa Kemal met his soon-to-be wife, Latife. And it was İzmir that bore the worst brunt of the war of independence. As the Greeks left Asia Minor, defeated at the hands of Atatürk's army, huge fires ripped through the beautiful old city. Almost all of it was destroyed.

These days, İzmir is known as a safe haven for Turks who want to kiss their lovers in public, wear revealing miniskirts or get raucous on their rakı. It's most likely down to the alchemy of two influences – the whiff of Greek culture that still hangs in the air, and the city's connection to Atatürk. İzmir is a totem for the CHP, Atatürk's party. 'What we need,' Barış Yarkadaş, the CHP deputy for my Istanbul neighbourhood, told me a few days after Erdoğan's referendum, 'is for the whole country to become like İzmir.'

A nice thought, perhaps, but deluded. İzmir is different; it feels as if it were built on ley lines. With a few exceptions – certain neighbourhoods of Istanbul and Ankara, for example, and other coastal cities with a view out towards Europe – Turkey is a conservative country. In the heartlands of Anatolia and along the northern Black Sea coast, life revolves around business, the mosque and the family. Even in the Kurdish lands of the east, where the PKK's leftism and feminism has stamped a big footprint, patriarchy and tribal politics rule.

Perhaps it is the rest of the country that will eventually creep into İzmir, not the other way around. In the summer of 2017, two young women dressed up for a night out in Alsancak, İzmir's central district, full of clubs and students, and were sexually harassed by men on a motorbike. They went to find the nearest police officers. But instead of helping the women, the officers told them they were at fault.

'Look at yourselves,' said one. 'You deserve more than that with those outfits.' And then they doled out what they deemed to be a fitting punishment – a slap around the face for each of the women. The incident was caught on security cameras and the women filed a legal complaint against the officers. One was arrested and charged with the attack but released on bail two days later.

But the İzmir I see as I accompany Göksel Kaya through the busy centre one afternoon is still the city where Atatürk rules. Decked out in a navy blue suit, with a crisp white shirt and a red hanky peeking out of his breast pocket, Kaya sails down the street to the amazed stares of onlookers. Some simply gawp. Others bound up and ask for a photo – and as soon as that happens, others flock to him so that, quickly, he is surrounded by a crowd. Kaya is used to it: he knows how to make a quick exit when the throng is getting out of control. '*Hadi!*' – Come on! – he shouts back to me as he bustles his way through.

His resemblance to Atatürk is striking but only, I suspect, because of the dye-and-contact-lens accoutrements and the anachronistic outfits. When we finally reach a coffee shop, and the waiters are done taking their selfies, I ask him how he realised his likeness to Turkey's most famous face.

'It was during my military service,' Kaya tells me. 'I put on my uniform for the first time, and – GAH! – my commander gasped.'

He pulls out his phone and begins reeling through the huge archive of photos that he keeps on it. It's true – in the leveller of khaki, he bears far more of a resemblance to Atatürk.

Kaya's odd career has taken him to the front row of some of Turkey's biggest events. He has often been in the first line of dignitaries at

the official celebrations for the country's national days. He has met
the head of the armed forces – and even Erdoğan, on a couple of
occasions. Small children, who are told by their teachers that Atatürk
sees them when they cheat, sometimes cry in Kaya's presence. It is
as if Turks want to kid themselves that Atatürk is still with them
– albeit several inches taller, several pounds heavier, and actually not
all that much like Atatürk really, once you take away the embellish-
ments.

Not everyone is a Kaya fan. Down in Hatay, Atatürk's descendants
are unimpressed. The friend I cadge his number from, who is part of
a powerful CHP family in Istanbul, harrumphs when I say I want to
meet him. 'That guy just uses Atatürk!' he says.

I've heard the same accusation levelled at many different people,
from the flag sellers to the CHP to the people who are campaigning
for the No vote in the referendum, using images of Atatürk on their
leaflets. Whenever Atatürk is invoked, and for whatever reason,
someone will accuse the one who has summoned the spirit of doing
so with cynical motives. Every Turk feels like they own Atatürk, and
none of them want to share.

Kaya, though, just seems to want to spread joy. Eight months after
our first meeting, he calls to ask if I fancy joining him on Victory
Day, the national holiday celebrating Turkey's defeat of the Greeks
in the final battle of the war of independence. He is leading a rally
of the city's classic car club from the Maltepe parade ground, where
leader of the opposition Kemal Kılıcdaroğlu held his justice rally six
weeks ago, to the ridiculously flamboyant Dolmabahçe palace, a
monument to the excesses of the late Ottomans and the place where
Atatürk died. The route will take them across the bridge where
Erdoğan's fanatics faced off against the coup-plotting soldiers. It is
to be a journey laced with symbolism – but also peppered with a
good dose of humour.

I turn up at the meeting point early on an August morning to
find a gaggle of people milling around rows of gleaming vintage cars.
Most have Turkish flags draped over their bonnets, and the owners

of those that don't are digging banners out of their boots and tying them on. There is one red Mercedes from the 1950s that is permanently patriotic. It has the star and crescent of the Turkish flag sprayed onto its roof, and a silhouette of Atatürk on the bonnet. A sticker across the front windscreen reads *Iyi ki varsın* ('It's good that you exist').

'I hate that saying,' mutters my Turkish friend, who has come along for the ride. 'It's from the shit we had to repeat in school every morning: *My existence is dedicated to the Turkish existence.* Fuck that.'

The car that Kaya will travel in is the centre of attention – partly because no one can get it started. It is a racing green Ford Phaeton from the 1930s, with gleaming silver trims and bug-eye headlamps and red number plates that read ATA, loaned to the club by a museum owner who has only driven it twice in the past decade. Militaristic music booms out over the car park from huge speakers strapped to the back of a pick-up truck. *'Sarı saçlı, mavi gözlü!'* (Blonde hair, blue eyes!) goes the refrain to one tune, repeated every three or four songs. My friend is in patriotic hell.

Most of the cars are huge American gas guzzlers, like props from films set in the 1950s. They are popular among Turks, the club's secretary, İlker Tayalı, tells me, because scores of them were sent to the country as part of America's post-Second World War aid package. Atatürk is popular here, too.

'We do these rallies on our national days because we adore Atatürk,' says Tayalı, as we sit in his 1961 Chevrolet Bel Air, waiting for Kaya to arrive and for the parade to begin. It is a gleaming slash of white with a varnished blue interior. Tayalı, who is forty-three, speaks about his hobby with a boyish pride. 'We also drive to all the cities that were important in the war of independence. We present our cars, we learn about the history, and then we eat and drink.'

The crowd here look similar to the one that showed up for the Justice March: educated, moneyed and Westernised. There are a few small dogs. Several women have come in form-fitting vintage dresses and cute high heels. Most others are wearing Atatürk-emblazoned

T-shirts. I ask Tayalı what the link is between the founder of the republic and Turkey's classic-car enthusiasts.

'We feel a kind of friendship with Atatürk,' he says. 'We like his etiquette, his education, his character. He is a symbol of the modern Turkish man, with his clothes and all his habits.'

Across town, there is another party in full swing. Istanbul's city government, which is controlled by Erdoğan's party, is holding a parade down Vatan Caddesi, a boulevard running through the heart of one of the city's most conservative districts. The mayor of the city is there along with scores of soldiers. Erdoğan, meanwhile, is at Anıtkabir, Atatürk's mausoleum in Ankara. He uses the occasion to reiterate his commitment to crushing the coup plotters and the terrorists. Tayalı is unimpressed.

'Now Erdoğan is trying to say that the coup anniversary is our national day – it's nonsense!' he cries. 'He doesn't want all of this. He openly doesn't like Atatürk. He knows that there are many people who are Atatürk fans, and that makes him nervous.'

Because of the state of emergency, Tayalı couldn't get official permission to hold his rally. Officially, it is illegal – all public gatherings and demonstrations must be approved by the government under the emergency laws. But he is going ahead with it anyway, knowing that Atatürk is the one man Erdoğan won't fight. Even if he is only here in the form of a lookalike, bumper stickers and T-shirts, that is enough.

There is a buzz around the car park as Kaya arrives, dressed in a sharp tuxedo and with a lashing of Brylcreem keeping every hair on his head in place. The car owners swarm around him. A preened TV news presenter rushes forward, dragging her cameraman after her, to get a prime shot of Kaya-Atatürk climbing into his car, which the mechanics have finally got going. Then, to the opening chords of the İzmir March booming through the pick-up's speakers, we swing out onto the highway.

On Bağdat Caddesi, a street where Istanbul's ostentatiously wealthy parade their riches, crowds pack out onto the streets to take photos, and cheer as Kaya passes. He waves regally. His fans hold up their cameras and snap photos. Old women pull silk scarves from their necks and wave them, blowing kisses with their other hands. The drivers honk their horns. We are causing a ruckus; a police car weaves its way into the convoy and pulls up beside us.

'You take the lead!' shouts Tayalı through his window to the dark-haired cop in the driving seat.

The young policeman looks unsure. He doesn't want to cut in front of a man who the crowds are cheering as if he really were Atatürk.

'That wouldn't be appropriate!' he shouts back.

So, as a compromise, he inches forward and pulls almost – but not quite – level with Kaya's car. The police stay with us past the Fenerbahçe football ground and along the highway right up to the bridge, their siren adding to the din of the horns and the cheering of the crowd. When we get to the bridge's entrance, we pull in to the side to regroup next to the memorial to the coup martyrs. As the mechanics pour cool water onto the engine of Kaya's car and the drivers get out to take photos against the backdrop of the Istanbul vista, a car speeds past with a young, shirtless man hanging out of the rear passenger-side window.

'RECEP TAYYIP ERDOĞAAAAAAAN!' he shouts, as he twirls his T-shirt round his head.

A retort flies back from a member of the convoy: 'Fuck off!'

Tayalı shakes his head sadly.

'We never used to be like this,' he says. 'It's Erdoğan who has made us like this, he has done it intentionally. He has polarised our society.'

## The legacy

Since he left no biological children or nephews and nieces, few traces of Atatürk's genetics were carried down the generations. Was that deliberate? Did he sense the dangers of leaving an heir? Turks need only peek over their borders to see what unchallenged dynastic power can bring. The Assads in Syria, the Aliyevs in Azerbaijan, the Barzanis

in the Kurdish region of northern Iraq – all of them are determined
to pass down their title along with their DNA, never mind what
turmoil that brings down on their people.

But how could Atatürk have known of the familial dictatorships
that would spring up in the old Ottoman lands decades after his
death? Everything we know about him suggests that he did not have
children simply because he wasn't that interested. His marriage to
Latife, the daughter of a wealthy İzmir trader, broke down in less
than three years because he spent too much time drinking and chatting with his old comrades in arms, the men with whom he was
building his new country. He never remarried, though stories of his
dedicated womanising abound. One of the more colourful is that he
took the virginity of Zsa Zsa Gabor, when he was fifty-six and she,
at twenty, was married to the first of her eight husbands. 'He dazzled
me with his sexual prowess and seduced me with his perversion.
Atatürk was very wicked. He knew exactly how to please a young
girl,' Gabor later wrote in her memoirs.

Despite his reputation as a womaniser, Atatürk also became self-
styled father figure to the Turkish nation, and adopted seven children.
His own flesh and blood, what few there were, could expect little in
the way of favours or fame. In 1938, as Atatürk was remoulding the
country, his cousin Abdurrahman took over the running of the local
railway station in nearby Dörtyol. Atatürk's sister, Makbule, moved
there too, and bought a small house next door to her cousin.

'Abdurrahman looked a lot like Atatürk, he was also blond and
blue-eyed and quite well-built,' says Şarap, his granddaughter. 'People
were amazed to see him, because he looked quite modern. Completely
different to the people down here! His wife was a proper Istanbul
lady. There were no cars here at that time, then she shows up driving
and wearing dresses from the city. Everyone here thought, *Wow!*'

Hatay was the newest and most controversial part of the country.
A thumb of land tucked away at the bottom of Turkey's
Mediterranean coast, it was initially handed to the French mandate
in Syria under the Treaty of Sèvres. The new Turkish state and the

Turkish population in Hatay never accepted it, however, and it functioned as an autonomous region to various degrees and in various forms from 1921 onwards. In 1938 it proclaimed itself an independent state under Turkish and French military supervision; a year later it was fully absorbed into the Turkish republic. Today the building where the short-lived parliament once sat houses an ice-cream parlour, a cinema, and the café where I held so many meetings with Syrian rebel leaders in 2013.

Atatürk made Hatay one of his personal projects. Its population was – and still is – a mix of Arabic-speaking Christians and Alawites, alongside a Jewish community that is now almost defunct. They might all have been happy enough to become part of the new Syrian state (though their descendants were definitely relieved that they hadn't when the civil war broke out there in 2011). But for Hatay's Turkish-speaking Muslim community, to be cut off from the new motherland was a tragedy. When Atatürk visited the nearby city of Adana in 1923 he was greeted by an Antakya woman dressed in black mourning. She held up a banner reading GAZI BABA SAVES US. Gazi is an honorific title for someone who has been injured in battle. Baba is the Turkish word for father.

The French rulers soon realised Atatürk's power, and banned any mention of him in the region's schools. But the Hatay Turks found ways to rebel. They followed Atatürk's reform of the alphabet from Arabic to Latin, and began abandoning the fez when his Hat Law decreed it. Meanwhile, Atatürk lobbied in Ankara and in international conferences for Hatay to become a part of Turkey. It was the last of his ambitions he would see achieved: four months before he died, the Turkish army marched into Hatay and its parliament voted to adopt Turkish laws.

Layer upon layer of history and blood shapes the contours of this region – the influx of Syrian refugees escaping the carnage over the border is only the latest coating. Just down the road from Feyzullah's apartment I spot the old French military cemetery packed with the bodies of men who died for imperial misadventure. Years before, on a lazy summer's weekend, my Syrian boyfriend and I took a trip to Vakıflı, a tiny mountain hamlet nestled between İskenderun and Syria and the last remaining Armenian village in Turkey. The people who live here are the descendants of a band of neighbours who refused to flee during the great expulsion and murder of millions of Armenians and other Christian minorities by Turkish and Kurdish soldiers in 1915, as the communities of the Ottoman Empire turned on each other. Instead, they gathered arms and holed up in their village high up in the mountains. Their suspicion and fear of Muslims has passed down through the generations; when my boyfriend and I went into a guesthouse to see if we could stay the night, the owner eyed his Arabic passport with misgiving. Eventually she agreed to let us stay; we guessed she assumed he was a Syrian Christian.

Late in the day, as the sun is setting over this complicated little corner of Turkey and after I've filled my notebook with his family's anecdotes, Ağca offers to takes me to The First Bullet Museum in Dörtyol, housed in the building where Atatürk – together with the leaders of the Hatay Turks – planned to bring the province into the republic.

As we drive the short journey over there from İskenderun, Ağca starts talking about how he once had political ambitions of his own. 'I studied public diplomacy at university, and under the old system I could have been a district governor after that,' he says. 'But then the AKP changed the rules. Now you have to have a political science degree. So I went to do my military service, and came back to work in an electrical appliances store.'

I wonder, though, if the rough, macho politics of the new Turkey is the place for any of this family. I've tried to push them on how they might vote in the referendum, and to introduce the topic of the president, and how he divides the country's opinion. They're having none of it. Feyzullah says he doesn't think that any leader of Turkey should be insulted, whether they are dead or alive. Others make noises about how it wouldn't be right for all the power to be with one person, but don't say who that person could be. When they do express strong opinions, it's within the safe borders of local government and parochial issues. I take the hint: they are scared. So I drop the subject of Erdoğan and the referendum, and go back to speaking about the past – a place where they seem far happier.

Ağca leads me into the small museum, an old Balkan-style wood-and-stone house, the upper floors overhanging the lower ones. Inside I find a very different view of Hatay's history to the one told in the bucolic wine houses of Vakıflı. The heroes of the story told here are not the Armenians who stood firm in the mountains, but the Turks who led the attack against them. The name has been chosen because Dörtyol believes itself to be the place where the first shot was fired in Atatürk's war of independence.

In the attic room, we find the obligatory waxwork of Atatürk – and Ağca and I take the obligatory selfie.

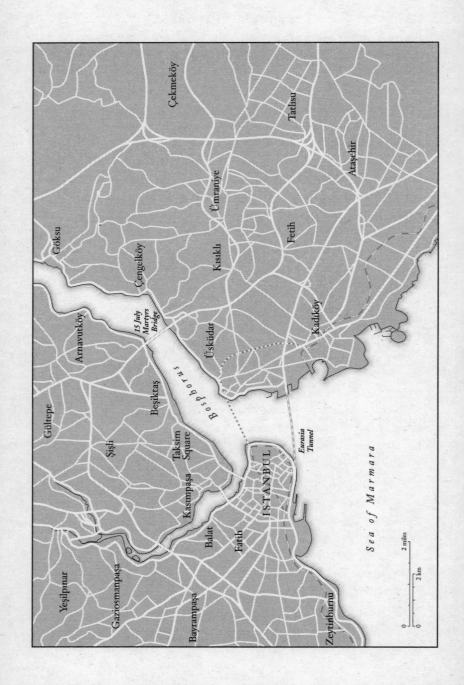

Çekmeköy

Tatlısu

Ataşehir

Göksu

Ümraniye

Fetih

Çengelköy

Kısıklı

Arnavutköy

15 July Martyrs Bridge

Kadıköy

Üsküdar

Gültepe

Beşiktaş

*B o s p h o r u s*

Şişli

Taksim Square

Eurasia Tunnel

Kasımpaşa

*Sea of Marmara*

ISTANBUL

Balat

Yeşilpınar

Fatih

Gaziosmanpaşa

2 miles

2 km

Bayrampaşa

Zeytinburnu

0
0

# 11

# ERDOĞAN'S NEW TURKEY

*April 2017*
*The referendum campaign*

Even if she were not who she is, Selin Söğütlüğil would draw stares. Petite and pneumatic, she is a five-foot column of curves wrapped in black and topped with a Medusa-like mane. Her eyes are dagger blue; tattooed butterflies flutter up her forearms.

'You know who I got the recommendation for the tattoo artist from?' she asks. 'David Beckham! A teacher at my daughter's school passed it on!'

Selin tips her head back and laughs, an infectious tinkle that floats above the music and the sound of glasses clacking on hardwood tables. I think how small and strange this world is, this elite international bubble where footballing legends share their tattooists' phone numbers with the descendants of revolutionaries.

Selin, a great-great-niece of Atatürk, is connected to the Aldırma and Kuzulu families in Hatay by a distant trace of blood. Hers is the branch of the family that stayed in Istanbul as the others moved on to Bursa and then Hatay. Today Selin flits between homes in Turkey and London: running marathons, writing poetry and editing a magazine, finishing her first novel and contemplating an entry into Turkish politics. She had already made a name for herself as a writer before she publicly revealed her blood ties to Atatürk in late 2016. Since then, she has played a starring role at many of the official days and celebrations linked to the founder, appearing in chic red outfits at Anitkabır to lay a wreath at the foot of his sarcophagus. But she is dejected with the state of the CHP, she says, and with Turkish party politics in general. I tell her I think there is still a chance that Erdoğan could lose the referendum, despite the odds stacked in his favour. Selin scoffs.

'It will be a yes,' she says. 'Trust me, I know this country.'

Tonight Selin and I are eating dinner in Istanbul's Soho House, part of the London-based chain of members' clubs for artistic and media types. It blends cool with old-school elegance in the same measure as any of its other venues in Manhattan, Miami or Malibu. Housed in a nineteenth-century Italian palazzo, it nestles in the centre of the twisting cobbled streets of Pera, a tiny triangle that has been the pumping heart of Istanbul's debauched nightlife since the late Ottoman era. Bounded by Taksim Square on one side, the grand boulevard of İstiklal on another and the dilapidated Kurdish neighbourhood of Tarlabaşı on the third, Pera is a web of brothels and basement drinking dens. When the Gezi Park protests kicked off in the spring of 2013, the demonstrators used Pera's maze to escape from the cops and the tear gas. One startled friend was saved from almost certain arrest by a group of transsexual prostitutes who flung open their door and pulled him inside at the last minute.

In its former life as the United States' Istanbul consulate, the walls of the palazzo were sheathed in white corporate plasterboard masking the building's exquisite eccentricity. When Soho House took over the lease they ripped away the façades to reveal a forest of faded frescos, vine flowers tangling around each other as they climb the ten-metre-high walls and ceilings. The floors and staircases are solid marble. The trimmings in the bathroom are antique brass, polished to a blinding gleam.

In the restaurant, Selin piles plates and plates of delicious mezzes towards me: a spicy, nutty paste of blood-clot red, a tabbouleh, halloumi. For the main course, we eat freshly caught sea bass that the waiters fillet in front of us. Selin's daughter and her friend, feisty and smart young women in their early twenties, join us. We talk for hours over fish and green tea about Proudhon's theory of anarchism, the erratic Turkish currency, and God.

After dinner, we go up onto the roof – the highest point of the highest hill in this part of Istanbul. From here, you can raise a glass of champagne as you soak in the outdoor swimming pool and look out over Istanbul's endless rolling suburbs to where frivolous Pera ends and Kasımpaşa – Erdoğan's steadfast loyalist home neighbour-hood – begins.

## Erdoğan's Istanbul

Kasımpaşa is a Black Sea town slapped down in the middle of the metropolis. Most of its residents are migrants from the region along Turkey's northern edge, who moved to Istanbul to make a better life. They brought their religiosity and straight-talking tough-man repu-tations with them. Today Kasımpaşa is packed with canteens serving Black Sea delicacies such as fried anchovies and a breakfast dish of gooey cheese, although Istanbul's modernisation has smoothed its grittiest edges.

Erdoğan's father, Ahmet, was one of those migrants. After moving the family to Istanbul from the Black Sea region of Rize he worked as a sea captain in the Bosphorus. At home he was a strict master, enforcing harsh discipline and instilling piety in his children. The legend goes that Ahmet's sternness could tip over into cruelty, and that young Erdoğan sold *simit*, sesame-encrusted bread rings, on the streets of Kasımpaşa to help his family survive. He appears to have been known as a moralistic yet tough child – at least if that film biography, *Reis*, is anything to go by. One scene of the film shows young Tayyip, having just performed another good deed on the streets of Kasımpaşa, drawing glowing admiration from the grown-ups but the envy of his peers. 'Why does everyone love Tayyip?' says one, clearly wishing that he could be more like the future president.

Erdoğan grew into a strapping young man, six foot tall. Away from politics, he became a semi-professional footballer, another tick on the Turkish macho credentials checklist. His nickname today is 'Uzun Adam' (Tall Guy); his rhetoric is pure bully-boy, filled with snide jokes at the expense of his opponents and solemn vows to crush perceived enemies.

It's a style his fanbase loves, because in an honour-based culture face-saving is everything. Turks, both those who support Erdoğan and others who do not, believe they have been humiliated by Europe with its hot-and-cold games. Meanwhile, the religious also feel humiliated by secularists, who thought they could keep their pious brothers and sisters out of politics simply by ignoring them.

Tayyip, their glamorous saviour, has turned their lot around and made Turkey a place where people from places like Dumankaya or Kasımpaşa can say that the guy in The Chair is one of them. Their fanaticism is partly due to religion. The doors of universities and the public sector have been opened to women who wear headscarves, and they have gratefully flocked through them. The religious high schools, known as İmam Hatips, are being expanded. New mosques are flying up everywhere.

But more than that, people of Dumankaya, Kasımpaşa, and other places like them love Erdoğan because he saved their honour.

'I am especially proud when he raises his voice against the world,' a sweetly smiling pensioner says at one of Erdoğan's huge rallies on the Yenikapı parade ground, before telling me how racist Europeans are and then in the next breath inviting me to his home for dinner. 'In the old days we used to watch our presidents bend to England and America. Now it is very different.'

## The suburbs

Rain slashes the grey plaza. I bundle some cash at the minibus driver, jump out, and race across it with my handbag over my head. The wide expanse of concrete I'm pacing over doesn't bring any feeling of space or light to this neighbourhood; on every side the traffic streams non-stop down polluted streets in a churning din. The apartment buildings and office blocks are dull, identikit, flaky concrete in pastel shades turned grubby in the places where car fumes cling. There is hardly anyone else on the pavement. I dodge huge dirty puddles as I sprint.

Çekmeköy is about as far from the postcard Istanbul as you can imagine. It's only taken me half an hour to get here from my picturesque waterside neighbourhood thanks to the minibus driver, an expert at weaving and butting through gummed-up traffic. We are still, geographically speaking, in the bowels of the metropolis; it would take us another couple of hours' drive to get through the rest of the suburbs. But the tourists never come here; even I, a committed Istanbul wanderer, have never visited Çekmeköy.

There is a glow from the centre of the square coming from a steamed-up box of glass and corrugated steel. The Evet Kafe ('Yes Café') has sprung from nowhere in the past few days, settling like a spaceship in the middle of this concrete desert. Inside the door I shake drops of rain from my hair and shrug off my jacket, which is far too light for the season. Perişah Uslu tuts and smiles when she sees my weather-inappropriate attire. I learn, to my astonishment, that she is forty-one – only eight years older than me. From her prim headscarf, her tabard and her motherly manner, I had put us in different generations.

Perişah hands me a small, tulip-shaped glass filled with strong steaming tea, and passes others to the old men gathered around the low tables. Without too much prompting she starts talking about the unpaid work she is doing for the man she adores.

'I am doing this for the future of our children,' she begins.

Perişah is a foot soldier in Erdoğan's army, one of tens of thousands of party volunteers who have flooded onto the streets ahead of Turkey's constitutional referendum. When we meet in March 2017 – three weeks before voting day – the polls put it neck and neck. Erdoğan's base and some followers of the nationalist MHP are rooting for the *Evet*, or Yes, vote, which would do away with the parliamentary system and hand executive powers to the president. Almost everyone who is voting *Hayır*, or No, to the changes is doing so because they fear Turkey will be taken another rung up Erdoğan's authoritarian ladder. The opposition are fielding a noisy grassroots campaign – but Erdoğan's guys have the resources. Posters for *Evet* have been hung on Istanbul's ancient city walls in blatant disregard for the rules banning parties from using state property for canvassing. The television channels friendly to (or frightened of) the government – and that is most of them – are running ads only for the *Evet* campaign.

In one of the most bizarre pre-referendum news pieces, TRT World, the Turkish state's English-language news channel, runs a vox pop with an apparent Erdoğan-loving cross-dresser in Taksim Square. The glamorous drag queens I've met would be appalled – the interviewee looks like a cameraman in a wig.

'I am gay, and I love Erdoğan!' he says, hammily and entirely unconvincingly.

But this is an exception, for otherwise Erdoğan's campaign team is smart. With sixteen years of experience they know how, and when, to press the buttons. The Evet Café is modelled on the traditional Turkish tea houses, where old men gather to gossip and speculate. Here, the political marketeers have created a perfect space for the faithful to reflect on everything their president has done for them.

'Recep Tayyip Erdoğan is the only hope for Europe to save itself from destruction. There is war in the Middle East, refugees, these are the most reported topics. We trust only him to stop the bleeding,' says İsmail Kaya, only thirty-five years old but a father of four and looking tired for it. 'Those people who don't like Erdoğan also don't want Turkey to develop itself. They have the same mentality as the people who don't want refugees.'

Perişah, a party volunteer for the past ten years, is firmly in charge here. As she brews the specially branded Evet tea (a blend of leaves grown in Rize, Erdoğan's home region), she tells me how she goes fishing every day at Eminönü, a central port district next to the Golden Horn. It is a man's world at the water's edge, where rows of weatherbeaten old guys line up with their fishing rods and their water-filled buckets ready for the little sardines they catch. It is an unusual place for a woman to spend her time. But Perişah tolerates no nonsense.

'Once someone cursed me, so I punched him,' she says. 'Then he twisted my finger and other people stepped in to separate us. He got the trouble for it! I have immunity as a lady in Turkey.'

Not every Turkish woman can be as free. Perhaps it is her no-bullshit personality, likely also the fact that she has brought up two children, one of whom is now serving as a soldier down in the restive Kurdish east. She has been faultlessly dutiful as a Muslim woman and gets to take her place alongside the men. She also believes Erdoğan to be the ultimate feminist champion, and insists that the AKP is the party of women's rights.

'He placed us over his head — may God be with him!' she smiles. 'Now headscarved ladies like me can go to school, be members of parties and organisations. These No campaigners, with their rucksacks and their leaflets like street sellers — they are the ones who are trying to oppress women!'

Truck driver İsmail Kaya, hardly looking like a poster boy for feminism, agrees. 'The most important thing that has changed under Erdoğan is that, before, women were invisible,' he says. 'Now, they've become our brains.'

Perişah and the men gather for a photograph and make the sign of the Rabia, the four-fingered salute of the Egyptian Muslim Brotherhood. Since Erdoğan was photographed with a startling Monty Python-esque statute of a Rabia hand on his desk, his supporters have adopted it, too. Perişah and the men have the demeanour of a group of liberal students – all entirely comfortable in this mixed-gender gathering and no one questioning that it is a woman who does most of the talking. It is not, I think, how Erdoğan's opponents like to portray his supporters.

Perişah offers me a final thought as she pours a fresh round of tea. 'We had really hard times – for so long – but now we have health-care, and medicines and comfort,' she says. 'The old Turkey is gone; we are progressing.'

Çekmeköy and districts like it are Erdoğan's Istanbul – his heartlands on the periphery of the city. Huge banners bearing his image sway limpidly between tower blocks, his face ten storeys high and his moustache stretching ten metres across. Visit Istanbul as a tourist and you will come away thinking it is a liberal, secular place where, outside the mosque-heavy historic quarter, people drink freely and transvestites mix with Syrian buskers in Pera. But those bohemian neighbourhoods are islands marooned in a sea of conservative suburbs; Çekmeköy is the real Istanbul.

The original Istanbul was very different. Until the 1950s it was a city of just under one million. The collapse of the Ottoman Empire sieved out some of its minorities, and purges of the Greek community in the 1960s and 1970s would homogenise it further. By the first decades of the republic it was a Turkish Muslim city rather than an imperial multicultural one, but its remaining residents were still cosmopolitan urbanites. The waterside districts they lived in had changed little in their layout for hundreds of years, even though they had been destroyed by earthquakes and fire and rebuilt countless times over. Istanbul lost its status as a capital when Atatürk founded the republic – but not its high opinion of itself.

'Istanbul is devious; its streets are dark, narrow and labyrinthine; its intrigues are still Byzantine; it is clogged by pessimism, eternally sponging itself in the fetid bath of its magnificent past,' wrote David Hotham, *The Times*'s correspondent, in 1962. 'No longer the capital,

A protester in Istanbul walks through tear gas clouds with a gas mask

A man recovers from the water cannons and tear gas used by Turkish police against protesters

Kurds wave a flag
of Abdullah Öcalan
as they wait for the
announcement of a
PKK ceasefire in
Diyarbakır, March 2013

Demonstrators in
Istanbul use slings and
improvised barricades
against the riot police

Erdoğan supporters celebrate his victory in the presidential elections, June 2018

Erdoğan supporters flock onto Istanbul's Bosphorus Bridge and attack surrendering soldiers as the coup attempt fails, 15/16 July 2016

Erdoğan cries during the funeral of Erol Olçok, his long-time friend and spin doctor, who was shot dead by coup soldiers on the Bosphorus Bridge

Erdoğan and former president Abdullah Gül carry Erol Olçok's coffin at his funeral in Istanbul, 17 July 2016

Opposition supporters join CHP leader Kemal Kılıçdaroğlu's Justice March from Ankara to Istanbul, July 2017

Kılıçdaroğlu walks from Ankara to Istanbul in protest at the arrest of a party deputy, July 2017

Erdoğan attends the Mausoleum of Mustafa Kemal Atatürk for an anniversary of Victory Day, flanked by former Prime Minister Binali Yıldırım

Post-coup 'Unity Rally' in Istanbul's Yenikapı parade ground, which the government claims draws a 5 million crowd, August 2016

...oğan emerges from the voting booth after calling a snap parliamentary ... presidential election, 24 June 2018

...e pictures of Erdoğan and Mustafa Kemal Atatürk hang side by side in Istanbul

[it] tends politically to be a nest of cynicism, pessimism and opposition. It can also devote itself more wholly to the pursuit of pleasure.'

But Istanbul was on the brink of change. Already as Hotham penned his flowery piece, migrants were pouring into the city from Anatolian villages. The ancient, narrow roads were choking up with motor cars. New luxury hotels of glass and steel were rising in the wealthy centre, yet at the same time squalid ghettos were spreading rapidly from the outskirts. Between 1950 and 2012, Istanbul's population grew more than ten-fold, and its area more than twenty-fold. The huge bulk of the new city was made up of unplanned, sprawling settlements built by newcomers who, culturally and aesthetically, picked up their villages and tacked them on to the edge of the free-wheeling metropolis: 'Turkish governments seem to regard any form of social housing as the thin end of the wedge of communism, so, in the true tradition of private enterprise, the poor build their houses for themselves.' wrote Hotham of the city's new appendages.

Çekmeköy began as one of the neighbourhoods known as *gecekondu*. Illegal constructions were hastily thrown up and left deliberately unfinished in anticipation of the growing family to be housed in future extensions. Photos from as recently as the 1990s show Çekmeköy as a place of jaunty self-built housing against a backdrop of green hills. The roads were dirt tracks. Sheep and cows wandered between the houses, constructed of unrendered brick and concrete. Without mains water, Çekmeköy's residents had to wait for a tanker to drive round each week to fill their plastic cisterns.

Now, only two decades on, almost nothing is recognisable. Even residents who have lived here throughout its remarkable transformation find it incredible to look back on photos from the recent past. 'When I came in eighty-seven all the roads were mud and there were no cars!' says Recep Kılıç, a fifty-year-old with a bristling moustache and hairdo like a 1980s football commentator.

We meet on a Saturday afternoon on a pedestrianised street outside a gleaming white mosque, where he has gathered with his uncle and cousins for an hours-long tea-drinking session. Today, Çekmeköy looks like any other neighbourhood in Istanbul's suburbia, with its repeating roll call of patisseries, cheap shoe shops and kebab houses. The shoppers bustling down the pavement are as Turkish a mix as you will find: women in black shawls with only their eyes and noses peeping out rush past harried-looking young mothers with bare heads and fashionable, cheaply made clothes. Engine revving and horn tooting blends into a constant background hum.

Çekmeköy has come a long way since the Kılıç family packed onto a rickety bus in the remote eastern province of Erzurum to begin the 800-mile journey westwards to their new life in the metropolis. By the late 1980s, the PKK had locked the Turkish security forces into a full-blown war in eastern Turkey. Erzurum lies north of the main Kurdish region, but the conflict played around its fringes. The Kılıç elders, themselves of Kurdish descent, saw their village's young men lured by the romanticism of the insurgency. And so, to remove their own children from the temptations of the militants, as well as to escape the region's dour poverty, they sent them to Istanbul.

'Eighteen siblings and cousins came with their families,' says Recep. 'We chose here for the cheap land. It was almost free! And we were so pleased with what we found. In Erzurum it is winter for eight months of the year. We had to dig tunnels through the snow to get from one house to another. Here, we found the forest!'

Çekmeköy at that time was a huddle of villages amid a sweep of pine forest heading north towards the Black Sea coast. In Ottoman times it had been prized hunting territory. Later, during the birth of the Turkish republic and the huge population swaps between Anatolia and Europe, Turks expelled from the Balkans settled here and began hacking down the trees to fuel the new factories that were springing up around Istanbul. The Kılıçs bought seventy houses and land from the Yugoslavs, as the Balkan Turks were then known, and opened some of the area's first businesses. Their photography studio is still trading opposite the mosque where we are sitting, catering mainly to the lower-middle-class wedding market. Pictures of soft-focus young brides in huge meringue dresses and thick make-up fill its windows.

Two things happened in 1994. First, Çekmeköy was recognised as part of Istanbul. Its population had erupted from just three hundred people in 1970 to around twenty thousand by the mid-1990s, and the villages had fused together. It was still not connected to the city's water system and the locals had to walk three kilometres home from the last bus stop, which served the nearby military base, each time they travelled to the nearest big district to go shopping. But as an official part of Istanbul it became amalgamated into the nearby municipality of Ümraniye, meaning that its residents could have a voice in the central Istanbul council. The village kiosk set up when the migrants started arriving in the 1980s became the Çekmeköy council house.

Second, an energetic young man with a growing reputation became mayor of Istanbul. Recep Tayyip Erdoğan won the city on a ticket that included a promise to build a mosque in Taksim Square. Across the country, his was one of twenty-two local victories for the Refah Party. After the 1980 coup the ruling junta of General Kenan Evren had permitted Islamist parties like Refah to combat the power of the leftists – as long as they stayed within strict parameters. An Islamist party would open, only to be shut down by the courts when it strayed too far from Turkey's secular path. Within months, another new party would spring up, usually populated by the same figures as the one that had been closed; different only in name. Now, though, the Islamist shapeshifter had moved into the halls of power. Erdoğan, Refah's candidate in Istanbul, won just 26 per cent of the vote in the 1994 municipal elections, but with the opposition parties riven by internal squabbles and corruption scandals, it was enough to hand him the mayor's office. His supporters touted it as historic.

'Kemalism is at an end,' Fehmi Koru, a columnist for Turkish Islamist newspaper *Zaman* told the *New York Times*. 'Before, people were afraid to say they were against Kemalism. Now the fear has gone.'

But in districts like Çekmeköy, the reasons why people voted for Refah were more basic. 'There were huge rubbish and water problems here,' says Recep Kılıç. 'They wouldn't have been sorted if it wasn't for Refah. When the party started winning local councils, Erbakan would call his mayors every week and ask them: "What have you been doing?"'

A thousand Anatolian migrants poured into Istanbul each day after Erdoğan became mayor – and as their conditions improved, so their loyalty to Refah deepened. The first pavement in Çekmeköy was laid in 1997, next to a park named after an army major killed by Kurdish militants. Two years later the district was connected to the city's water supplies and bus services; the streets were paved, the houses properly built. If residents had grievances, they could take them straight to the top – Erdoğan held open surgeries every Friday.

Recep Kılıç's cousin, 43-year-old Erdem Kılıç, emigrated to the United States in 1990. By the time he returned seven years later, his Midwestern drawl peppered with sharp Turkish consonants, his former village was unrecognisable.

'I couldn't find my house. I was shocked!' he says, the only member of the family left behind while the others park their teas to attend prayers at the mosque. His years overseas have, he says, changed his outlook on both Turkey and God. 'I stood on the road – it was just a mud track when I left – and I tried to see where I lived. I couldn't! Everything had changed.'

Then something else happened, which would turn Çekmeköy from a suburb into a bona fide city district. On 17 August 1999, a huge earthquake measuring 7.6 on the Richter scale hit İzmit, a city sixty miles south-east of Istanbul. The metropolis itself was rocked, with hundreds of buildings collapsing. Istanbul's solidly built ancient mosques and palaces survived; it was the newly built apartment blocks on the fringes of the city, most of them thrown up without quake safeguards, that were the worst affected. But although the earth shook in Çekmeköy, the buildings remained standing. The ground here was discovered to be solid rock – a sound foundation. The developers and new residents rushed in at an even greater speed and by 2009, with the population now above 150,000, it was granted full status as a city district in its own right.

Today Çekmeköy's population stands at 240,000 – a city the size of Derby – from almost nothing in less than fifty years. It has its exclusive neighbourhoods, where designer-clad young couples live in gated developments with swimming pools and only see the rest of the area through the smoked windows of their 4x4s. Most of the district, though, is somewhere in the middle: not rich, not poor, just riding the economic boom that Erdoğan brought to the whole of Turkey when he traded up from mayor of Istanbul to become prime minister of the country in 2003. His tenure at the top has brought a wave of both construction and credit – the main recipients being people like those who live in Çekmeköy. Rather than living with relatives until they have scraped together the money to buy a house outright, they can take out mortgages (the lowering of interest rates in 2001, followed by reform of the housing laws in 2006, opened up mortgages to the masses). Thirty years ago they came to the city with nothing; now they have cars, household appliances, and ambitions.

'One of my grandchildren is an engineer, another a teacher, another an economist!' says Sadrettin Kılıç, Recep's 73-year-old uncle. It would all have been unthinkable back in Erzurum.

Recep Kılıç and his cousins don't credit Erdoğan for all that has happened here. Erbakan was the brains, they say, and the 1999 earthquake the real trigger for Çekmeköy's dizzying rise. But somewhere along the way, it is Erdoğan who became the figurehead for this generation. His government is still ploughing money into huge development projects – the country's first driverless train line is currently being built and its terminal will be in Çekmeköy. But their love for the man who is now president is based on something more ethereal than sewage systems and train tracks.

'Now, if you go into any girls' class in an İmam Hatip school, you won't find a single male teacher,' Recep beams. In his eyes, that is progress.

## Erdoğan's elites

Back in a swerving minibus, it's only a ten-minute drive to the other side of Erdoğan's Istanbul. The sun has come out in Kısıklı, a hilltop neighbourhood of wooden villas clustered around a picturesque stone mosque. It's a quaint area despite being in the middle of a city district. The roads are narrow and winding and there are boutiques and luxury coffee shops. Erdoğan has a villa here, his private residence when he is in Istanbul. It's a very different neighbourhood to Kasımpaşa, and a world away from Çekmeköy. His daughter, Sümeyye, runs a women's organisation headquartered out of another of the area's mansions.

Kısıklı embodies the quieter side of the Erdoğan revolution. You would be unlikely to find this neighbourhood's genteel residents out on the streets in Erdoğan T-shirts, or shouting and waving their fists at his rallies. Yet the support of this moneyed, pious elite is every bit as crucial to his success as that of the disenfranchised masses. Under Erdoğan's rule, a whole new class of rich, conservative Turks has assumed the trappings of wealth the secularists once guarded so jealously: the cars, the designer fashion, the glittering weddings and the luxury homes. But they do all of it with a religious twist that makes the old elites gasp. Women buy silk headscarves from designer labels and families go on holidays in exclusive halal resorts, where not a drop of alcohol can be found on site and the women's bathing areas are completely off-limits to men. At Islamic society events, jewel-encrusted crowds make their toasts with fruit juice and then pray.

I peer into an estate agent's window on Kısıklı's high street, trying to gauge the prices of villas like Erdoğan's. They don't come cheap – a wooden mansion down the road is on sale for three million lira.

'This area has changed a lot, but construction here is limited because it's classed as a green region by the municipality,' says the estate agent, Necat Karakaş, when I go in to gently dig about the local market and what Erdoğan might have paid for his place. 'Fifty years ago people wouldn't go to the water for their entertainment, they would come here to picnic. There are few areas left like this in Istanbul. This is one of the most exclusive neighbourhoods.'

Karakaş is seventy-eight and has spent forty-one of those years running this estate agency. Stepping into it is like entering a time machine. He is settled back into a green leather chair, and the walls around him are panelled in dark wood. There is a Turkish flag on the wall, and a calendar issued by the Diyanet, the state agency in charge of religion. Through his gleaming plate-glass frontage he has a perfect view of the mosque, where Erdoğan often goes to perform Friday prayers.

'They buy,' Karakaş continues. 'There is no economic problem here in Turkey. Our economy is great. The restaurants are full, even doormen have cars, even cleaning ladies have cars!'

Maybe Karakaş avoids news from anywhere outside of Kısıklı, this old-world, salubrious bubble. On the government-controlled news channels, and in growth figures alone, the Turkish economy appears to be booming. Construction is everywhere, especially in Istanbul. A road tunnel under the Bosphorus and a third bridge over it have been opened in the past year. Metro extensions are snaking out of the old centre and spreading out into districts that didn't exist twenty years ago. But look close, and you see that everything, from huge state-funded development projects to starter-home apartment blocks for the ascendant lower middle class, is built and bought on borrowed cash. The economy is faltering by the spring of 2017, as investors start to realise that Turkey's construction-credit economy is a hollow bauble. The lira is falling in value and unemployment is rising, especially among the youth. The educated are trying to leave the country, and those without an education are left with few well-paid options outside the police force and army, which are the only employers recruiting in large numbers. Everything is getting more expensive in the shops, and the tourism industry has been decimated by terror attacks and the political unrest since the coup attempt nine months ago. The lady who comes to clean my flat once a fortnight travels for an hour in a public minibus.

The people down the road in Çekmeköy may be delighted with the improvements they have seen in their fortunes over the past thirty years, but neighbourhoods like Kısıklı have shot further out of their reach in the same time period as the gap between rich and poor has widened. Meanwhile, the mega-projects keep coming. The huge new airport to the north of Istanbul has enraged the city's few beleaguered environmentalists, who are aghast at how much of the apparently protected forest around the metropolis is being hacked down for these schemes. Most controversial of all is the one Erdoğan calls his 'crazy project' – a man-made canal linking the Sea of Marmara to the Black Sea that will run parallel to the Bosphorus and turn the European side of Istanbul into an island. Experts are warning that it will cause an ecological catastrophe, both on land and at sea.

Three weeks from referendum day, these are all big issues. I'm trying to inch Karakaş from the housing market to the economy and then towards politics. He begins talking down interesting lines, about how he has known Erdoğan since the 1970s. He is obviously both an admirer and a pious man. He credits his youthful looks – which are remarkable – on the fact that he has never drunk alcohol nor smoked, and is blessed by Allah for it. And then, suddenly, he clams up. He doesn't want to talk about politics any more, and he doesn't want me to take notes. Just in time for him, the mosque sounds the call to prayer.

'And now,' he says, 'I must go.'

My friend and I are confused by Karakaş's sudden change of mood. He had been hospitable, if not exactly friendly, and none of the Erdoğan supporters I have spoken to during the referendum campaign has been backwards about saying so – it's the people who oppose him who have reason to be wary about speaking to journalists. We try to work it out over coffee in the tea shop next door as the worshippers file into the mosque. Maybe Karakaş is full of the same mistrust of Western reporters that so many of Erdoğan's fan club harbour – only better at hiding it beneath his urbane finish. Or maybe he suddenly realised that he was about to give away too much. Whatever, we decide, on to the next. We head to Kısıklı's florist.

But our day is about to take a different turn. We are just ten seconds out of the coffee shop when six plain-clothes police officers come up to us from behind. One flashes his identity card, and we stop. I reach for my papers – passport, press card and Turkish residency – thinking this can all be sorted in minutes. But the officer doing the talking, a small guy with sharp eyes and a scar running down the length of his nose, has different ideas. He herds us towards a tea shop, sits me down at one table with an officer watching me, and my friend at another metres away. Then comes the moment when everything changes. My friend, who is six foot six tall and is asked every day whether he plays basketball, stands up to get his cigarettes out of his pocket, towering over the diminutive cop.

'*Otur!*' – Sit! – the policeman shouts suddenly. I realise immediately that he feels his masculinity has been threatened, at some kind of Darwinistic level, and that we are now here for the long haul.

An hour into our questioning, a couple of policemen lead my friend away to a nearby car. They have already called my papers in and I am sure that by now they know I am an accredited journalist. They have done a preliminary search of both of us, and asked some questions about what we are doing. I tell them everything we have done this morning. Çekmeköy and Perişah's cosy café feels like a long time ago.

'And what have people been telling you?' asks a policeman with his arm in plaster and a lazy eye.

'That they will all be voting yes in the referendum,' I reply dutifully, hating myself even though it's the truth.

'Of course they will!' says the policeman happily. 'We all love Mister President.'

I ask where they are taking my friend, and why. They pretend not to understand.

'*Gel*' – Come – says the short one with the scar, and bustles me to a separate car. Now I am panicking. I take out my phone and send a short message to another friend. I am in the back of the car and there is a policeman on either side of me, as if they think I might try to escape. The short one is looking over my shoulder as I send the message. I douse it in British slang so that if he does speak any English, he won't have a clue what I'm writing.

*Being taken by the rozzers*, I write. *Call paper if I don't msg in an hour.*
*Oh, shit*, my friend replies.

I reply with a pin of my current location.

The thing I'm terrified of is being taken over the bridge to the
other side of the city, and to the Vatan – Istanbul's central security
building. This is where the serious interrogations go down, and where
the ordeals of foreign journalists who have been arrested and kicked
out of the country over the past few months have generally started.
It is also where those of the dozens of Turkish journalists who are
now slammed in prison began. The charges are always the same,
revolving around support and propaganda for terrorist groups. But
everyone knows what their crimes really are – writing stories that
displease Erdoğan. The state of emergency after the coup attempt has
still not been lifted, endowing the police with powers to detain
suspects for up to thirty days without charge, and without access to
a lawyer for the first five.

'Where are you taking me?' I ask.

'Somewhere warm,' the short one replies. If this is meant to be
comforting, it is not. They have already ticked me off for asking
questions so close to the president's house, even though I weakly
protest that it is a public area. I wonder what roused their attention.
Did I get too close to Sümeyye's foundation when I went to take a
look at the brass plate on its door? Did the estate agent have a quiet
word in the cops' ears as he made his way to midday prayers? Was
it enough just to be a strange blonde and a beanpole wandering
around this insular, conservative neighbourhood?

Whatever has happened, my credentials and explanation have not
been enough for them. But I feel my stomach settle a little as the
car swings into a local police station after a mere ten-minute drive.
Although I don't know it, my friend has been brought here, too, and
is watching me being escorted through the entrance hall. He will
spend the next few hours fielding a litany of ridiculous questions
about me.

'What are her politics?'

'Have you been to her house?'
'Why don't you marry her?'

I am led into a small ground-floor office cluttered with file boxes, and which boasts a sweeping view of the Bosphorus. The short cop has been charged with watching me. He spends most of his time smoking out of the window, fiddling with his pistol, which is strapped into a leather holster that crosses his chest, and asking about my social and love life in Istanbul. What might have been the end of my career as a Turkey correspondent and the start of several days in a prison cell has thankfully descended into farce. By hour three, I am smoking the policeman's cigarettes and commiserating with him on his failure to find a decent woman to marry. Boredom replaces fear. I look at the seagulls skirting the water's surface and think how lucky they are to be there, rather than sitting in a cramped, smoky office making small talk.

After five hours, the policeman tells me I can go. The presidential guard – Erdoğan's elite protection – have been called, but when they arrive they say they don't need to speak with me. As I leave I catch the eye of one of them, a tall, grey-haired guy wearing a black trench coat. Then I turn back to the short cop, and take one final stab at finding out what started this whole rigmarole. Though he has become friendly, he won't give anything away.

Maybe he barely knows himself. 'Because,' he says sheepishly, 'Mister President.'

## 16 April 2017
### Referendum day

The referendum results are in: a victory for *Evet*. A last-minute rule change has shifted an ultra-fine balance: two hours before polling booths close, the electoral board announces that ballot papers without the official stamp that officials use to mark those that have been filled and validated will be included in the count, rather than disqualified. No reason is given for the decision, and four days later the head of the union of Turkish bar associations tells Reuters that there is no way of knowing how many unstamped ballots were added. No records were taken, although bar associations across the country fielded thousands of calls on voting day from observers telling them box-stuffing was happening. The provisional result shows 51.4 per cent for *Evet*, a victory margin of 1.4 million votes, and Erdoğan calls it as a win. Unsurprisingly the opposition cries foul. So too do international election monitors. Erdoğan accuses them all of bias.

My Turkish friends watch with a sad resignation. 'I told you they would never let the No vote win,' says one.

I watch the count live on state television in a tea shop in Kasımpaşa, Erdoğan's home district. The burly men playing backgammon around me seem mostly uninterested in the presenters' breathless commentary, but when the result is called, young men start speeding around the neighbourhood in their cars, blaring their horns and waving Erdoğan flags out of their windows.

Once I've filed my first story for the morning's paper, balancing my laptop on my knees as the waiters refill my tea cup, I make my way down to the AKP's Istanbul headquarters. The crowds are flocking down the dual carriageway along the bank of the Golden Horn, some on foot, others on motorbikes with flags flying, a few brave ones waving lighted flares from the windows of their cars. The trinket sellers are out already, having predicted this result. Their roadside stalls are heavy with Ottoman banners and Erdoğan scarves.

A light drizzle begins to crack the glow from the floodlights into crystalline beams of light in the forecourt of the headquarters. The party's local representatives are here already, addressing the crowd from the top of a bus. Now the economy will be bigger, they promise, the development faster, the fight against enemies both internal and external stronger. The crowd is dancing, cheering, swaying – ecstatic and, for once, happy to speak to a foreign journalist.

'Erdoğan is the most powerful leader in the world! Now no one can bring him down,' says Hüseyin Apolu, a middle-aged man wearing an *Evet* baseball cap.

At a quarter past ten, the hysteria reaches fever pitch: Erdoğan appears on the big screens from Ankara to address his people in victory.

'Today, Turkey gave a historic decision on its governance system, which has been an immemorial matter of debate for two hundred years,' he says. 'April sixteenth is the victory for all Turkey, with everyone who both voted yes and no.'

When I finally make it back through the snarled-up traffic to my neighbourhood, liberal Kadıköy on the city's Asian shore, I find another set of gathering crowds. For weeks I have watched the streets outside my door turn into a gallery of opposition artwork. Stencilled images of Atatürk have been spray-painted onto pavements and walls, and posters tacked up.

*Istanbul hayır diyor!* – Istanbul says no! – reads one, above the logo of the Turkish communist party.

*Tek adam rejim!* – A one-man regime! – says another.

Just as they did during the Gezi protests four years ago, old ladies are hanging out of their windows and banging their pots and pans in a dignified and domestic show of protest. On the streets below, the secular youth are gathering in their hundreds for a slow, funereal march. It is past midnight and the weather is miserable, but the throng swells by the minute.

Maybe Erdoğan, even if he knew what was happening in Kadıköy, wouldn't care too much. This neighbourhood, this bastion of Kemalism, has hated him from the get-go. It is a stronghold of the opposition party, the CHP, where the bars are full of rakı-drunk Turks every night and the mosques always empty on a Friday. It has voted 81 per cent for No – of course it has. It is filled with tattoo shops and hipster cafés and dog owners, not to mention those glamorous old ladies and their husbands, with their tired old ideas about what Turkey is and should be. Why should Erdoğan care what Kadıköy thinks?

But news is creeping through of bigger losses behind his victory.

The No vote has won in the three biggest cities – Istanbul, Ankara and İzmir. The first will deliver a particular sting. Erdoğan's home city, his power base, the place where his political career began – Istanbul has turned its back on him for the first time. And while the biggest opposition turnout has come from these predictable secular neighbourhoods, others have also handed him shock defeats. Fatih, the ultra-Islamic district that includes the historic Ottoman heart of the city, has voted No. So too has Üsküdar, where the upscale neighbourhood of Kısıklı and Erdoğan's villa lie. Earlier in the day, as the votes were being cast, Erdoğan's supporters told me they were expecting an 80 per cent win for the Yes vote. AKP insiders had said privately that they would be disappointed at anything less than a 60 per cent victory. Behind the smiles and the bombast, they must all be stinging now.

'Liar, thief Erdoğan!' the crowd chants as it weaves through the narrow streets. 'Kadıköy will be your graveyard, Erdoğan!'

# I 2

# SPIN

From the deck of a pleasure boat cruising down the Bosphorus, the white house looks like any of the old Istanbul mansions on the water. Intricate wooden trellis-work frames its windows and gables, and its terrace doubles as a private jetty. Peer through its windows and you might catch a glimpse of serious twenty-somethings hammering at their computers, or suited men and headscarved women locked in animated discussion around the conference table. Visitors enter through a small doorway on the other side of the building, next to a busy main road. There is little to suggest what is housed here, other than the security camera looming over the doorbell.

Erdoğan's daughter is a regular visitor to the white house. So too are several of his closest party allies, and although the president himself wouldn't be so indiscreet as to be seen here in person, his name and spirit is ever-present in its high-ceilinged rooms. Because this mansion on the water, built as a summer retreat for an elite Ottoman family before Istanbul swelled up and swallowed it, is the nerve centre of a huge propaganda operation. From within these walls a prime minister has been toppled, British politicians have been courted, and a clique of ambitious young men and women have secured their positions as the most powerful political influencers in Turkey.

## The spin operation

The Bosphorus Centre for Global Affairs, the organisation that rents out the white house, markets itself as a think tank, its mission to 'bring different groups of society together to address national and international political, social, cultural and economic issues and come up with sustainable solutions'. It hosts foreign journalists and politicians at roundtables together with Turkish government figures, and runs a plethora of 'fact-checking' websites and social media accounts in Turkish and English which, it says, aim to push back the morass of fake and biased news about Turkey – and Erdoğan – in the international press. There was plenty for the centre to sink its teeth into when it opened in late 2015.

'I had started catching lies on social media and fact-checking during Gezi,' said Fırat Erez, who was headhunted for a job at the Bosphorus Centre. Erez's background might suggest that he would have taken the side of the protesters during that spring of demonstrations against Erdoğan's government in 2013: he is an artist, a self-described atheist, and an old communist who has mellowed into liberalism in middle age. The living room-cum-studio of his house in a ramshackle old Roma neighbourhood of Istanbul is packed with flea market artefacts, and a sketch of a female nude is pinned to the fridge. But it was the conservative, Islamist Erdoğan who Erez ended up siding with during Gezi.

'At that time I saw that Erdoğan's government was opening up Turkey to the West, ending torture, enlarging our freedoms,' he said. 'They had improved transparency, started a peace process with the PKK. And meanwhile they were also under attack from all the rotten old ideologies – Kemalism, socialism. I supported Gezi when it was about saving the trees in the park. But then it turned into a kind of attack on the government, a coup or an uprising.'

As Erdoğan sent the riot police into Taksim, the Gezi protesters turned to social media to spread their message to the world. Turkey's television channels shut them out; even the independent CNN Türk broadcast a documentary about penguins as Gezi Park erupted in a swirl of tear gas. But falsehoods quickly crept into the ungoverned internet space. Some Gezi protesters claimed that the government had deployed Agent Orange in the heart of Istanbul. Others said that the cops were deliberately shooting to kill protesters. Erez started using his Twitter feed to argue back.

'And the leftists crucified me,' he said. 'All politics in Turkey is so tribal. I became estranged from my own friends, and after Gezi I started to feel that I am pro-AKP.'

After Gezi, Erez approached local AKP officials with the idea of setting up a fact-checking project. He landed gigs writing columns for *Karar*, an Islamist-leaning newspaper, and often appeared on state television as an analyst. When the Kurdish peace process collapsed, Erez turned to deconstructing the disinformation coming from the PKK's social media propagandists. His first score came when he revealed that an apparent police special forces officer, who the guerrillas claimed they had captured and paraded on camera, was actually a homeless man from the eastern city of Elazığ, known locally as Crazy Ersin. Kurds on Twitter rounded on Erez and accused him of carrying out psy-ops for Turkish intelligence. Then, in September 2015, he received a phone call from Hilâl Kaplan, a columnist at *Sabah*, a rabidly pro-Erdoğan newspaper.

## The mouthpiece

*Sabah* has the look of a downmarket tabloid and a reported circulation of more than 300,000 – the biggest on the newsstands. Its sensationalist headlines are filled with outrage at whomever it has decided are Turkey's enemies of the today. Meanwhile, *Daily Sabah* – its English-language counterpart – models itself on a dry US broadsheet with a sensible typeface and lots of text. It boasts a circulation of just 7,000, but presidential advisers and AKP politicians flock to pen opinion pieces in its pages. The articles here may be more erudite than their Turkish-language cousins, but they pursue the same themes – foreign meddling, domestic plots, and praise for the man who is battling both.

Hilâl Kaplan is *Sabah*'s star writer, a headscarved woman from the conservative fringes who made it to Istanbul's prestigious Bilgi and Boğaziçi (Bosphorus) universities. In 2004, when she started her first degree, the headscarf was still banned in the halls of learning. So too was the Islamic beard, as sported by Soheyb Öğüt – her fellow student and the man she would later marry. Kaplan had grown up in Fatih, Istanbul's ultra-conservative inner district where women roam in black shawls with only their eyes and noses peeping through. But when she walked the smart streets around her colleges, people would stare at her colourful headscarf, teamed with a modest fitted coat – the outfit that felt so modern in Fatih – and whisper. In class she covered her headscarf with a hat. Once, in the street, a drunk tried to pull the scarf off her head. It was an attitude she had lived with all her life; when she was five or six years old, she heard a Turkish man telling her covered mother to 'Go back to Iran.'

At university Kaplan joined the *Genç Siviller* (Young Civilians), a small activist group that pulled social liberals together with conservative Muslims in an alliance against the Kemalists. They wanted Turkey to democratise by breaking free of its secularist dogma and military custodianship, and the headscarf was high on their agenda. Kaplan turned it into a feminist issue, telling an online news outlet in 2010:

I believe it's wrong to associate taking off your headscarf with freedom. It's said that taking off your headscarf is liberating for a woman. However, there is a lot of media related propaganda against women who are not covered. There are moulds that are hard to fill, such as the weight and height women should be. Sadly these are set from a man's point of view and are commodifying women. This situation is increasing the amount of women suffering from conditions such as anorexia and bulimia. There are also millions of women who are having plastic surgery in order to free themselves from societies, which is ruled from a male point of view, comments etc . . . Whether she is covered or not, every woman tries to be free.

Kaplan struck an eye-catching note on the issues: personally pious, socially liberal. Religious classes in schools should be available but optional, she argued. She said her biggest inspiration was Hrant Dink, a Turkish-Armenian journalist murdered in 2007, most believe for his outspoken work on the massacres and deportations of Anatolian Christians by Turkish and Kurdish soldiers in 1915.

In 2008, in power for six years and having defeated the Kemalists over the nomination of Gül as president, the AKP started moving to lift the headscarf ban in the universities. In his speech to a party congress that year, Erdoğan hit the same note as Kaplan: 'What do they say – only citizens without headscarves can be secular? They are making a mistake falling into such segregation. This is a society of those, with and without headscarves, who support a democratic, secular social law state.'

Liberals and the religious bloc applauded. But although the law was changed to allow covered women through the doors of the universities, most rectors – largely CHP sympathisers – refused to recognise it. The CHP started a case at the constitutional court, seeking for the law to be blocked. Amid the furore, Kaplan and another *Genç Siviller* member drafted a communiqué stating that they would not be happy going into the universities with their heads covered until Turkey also addressed its problems with discrimination against Kurds and religious minorities. It was a genius move. Now, the issue was about all of Turkey's democratic flaws, not just its attitude to the pious. The court ruled that the headscarf ban should stay, but Kaplan had become a revolutionary figure. Already making a name as a newspaper columnist, her rise began.

The headscarf ban was finally overturned in the universities in 2011, in public offices in 2013, and in the police and civilian sections of the armed forces in 2016. Kaplan, meanwhile, is no longer a revolutionary underdog but a firm part of the Erdoğan establishment, sitting at the top of a new journalistic elite. Her private office in *Sabah*'s building on the European side of İstanbul comes with a sweeping view of the Bosphorus and its soaring bridge. She is often at Erdoğan's side as he travels around the world, a member of the select press pack allowed on his presidential jet.

Like the newspaper she works for, Kaplan has two sides. In English, she comes across as polite and reasonable even if it is always clear where her views lie. In Turkish, she can be abrasive, combative and often downright aggressive. Twitter is her domain – she is one of an army of pro-Erdoğan journalists who open fire on anyone who might criticise their man. She churns out dozens of tweets a day to her nearly 500,000 followers.

Fırat Erez says that when Kaplan approached him to join the Bosphorus Centre in September 2015, she sold it to him as an independent think tank, with no political links or funding. She told him that the money was coming from Medipol, a private business conglomerate with close ties to Erdoğan. But it was clear what the centre's role would be: to fact-check critical stories about Turkey in the international media, and to highlight the positive things that the AKP was doing in social welfare and for Syrian refugees. Erez was offered the position of creative director, and was made head of the fact-checking department in October 2015. He lasted in the role for just five months. In January 2016, a group of 1,128 Turkish academics signed a petition calling on the government to end the fighting with the PKK, which was mushrooming from street skirmishes into full-blown civil war. Erdoğan exploded, calling the signatories 'enemies of the state' and demanding that they be punished. The arrests and sackings started almost immediately. Erez believed Erdoğan was taking the wrong course of action against the academics, and said so openly in the office – to the chagrin, he says, of Hilâl Kaplan. Two months later, in March 2016, he was fired. Soon after, the Bosphorus Centre would soar to national notoriety.

*May 2016*
*Ahmet Davutoğlu's political assassination*

Ahmet Davutoğlu, the foreign minister with whom Erdoğan had forged Turkey's expansionist Middle East policy, was the man he handpicked to take over as prime minister when he stepped down to become president in August 2014. On paper, Davutoğlu was now the most powerful man in the country – officially, the office of president was ceremonial and non-political (Erdoğan also had to resign from the AKP when he took the job). But when Erdoğan selected his diminutive sidekick the rationale was clear: meek-mannered Ahmet might have ideas, but he would never have the balls to try to outshine Tayyip, the real rock star.

The parliamentary elections of June 2015 were Davutoğlu's first test: he must win them for the party, of course, but he must not do so with any great charisma. The AKP's final election rally on Istanbul's Yenikapı parade ground a week before the election was a double headliner. Davutoğlu spoke first, but he was just the warm-up for the main act. Erdoğan had been campaigning for the party despite his new non-political role, using endless official openings of public buildings and infrastructure projects as a thin cover to make almost daily speeches. It was a clear flouting of the rules. So too was the party's use of two fighter jets from the air force's aerobatics team, the Turkish Stars, which screamed overhead pumping out red smoke behind them as the crowds swelled onto Yenikapı.

I looked around at the merchandise stalls as I shuffled towards the parade ground with the crowd. There were the usual Erdoğan T-shirts, headscarves and banners, but though I searched high and low for some Davutoğlu tat, there was none. When he took the stage, the prime minister – who always seems to be smiling under his grandad moustache – tried to affect the booming vocal style of his boss. It was comical, almost tragic. His voice is too high and too gentle, and he winced as if his vocal cords hurt. After half an hour, Davutoğlu wrapped up to weak applause and Erdoğan came to the stage to show him how it should be done. The crowd erupted ecstatically.

The AKP had all the advantages and took the largest share of the vote, but not an outright majority of parliamentary seats. It was the first time since 2002 that this had happened – and the first time Tayyip had tasted anything less than total victory since he last lost an election in 1989. Selahattin Demirtaş's party, the Kurdish-rooted HDP, had managed to bust through ethnic identity politics to build a broad coalition of leftists and social liberals. It was roughly a partial and evolved Gezi movement, two years on. Demirtaş opposed Erdoğan's plans to introduce to Turkey a presidential system, and included gay rights in his manifesto – a first for any party in the history of the republic. The HDP took more than 13 per cent of the vote, crashing through the 10 per cent threshold that had previously kept the narrowly focused Kurdish parties out of parliament. Their gain came at the AKP's expense. In the south-east, and the liberal neighbourhoods of the western cities, street parties stretched into the night as the results were called.

Now the AKP had to form a coalition in order to govern, for the first time in its history. Davutoğlu got to work, sitting down to endless meetings with the CHP, the nationalist MHP, even the HDP. All the talks failed – Erdoğan, alien to the idea of sharing power, opposed them all. Another election was called, and in the meantime the PKK called off its ceasefire. As the casualties started mounting, the HDP's Turkish voters in the west of the country waited for the party to oppose the PKK's new violent campaign. The denunciation never came. By the time the fresh elections came round in November 2015, the HDP's support outside its Kurdish base had withered and the AKP took back its majority. June's heady optimism gave way to a glum sense that nothing ever really changes in Turkey.

Davutoğlu had finished the job and restored the AKP's majority, but his own political future now looked bleak. He had started to speak his mind and wanted to shake things up – to reconstruct Turkey's entire political structure and culture to make it more democratic and less personality-led. Everyone could see that a collision was coming.

'Davutoğlu is a bureaucrat. He is intelligent and he is hard working. But he is not a politician and he will never be,' said Davutoğlu's former adviser, Etyen Mahçupyan. An Armenian Catholic by descent and a liberal ally of the Islamist centre since the Refah Party era of the mid-1990s, Mahçupyan was perhaps the last outspoken voice within the AKP. His tenure with Davutoğlu lasted just six months, from October 2014 to March 2015. In that time he managed to repeatedly irk Erdoğan's inner circle by loudly criticising many aspects of the party's workings and policy.

'Erdoğan's advisers had decided that the person to be chosen' – that is, chosen to become prime minister once Erdoğan stood down – 'was also going to be the leader of the party. One of those advisers came to me and asked my opinion on Davutoğlu. I said I thought he would be a very good prime minister but an awful leader . . . He cannot manage the semi-corrupt rules of the politics of the party. There was also . . . a clash between Erdoğan and Davutoğlu; a mismatch of characters. Davutoğlu is full of himself. There is no doubt in his mind that whatever he says or thinks is the ultimate truth. He has this disadvantage. On the other hand, he is the most educated and knowledgeable person. Without anyone to challenge him, he started to believe more and more in himself. I have spoken to Davutoğlu many times and he said that the job of prime minister was not in reality as it was promised to him. Erdoğan could say something today and change his mind tomorrow. Davutoğlu was frustrated so he stopped giving information to Erdoğan. That pissed Erdoğan off, and it escalated . . . But what happened then was very humiliating.'

In May 2016 the AKP's executive board voted to strip Davutoğlu of his powers to appoint provincial officials. They moved while the prime minister was out of town, and when he returned to Ankara to face his party it became apparent that this was really a power tussle with Erdoğan. Following an hours-long meeting with the president, Davutoğlu then faced the AKP's executive committee. In the press conference that followed he appeared shaken and defeated. He would be stepping down, he said, at the party's upcoming congress, scheduled for just two weeks later.

'I decided that for the unity of the party, a change of chairman would be more appropriate,' said Davutoğlu as he gripped the podium with white knuckles. Ever the diplomat, he betrayed no malice towards the man who has always remained his boss. 'I will not accept any speculation over my relationship with Mr Erdoğan. We have always stood shoulder to shoulder. His honour is my honour.'

## The blog post

*Pelikan Dosyası* – The Pelican Brief, named after the 1990s book-to-film legal thriller – is 2,700 words of pure bile and intrigue, published on the most basic WordPress template a week before Davutoğlu was ousted. In florid and often opaque language, it outlines twenty-seven points of conflict between Erdoğan (whom it dubbed Reis, or boss) and Davutoğlu (Hoca, or teacher). There is the jailing of critical journalists and academics, which Davutoğlu was known to be uncomfortable with. There is the Dolmabahçe agreement to permanently end the war with the PKK, which Davutoğlu announced and Erdoğan then retracted. And there is the proposed switch to a presidential system, on which Davutoğlu is far from convinced.

'This is a fight,' the blog post ends, addressing Davutoğlu directly. 'It is certain you will lose!'

*Pelikan Dosyası* went viral on Turkish Twitter almost as soon as it was posted. Suspicion about who wrote it fell immediately on Soheyb Öğüt, Hilâl Kaplan's husband and the director of the Bosphorus Centre. He had written a strikingly similar article eleven months earlier – three weeks after the AKP's humiliation in the June 2015 elections – in the now-defunct magazine *Actuel*. Titled 'Bravo, *hocam*, bravo!' it accused Davutoğlu of betraying Erdoğan in starkly similar tones to the later *Pelikan Dosyası*. As Twitter speculated, I requested a meeting with Hilâl Kaplan.

Six days after Davutoğlu's dismissal I arrived at her *Sabah* offices. Kaplan is pale-skinned with hypnotic green eyes, and if it were not for the tight headscarf and full-length buttoned-up coats I am sure she would turn heads. Despite her reputation as an attack dog, she was disarmingly likeable and funny, chain-smoking as she told me why Davutoğlu fully deserved his cruel fate.

'They have been working together since 2009 – Davutoğlu was Erdoğan's adviser, then his foreign minister. They were working very closely and Erdoğan trusted him. Davutoğlu is not a good orator, but he has the image of a Hoca. He smiles a lot, and Erdoğan wanted him to use those qualities. But in the end he had a know-it-all attitude. Erdoğan won the November 2015 elections, but Davutoğlu acted like it was all his success . . . Erdoğan has huge credibility among the AKP. The opposition may hate him, but he has huge credibility. He is the centre of the state because he takes his power from the people.'

Kaplan dismissed the possibility that there might be another round of elections to give the public stamp of approval to whoever was anointed Davutoğlu's successor: 'Erdoğan does not like snap elections. During Gezi Park some members of the party thought it would be good to hold snap elections. He said no, we should follow the routine elections.'

To replace Davutoğlu there were three options, Kaplan told me: Bekir Bozdağ, the justice minister, Binali Yıldırım, the transport minister, and Berat Albayrak, Erdoğan's son-in-law and energy minister. All three are arch-Erdoğan loyalists.

She thought Yıldırım would get it. He had worked with Erdoğan since the 1990s, when Erdoğan was mayor of Istanbul and Yıldırım his loyal ferries chief, in charge of the passenger ships that criss-cross the Bosphorus. 'He has great support among the party's base,' she said. 'And great experience.'

Whether she was involved in Davutoğlu's end or not, Kaplan was right about Yıldırım's rise. Days later, the AKP's executive committee appointed him prime minister and leader of the party. He quickly established himself as a wider-smiling, more jovial, even greyer figure

than Davutoğlu. And as for the former prime minister, now gazing
down his path into the political wilderness?

'Davutoğlu will go on being a party member,' Kaplan said. 'He
will rebuild his credibility. He will continue a path in politics. But
I don't think he will succeed.'

## The son-in-law

Berat Albayrak, the smooth-browed, half-smiling businessman who
married the president's daughter Esra Erdoğan in 2004, was perhaps
too young and inexperienced to take the job of prime minister after
Davutoğlu's ousting. It would have been hard for the party ranks to
swallow, too openly nepotistic a move. But there was no doubt that
he was at the start of a sharp ascendant.

Albayrak is well connected, and his addition to the Erdoğan
family has allowed the president to reach out into areas beyond the
state. Albayrak's brother, Serhat, is general manager of Turkuvaz
Media Group, which owns *Sabah*, Hilâl Kaplan's newspaper, and a
clutch of other virulently pro-Erdoğan news outlets including the
shouty, caustic television news channel A Haber, always the first to
land the political exclusives. Turkuvaz's titles were once left-leaning
opposition voices, before the group was seized by the government
in April 2007 as part of a debt-collection action against the conglomerate that owned it. A year later Turkuvaz was sold at auction to
Çalık Holding, the conglomerate of which Berat Albayrak was then
CEO, a quarter of its $1.1 billion price tag being covered by a state
loan (the other bidders had all dropped out by the time the deal
was awarded). Serhat Albayrak was appointed vice-president of the
board of Turkuvaz, and instantly, *Sabah* and A Haber became
Erdoğan's principal media flag-wavers, though they failed to bring
in profits for their owners. Over the next four years, they accrued
losses of $200 million, and while international media giants
including Rupert Murdoch's NewsCorp and Time Warner Inc.
expressed interest when Çalık Holding put Turkuvaz up for sale in

2012, they backed off when they saw the books. In the end, Turkuvaz was sold in a closed deal brokered in Erdoğan's house. The buyer was the Kalyon Group, a Turkish conglomerate that is one of the major contractors for Erdoğan's huge state construction projects, including Istanbul's new airport. Kalyon set up a subsidiary called Zirve Holding to buy Turkuvaz, and the sale was approved by Turkey's competition commission in December 2013. Eleven days later, Berat Albayrak resigned as CEO of Çalık, and began writing occasional columns in *Sabah*.

Today, Turkuvaz also owns *Fotomaç*, the biggest-selling football weekly, which often carries AKP adverts in its pages, and the down-market *Takvim*, which once carried a half-page picture of me claiming that I was a British agent. That puts me in good company with other foreign journalists; those who have displeased the president's circle have often enjoyed the same treatment.

## Berat Albayrak and the Bosphorus Centre

Eighteen months after he resigned from Çalık Holding, Berat Albayrak's political career took off – he was handed an AKP seat in the June 2015 elections. The Bosphorus Centre launched two months later, in August 2015. Two months on again, in October, Albayrak was appointed energy minister, and soon it was whispered that Erdoğan was grooming him to be his heir. Finally, in May 2016, Davutoğlu as prime minister was toast.

In December 2016, the web of ties between Berat Albayrak, Soheyb Öğüt, Hilâl Kaplan, Turkuvaz and the Bosphorus Centre was revealed when WikiLeaks spilled a tranche of Albayrak's emails – a cache it dubbed 'Berat's Box'.

One email, from an executive at Turkuvaz to Berat Albayrak and dated 5 October 2015, revealed that Turkuvaz was employing a network of more than 600 people to bump up the circulation of its titles. 'A total of 200,000 newspapers are distributed every day in 79 cities and 290 districts,' the report reads. 'The distributions are mainly made in cafés, coffee shops, patisseries, restaurants, taxi stands, town halls, hairdressers, private hospitals, hotels, bus companies, various artisans, student dormitories, etc.'

An attached spreadsheet details the exact locations, and the number of each title distributed in each, the kind of painstaking detail the AKP excels in. The freebies push *Sabah*'s real circulation down to just 100,000 – fourteenth place on the newsstands, rather than first.

On 5 September 2015, Soheyb Öğüt emailed Berat Albayrak, just weeks before the launch of the Bosphorus Centre and two months before Albayrak was appointed energy minister. 'One-off costs,' Öğüt's email begins, before moving into a delightfully pedantic list.

All the details on it, from the staff to the location of the office to the furniture, match those I have seen on four separate visits to the centre. It includes £4,550 for 'high quality furniture as possible to accommodate the ambassadors, international media representatives and politicians in comfort'; a regular monthly budget for 'Foreign and Domestic Transportation; reception of guests (food, drink, transportation, gift); printing banners and booklets', and a 'vettori chester sofa set' at £777. According to the exchange rate at that time, the whole lot – from teaspoons to the director's salary – totalled £70,000 in set-up and first-month operating costs, followed by a monthly stipend of £27,250. This was the sum requested by a purportedly independent think tank of a man who was already a parliamentary deputy and Erdoğan's son-in-law, and who two months later would become a high-ranking minister.

Hilâl Kaplan, although often present at the centre and deferred to as a boss by its staff, flatly denies any official involvement. Another leaked email suggests otherwise, at least in the conception stage. Again addressed from Öğüt to Albayrak and dated 8 September 2015, this one lists the suggested names for the centre's management board. Kaplan's is at number four.

In a blog he has started since leaving the Bosphorus Centre, Fırat Erez has publicly described the *Pelikan Dosyası* and the expulsion of

Davutoğlu as a 'right-wing coup': the moment when ultra-loyalist forces in Erdoğan's court – the clique gathered around son-in-law Albayrak – took over the party, the government and ultimately the country. The trigger for Davutoğlu's banishment, Erez says, was the arrest of Reza Zarrab, the kingpin of the alleged Iranian sanctions-busting plot, in the US in March 2016. According to Erez, that was when the organisation shifted its attention away from semi-genuine fact-checking and a bit of light spin to 'building a wall against the West' – stoking Turkish public scorn towards the US and Europe, so that any allegations against Erdoğan emerging from Zarrab's trial in the near future could be dismissed as part of a plot against Turkey.

'The liquidation of Davutoğlu was very important because it was him who got the promises from the West on the refugee deal,' Erez said. 'He had pulled the date for visa-free travel in the Schengen zone earlier. Even the Turkish opposition accepted Davutoğlu's successes and prestige in the West.'

On 6 May 2016, five days after the *Pelikan Dosyası* was published and a day after Davutoğlu stepped down, Erdoğan made the first of many speeches that would turn Turkey's relations with the EU toxic, blowing up all the bridges that his banished prime minister had built. 'We'll go our way, you go yours,' the president told EU leaders. He delivered the message not in the cordial and closed-doors meetings that Davutoğlu had held with European heads of state, but in his preferred arena – in front of the television cameras and baying throngs of his fanatics in Istanbul.

## *June 2016*
### *Britain's referendum and Boris Johnson's Turkophobia*

At the other end of Europe, another difficult partner was also entering torrid waters with the bloc. Britain had always been one of Turkey's best allies in the European Union, consistently supporting its ambitions to join. Yet, when it came to the referendum on leaving the EU, Britain's Eurosceptics latched on to the possibility of Turkish membership as one reason why the UK should leave the bloc as soon as possible. Then they took that unlikely prospect and twisted it into imminent danger.

12 MILLION TURKS SAY THEY'LL COME TO THE UK! screeched one front-page headline in the *Sunday Express* in May 2016. Its evidence, revealed in paragraph two, was predictably thin. Sixteen per cent of 2,500 Turks questioned said they would consider relocating should their country join the bloc – a fast-fading possibility now that Davutoğlu had been booted and Erdoğan's hate-bombing campaign on Brussels had begun. Two months earlier UKIP had released a party political broadcast based entirely on scaremongering about what might happen should Turkey join the EU in 2020, bringing its huge and growing Muslim population with it (the blonde and furrow-browed presenter was superimposed over background footage of Istanbul, and explained that the growing crackdown on the press in Turkey meant she was far more comfortable recording her assertions about the country without actually visiting it).

Such hyperbole and misrepresentation might be expected of the *Sunday Express*, a newspaper chiefly concerned with jingoism and Princess Diana, and of UKIP, a party founded on a single nativist objective. But what about Boris Johnson, who in June 2016 co-wrote with his fellow Leave campaigner Michael Gove a letter to then prime minister David Cameron, demanding assurances that the UK would use its veto powers in the EU to halt Turkey's accession talks and block the visa-free travel arrangement – everything that had been hard-won by Davutoğlu only three months earlier? 'If the Government cannot give this guarantee, the public will draw the reasonable conclusion that the only way to avoid having common borders with Turkey is to vote Leave and take back control on 23 June,' the letter concluded.

Vote Leave, the lobbying group fronted by Gove and Johnson, also produced a billboard poster claiming that a vote to stay in the EU was akin to opening the door to 76 million Turks. It was Vote Leave who commissioned the survey that led to the dodgy headline in the *Sunday Express*. And evidence submitted by Facebook to the House of Commons committee on culture, media and sport's inquiry into fake news in July 2018 showed that Vote Leave had hired data company Aggregate IQ (a Canadian firm linked to Cambridge Analytica, the political consultancy famed for mining voters' data during the 2016 US presidential elections) to place targeted ads on the pages of British voters with the strapline ALBANIA, MACEDONIA, MONTENEGRO, SERBIA AND TURKEY ARE JOINING THE EU. SERIOUSLY. Another claimed that 'Turkey's 76 million people are joining the EU', next to a graph showing the average wages of Britons (£25,692) and Turks (£7,368). Viewers were invited to vote yes or no on whether this was 'good news'. Other ads claimed that 'Turkey's 76 million people are being granted visa-free travel by the EU', that Turkey was joining the EU, meaning that 'Britain's new border is with Syria and Iraq', and that furthermore 'We're paying Turkey £1 billion to join the EU'. A graphic showed the money flowing east from Britain to Turkey. Under repeated questioning from the committee, Rebecca Stimson, Facebook's UK head of public policy, eventually revealed that the adverts generated by Aggregate IQ were likely to have reached 'most' of the site's UK users.

Such Turk-hate proved good – perhaps winning – campaign fodder in referendum-era Britain. James Kerr-Lindsay, an academic at the London School of Economics, concluded his study of the campaign saying 'there is a good case to be made that the unfounded claims made by the Leave campaign about Turkish membership of the EU have ultimately cost Britain its own membership of the Union'.

Boris Johnson got stuck into his new role as Brexit campaigner-in-chief in February 2016, when he officially threw his considerable weight behind the Leave campaign. At first he spoke cautiously on Turkey. 'I am certainly very dubious . . . about having a huge free travel zone,' he said in March 2016 when asked about the visa-free promise that Davutoğlu had just clinched under the migrant deal.

Boris turned combative as soon as he stepped down as mayor of London on 8 May 2016 and launched his rebrand as a Leave campaigner. Ten days later, he won a contest set by the *Spectator* to write a rude poem about Erdoğan. Johnson's limerick, published in the magazine and widely circulated, refered to the Turkish president as 'the wankerer from Ankara' and suggested he had intimate relations with goats. But inside Berat's Box and the forgotten news cuttings of a time-not-so-long-ago, there is proof that Johnson is no Turkophobe.

Boris had been making a good impression on Turkey, and vice versa, since he first campaigned to become mayor of London. In 2007, on the BBC's pop-genealogy programme *Who Do You Think You Are?*, he revealed that his great-grandfather had been an Ottoman diplomat kidnapped and hanged by Atatürk's agents in 1922 for his continuing support for the Sultan. This disclosure propelled Johnson to the top of a small but prestigious group of Britons with Turkish origins (others include artist Tracey Emin and Lords member Baroness Hussein-Ece). Johnson was appointed (and remains) the president of the Anglo-Turkish Society. Almost as soon as he was voted into the mayor's office in May 2008, he took his family on a sailing holiday to Turkey's Mediterranean coast, where the local newspapers reported that he was pondering buying a villa, and he was gifted a rug, table cloth, coffee pot and cups and saucers by the mayor of the resort town of Göcek. The mayor of Istanbul, AKP man Kadir Topbaş, visited London two months later, when according to records from City Hall he presented Johnson with a 'paperweight and plate'.

Over his eight years as mayor, Turkey lobbied Johnson harder than any other country bar Qatar, sending AKP deputies, ambassadors and PR firms to his office. Meanwhile, a network of London-based Gülenists with high-level connections back in Ankara went out of their way to schmooze and flatter him. In September 2009, the Business Network, an organisation run by Gülenists to serve their supporters setting up businesses in the UK, put Johnson on the front cover of the inaugural issue of its glossy magazine with the splash THE TURKISH MAYOR OF LONDON. Interviewed inside, Boris said he believed that Turkey's entry to the EU would 'contribute enormously to a better Europe; indeed it will help recognise the considerable contribution they currently make'.

A year later, the Business Network awarded him the 'Most Supportive British' prize at its annual Most Successful Turk Awards, held in the Banqueting House in Whitehall. The glittering ceremony was attended by Ünal Çeviköz, Turkey's ambassador to the UK, and Aliye Kavaf, the Turkish families minister and previously the long-term president of the AKP's women's branch. Although Johnson didn't attend that year, he was the keynote speaker at the 2011 awards, which Turkey's deputy prime minister, Ali Babacan, and Ahmet Davutoğlu, then foreign minister, both attended.

In February 2013 Egemen Bağış – a close ally of Erdoğan, and at that time Turkey's Europe minister and chief negotiator with the bloc – travelled to London for a meeting with Johnson, who was fresh from the success of the London 2012 Olympics. The two discussed Erdoğan's own mayorship of Istanbul in the 1990s, the huge development projects planned for the Turkish city, and its bid to host the 2020 Olympics. They also talked about Johnson's Ottoman heritage, and his call for the people of London to fast for a day to get a better understanding of their Muslim neighbours' endeavours during the holy month of Ramadan. Bağış's emailed account of the meeting to Berat Albayrak is full of praise verging on eulogy for the mayor of London:

> [Johnson] wholeheartedly supports Turkey's membership of the European Union, even against those who try to block it. He does not hide his admiration for Istanbul . . . He said he was following the growth of Istanbul closely. I asked him for his support on Istanbul's Olympic bid, and he gave his support without hesitation.

Details of the conversation were immediately leaked to London's tiny but vibrant Turkish-language press, which, just a day after the meeting, reported that Boris backed Istanbul 2020. Bağış was forced to resign seven months later, in December 2013 – he was one of the ministers implicated in the Iranian gold-dealing scandal. But although he was no longer in the cabinet, he retained his seat in parliament until June 2015 and even after that has continued to serve as one of Erdoğan's most loyal enforcers within the AKP. According to Fırat Erez, Bağış was a regular visitor to the Bosphorus Centre in the months after it was founded.

In February 2015, as he entered the final year of his second term in the London mayor's office, Johnson was still full of praise for Turkey, saying that he hoped to visit the country again before he stepped down. Then, a year on, he announced he was backing the Leave campaign – and everything changed.

Although Prime Minister David Cameron repeatedly tried to assure the public that there was no imminent prospect of Turkey joining the EU, Johnson and the other Leave campaigners pumped up the threat of mass Turkish immigration in their campaign rhetoric, their claims growing more absurd and divorced from the facts as the Brexit battle reached its bloody crescendo. Theresa Villiers, the secretary of state for Northern Ireland, claimed that six hundred Isis fighters who had left Syria for Turkey would soon enjoy visa-free travel in the EU. Penny Mordaunt, later to become Britain's first female defence secretary but then a backbencher, said that levels of criminality in Turkey were far higher than in Britain (leaving it to be implied that Turkish criminality would inevitably wash over into the UK if Britain failed to exit the EU). Iain Duncan Smith, the former Tory leader, claimed that Ankara had been promised accelerated membership.

As the Brexit campaigning progressed, back in Turkey the knives were gathering behind Davutoğlu and his refugee deal was being dismantled. The numbers of migrants landing on the Greek islands started to creep up again, and Erdoğan openly threatened to open his borders unless Brussels handed Turkey more money. It all fed into the Brexit camp's rhetoric about the dangers of imminent Turkish membership of the EU, even though events in Ankara and Erdoğan's increasing Europhobia made it less likely, not more, that Turkey would join the bloc at any foreseeable point. On the same day as Johnson's poem was published in the *Spectator*, Turkish foreign minister Mevlüt Çavuşoğlu insisted that Turkey would not amend its anti-terror laws to satisfy the EU's human rights rules, effectively quashing the promised visa-free travel arrangement that Davutoğlu had won.

After the Leave campaign won and David Cameron resigned, the new UK prime minister Theresa May appointed Boris Johnson foreign secretary. His first visit was to Turkey, where he was tasked with nurturing new trade ties of the kind that would be key to Britain's economic success post-EU. In front of the press pack in Ankara, Johnson praised his Turkish-made washing machine, dismissed his *Spectator* poem of five months ago as 'trivia', and restated the UK's support for Turkey in the wake of the coup attempt, which had unfolded just three weeks after the Brexit vote.

'The United Kingdom is totally behind the Turkish people and the Turkish government in resisting the forces that tried to overwhelm your democracy,' Johnson said. 'It was great to see the way that the Turkish people responded to that challenge and of course we discussed the importance of a measured and proportionate response now to what has taken place, and I believe it's overwhelmingly important that we support Turkish democracy.'

A year later, in August 2017, Johnson was back on another sailing holiday in Turkey, his anguish at the thought of hordes of Anatolian peasants flocking to Britain apparently overridden by the lure of the turquoise coast. Meanwhile the Business Network, which had once hosted him as guest of honour at their sumptuous and influential awards ceremonies, has been driven underground in London and is now helping some of the Gülenist businessmen who have fled Erdoğan's crackdown into exile in the UK. In early 2016, it was through an intermediary on a Business Network email address that I conducted my convoluted interview with Akın İpek, one-time owner of the halal Angels Resort and the *Bugün* newspaper, after his businesses had been seized and his brother arrested. İpek remains in

London, despite attempts by Turkey to have him extradited to face charges at home.

In January 2019 Johnson delivered yet another volte-face on Turkey, claiming in a public speech that he had never raised the issue of the country's membership bid during his Brexit campaigning. By now, he had quit the Foreign Office and set his sights once more on the Tory leadership and Number 10 – and so he attempted to drop his very recent xenophobia into the memory hole. Too bad for Boris that the British press and public have memories that can reach back two years; he was immediately called out and ridiculed. But maybe we shouldn't have been so surprised at Boris's frequent changes of heart on Turkey, his fickle relationship with the Turkish community in London – or at Erdoğan's unprecedentedly laid-back response to his poem. Because Johnson and Erdoğan have more in common than divides them – they are playing from the same rulebook. For populists like them, winning is the only part of democracy that matters. It doesn't matter how many lies you tell, how often you change your ideological course, so long as in the end you take your place on the winner's podium.

*Britain and Turkey: the bottom line*

To fully understand Britain's relationship with Erdoğan's Turkey, you need to look beyond Boris Johnson to the bottom line. In its post-Brexit era, as the UK gropes for new trade relationships to keep its economy afloat, Turkey is turning into an increasingly important ally. Bilateral trade between the two countries is worth $20 billion annually in 2019, more than double what it was a decade ago. Theresa May's second visit on becoming prime minister was to Ankara in January 2017 – she flew straight to her meeting with Erdoğan from Washington, her first overseas destination. In Turkey, she signed off on arms deals worth £100 million and said almost nothing about Erdoğan's escalating post-coup purge or war against the PKK, to the horror of human rights campaigners. Diplomats insist that May aired her concerns behind closed doors.

Four months later, in May 2017, British defence companies and trade bureaucrats flocked to the cavernous halls of the World Trade Centre close to Atatürk airport for Istanbul's biannual arms fair. Here, more deals were struck between Rolls-Royce and Kale, a Turkish defence company, for a project to help Turkey produce its first indigenous jet engine. Come summer, when the British embassy in Ankara hosted its annual garden party to mark Queen Elizabeth's birthday, the manicured lawns and gilded rooms of the grand main building were scattered with adverts for iconic British brands, from JCB to Aston Martin (several Turkish cabinet members and scores of Erdoğan's advisers attended). In May 2018, even as Erdoğan spat venom against other European countries and leaders, he was welcomed in London for a two-day visit that stopped just short of full state honours. After speaking with investors and attending a string of lunches and dinners thrown in his honour by the London branches of the AKP's various lobbying groups, he went to Buckingham Palace for afternoon tea with the Queen.

The roots of the special business relationship between Britain and Turkey go back to July 2010, when David Cameron, elected prime minister two months earlier, visited Ankara. Following his meeting with Erdoğan, he gave a speech setting out the future shape of relations: 'I have come to Ankara to establish a new partnership between Britain and Turkey. I think this is a vital strategic relationship for our country. Turkey is vital for our economy, vital for our security and vital for our politics and our diplomacy . . . Today the value of our trade is over $9 billion a year. I want us to double this over the next five years.'

That speech kick-started a flurry of economic diplomacy, with much of the legwork on the British side being carried out by the City of London Corporation, the opaque administration that governs the heart of the UK's financial sector in the ancient warren of the Square Mile. It is the only part of the country over which Parliament has no jurisdiction: a unique cross between local municipality, business interests

lobby and charitable organisation that has existed for more than a
millennium. Although separate from UK government, the work of
the City often overlaps with that of Whitehall, most frequently when
it is used as a soft power arm by the Treasury and Foreign Office as
they nurture relations overseas. Other financial centres, from Wall
Street to Tokyo, may command more capital than the City of London,
but none can compete with its gothic dining halls, medieval guilds
and sumptuous costumes. It is the Lord Mayor of London (not to be
confused with the Mayor of London), successor of Dick Whittington
and wearer of fur-trimmed capes and gold chains, whom Britain sends
on trade missions to the countries it wants to impress.

Six months after Cameron's speech, Lord Mayor Michael Bear visited
Turkey together with a thirty-strong business delegation. It was his
first major foreign trip of the mayoral year, and he hosted a series of
events in Istanbul and Ankara, including a reception in the capital 'to
meet contacts working in the infrastructure and construction sectors
and "set the scene" for the discussions focused on opportunities for
UK firms', according to the official report of the Lord Mayor's visit.

Those opportunities centred around Turkey's growing public–
private partnerships (PPP) sector, the investment model powering the
wave of mega-projects that have transformed the country, beyond
recognition in many places, and defined the later Erdoğan era. Since
the AKP took power, it has built eleven new airports (and fully
refurbished as many again), thousands of miles of new roads and
railways, and extended a once-minuscule metro system across Istanbul.
Erdoğan and his ministers hail these projects as the crowning proof
of their success. Their devotees believe them.

The PPP funding model is based on the private finance initiatives
– or PFI – dreamt up by the UK's Conservative government in the
1990s, and brought to full fruition in the Tony Blair era of the 2000s.
Private companies are contracted to build and service public assets
such as hospitals, schools, waste disposal facilities and roads. The
government does not have to pay anything up front, but the state is
locked into decades-long payback agreements, under which the

taxpayer ends up shelling out many times more than the original construction would have cost due to the high rates of compound interest and non-competitive servicing deals. PFI is a classic example of instant gratification on a grand scale – the government of the day takes credit for the sudden explosion of shiny new public facilities, the debt stays off the books, and the country is left paying for it long after the politicians who signed off on it have retired. In 2015, the UK's National Audit Office found that PFI projects end up costing the taxpayer more than double what they would if the government borrowed the money directly and built them itself.

In the UK, the PFI model has been largely discredited and abandoned. After the financial crash of 2008, credit lines dried up and so did Britain's construction boom – and at the same time, the number of new PFI projects fell off a cliff. But as the rich Western economies tightened their belts, global lenders started flooding emerging economies, including Turkey, with cheap money, allowing them to launch their own construction booms, and for their governments to start toying with the PFI model. Companies that had grown rich from PFI projects in the UK started turning their attention overseas, where they marketed themselves as originators and experts in the field. In doing so they were supported by the British government, which through its embassies and consulates promotes the PFI model, the UK as a centre of PFI expertise, and British private companies that can advise on and deliver the projects to foreign governments.

Two years after the Lord Mayor's visit, Turkey's PPP projects had more than doubled. By January 2018, it had over two hundred completed or in progress, with a combined value of $135 billion – among the highest of any country in the world. The largest and most expensive of these is also the most recent – the new Istanbul airport, which opened in April 2019 after months of delays.

British companies have done well out of Turkey's PPP spree – at least partly thanks to the Lord Mayor's visit. 'The Lord Mayor met with the Minister of Transportation and Communications, Binali Yıldırım,' the report notes. 'He was keen to work with UK firms on implementing key projects focusing on maritime infrastructure (including ports), roads (including highways and interstates), rail (both urban and intercity fast rail), airports and an advanced metro system in Istanbul.'

In the wake of the 2011 visit, Turkey passed a package of PPP laws based on British legislation. Since then, Arup, a major British construction and consultancy firm that hosted the networking reception where Lord Mayor Bear met Yıldırım, has won contracts on scores of Turkish PPP projects including the new Istanbul airport. Ankara launched its £8 billion PPP healthcare scheme in 2014 following a visit, sponsored by the Foreign and Commonwealth Office, to PFI-funded hospitals in the UK for Turkish ministry of health officials and businesspeople. Mott McDonald, a consultancy firm, was appointed as an adviser on Turkey's first six hospital PPP projects. In 2015, the Treasury estimated that the scheme would be worth £2.5 billion in contracts to UK firms.

For Turkish taxpayers, Erdoğan's mega-projects – which he wields constantly as proof of his success – are costly monuments to the vanities of a leader who increasingly has little else to offer. As Erdoğan's erraticism, domestic crackdowns and foreign misadventures dent both Turkey's image on the world stage and its economy, these credit-financed projects are turning into his sole plan for sustaining economic growth and keeping his domestic image afloat. His support base, who once venerated him for keeping the rubbish collection going while he was in the Istanbul mayor's office, now cheer when they hear how his government builds the longest tunnels, the biggest hospitals and the most new roads. So, even in the face of a looming recession and a huge crash in the value of the Turkish lira, Erdoğan is determined to push on. It is unclear where the money might come from; the European and World Banks were once keen to pour money into Turkey's PPP projects, but the gush of international funding has slowed to a trickle since 2016.

It is certain who benefits as the projects keep coming. Worldwide, five of the six private construction firms with the most government contracts by value in 2018 were Turkish. The top two – Cengiz and Limak Holdings, both of them owned by pro-Erdoğan businessmen – are part of the group that won the contract for the new Istanbul airport. So too is Kalyon Holding, at number five – the conglomerate that owns Turkuvaz Media. Those figures are even more remarkable in the context of Turkey's global rankings among international contractors. Based on the value of contracts won outside their home country, Turkish firms come way down the list. In 2018 only eight Turkish construction companies made it into the top 100, with Rönesans Construction the highest ranked at number thirty-six. Cengiz Holding, the world's biggest recipient of government construction contracts, is at 225.

Back in the City of London, the blossoming financial relationship between Turkey and the UK has been sweetened with the kind of glamour and prestige that the Corporation excels in. Amid the crooked alleyways and gleaming glass towers, members of Erdoğan's circle have received a string of honours, continuing even as he has burned almost every democratic check and balance in his country. In November 2011, the Corporation held a banquet in honour of President Gül during his state visit to the UK. In April 2016, Turkey's ambassador to Britain, Abdurrahman Bilgiç, was awarded the Freedom of the City of London. It is a title first presented in the thirteenth century to individuals who were recognised masters of their trades, and allowed them privileges including the right to drive sheep across London Bridge and to be hanged with a silk rope if they faced execution. Over the years, it has been opened up: starting in the nineteenth century, you could be awarded the honour 'by redemption' if you made a cash donation to the City, and since 1996 foreign nationals can also apply. Bilgiç took advantage of both liberalisations, and was nominated for his honour by Emma Edhem, a British barrister of Turkish-Cypriot descent who has served as a City of London alderman, and had represented Erdoğan in a defamation case against the *Daily Telegraph*. (The newspaper had claimed that the AKP had taken a $25 million campaign donation from Iran; Erdoğan settled in March 2011 for an undisclosed sum.)

On the evening of 11 September 2018, guests at the Global Donors Forum awards ceremony at Mansion House – the official residence of the Lord Mayor, owned by the City of London Corporation – were startled to see Emine, Erdoğan's wife, receive an award 'in recognition of her humanitarian service'. It was given to her, the organisers said, for her championing of Rohyinga refugees who had escaped genocide at the hands of the army in Myanmar – and was well trumpeted in Erdoğan's tame media back in Turkey. 'The true owner of this meaningful award, which I will be honoured to cherish for the rest of my life, is my country, my state and my nation which respond to any cry for help no matter where it comes from and regardless of religion, language or race,' the first lady gushed as she was handed the solid glass trophy.

Back in Turkey, on the same day, Emine's husband had appointed himself head of the country's sovereign wealth fund, where the assets stripped from businesspeople accused of being Gülenists are pooled, and sent his intelligence services to Moldova to seize and extradite Turkish citizens accused of links with the group. In Ankara, a leftist Turkish-Austrian activist had been arrested on terrorism charges, prompting the Austrian government to demand a full explanation from Erdoğan's government.

A second award at the same event was handed to the Turkish Red Crescent, which describes itself as 'an auxiliary to the Turkish government', while Turkish Airlines, which is 49 per cent owned by the Turkish state, was handed the 'creative philanthropy award' for its campaign of sending cargo planes loaded with food to Somalia.

While these awards were nominally organised by the Global Donors Forum, which describes itself as 'the biannual convening of the World Congress of Muslim Philanthropists', it was at least partly the brainchild of the City Bridge Trust, the City of London Corporation's charitable fund. Minutes from the Trust's meeting on 2 May 2018 reveal that its representatives had met with the Global Donors Forum and proposed to host the September event 'as part of a range of international relationships we are building'.

London's relationship with Ankara, and its prioritisation of business over human rights and democratic values, is a harbinger of the kind of mercantile foreign policy that the UK will be pursuing in its post-EU era. But it is also a glance into the future, at how all of the old order might be forced to deal with the new. Erdoğan is no longer the only populist in Europe, and Turkey not the only country that was recently deemed to be democratising but is now backsliding. Hungary and Poland, both EU member states, are led by men with autocratic tendencies who have stifled the media and captured the judiciary. The far right is on the rise in Italy, Germany and Spain, while on the periphery of the bloc most of the Balkan states are ruled by nationalists who would be happy to drag their region back to war. Even Britain and the US, cradles of liberal democracy, have been rocked and reshaped by their own brands of populism. Europe is well beyond the point where the forces of illiberalism can be ignored or contained. As the power and influence of the old global centres declines, it is countries like Britain who are on the back foot – growing poorer and weaker and desperate for friends, and so forced to keep taking tea with Erdoğan and his ilk.

## Celebrity endorsement and political courting

Since Davutoğlu's deposition, the Bosphorus Centre has focused on producing coup-themed propaganda, launching social media attacks against critical journalists and academics and, right after the coup attempt, enlisting Hollywood wild child Lindsay Lohan as Erdoğan's chief celebrity admirer. In the autumn of 2016, Lohan made the first in a series of bizarre appearances in the Turkish media when she visited a refugee camp in Nizip, close to the Syrian border. The camp, which has since been closed, was stunning; the Syrians living there

were housed in caravan-style homes with beautifully tended patches
of garden often attached. Angela Merkel visited in March 2016 and
spoke with the delighted, grateful and handpicked residents. Every
foreign dignitary and celebrity who saw Nizip came away chattering
about how generous and hospitable the Turkish government is to the
refugees it hosts. In many ways that is true, but Nizip was not representative. Less than 10 per cent of the 3.5 million Syrian refugees in
Turkey live in government-run camps, of which many are squalid,
isolated and overcrowded.

Lohan gave interviews to the Turkish press at the Nizip camp, her
head swathed in a Turkish-style headscarf, Hilâl Kaplan at her side.
'[An aid worker] saw that my eyes lit up when I told her that her
headscarf is beautiful. She waved to me and said, come with me, I
followed her and she gifted it to me. I was so moved and touched
by this that I wanted to wear it in appreciation for all of the generosity and love I received from everyone at the camp . . . We can do
more for each other, we should do more for each other. And we can
start by giving support to Turkey which did its part in this huge
human tragedy called Syria by welcoming three million refugees.'

Next, Lohan met with Erdoğan. In January 2017 she arrived at his
palace for an audience with him, his wife Emine, and a little girl from
Aleppo who had become famous for her tweets under siege. Lohan
posted the pictures on her (now-wiped) Instagram page: 'What a dream
it is for Mr President Erdoğan and The First Lady to invite me to
their home. Their efforts in helping Syrian Refugees is truly inspiring.'

Her agent, Scott Carlsen, who was also present at the meeting,
posted his own image from the day on his Facebook page: 'Had the
chance to sit down and chat with the president of Turkey and First
Lady a week or so back. Feeling very grateful and thankful for the
opportunity,' he captioned it.

Hilâl Kaplan claimed that the Lohan connection had come about
by pure chance through a mutual connection, and that the Nizip trip
had happened because the actress genuinely wanted to meet refugees.
But the arrangement quickly turned into one of mutual benefit for

a president struggling with his international reputation and a celebrity with her career on the rocks. Soon after her visit to Nizip, a source inside a soft drinks company for which Lohan is a paid 'brand ambassador' told the press they would be donating to refugees for each order placed online. Then Lohan gave an interview at the opening of her new nightclub, Lohan, in the Greek capital Athens. She was bleary-eyed, rambling, and intent on telling the interviewer about her work with refugees.

Most fascinating, though, was her awkward insertion – twice – into the interview of an Erdoğan catchphrase, 'The world is bigger than five'. It refers to the UN security council's five permanent members – China, France, Russia, the United Kingdom and the United States – and the unfair influence the Turkish president believes they wield over the rest of the world. The phrase originated as the brainchild of a group of pro-AKP activists in 2015, and is now repeated by Erdoğan at every opportunity. It is the title of a series that began airing on the state-controlled television channel TRT in September 2017 and 'deals with global conflicts and crises as new rivalries and alliances are formed as the era of a unipolar world ends'. It is the theme of a tuneless song with a glossy video that features people from the smaller nations, angry that the five make the world's decisions without them. And it is the title of a book, *The Vision of New Turkey: World is Bigger than Five*, that Erdoğan often presents to foreign visitors at his palace.

Lohan made plenty of other pro-Erdoğan and AKP comments during her six-month love-in with Turkey, both on her social media accounts and in interviews with Turkey's pro-government press. Since then, the friendship appears to have gone quiet. When I approached her agent for comment in February 2018 he told me they were 'not doing interviews at the moment'.

The Bosphorus Centre has also shifted focus to Britain. In December 2017 it brought British Labour MP John Woodcock to Turkey to visit the country's flagship camp for Syrian refugees and to meet with interior minister Süleyman Soylu. In an interview with *Daily Sabah* at the end of the trip, Woodcock was pushed to give his views on why Turkey and its fight against Kurdish militancy is so misunderstood in the West. Back in 2015 he had sponsored a Westminster event hosted by the PYD, the political wing of the Syrian Kurdish militia, the YPG. Now was his time to repent.

'I will be painfully honest – I was ignorant back then of the scale of the links between the PYD and PKK. This visit to Turkey has reinforced my new understanding of the reality and I am keen to work with our Turkish allies to spread that understanding in the UK so fewer British parliamentarians make the mistake I did,' Woodcock said.

Woodcock listed the visit in his register of interests, as is required of every Member of Parliament for all earnings, gifts and hospitalities they receive. He estimated the cost of the four-day trip at £3,941.08, all of it covered by the Bosphorus Centre, and recorded the purpose of the visit as '[A] fact-finding delegation to meet officials and activists, to learn more about Islamist radicalisation, Isis and Turkey-Syria regional dynamics. Visited camps for internally displaced people.'

Two months afterwards, in late January 2018 – as Turkey was launching a cross-border offensive against the YPG in the Syrian region of Afrin – the centre brought another delegation of British politicians to Turkey for a three-day visit. Lord Stuart Polak, Lord David Trimble, Lord James Arbuthnot and Baroness Pauline Neville-Jones met with 'politicians, artists and businesspeople' during their stay. They visited the parliament, which had been bombed by rogue fighter pilots during the 2016 coup attempt. And, for the finale, they met with Erdoğan in his presidential palace.

All filed the trip on the register of interests, but without the estimated value of the hospitality: 'visit to Istanbul and Ankara, Turkey, 29 January–1 February 2018, to hold meetings with government, political and business leaders and build relations with Turkish civil society and media with view to deepening understanding of Britain-Turkey relations; flights, local transport, food and accommodation provided by local NGO Bosphorus Center for Global Affairs.'

Hot on the heels of those four Lords members came another – the

Archbishop of Canterbury, Justin Welby. In February 2018 he flew into Turkey and met with Erdoğan. The meeting was trumpeted in *Sabah* and other pro-government titles, but kept quiet by the archbishop's office back in London. Turkey's small band of Anglican priests said they were not told about the visit, and were 'mystified' as to why it had taken place now. Because as Welby met Erdoğan, Andrew Brunson, an American pastor who had been preaching to a tiny Protestant congregation in İzmir since the 1990s, was spending his seventeenth month languishing in a Turkish prison cell. He had been arrested in October 2016, accused of links with the Gülenists, and Erdoğan had then tried to trade him with the US government for Gülen, who was still hiding out in Pennsylvania. Weeks after Welby's visit, Turkish prosecutors announced that they were aiming to ensure Pastor Brunson received a life sentence for 'seeking to overthrow the constitutional order'. (Brunson was finally released from custody and handed back his passport in October 2018, but only after sanctions imposed by the US over the case sent the Turkish lira crashing to its lowest level in fifteen years.)

'We have no doubt that Archbishop Welby's visit was well-intentioned, though seen as deplorable,' Canon Ian Sherwood, the chaplain of Christ Church Istanbul told the *Church Times* as news of the archbishop's trip leaked out. 'The Diocesan Bishop responsible for Turkey as well as HM Embassy in Ankara could not add any further light to the situation. We look forward to hearing about it. So far we have heard not a peep.'

When I called Lambeth Palace to find out why the archbishop had made the visit, I was told he had done so in a personal capacity. Welby has not only not revealed his motives for visiting Erdoğan, but has also not recorded his visit on his Lords register of interests. John Woodcock declined to comment. Meanwhile, the other Lords members did not answer my request to ask a few questions about their visit; instead, they forwarded my email to Hilâl Kaplan.

# 13

# THE MISFITS

Welcome to New Turkey, a place where election rules bend like plasticine and news anchors lie like they breathe. Here, in this reborn country, we are transfixed by cute kitten compilations playing on the metro's public video screens, as hundreds of thousands of people are arrested above us. No one talks about things that happened a few years ago, and after a while you forget all about them. It is a place where the people in power say they are the oppressed, and where corruption comes with God's blessing.

New Turkey moves fast. Bridges, airports and mammoth housing blocks appear as you blink, and truth today can be lies tomorrow. It creeps up on the people who didn't pay close attention, because they were either uninterested or still hopeful. Police officers raid university professors and newspapers as often as they bust drug dealers and terrorists. Village boys too poor and guileless to wriggle out of military service are whipped and denounced as traitors, while powers grapple unseen around them. New Turkey has consumed the actors, writers and musicians who are blocked from almost any big commercial job unless they pay some respect to Tayyip on Instagram.

The way to the top is fast and simple: block out the naysayers, wave the New Turkey flag, and prove your allegiance as often and as loudly as possible. If Tayyip says that America is waging economic war, go out there and burn piles of dollars in the streets. If your neighbour has put up a picture of Tayyip in their window, stick a bigger one across your balcony. At rallies arrive early, shout hard and sing along to all the songs. The rewards are rich, and it is easy to prosper when you are ready to suck up lies. But across the country there are scores of others who don't fit into New Turkey, like those who crowd into the theatre of the last Jewish school in Istanbul on a dark Wednesday evening in February – singing, gossiping, and dressed up in their finest. Quietly, stoically, they are clinging on to the old Turkey amid Erdoğan's wave of social reform, bracing as New Turkey crashes over them.

## Turkey's Jews

The Ottoman Empire was a place of sanctuary for the Jews. When Spain's Catholic monarchy drove them out of the Iberian peninsula in the fifteenth and sixteenth centuries, the sultans opened their arms. Mehmet II – better known as Fatih Sultan Mehmet or Mehmet the Conqueror – had stormed into Istanbul from the east in 1453, expanding the Ottoman Empire into territories where there were already significant communities of Arabic- and Greek-speaking Jews. In the Jews fleeing the Spanish Inquisition, Mehmet's son Bayezid II saw an opportunity to turn the new Ottoman capital into an even more cosmopolitan hub. In 1492 he sent the Ottoman navy to Spain to pick up the Jews and bring them to their new home. By the start of the 1500s, the Ottoman Empire boasted the largest Jewish population in the world. Some 150,000 had settled, overwhelming and absorbing the native Jewish populations. They were granted citizenship, and cultural, religious and linguistic freedom, and were soon helping to make the Ottoman Empire the most powerful and prestigious in the world. In 1493, the same year the first group of Spanish Jews landed in Istanbul, they established the empire's first printing press.

Separated from their homeland, the Spanish – or Sephardic – Jews mashed their native language with Turkish to form a creole known as Ladino. While back in Iberia the other Spanish dialects merged to form Castilian, Ladino developed along its own path. At first it was written in the Hebrew alphabet, then the Rashi script – a Hebrew variant – and finally, at the start of the twentieth century, in Latin letters. In its grammar, it retained the characteristics of fifteenth-century Spanish.

'How does Shakespeare sound to you?' asks Karen Şarhon, the world's leading Ladino expert, in her cluttered attic office one Wednesday afternoon.

'Understandable but weird,' I reply.

'Exactly!' she cries. 'That's exactly how Ladino sounds to modern Spanish speakers.'

Karen is one of the most vocal and visible members of Turkey's Sephardic Jewish community. She attacks her wide-ranging projects with an unabating, infectious energy – at once, she is an academic, the editor of *Shalom*, a newspaper publishing in Ladino and Turkish, and the founder of Istanbul's Sephardic Centre, an archive documenting the history of the community. She also plays the female lead in *Kula 930* – the world's only Ladino-language musical.

*Kula 930* tells the story of a group of bawdy, gossipy Jewish mothers in an unnamed Istanbul suburb. Karen's character, Bulisa, goes further than the others and cheats on her husband with a fishmonger. She is caught red-handed in her nightie and forced into a shameful exile. It is a character Karen plays to perfection – so well that after the show's early performances, years ago, Istanbul Jews would approach her on the street and tell her she must behave better when she marries. Now in her fifties – well-preserved, glossy-haired, and with a face aged through laughter rather than trauma – she brings rich dashes of camp humour to her lines.

*Kula 930*'s final performance takes place on a drizzly evening in February 2018 – Karen says they will not perform it again as they have done, every few years, since the late 1970s. The audience is dying out and the venue, the Ulus Özel Musevi Okulları (Ulus Private Jewish School), is the last of its kind in Istanbul. Security is tighter than at an airport. First we pass through the heavy door in the gunboat-grey outer fence, topped with a mess of razor wire and security cameras. Then we queue to go through a second door, where security guards are letting in groups of four at a time to make sure no one slips through unchecked. They ask for our names and ID cards.

'You're not on the list,' one insists, and I dig out the text message invite from one of the actors to show I'm legit.

Once he is satisfied, our bags take a slow roll through the scanner and we walk through a metal detector way too big for the cramped anteroom. A female officer pats me down and her burly colleague asks my friend to switch on his camera to show that it works. And then, finally, we are in, and we make our way through spotless corridors, painted in relaxing colours and lined with students' artwork, to the plush theatre down in the basement. From the outside it could pass for a prison, especially with the two police cars parked outside day and night. But inside it is much like any other private school – clean, well-equipped and revelling in its history. There is a wall tribute to Atatürk in one of the spacious public areas – the school's website says its mission is to 'cultivate moral youth who follow Atatürk's reforms and principles'. Children can attend from reception right through to their Baccalauréate exams.

I have brought along a Turkish friend who is a Sephardic Jew on his mother's side ('and a Kemalist on my father's!' he tells me as we take our seats among pensioners wrapped in sparkly shawls and dapper suits). Many of them sing along to the songs in perfect Ladino. For those who don't know the language, a simultaneous Turkish translation flashes onto an LED screen above the stage. That is a modern addition: when *Kula 930* was first performed in 1978, there were still enough Ladino speakers that translation was not necessary.

'Ladino was born in the Ottoman Empire and it is dying in Turkey,' Karen says. 'I am in the last generation of native speakers. It's a phenomenon, because nowhere in the world has such a language been preserved for so long. Usually, newcomers are assimilated and the language disappears within four generations. But my father, for example, he only learnt Turkish when he went to military school!'

The Ladino language has recently been dealt several death blows, some of them self-inflicted. In the 1860s, the French-Israel Institute opened fifteen schools across the Ottoman Empire, which quickly became the choice of the Jewish elite. The language of instruction was French – and it was here that Ladino speakers had their first contact with the Latin alphabet. Such was the sustaining pull of the French schools that Karen herself was educated in one in Istanbul a century later – and today she speaks five languages with a melodic fluency that comes out best when she skips across several of them in the same sentence. But the institutes created a two-tier Jewish community, with French the language of the upper classes and Ladino the tongue of the lower.

'Until I was five, I only spoke French!' Karen laughs. 'On my first day at school I didn't understand anything. And the teachers suggested to my parents that, you know, they might want to start speaking Turkish to me at home.'

The next step came in 1925, two years after the foundation of the republic, when the Jewish community announced that it was collectively renouncing its minority rights to become full Turkish citizens. The statement read:

Seeing that the political and general order of the Turkish Republic is completely based on the separation of religion from things of this world, the Jews, who consider themselves at all times to be true children of this fatherland, cannot conceive of a situation of incompatibility concerning the application against them of separate arrangements which are in contradiction to this principle and to the duties of patriotism. As a consequence, we, as Jewish Turks, express the view that we will benefit from secular laws and arrangements as well as from all other civil laws which the republican Government intends to promulgate in reference to personal status and to family laws, and we present to the Government the feelings of our unwavering gratitude.

Under the Ottoman Empire, religious minorities had been mostly left alone to organise their affairs. Now, though, being a citizen of Turkey meant allowing your minority identity to fall within the shadow of Turkish nationalism. The Sephardic community could no longer have its own schools teaching in the Ladino language, because all schools run by the state taught in Turkish. Furthermore, all Jewish hospitals, orphanages and synagogues were now classed as independent institutions and had to pay taxes to the state.

The move was championed by Jewish intellectuals, some of whom formed a society to encourage the spread of the Turkish language among the Sephardic community. Jews were also represented among the principal ideologues of Kemalism, the political philosophy of Atatürk. One such intellectual was Moiz Cohen, born in Atatürk's home city of Salonica two years after Atatürk himself. After changing his name to the Turkified Munis Tekinalp during Atatürk's era of language reforms, he joined the CHP and the Turkish Language Association, and lobbied furiously for the new nation's minorities to assimilate.

Atatürk's views on the Jews appear to have shifted as his Turkish national project progressed. In 1923, eight months before the foundation of the republic, he stated that all religious minorities would be guaranteed protection. A year later, however, he told the *New York Herald* that the authority of the Greek and Armenian patriarchs and the rabbinate must be removed at the same time as the Caliphate was abolished. Then in 1931 he launched the 'Citizen, speak Turkish!' campaign, followed up by the alphabet reform of 1934. Meanwhile, the Jews' renunciation of their minority rights almost brought financial ruin for the chief rabbinate of Turkey, which no longer even had the authority to control and verify kosher meat.

In 1942 Atatürk's anointed successor, İsmet İnönü, levied a punitive wealth tax that hit minorities disproportionately hard. Officially, its purpose was to fill the coffers to insure against Turkey's financial ruin should it be dragged into the Second World War. In practice, it was a strike against the groups who had been promised equality under Atatürk's constitution only two decades earlier. Before the tax was imposed, the press filled with (fake) news of how businessmen from the minorities were hoarding their wealth and profiteering, even as the country was scrimping and saving lest it be forced into the conflict. The prime minister, Şükrü Saracoğlu, initially announced that the tax would eliminate foreigners from the Turkish market and put Turks in control of their own economic destiny. He was forced to retract when the foreign consulates cried out in dismay – but Turkey's minorities had no such powerful friends lobbying for them. Officials charged with gathering the tax were ordered to pursue payments at higher rates from non-Muslims, while the arbitrary assessment of incomes, which formed the basis for the taxes individuals were charged, left plenty of room for discrimination. Faik Ökte, Istanbul's finance director at the time, revealed that non-Muslims were being charged taxes around four times higher than Muslims. Payments had to be made in cash within two weeks of the notice being served, and anyone who couldn't pay was taken to a labour camp. Many sold everything they had to avoid that fate – and one study found that almost 40 per cent of the real estate sold to pay the wealth taxes had been owned by Jews, while a further 30 per cent was sold by Armenians and 12.5 per cent by Greeks. Around 30 per cent was bought by the state – and the rest by Muslim citizens.

The wealth tax had sombre implications for the whole country beyond the minorities. The liquidated businesses tended to be older and better established, and their replacements far less productive ventures run by inexperienced owners. Many quickly went out of business and the turmoil stunted the economy for decades. For the minorities the tax was devastating: around 30,000 Jews and 20,000 Orthodox Christians left Turkey in its wake.

## Pluralism à la Erdoğan

Cosmetically, Erdoğan has brought some relief to Istanbul's Jews. The president, keen to prove his credentials as a leader for all of Turkey, sends warm messages of congratulation on the Jewish and Christian holy days, and regularly meets with the country's top rabbis and priests. One Ottoman-era synagogue and fourteen churches have been restored in the AKP era – projects that have been widely trumpeted by the pro-Erdoğan press.

But such gestures look token next to the expensive facelifts bestowed on scores of the country's old mosques, and by the more than 17,000 new mosques built around the country since 2002. Meanwhile, what is said over the religious feasts is not what the masses are hearing. While Erdoğan's assurances of togetherness stroke the feathers of the rabbis with one hand, he stirs the boiling pot of Islamic victimhood with the other, nourishing a fierce sense of otherness among Turkey's pious. The sentiment can be expressed in ways that make sense for the faithful, from the top rung to the bottom. *Sabah* columnist Hilâl Kaplan believes it is the Kemalists running Turkey's universities who are keeping her husband from completing his Ph.D. The masses at Erdoğan's rallies believe it is the West – various European states and America, cyclically – that is plotting to hold Turkey back. Erdoğan's genius is that he manages to present himself as the antidote to both – as well as to problems afflicting the rest of the Sunni Muslim world.

'I thank my friends and brothers all over the world who prayed for our victory,' Erdoğan boomed to his supporters from the balcony of the AKP's headquarters on the night of his victory in the presidential elections of August 2014. 'I thank my brothers in Palestine who saw our victory as their victory. I thank my brothers in Egypt who are struggling for democracy and who understand our struggle very well. I thank my brothers in the Balkans, in Bosnia, in Macedonia, in Kosovo and in all cities in Europe who celebrate our victory with the same joy we have here. I thank my suffering brothers in Syria who pray for our victory although in a great pain, facing starvation and under bombs and bullets. I express the gratitude of my people to all our brothers and friends who gave a support to Turkey's independence struggle just like before the Independence War of Turkey.'

In Palestine Erdoğan has found his perfect cause. Until the AKP era, Turkey had been one of the few Muslim-majority states to enjoy a close military and intelligence relationship with Israel, though not without occasional scuffles. That all changed in 2009, when Erdoğan used Davos, the annual gathering of world leaders in the glitzy Swiss alpine resort, as his stage to pick a fight with Israeli President Shimon Peres.

The two men were on a panel discussing Middle East peace and Gaza, the strip of Palestinian land where the never-ending conflict with Israel plays out. Peres had just finished talking about his nation's right to defend itself – the perennial answer to anyone who questions Israel's policy of punishing all Gaza's civilians for the actions of its militants – and the moderator was wrapping up when Erdoğan launched into a diatribe:

'When it comes to killing, you know well how to kill. I think that you feel a bit guilty and that's why you have been so strong in your words. I remember the children who died on beaches. And I remember two former prime ministers of your country who said that they felt happy when they were able to enter Palestine on tanks. The Old Testament's sixth commandment says "Thou shalt not kill". There is murder here.'

Then things got really scrappy. Erdoğan batted away the hand of the moderator who was trying to stop him by nudging him on the shoulder. He continued to speak, shouting over him.

'One minute, one minute,' the president cried in accented English before switching back to his booming Turkish. 'Thank you very much – I don't think I will come back to Davos after this. Because you don't let me speak! The president [Peres] spoke for twenty-five minutes – I have only spoken for half of that.'

Erdoğan gathered his papers and stalked off stage, followed by a gaggle of press photographers and stopping only to embrace Amer Moussa, the secretary-general of the Arab League, on the way out.

Back home, reactions were mixed. Some columnists and political analysts warned that Erdoğan's outburst had shunted Turkey out of its influential position as a moderator between Israel and other Muslim states, potentially for good and with dire implications for both Ankara

and the region. But for conservative Turks his outburst was another
sign that he was one of them, thinking as they thought and refusing
to kowtow to the rest of the world. When he landed back in Istanbul
that night, thousands of supporters were waiting for him at the
airport.

TURKEY IS PROUD OF YOU! read the placards, while the crowd
waved Turkish and Palestinian flags. On the tarmac, Erdoğan deftly
turned his performance at Davos into a nationalist triumph, claiming
that he had 'protected the honour of the Turkish nation' to rapturous
cheers. 'To be honest,' he said, 'I come from politics, not from diplomacy. Therefore, I do not speak like a diplomat . . . I am not just
some leader of some group or tribe. I am the prime minister of the
Republic of Turkey. This is my character and my identity.'

In the rest of the Muslim world, support for Erdoğan's actions at
Davos tipped over into full-blown adoration. Hamas, the Palestinian
group that rules Gaza and whose armed wing is listed as a terrorist
organisation by many Western countries and institutions, praised his
'courageous stand'. 'The Palestinian people, the resistance and Hamas
salute you, Erdoğan,' Hamas's leader Khalil al-Hayya told a rally the
same day as the Davos incident. A newspaper in the Gulf ran a front
page saying that Erdoğan had exposed the Israeli 'holocaust'. Iran's
former president Ayatollah Akbar Hashemi-Rafsanjani thanked him
during Friday prayers.

Meanwhile Israel flailed to smooth things over, desperate to maintain relations with one of its only Muslim allies in the region. So too
did the Turkish army generals, who were unwilling to let a rabble-
rousing prime minister wreck the valuable military alliance with
Israel they had spent decades nurturing. But things were about to
get much worse.

On 21 May 2010, Israeli commandos stormed a Turkish-flagged ship
sailing towards Gaza. The *Mavi Marmara* was carrying pro-Palestinian
activists brought together by *Insan Hak ve Hürriyetleri ve Insanı Yardım
Vakfı* (the People's Law and Freedom Assistance Association, or IHH),

an Istanbul-based Islamist charity with links to the Muslim Brotherhood and given the tacit blessing of Erdoğan. Their aim was to break the Israeli blockade on Gaza by entering its waters. When Israel sent in its crack troops to stop them, pitched battles broke out on the *Mavi Marmara*'s decks. Nine Turkish citizens were killed, and Ankara severed relations with Israel.

It took Turkey and Israel six years to recover from the incident; during that time the rusting hulk of the ship remained moored in public view in Istanbul, still hung with its protest banners. When the two countries formally reconciled in June 2016, the survivors paid the price. Turkish prime minister Binali Yıldırım agreed to a deal under which Israel would 'donate' $20 million to the relatives of the dead, all of whom were Turkish. But for other survivors who were on the ship, all legal actions against the Israeli state were blocked. Alexandra Lort Phillips was one of thirteen British citizens midway through a case against Israel in the Turkish courts when the decision was made. 'I understand that they have to do diplomacy, of course political processes carry on, but I don't feel that the Turkish government has taken other victims into account,' she told me as she contemplated the sudden end of the years she had spent in the Byzantine Turkish justice system. 'To dismiss the case at this point just seems wrong.'

Among Erdoğan's home fanbase the half-hearted reconciliation has barely been noticed. He is still the unbending champion of Palestine, the man who stood up to Peres – but that comes with consequences for Karen Şarhon. 'All over the world, whenever something negative happens with Israel, the Jewish community is always associated. They think the chief rabbi has power enough to phone the prime minister of Israel and say, "Hey! Come on! What are you doing? Don't do that any more!"' she says, good-naturedly rolling her eyes at the idiocy of it all even though she has been putting up with it for decades.

Karen receives daily death threats from militant pro-Palestinians who believe the Jews of Istanbul are to blame for policies made in Jerusalem. The majority of Turkey's remaining 15,000 Sephardic Jews live in the city, mostly in upmarket neighbourhoods where they might be mistaken for secular Muslim Turks. They largely keep out of politics, but still politics finds them. And so, to enter the offices of *Shalom*, on a small side street of swish bars in a neighbourhood packed with boutiques and plastic surgeons' offices, I also have to go through security. Paranoia? Probably not. In November 2003, fringe Islamist militants drove truck bombs into two of Istanbul's biggest synagogues, killing twenty-three people. It only takes one of the poison-pen writers to be a committed terrorist.

'They need to realise that we are Turkish – full-fledged Turkish citizens! People don't realise that we are not Israeli,' Karen says. 'It's not something specific to Turkey, I'm sure it happens in France, too. But obviously because of the affiliation with the Arab countries, they probably say . . . you know. Plus now, with the radicalism going on . . .'

## The LGBT *community*

Karen will take new citizenship, but she will not leave Turkey – after all, she can trace back her roots here further than most other citizens. 'No way!' she affirms, and resettles herself in her chair to prove her point.

In 2015 Spain and Portugal both began offering citizenships to Sephardic Jews. So many have taken them up that the system has snarled and the waiting list now stretches to several years. But it is a golden opportunity in uncertain times. Karen's daughters have accepted the offer so that they can study in Europe. She applied so that she might visit them more easily. She has never been tempted to take up her right of Israeli citizenship.

But people are leaving. The intellectuals. The youth. The comedians and the freaks, and the people who do not fit Turkey's increasingly conservative mould. Not so long ago Istanbul was a haven for gay and transgender men and women from across the Middle East, who had been forced from their home countries by bigotry and war. In

June 2013, during the last spurts of the Gezi protest movement, I joined the Istanbul Pride parade surging from Taksim Square down İstiklal, sweating and dancing under the humid canopy of a fifty-metre rainbow flag. An estimated 100,000 people attended that year, and the police stepped back and let them do their thing. Two years later – after Erdoğan had taken the presidency – the Istanbul governor banned Pride at the last minute, saying it was inappropriate to hold it during the Islamic holy month of Ramadan. Each year since then, Pride has been banned on various pretexts, and the numbers showing up to have a crack at it anyway have slid. In 2017 it was a huddle of just a few hundred who gathered in the side streets off İstiklal, determined to at least shout a few slogans before the police steamed in with their tear gas and batons.

When it came to it, no one was willing to stick up for Turkey's LGBT community – they didn't fit into anyone's tribe. When the Kurdish-rooted HDP made equality for all sexualities a part of their manifesto for the June 2015 elections, it was a first for any party in the history of the Turkish republic, but from the trenches it looked like a sop. Ümit Manay, a poet and gay activist in Diyarbakır, told me in early 2016 how he had endlessly requested meetings with the party's local branch. He wanted to discuss the precarious position of gay and transgender people in what is still a deeply conservative city, and push to get funding for a crisis shelter. They ignored him, preferring to focus instead on issues relating to Kurdish identity. Elsewhere, as Turkey's rhetoric grows more stridently Islamist, the people who once partied at Pride and in Istanbul's gay clubs are now hiding themselves away, trying to keep a low profile. In July 2016, as Erdoğan's Turkey spiralled high on the fervour of having beaten the coup attempt, a gay Syrian man was murdered and beheaded on his way to his job as a hospital cleaner. His flatmates, who are also gay, said they received messages threatening the same fate. A month later a transgender woman was raped, tortured, murdered and then beheaded by a mob in a conservative suburb.

The bravest men I have met in Turkey are the three gay Syrians who stood in front of the hundreds-strong audience at the Istanbul Film Festival in February 2018, to speak about the documentary that had just been screened. *Mr Gay Syria* follows them as they prepare to compete in the 2016 Mr Gay World championships in Malta. All had been cast out by their families and abused in the street. Some were married with children in an attempt to cover their sexuality, and coming out meant losing their kids. With the double blow of being refugees and gay, they know they can expect little help from the Turkish government or authorities. 'I see a lot of sadness in this room,' one of the main protagonists told a support meeting at the beginning of the film.

Most LGBT refugees in Turkey have registered with the UN for resettlement, and hundreds have been offered asylum in Europe and Canada. But for those who remain, the future looks bleak. In November 2017 the governor of Ankara banned all screenings, festivals and events organised by LGBT associations. The producers of the Istanbul Film Festival rebranded *Mr Gay Syria* as *Halepli Berber* (*The Barber of Aleppo*) so that it might slip past the government censors.

Some days it feels like almost everyone I speak to is plotting a way out. There is the highly educated and privileged young media graduate with flawless English who is planning to go to the UK to work in a restaurant kitchen. My friend thinks about rediscovering his Sephardic roots so that he can take Spanish citizenship. When the Turkish government launches an online genealogy service in early 2018 that allows Turks to search for their heritage, it is so popular it repeatedly crashes. Many are checking for pre-Republican roots that might let them claim a second passport. A website portal that lets prospective students search for overseas opportunities reports that its traffic from Turkey tripled in the days following the coup attempt.

But then I go to the other side of the country – sometimes just a few hundred metres down the road – and people tell me how Turkey is now stronger than it's ever been. In Çekmeköy and the other *gece-kondu* districts, in the rallies at Yenikapı and in the villages of Rize they say that Erdoğan has broken the country's old shackles, and nothing will be the same again. It can be disorientating to shift between the two worlds too quickly; like stepping through Turkey's looking glass. But even as some Turks grasp at chances to leave, desperate to jump before the country they once knew disappears, there are others who are desperate to come and live the New Turkey dream.

## New Turks: the Ahiska

When I ask Nesibe Aliriza about her plants, her defences drop and she transforms from a shy housewife into a woman with passion in her ice-blue eyes. The blooms are everywhere in her spotless, two-storey house; lined up against the French windows to absorb the winter sunshine, on small side tables dotted around the front room, and tucked into corners that would otherwise look bare and cold. Out in her front garden there are the skeletons of rose bushes that will burst into colourful flower when the spring comes. To the back of the house, a spacious plot has been turned and fertilised ready for planting with tomatoes and squash. 'These plants are like my children,' she says, her eyes shining and the gold teeth on her bottom row glinting as she smiles. 'I love them, I can't describe it. I've kept plants ever since I was a young girl. But I had to give most of them away before I moved to Turkey.'

All that Nesibe managed to bring from her garden in Ukraine were some tulip and rose bulbs. Now they are nestled in the earth of Turkey – her new home – readying green shoots to burst through the soil.

Nesibe and her family – her husband, two children and four grandchildren – have always thought of Turkey as the motherland. They are part of the Ahiska Turk minority, who originated in Georgia but endured a seven-decade exile across the former Soviet Union after they were deported east by Stalin in 1944. The Aliriza family were among around ten thousand Ahiska Turks who eventually settled in eastern Ukraine after the Soviet Union collapsed in 1989. Life was good there, the family say – until the area was annexed by Russian militias in 2014. A missile fell through the roof of their house in the town of Donetsk and exploded in the kitchen, and they went to stay with relatives nearby. It appeared that they were set to endure another era as refugees on the run. Then, a saviour stepped in.

'In May 2015 we heard that Recep Tayyip Erdoğan was going to visit Kiev [the Ukrainian capital]. So we asked for an appointment with him through the Turkish embassy,' says Nesibe's husband, Vahid. 'He agreed, and he promised us he would look out for us and provide homes for us in Turkey. We were thrilled! He had welcomed us and spoken to us as if he was one of us, not a president.'

Six months passed, and Ukraine's Ahiska Turks wondered if the promise had been forgotten. But in December 2015 they got a call from the Turkish embassy in Kiev and were told to pack their bags. They were to be resettled in Turkey, and were allowed to bring just thirty kilograms of luggage each. Their flights were booked for Christmas Day of that year.

'We didn't expect it to happen, we couldn't believe it,' says Vahid, his Turkish bearing a hint of a Russian accent and his skin white from a lifetime in colder climes. 'For the past seventy-three years we have been on the road, no state has ever stood up for us. But with Erdoğan, we are like a child holding the hand of its mother.'

Most of the Ahiska Turk newcomers have been resettled in Üzümlü, a small village in the mountainous eastern Anatolian province of Erzincan. The area is famous for its waterfalls, ski runs and little else. When I tell my friends in Istanbul that I am going there, they are impressed – it's a part of the country few Turks have seen. The airline steward who checks me in tells me I am the first Briton he has ever seen flying there.

It is only 250 miles from Erzincan to the Georgian border, and even less to the place where tens of thousands of Turkish soldiers died in the snow as they fought the Russian army over the winter of 1914. The struggle between the two great powers for this unforgiving patch of the Caucasus was the prelude to the Ahiska Turks' tragedy; when Turkey's borders were drawn after Atatürk's war of independence, their lands fell outside the boundaries. Although they continued to identify as Turks, speak Turkish and practise Islam, the Ahiska Turks now lived in the Soviet Union.

For two decades they stayed in their homes. But in November 1944 Stalin – by birth a Georgian himself – decided that they were a threat to his empire. The entire Ahiska Turk population – 115,000 people including the elderly, women and children – was rounded up onto cattle trains and deported to central Asia.

I sit around a plastic table in the sharp sunshine of a November morning in Üzümlü with Vahid Aliriza and two other Ahiska Turk men. The light sparkles on the snow capping the mountains either side of the village, and when I suck in the air it is cleaner than any I have breathed in Turkey. It is warm enough in the sunshine to sit outside and bright enough to warrant sunglasses, and as we drink round after round of strong tea I get a richly textured personal lesson in the history of the Ahiska Turks. Fifty-two-year-old Vahid and 64-year old Hasan Bahtiyar tell the second-hand stories of what their parents endured on that journey. Ilham Raminov is seventy-seven; the story he tells is his own. He has been happy and vivacious up to this point, but now his blue eyes, with their burst of yellow-green around the pupils, are clouding.

'I was three or four years old when the exile happened, and I was on the train. Since it was a train built for livestock, there were no toilets. We had to make holes in the floor, but still many of the women were too ashamed to go to the toilet in front of everyone else. Some of them died because of that. Every time someone died, the soldiers would throw them off . . .

'After the exile, my mother lived forty days and then died. My father passed away in Azerbaijan in 1986. He had moved there because he wanted to be as close as possible to his birthplace.'

Around eighteen thousand people are estimated to have died on the trains, their bodies discarded along the route. At the time no reason was given for this crime against the Ahiska Turks, and the deportations were covered up by the Soviet leadership. The dead were never given proper burials; their families were never allowed to return to find them. But in 1968, fifteen years after Stalin's death, the Ahiska Turks finally got an official explanation for their suffering. It was revealed that Stalin, drunk on his victories on other Second World War fronts, had planned to declare war on Turkey. The Ahiska Turks were potential enemies within.

The families of all three men ended up in Uzbekistan. The Ahiska Turks were not allowed to live in the cities of the regions they were exiled to, and under Stalin's harsh communist system no one was allowed to practise religion. But their parents and grandparents kept up the rituals of Islam in the secrecy of their homes, and continued to speak Turkish between themselves. 'After the exile it was forbidden for us to even travel from one village to the next, so relatives didn't see each other for decades,' says Vahid. 'Once Stalin died the laws started relaxing and we began getting together again. Then in 1989 there was the second exile.'

As communism collapsed, many of the Soviet Union's ethnic groups began turning on each other. For decades they had been told they were all socialist brothers, but the heavy hand of the system had simply been holding a lid on bubbling tensions. A scrappy civil conflict between the ethnic Uzbeks and the Ahiska Turks, who had lived alongside each other for forty-five years, began with a random street fight in which an Uzbek was killed. Some believe it was started by the agitation of the KGB, although that has never been proven. Huge violent riots broke out, leaving up to 1,500 people dead and the houses of thousands of Ahiska Turks torched.

The Soviet army moved all the Ahiska Turks to a military base, where they held them for seventeen days before evacuating them to western Russia. Most had nothing apart from the clothes they were wearing. Everything they had accumulated over two generations in Uzbekistan – their houses, their cars and their land – was lost. Over the course of the following year, the whole population of ninety thousand Ahiska Turks fled the country. Some moved on to Azerbaijan – and some went to eastern Ukraine.

For almost three decades, life was good there. The Ahiska Turk elders sent their representatives to the Ukrainian towns first to check if they would be welcoming, and found the Ukrainians open to anyone who had suffered under Soviet Russia. The Ukrainians, too, had been appallingly treated by Stalin, both deported and starved in the early years of his reign and forbidden from speaking their own language. Vahid Aliriza, who was twenty-three when he arrived in Donetsk with his parents, attended the police academy and joined the Ukrainian force. If it had not been for the outbreak of the conflict in 2014, he would have been happy to stay there for the rest of his life.

'I wouldn't have wanted to move from anywhere,' he says. 'Even though Donetsk was not our motherland, we treated it as if it was. We are so thankful to the Ukrainians. They have never treated us badly.'

But the new war with Putin was the last push they needed to return to the place they had always thought of as home. In the weeks before their journey to Turkey, Ankara sent bureaucrats to Donetsk to take full notes on all the families who would be coming. When they arrived in Üzümlü they were taken to houses fully furnished and with the heating already turned on – a literal warm welcome awaited them. Inside, workers from the local council handed over the keys to their new homes. To date, more than three thousand Ahiska Turks have taken up Erdoğan's offer of resettlement in Turkey, with all of them guaranteed fast-track citizenship. Plans are underway to extend the right to all the quarter of a million Ahiska Turks scattered around the world.

Vahid takes me to his home, a doll's house-style villa in the middle of a sprawling new estate. All the others in this neighbourhood are exactly the same: four steps leading up to a small front porch, dun-coloured walls and white trim around the large windows, red pitched roofs at a gentle gradient. The village mayor tells me they were built by TOKİ, the Turkish state housing company, in early

2015 but had lain empty since then; no one had been interested in buying them, even at the bargain price of 125,000 lira (around $40,000) spread out in fixed instalments over twenty years. Üzümlü's geographical isolation probably has much to do with it. Though it is beautiful, there is little to do here. Most young people eventually leave for the big cities.

Now, New Üzümlü is being filled with newcomers. A sign at the entrance to the estate points the way to the Ahiska Market, set up as a franchise by the canny owner of the general store in the village centre. Boxy Ukrainian-plated Ladas dot the edges of the near-silent boulevards. Vahid and Nesibe have made a few changes to their house in the nearly two years they have been here; in addition to the plants, they have repainted, and bought a small television and some knick-knacks. On the walls they have hung framed pictures of the men they thank for their new life – Erdoğan and his old prime minister, Binali Yıldırım.

There was little to adjust to here, they tell me – they had even clung to the Turkish cuisine during their years in exile. But the creamy homemade pasta with chicken and sweetcorn that Nesibe serves for lunch is different to anything I have tasted in Turkey before. Vahid admits that he still prefers Ukrainian vodka to Turkish rakı.

For Nesibe, a true believer, the biggest thrill of being in Turkey was hearing the Islamic call to prayer for the first time in her life on the day she touched down in Erzincan. Although they had been able to practise freely all the time they lived in Ukraine, there were no mosques in Donetsk and they prayed in each other's houses. At Ramadan, the Alirizas hosted all their friends and neighbours. Now, for the first time in their lives, they have their own neighbourhood mosque. 'We arrived here on a Friday and we all went to the mosque together and prayed,' Nesibe says. 'Even the children were really curious. It was overwhelming for me – that is when I thought, *This is real!*'

Although she had prayed five times a day in Ukraine and studied the Qur'an to the level where she could recite it by heart, Nesibe had never felt she could show the full trappings of her faith in Ukraine. She kept her head uncovered there and wore knee-length skirts. 'There was no law against covering, but people would look at you in a funny way,' she explains.

On the flight to Turkey, she covered her head with a hijab for the first time. She has never left the house without it since she arrived, she adds – though I can tell by the few strands of hair peeking out from the Lycra headband underneath that she is not fully used to wearing it. When I meet her she is wearing a soft lilac headscarf with a sleek fitted black dress embroidered with flowers around the sleeves. It covers her fully to the ankles and the wrists and is both more conservative and more delicate than the usual Turkish pious style. The Turkish government has laid on free Qur'an courses for the Ahiska Turks, she tells me – but she needs no educating about her faith.

Religion aside, Vahid says they are doing all they can to fit in. It is what the Ahiska Turks have been doing for the past eight decades, after all – their way of self-preservation in each new and uncertain resting place. But this time, they feel they have come home for good.

Vahid sips his tea and offers plates full of delicious cakes as his cute grandchildren, fluent in Ukrainian and picking up Turkish at a rate I both admire and envy, play around his feet. One day they, like the other young Turks of Erzincan, will head for Istanbul, sucked into the metropolis where all the politics and intrigue and money is made. And if their loyalty to the man who has given them this new life is sealed, he can rely on their votes in the future. Here, there and everywhere, Erdoğan is picking up new voters. Three hundred thousand Syrian refugees have been promised Turkish citizenship, while the requirement to learn the Turkish language has been dropped. Since 2014, Turkish citizens living abroad, the majority of them AKP voters, have been allowed to cast their votes in Turkish embassies in their adopted countries. As his margins, always ultra-fine, slip further towards the centre line, such numbers could be enough to nudge elections.

This new Turkish family is content to simply stroll the mountain paths and settle in to the country that has embraced them. 'There is a blessing in everything that happens, and this is our blessing,' Vahid says. 'We are trying to set a good example here so the gate will be open for all the others.'

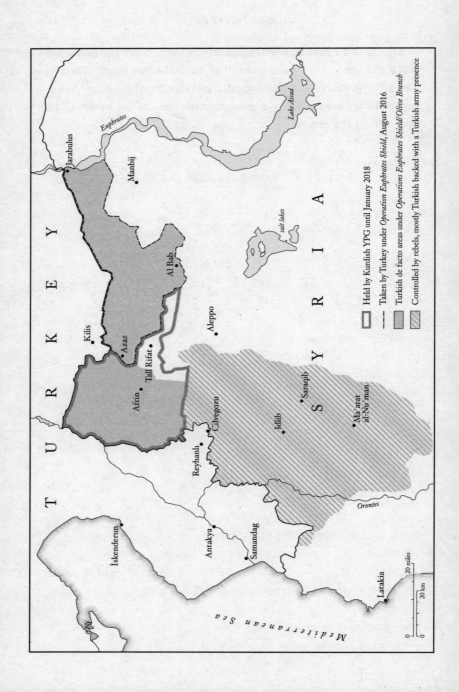

Held by Kurdish YPG until January 2018

Taken by Turkey under *Operation Euphrates Shield*, August 2016

Turkish de facto areas under *Operations Euphrates Shield/Olive Branch*

Controlled by rebels, mostly Turkish backed with a Turkish army presence

TURKEY

SYRIA

Euphrates

Lake Asad

Jarabulus

Manbij

Al Bab

Kilis

Azaz

Tall Rifat

Afrin

Aleppo

salt lakes

Saraqib

Idlib

Ma'arat al-Nu'man

Cilvegozu

Reyhanli

Orontes

Antakya

Samandag

İskenderun

Latakia

Mediterranean Sea

0    20 miles

0    20 km

# 14

# THE WAR LEADERS

*Atatürk's end*

At five past nine in the morning, every 10 November, cannons
fire and air-raid sirens sound across Turkey. Public offices blast
out the national anthem and a mournful drone of foghorns strikes up
from the ships on the Bosphorus. Almost everyone stops what they
are doing and stands to attention.

It's an eerie sight, none more so in the sprawling metropolis of
Istanbul where the drivers, who would generally run over their own
grandmas to get somewhere a little quicker, stop dead and sound their
horns. But it is nothing compared to what happened on 10 November
1938, when Mustafa Kemal Atatürk, the great Republican reformist,
breathed his last in an upstairs bedroom in the annexe of the Dolmabahçe
Palace. You can still visit the room today, left exactly as it was the day
he died with a Turkish flag draped over the bed. Strikingly small and
cold compared to the cavernous gold-trimmed halls of the palace proper,
Atatürk lay dying here for weeks. Nightly bulletins from the palace
detailed the exact statistics of his condition – temperature, pulse,
breathing rate. A team of eight doctors attended him, and on some
days he seemed to be improving. But the liver failure nurtured by his
years of copious consumption finally overwhelmed him.

'A great soldier, statesman and leader has passed away,' ran *The Times*'s editorial on Atatürk's death:

Of the leaders whom the new Europe has seen emerge from the confusions of war and revolution, none has accomplished more, none faced greater difficulties. He leaves his people in mourning. It may at least console them to know that in this country [Great Britain] their old opponents, now turned friends, who admired him as a redoubtable enemy, deeply regret the loss that Turkey and Europe have sustained in the death of so great a man.

Six days after Atatürk died, the Dolmabahçe Palace was opened to the public to allow Turkey to pay its respects. Within three days, an estimated 400,000 had filed past his body. Twelve people were killed and thirty injured as the huge crowd waiting outside the palace surged in panic on the evening of 17 November. Inside, the mood was different. His ebony coffin, surrounded by torches, was draped in the Turkish flag and garlanded by wreaths placed by İsmet İnönü, his prime minister and now the new president, representatives of the army and of the Kamutay, the national assembly.

'The dimly lit room is most simple and impressive,' wrote Jack Kernick, *The Times*'s correspondent, who joined the throng. 'Army officers, officials, students and long queues of men and woman of all classes and ages, filing past, bow silently, deeply moved and whispering prayers for the dead leader. The former King Amanullah of Afghanistan arrived this morning and passed incognito among the people, praying before the coffin.'

Ten days after his death, the body of Atatürk was transported to Ankara, the village he had turned into his capital. His coffin was loaded onto the Turkish battleship *Yavuz* and carried to the port of İzmit, escorted by HMS *Malaya* and ships from the French, Russian, German, Greek and Romanian fleets. In İzmit his coffin was transferred to a train. At Ankara station a team of soldiers placed the coffin on a howitzer carriage drawn by six black horses and escorted by six

generals with drawn swords on either side. In contrast to the mael-
strom that had engulfed Istanbul, the streets of Ankara were deserted;
residents had been cleared from the whole route to the Kamutay,
where a fifty-foot platform had been constructed and painted red.
There Atatürk's body lay overnight, as still more mourners filed past
to pay their respects. 'Orderly and generally mute,' Kernick reported,
'but there is obviously much stifled emotion.'

Atatürk's funeral was held the next morning under a steady late
autumn drizzle. Soldiers wept as they saluted the passing cortege.
Detachments of foreign armies marched in procession behind the
Turks, with the British turning out the largest, of 266 troops including
60 Royal Marines. Fifteen generals flanked Atatürk's coffin, while
another walked behind carrying a cushion pinned with the leader's
medals from the war of independence.

At midday the procession reached the Ethnography Museum, where
Atatürk's coffin would lie as it awaited its final home. Chopin's funeral
march – a symbolically European choice – accompanied this final
ritual. It would be played by the military band at the funerals of all
Turkish soldiers and statesmen for the next seventy-nine years.

## Erdoğan: from civilian to commander in chief

Erdoğan – the born orator, masterful politician and genius populist
– has never made a natural commander in chief. Photos from his
military service in the early 1980s show a gawky, startled-looking
young man cradling his rifle awkwardly. From time to time since he
first became prime minister the pictures have been printed in the
Turkish press, but he is always careful not to over-egg it. After all,
he is the scourge of the military, the man who ascended the ladder
of Turkish politics promising to quell the might of the generals. His
power lies in his image as a civilian, not as a man in uniform.

But post-coup Erdoğan is wearing his commander-in-chief role
with aplomb. When the state of emergency was brought in, allowing
the government to rule by decree, it was the security services Erdoğan

turned to first. He brought the gendarmerie and the coastguard under the control of the interior ministry, alongside the police, and announced that he would be closing down the military high schools – the training grounds of the officers since the Ottoman era. The military was brought under the command of the ministry of defence, and its ministers now – for the first time – sit alongside generals on the appointments council.

Two days after the revolt almost three thousand soldiers were dismissed. The government insists that only 1 per cent of the military took part in the coup. But the raw numbers hide the real story: the sackings and arrests soon hit the top brass hardest. Within four days, 110 generals and admirals were purged from postings all over the country, many of them places the coup did not even touch. And, as Erdoğan's military clearout continues, even those who were not in the country on the night of 15 July find themselves in his sights.

In November 2016 I was approached through an intermediary by a group of Turkish officers who were on NATO postings in Europe as the coup played out. They had all been recalled to Turkey following the putsch, told they would be reassigned. But when those who heeded were arrested within days of their arrival, the others decided to stay in Europe and claim asylum. Overall, 650 of the 900 Turkish officers in NATO had been purged by the time the officers contacted me. Stripped of their positions and denounced as traitors, they decided to break their silence.

'I and my colleagues were informed that our tours were terminated unexpectedly and called back immediately to our country with no further explanation,' said one officer, who had been based in the UK and used the pseudonym 'Kemal'. 'I learned that criminal investigations were made in my former residence address in Turkey. They cancelled my diplomatic passport. I requested many times with phone calls and written official letters that the Turkish armed forces inform me about the bizarre order and charges against me. However, Ankara was earless to my appeals and gave no response. I contacted many lawyers in Turkey but none of them undertook defending me before the courts. Under these circumstances I refused to go back to Turkey as I feared I would be imprisoned with no fair trial, since this is exactly what has happened to all the other members of Turkish military who went back. I know at least thirty-two of them personally.

'A few weeks after I was called back to Turkey, I learned from the Turkish official gazette on the internet that I, along with 15,653 other people, no longer had a career, any income or any benefits. I was dismissed disgracefully. I was declared guilty of terrorism and punished without any evidence, accusation, legal process or opportunity to defend myself. They destroyed my honour and reputation by a smear campaign, which accused me of being a supporter of a terrorist organisation.'

As Erdoğan's purge of NATO officers continued, General Mehmet Yalinalp, a former Turkish brigadier general and NATO's former Deputy Chief of Plans of Allied Air Command, sent an email outlining his concerns to General Curtis Michael Scaparrotti, the current Supreme Allied Commander Europe of NATO Allied Command Operations:

As the historical purge of thousands of military personnel takes a faster speed, I and my Turkish colleagues observe a considerable rise of ultra-nationalist, anti-western sentiments within our military and throughout our state departments. It is very worrying to witness that some of the newcomers from Turkey to NATO have a radical mindset, some question the values of NATO and even hate western organisations while holding pro-Russia/China/Iran sentiments. For example, during an address to tens of Turkish NATO officers, a Turkish SNR from a NATO Headquarters located in Southern Europe, stated that there are currently two types of Turkish officers within our military; those who are loyal to NATO and those who are loyal to their nation, and the cleansing is carried out to replace the former ones.

Erdoğan's post-coup new guard are a mix of loyalists at the start of their careers, and ultra-nationalist officers purged under the trials spearheaded by Gülenist judges and prosecutors back in the 2000s, who have now been brought back into the fold. Meanwhile, as the military is decimated, the president is building up an alternative security force, the Polis Özel Harekat (PÖH, or special operations police). Founded in 1982, while Turkey was still ruled by General Kenan Evren, leader of the 1980 coup, the unit's broad remit is anti-terror operations. It recruits from the regular police force, sucking in the fittest, the bravest and the most dedicated, and trains them in purpose-built facilities in Ankara and the Aegean province of Balıkesir. In the mid-1990s, the head of the unit was entangled in a scandal that blew open the links between the police, the government and the right-wing mafia. In 2010 Erdoğan instructed the interior ministry, which oversees the PÖH, to restructure it and pour more resources in. At that time, the number of PÖH officers stood at around 11,000, armed with machine guns, assault rifles and pistols.

When the Kurdish peace process broke down in mid-2015, it was the PÖH who led the fight against PKK insurgents in the towns and cities. The government announced in March 2016, eight months into the renewed violence, that it was increasing their numbers in response to the terror threat. When I arrived in ruined Kurdish towns where curfews had been newly lifted, I would find their graffiti – PÖH KOMANDO – scrawled all over the rubble.

In April 2016, three months before the coup and as the terror attacks were at their height, I saw the heavily armed PÖH officers in their camouflage uniforms and black balaclavas on patrol in Istanbul for the first time, guarding the entrance of the high-class Marmara hotel in Taksim, the heart of the city. Around the same time, a military adviser told me that Erdoğan was 'giving the PÖH everything, turning them into Tayyip's boys'. The military was growing concerned with the creeping power of the police, the adviser added, and they believed that the conflict in the Kurdish south-east was being used as the PÖH's training ground. On the night of 15 July the special units proved their mettle: the PÖH's Golbası head-quarters in Ankara was bombed by rogue pilots, while the special forces officers led the fightback against the revolt. A few months later, one of Erdoğan's advisers let slip to me that the PÖH and their gendarmerie counterparts, the Jandarma Özel Harekat (JÖH) are the only officers the president trusts. By 2017, their combined numbers had soared from 11,000 to an estimated 40,000, an almost four-fold increase in seven years.

Their rigid selection process – recruits must be able to run 2.5 kilometres wearing a ten-kilogram backpack in less than fifteen minutes – precedes gruelling training. Over sixteen weeks, the PÖH recruits are schooled in advanced weapons techniques, sharpshooting, waterborne operations, reconnaissance and intelligence gathering, and hostage rescue. At least some of that training is now conducted by a shadowy private company with close ties to Erdoğan.

SADAT, a defence and consultancy firm, was established by a group of former Turkish military officers. It is headed by Adnan Tanrıverdi, a one-star general who was forced into retirement in 1996 due to his suspected Islamist sympathies. He told journalists at the time of SADAT's incorporation in 2012 that the company's focus would be African and Middle Eastern countries, and that it would provide services solely to state institutions, not private individuals. A banner on SADAT's website warns that it will only work with the police and militaries of 'friendly countries'.

SADAT says it operates in twenty-two Muslim nations, although it doesn't specify which ones. The world map on its logo shows Turkey coloured in red, and in Islamic green a swath from Senegal in the west to Kazakhstan in the east, taking in the Arab peninsula and some isolated areas: Bangladesh, Indonesia, the Muslim parts of the Balkans. Independent reports claim that SADAT won a contract in 2016 to train the Saudi Arabian air force, and bid unsuccessfully for one with militias in Libya in the same year. Meanwhile the company's brochure, which I picked up from its stand at the biannual Istanbul arms fair in May 2017, reveals a deeply anti-Western undertone to its mission. The bald, grey-bearded Tanrıverdi writes in his introduction to the company:

Today, there are around seventy 'International Defence Consultancy Companies' which are controlled by Western developed countries and which provide service in parallel to and under the control of the armed forces and foreign affairs departments of their countries.

All of these companies were established after the World Wars I and II, and they operate in around 20 Muslim countries. They carry out the most confidential military operations of countries in which they operate. Some of them instigated the civil war in their countries by means of impudent leaders while some turned neighbouring Muslim states into enemies, some were left behind to maintain control in lieu of the armed forces that retreated after the actual occupation and some others committed major crimes against humanity with their 'hired armies'. As a result, this area was used as a means of exploitation by the West. This situation imposes a liability on us. When other countries needed a military personnel, who have served for the long-established Turkish armed forces with a view to build, train and arm the military forces of friendly and Muslim countries, we were encouraged to form SADAT in order to ensure such countries find the opportunity which organises skilled and idealist commissioned and non-commissioned officers who will attach primary importance to the national interests of such countries and the joint interests of the World of Islam.

In August 2016, a month after the coup attempt, and as the pro-Western generals were being purged from the Turkish military, Erdoğan appointed Adnan Tanrıverdi as his senior adviser. Then, seven days later and with the military chain of command brought firmly to his heel, Erdoğan launched a war he had long been craving. Turkish special forces and allied Syrian rebels stormed across the border into Syria, with the stated aim to drive Isis out of the borderlands. Days earlier, though, the Kurdish YPG had taken the nearby town of Manbij from Isis. In fact, Erdoğan was desperate to stop them advancing further towards the Turkish frontier.

The generals had always blocked Erdoğan's demands to put troops on the ground inside Syria, fearing they would get sucked into the quagmire. But the Second Army – based in the eastern city of Malatya and in charge of protecting Turkey's southern borders – was stripped out entirely in the post-coup purge. General Adem Huduti, the commander of the Second Army, had previously briefed junior staff officers that he would not allow an incursion into Syria; he, and all of the 150 brigade commanders along the Syrian and Iraqi frontiers, were arrested and decommissioned straight after the coup attempt even though there had been almost no coup activity in those areas.

Erdoğan's Syria operation in August 2016, codenamed Euphrates Shield, progressed quickly in its early stages and then became bogged down. The town of al-Bab, twenty miles inside Syrian territory, was an Isis stronghold where the jihadists had dug in. Turkish forces had not managed to set up a fully functioning supply line from the border by the time winter descended. The death toll began to mount: almost every day, another Turkish soldier died. On the bloodiest day, fourteen were killed in one bomb blast on the outskirts of al-Bab. Days later, Isis released one of its glossy, gruesome propaganda videos. Two Turkish soldiers captured by the group in the borderlands in 2015 were shown shaven-headed and dressed in orange jumpsuits, shackled by their necks and caged. They were dragged out on leashes by an Isis fighter who was also Turkish, forced to read statements to camera, and then doused in petrol and set on fire. 'If you do not retreat, this will be the end of all your fighting soldiers,' the Isis terrorist, who called himself Abu Hassan al-Turki, told the camera.

The Turkish government claimed the video was a fake, and shut down Twitter and YouTube for four days to stop it spreading. They never made any more official statements, wagering that it would be quickly forgotten. They were right; few Turks I mention the video to today have even heard of its existence.

## Afrin: Erdoğan's second Syrian war

In January 2018, Erdoğan launched Operation Olive Branch, his second war in Syria. This time his target was a mountainous pocket of Kurdish territory in the north, just across the border from Antakya and controlled by the YPG.

Erdoğan's already shaky relations with the militia and its US backers had crumbled further in the wake of Operation Euphrates Shield. Once Isis was routed from al-Bab the Turks started threatening to attack nearby Kurdish positions. There were minor skirmishes, and the Pentagon eventually made clear that it would not be withdrawing its own special forces from that area. Erdoğan had hoped the flaky new US president, Donald Trump, might be talked into withdrawing support for the YPG. Trump mulled it over, and then went in entirely the other direction, upping US weapons shipments to the Kurds.

Erdoğan had threatened a full-scale attack on the Kurds near al-Bab but knew it would also lead him into a fight with US troops – and an internecine NATO clash of the type last seen in the Cyprus war of 1974. Instead he swung his guns on Afrin, an isolated bubble to the west of the Kurds' main territory, where the YPG was supported by Russian advisers in early 2018, but not by American special forces. The YPG occasionally fired rockets into Turkey from Afrin and killed soldiers at the mountainous border posts, provocation enough for Erdoğan to claim they posed a threat to the nation. Public support for the Afrin operation was overwhelming, despite the fact that, again, Turkish soldiers were dying almost daily. In Istanbul, shopkeepers plastered on the walls of their arcades billboards cheering on the Turkish troops, and thousands turned out to the funerals of slain soldiers, turning them into nationalist PR events for Erdoğan's second war. One month in, with the offensive progressing less rapidly than hoped, the government announced that it was sending PÖH and JÖH officers to join the fight alongside the army in Afrin.

*

Erdoğan declared victory in Afrin on 18 March 2018, Çanakkale (Gallipoli) Day, the 103rd anniversary of Atatürk's defeat of British and Australian troops in 1915. In his speech to mark the day the president deftly blended past and present, while praising again the might of the Turkish people during the coup attempt and throwing in a swipe at the Kurds' Western backers: 'They assumed that our nation no longer had the courage and perseverance which it had back in Çanakkale. They assumed this nation no longer harboured that unwavering faith. However, they saw in every step they took that they were mistaken.'

The YPG's fighters had eventually turned and fled from Afrin when they realised the US bombers would not be coming to save them. What could have turned into a months-long urban battle had come to a thankfully swift end – although almost a hundred thousand civilians fled and hundreds were killed. It is a scandalous mark of the scale of Syria's plight: a small city's worth of people are forced out of their homes and it barely registers with the rest of the world. Kurdish activists worldwide shrieked that no one was protesting about Afrin because no one cares about Kurds. But that was not what was behind the ghastly silence. Seven years in, more than half of Syrians have been displaced. No one protested about Afrin because ruined towns and the sight of their fleeing inhabitants have become ubiquitous and mundane.

Forty-five Turkish soldiers were among the dead. The news filled with jingoism, mock-ups of the battle and stories of the army's glorious progress through the mountains of north-western Syria. 'More towns cleaned of terrorists!' the headlines screamed. 'More terrorists neutralised!'

'The notion of martyrdom is very different in Turkish culture,' said Faruk Loğoğlu, when I asked him how many Turkish soldiers must die before public opinion started turning against Erdoğan's Syrian adventures. 'Look at the parents of those who lost their lives in the operation. They are saying that if they had another son they would send them there, too. It is what I called a magnetic effect of the *Mehmetçik'* – 'Little Mehmet', like the 'Tommy' of the British army. 'Everybody lines up behind that notion. And the media keeps pumping this.'

The government issues Turkish journalists with a list of exacting instructions for covering the battle. They are not to trust any reports of civilian casualties coming from the Kurdish enemy, either armed or civilian – those are just 'information pollution'. Neither are foreign journalists' reports to be trusted. Anything that might 'boost the morale' of the other side is banned, and readers and viewers should at all times be reminded that the operation is being conducted with newly hatched, Turkish-produced weaponry. It is a campaign designed to stir nationalist hearts. Since the coup attempt, Erdoğan has repeatedly claimed that Turkey is embroiled in its second war of independence.

The international press corps is less easy to control, but the government's media men are trying. We get a flurry of emails from the press ministry, pictures with big green ticks and red crosses showing us how the YPG is circulating fake images of dead children. The main press spokesman reminds us that if we try to embed with the Kurdish militia, we will be enabling the terrorists' propaganda and will be treated accordingly. In lieu, a select few foreign journalists are offered escorted trips across the border with a Turkish government minder, to look at the sprawling refugee camps Ankara is bankrolling and meet families who insist they are pleased the Turkish army is coming. Two weeks into the offensive, a handful of us are called to a meeting with İbrahim Kalın, Erdoğan's spokesman, in Istanbul's Yıldız Palace.

I ask Kalın a question about the prestigious Turkish Medical Association and its venerable board, all of them arrested and jailed for an anti-war statement published on their website during the first week of the Afrin operation. The statement, which did not mention Afrin, nor Kurds, nor Turkey, was the broadest kind of protest against harm to civilians. The Turkish government says it was terrorist propaganda.

'Did they oppose any other war before this one?' Kalın asks. 'No. So they are doing propaganda for the terrorists.'

I try arguing back, but Kalın's wall comes down. More than three hundred people have been arrested for criticising the Afrin operation, yet they find little sympathy from their countrymen. The war is an easy sell. The YPG's affiliate, the PKK, have wrought chaos in eastern Turkey for three decades. Many of its leaders and fighters in Syria, especially in the earliest days, were Turkish Kurds. The group spits hatred into Turkey from its Syrian stronghold and occasionally fires rockets across the frontier. Even secular Turks who are no fans of Erdoğan's government fill their Instagram pages with patriotic messages and pictures of Turkish soldiers kissing the flag.

Having fended off an hour of journalists' questions with the skill of a practised propagandist, Kalın switches seamlessly into another role – that of impeccable host. The Yıldız Palace is where the Ottoman sultan Abdülhamid II holed up as his empire withered and a group of scheming officers, including Mustafa Kemal, plotted a coup. Abdülhamid had been scorned and ridiculed in the early Republican era as a man who squandered both the power of the empire and his own dignity. The liberalising Ottoman reforms of the 1830s were rolled back under his rule, and he dissolved the empire's first parliament and constitution. He tried to muzzle journalists who criticised him and cartoonists who made fun of his big nose. He saw conspiracies everywhere – some of them real. Several revolutionaries tried to assassinate him, and in the end he was unseated by the officers.

But Erdoğan has rehabilitated Abdülhamid II. A glossy, hagiographic TV series, *Payitaht*, tells a version of his story so whitewashed it makes historians cringe and swear. Erdoğan says Turks should watch it to learn about their history. In the same week that Kalın called us to the Yıldız Palace, the new Turkish establishment marked the centenary of Abdülhamid's death. All of the sultan's descendants – who had been banished from the republic but have recently returned to the limelight singing Erdoğan's praises – were handed Turkish citizenship.

To celebrate, we are served a halva dessert that was a favourite of the sultan's. And as I suck the sugary paste from the spoon, I study Kalın's intellectual face and wonder what he really believes.

## Turning war into myth

Erdoğan's transformation to war leader is complete; in April 2018, two weeks after the Turkish victory in Afrin, he tours the troops at the Syrian border. Herds of celebrities are bussed in, including Ibrahim Tatlıses, a much-scorned singer of kitsch Arabesque music who tends to attach himself wherever power lies. Erdoğan wears the same uniform as the rank-and-file soldiers who line up to shake his hand – drab camouflage, with his name patch over the right breast.

There are murmurs of early elections. The presidential and parliamentary ballots are scheduled to be held in November 2019 – seventeen months from now – but the economy is sliding fast and Erdoğan knows it. After the next polls, Erdoğan's reformed constitution will take effect. Whoever gets the keys to the presidential palace will be running an almost one-man show. And right now, in the wake of Afrin, Erdoğan is riding a wave of nationalist fervour.

'They are now playing the war game,' Faruk Loğoğlu tells me. 'They are using this entire episode for domestic political reasons.'

The Erdoğan-hating part of the country snickers; the president still looks out of sorts in fatigues. He wants to be the war hero, that is clear – but he will never quite pull off the look. The jokes are made behind closed doors, at private dinner parties that are becoming more uproarious as Turkey's public spaces become small-talk-only zones. These days, my friends and I use code words when we discuss Turkish politics in cafés or on buses. In the evenings, within the comfortable circles of close friends, all the words and thoughts and hilarities we have been bottling up all day spill out. With the dearth of reliable information about what is going on in the country, and all the TV channels churning out minor variations on the government's line, we delve into conspiracy thinking. It's probably not true but it could be – and we can never know either way.

'OK! I have a new theory,' says a friend. 'How about if, actually, the coup succeeded and now the army is in charge and keeping Erdoğan drugged all the time, and wheeling him out for these appearances!'

We laugh until we cry.

Ayşe Hür, a radical Turkish historian, is unimpressed by Erdoğan's latest rebrand. When I meet her in a bustling diner on Taksim Square, three weeks after Erdoğan's appearance in military garb, she has just been slapped with a five-year suspended prison sentence for tweeting that she doesn't believe the PKK is a terrorist group. She must have known it would land her in trouble.

'What am I meant to do?' she says with a broad white smile. 'Somebody asked me what I thought of the PKK and I answered. Somebody asked me and I felt obliged to give a correct answer. Maybe I am a Christian. Even if somebody asked and there was a police officer next to me, I would answer. People are asking questions and I am a historian journalist writing about historical issues. I should answer these questions correctly. It is my job.'

Hür has made her name by questioning all of Turkey's dodgy historical narratives, from the Kemalists' pseudo-scientific explanations of who the Turks are, to the details of what really happened during the ethnic massacres of 1915. She calls it the history of the underdog – and back when Erdoğan was the underdog, he was a fan. These days, when she has turned her attention to unpicking his own fabrications, he is less enamoured. In a witty internet post from April 2016 titled 'Erdoğan's ignorance in history and numbers', Hür forensically examines occasions when the president has played with the facts. In 2003, he claimed that during the Battle of Manzikert (modern Malazgirt) in 1071 – the Ottomans' first victory in Anatolia – the invading Sultan Alparslan had cried out 'Allah, Allah!' and 'Vatan!' (Motherland). Hür pointed out that the word 'Vatan' did not exist in the Turkish language until the eighteenth century, and even after that there are no recorded instances of it having been cried out during battle.

Then, in 2011, Erdoğan claimed that his great-grandfather was one of the seventy thousand Turkish soldiers who had frozen to death while battling Russian forces in Sarıkamış in the winter of 1915–16. 'My great-grandfather, Rize Güneysulu Kemal Mutlu, was martyred here in Sarıkamış and embraced with the mercy of Allah. My elders told me, saying: They wrapped around their guns, we saw they had been martyred by freezing, and their tears were like dripping drops of ice,' he said at a speech to commemorate the tragedy.

Armed with the name, Hür went to the defence ministry archives and scoured the five volumes of records about the Sarıkamış martyrs. The name of every soldier who had died there is listed. Erdoğan's great-grandfather was not among them.

The questions that really haunt Erdoğan, following him around like a mosquito he can't swat away, are the ones about his university degree. He claims to have graduated from the business school at Istanbul's Marmara University in 1981. In 2014, as he prepared to run for the presidency, members of the opposition started to investigate. The president must, by law, have a university degree. The university's rector produced a degree certificate. But Marmara was only incorporated as a university in 1983, and the questions linger on. Ayşe Hür is one of the people looking into it.

'I asked Marmara University [to look at their records] but there is an internal law and they cannot give information. I applied to the university asking if there was ever a student by that name there. The answer was that it was about somebody's private life and that they could not answer,' she says. 'Then I asked a teacher's assistant at the university to check. He researched and it was not there. Erdoğan does not exist in any documents. When I started to research a guy who claims to have taught Erdoğan there was no information and when asked more was told that it was private information. That guy is now living in Israel. I contacted him and asked how Erdoğan was as a student. It turned out it was also bullshit. There are no school friends, no photos. The research assistant found a yearbook from 1983. There is a Recep Tayyip Erdoğan but with no photo. On another yearbook he is not mentioned.'

Those awkward old military service photos also throw doubt on Erdoğan's claims about his degree. In them he is wearing the uniform of a private – entry level for non-graduate enlistees. If he had indeed graduated, he would likely have been an officer.

The furore died down as Erdoğan's grip tightened, and these days the degree question is just one on a list of many others that no one talks about. There are the tapes of Erdoğan and his son discussing how to hide money that emerged during the December 2013 Iranian gold-dealing scandal. Or Erdoğan's second son – not Bilal, the model child who organises traditional Turkic sporting events in the mass rally ground at Yenikapı, but Ahmet, who killed classical musician Sevim Tanürek in a hit-and-run car crash in 1998. Ahmet Erdoğan did not have a driver's licence and was found guilty on three of eight counts in his first trial. At appeal he was cleared and flew to America. No one talks about him now. Younger Turks might never have heard of him.

It's little surprise, then, that Erdoğan is also trying to rewrite the history of coup night and its aftermath. The people injured on the night, and on his side, are given the honorific title of 'Gazi' (meaning veteran – and also bestowed on Atatürk), and cards that allow them free public transport and other benefits. Now, he is trying to recast his own military history, claiming status as a war hero – not as the timid, cowardly man remembered by those who knew him in the early days.

'He is trying to identify himself with Atatürk and make them the same,' says Hür. 'People do not get it. In Çanakkale the Allies were attacking us. He is saying the same about Afrin even though we are the attackers there. There is false information. Nobody knows about the true genuine facts.'

In a small glass case in the museum at Anıtkabir you can find the first known portrait of Atatürk.

It is an expressionist oil painting depicting him from mid-chest upwards, face turned slightly to the right, his eyes fixed on a point

in the distance. It was crafted in October 1915 by Austrian artist
Wilhelm V. Krausz, famous for his depictions of Ottoman and Austro-
Hungarian rulers. At the time Mustafa Kemal was an Ottoman officer
fighting in the First World War; six months earlier he had won the
glorious victory over the British and Australian troops at Gallipoli,
establishing himself as a hero among his men and the Turkish press,
who dubbed him 'the saviour of the Dardanelles and the capital'. But
back in Istanbul, Atatürk did not receive the praise he believed he
deserved. His relationship with Enver Paşa, the general who led the
Young Turks, was fraught. Mustafa Kemal considered Enver incom-
petent, and Enver viewed Mustafa Kemal as an upstart to be watched.
He dispatched him to the Caucasus front, out in the eastern wilds,
400 miles from Istanbul.

I'm fascinated by this depiction of a future icon. The canvas is less
than fifty centimetres high, and none of the facial features that would
later stand out so strikingly seem remarkable. A messy moustache
cancels out the sharp cheekbones; the blue eyes seem watery rather
than sharp. His rank is not visible, and there is no indication of his
achievements.

It is difficult to imagine this soldier's portrait being replicated
millions of times on posters, tea sets and lighters, as Atatürk's more
famous later images subsequently were. By the end of the twentieth
century it had occurred to the Kemalists that the old forms of Atatürk-
worship – mass rallies in sports stadiums; dour official portraits
looming over public squares; above all, harsh punishments for anyone
who did not comply – were no longer working. The rising Islamists
– men like Recep Tayyip Erdoğan – were forging genuine bonds with
the people through their common touch. Thus, the Kemalists decided
to bring Atatürk into the private realm. For the seventy-fifth anniversary of the republic in 1998, new official exhibitions displayed
Atatürk's evening wear for the first time, and historians went to the
archives and started pulling out new photos of him – drinking,
laughing and swimming.

Esra Özyürek, a Turkish anthropologist who had lived in the States

for many years, noticed a profound change in her people's relationship
with Atatürk on her return to Turkey to study the celebrations in
1998. She writes in her 2006 book, *Nostalgia for the Modern*:

> Although I grew up under the perpetual gaze of the founding
> father, I was astonished by the omnipresence of Atatürk images on
> my return to the country after several years' absence. What startled
> me most was not the multiplication of his image, but his appear-
> ance in strange, new places and in novel poses – the very
> commodification of the leader. Kemalist entrepreneurs and
> consumers had creatively adopted the founding father into their
> personal lives and ventures . . . Most surprisingly in the newly
> popular images, Atatürk appeared smiling, much in contrast to his
> fierce looks in pictures that decorate state offices.

Back in those days, when Erdoğan was still the rebel upstart, Ayşe
Hür spent most of her time battling against the Kemalists' myths.
Over strong coffees she destroys one after another little parts of the
Atatürk story that I have taken to heart over the past six years: 'He
has fake photographs, like the one where he is sleeping on the snow,'
she says, referring to a famous grainy black-and-white picture of
Atatürk on the battlefield. 'It is staged . . . There is a story about
Atatürk getting hit by a bullet and it bouncing off his watch. This
is probably also fabricated. Most of my career has been about deconstructing the Kemalist reading of the era. Over the last ten years,
people started to get pissed off because now everyone expects me to
give only a critical review of the AKP period. Sometimes I tweet
something about Kemalism and people ask what I am doing. They
say that this is not the time to be criticising Kemalism!'

We have been speaking for three hours over the din of the coffee
shop, our conversation curving through Atatürk and Erdoğan, then
back to Atatürk again. Both men are more fictions than fact, we
conclude – but Atatürk has one claim over Erdoğan: 'Atatürk joined
the war,' Hür says. 'Erdoğan would never do that!'

She gathers her things to dash to her next meeting through the rush-hour crowds on a warm April evening in Taksim. On one side of the square the brutalist Atatürk Cultural Centre – a symbol of the modern republic – is being pulled down by digger trucks to make way for a new opera house. Turkey's secularists are horrified, seeing it as a metaphor for Erdoğan's drive to pull apart the nation that Atatürk created, and to refashion Taksim just as he is trying to remould the minds of the people. They will not be soothed by what is happening on the other side of the square, exactly facing the demolition site. Here, the skeleton of a new mosque is rising in exact sync with the razing of the Cultural Centre. It is the project that Erdoğan has been promising for a generation, since he first became mayor of Istanbul.

Just after Ayşe and I say our goodbyes, news comes in. Snap elections have been called, even earlier than everyone was expecting. In two months, on 24 June 2018, Turks will go to the polls seventeen months early to pick both their president and parliament. Either way, the decision they make will reroute the country's future. Once the winner is called, Erdoğan's new constitution will come into force, sweeping away Atatürk's legacy of parliamentary democracy and handing whoever takes the presidency almost unbridled power to shape the country as he, or she, sees fit. The opposition must now scramble to find their candidates. Erdoğan doesn't have to announce he is standing: it's a given.

# 15

# ERDOĞAN'S ENDGAME

*24 June 2018*
*Election night*

Defeat and the death of democracy wears an ashen, sickened face. On the top floor of a draughty old Istanbul building, men cluster around a small television set as a map of Turkey turns Erdoğan-yellow.

All of them smoke and few of them talk. Those that do murmur vague protest.

'The count isn't finished yet!'

'Their numbers don't match with ours!'

'There's still time!' This last in a small, desperate whisper.

Hope's dregs gurgle away as the count nears its finish. Erdoğan wins it outright, calling victory at 9.30 p.m., only four and a half hours after polling booths have closed. And that is the end of parliamentary democracy in Turkey.

As soon as it was settled it all seemed so obvious: of course Erdoğan would never lose. Every weapon in this battle had been his for the choosing: the media coverage, the resources, the power to lock up his opponents – everything he had gathered over the past fifteen years. But the outcome is no longer the real point of an election in Turkey

– it is all about the journey, the show. The June 2018 elections had turned into the greatest test of his flock's loyalty since the coup attempt: a challenger rose, Erdoğan faltered, and for the six weeks of campaigning his opponents started believing that things could change. And so, his devotees came out stronger, fought tougher, and played dirtier. And when he defied all the doubters and won it again, they lauded him more fiercely than ever. Jeopardy was not the process here but the goal – and payoff came with proof that, once again, the most skilled and practised populist in the world could rally his army and march on.

## The campaign

The June 2018 election campaign was a masterpiece of black comedy, timing and suspense: the opposition's last chance to stop Erdoğan, the endgame. He knew he couldn't wait much longer to set the last pieces of his plan in motion: the economy was stuttering, the currency weakening. Everything he had built his support on was going into reverse. Ever the gambler, Erdoğan was gambling on an opposition in shambles, and a country flying high on the jingoism of Afrin.

'Who's getting ready? Making preparations? Working ten hours a day? Touring the provinces? Making alliances? Recep Tayyip Erdoğan. Who else is doing that? No one,' a former member of his circle told me a month before the elections were called. 'It is his big asset – he knows what the mood is. Aged thirteen he started giving speeches. Since then he has been dealing in politics. It is the first time that we have a natural-born politician. Atatürk didn't have to win popular support, it was narrower elite politics when he ruled, he was managing groups. But Erdoğan grew up being a populist. He is a deal-maker, a deal-breaker. He keeps his constituency under strong control. His family lives politics twenty-four-seven, even on holiday. It is defensive politics at home. Do they go on holiday? Never. Never happened in that family. In the past, ministers would dream of retirement. His only relaxation is maybe playing with his grandchildren. Maybe

Islamist politicians are like that because they are defensive. It is their style of engaging with life – politics is everywhere. It is twenty-four-seven, without an exit strategy. They believe there is an afterlife, maybe that is their holiday.'

Turkey had no shortage of issues in the spring of 2018. Soldiers were dying in Syria and the educated youth was deserting the country. Construction projects were stopping midway, cranes frozen, as companies' credit lines dried up. Their huge skeletons loomed over the cities' highways like the concrete ghosts of Christmas yet to come, a warning of what the future surely holds as the backlash of the AKP's obsession with borrowing and building begins. But all else was pushed aside in the spring of 2018, because there was only one issue in this election – a Turkey with Erdoğan, or without?

All the main opposition candidates pledged to scrap the results of his referendum should they win and rewrite the constitution – again. The nationalist Iyi (Good) Party had Meral Akşener, a glamorous grandmother with hennaed hair and a problematic past; she was interior minister in the 1990s, at the very time that the Turkish state was committing its worst atrocities in the Kurdish south-east. She reinvented herself by replacing the wolf's-head hand gesture of the ultra-nationalists with pearl earrings and a hennaed star and crescent on her palm to match her hair, but the Kurds would never forget.

Saadet, the rump Islamist party left behind when Tayyip and the other young guns broke away to form the AKP, had the aged Temel Karamollaoğlu, a grandfatherly, grey-bearded figure. The party's campaign video featured a cartoon Karamollaoğlu depicted as Superman, swooping down to stop a car steered by Erdoğan from driving off a cliff.

'The first ever Islamist with a sense of humour!' one friend remarked.

Selahattin Demirtaş, the first major politician to oppose Erdoğan's presidential system, stood for the HDP. He had been in prison for seventeen months but was still by far the most popular Kurdish politician. If convicted before election day on any of the seventeen terrorism charges he faced his bid would be finished. He was not able to hold rallies or speak to his followers apart from through statements handed to his lawyers. Then, seven days before the election, state television decided to grant him a ten-minute slot. The pro-Erdoğan press heralded it 'a first for democracy!'

The outsider was Doğu Perinçek, leader of Vatan – a neo-Maoist, ultranationalist party so marginal it never gleans more than 1 per cent of the vote. And the CHP had Muharrem İnce, a 54-year-old former physics teacher who had challenged Kılıçdaroğlu for the leadership of the party a year earlier.

İnce was a witty orator, well used to controlling a classroom full of bored and gobby teenagers. The Turkish paparazzi snapped him enjoying a beer and performing the Zeybek, a traditional Aegean dance. Such leisure pursuits marked him down as a full-blooded Turkish secularist – though his mother and sister wore the headscarf. As he announced his candidacy İnce took off his CHP lapel badge, his tribal marker, and promised to be a president for the whole of Turkey.

The AKP media sneered. 'He couldn't even win the CHP leadership elections,' scoffed one commentator. 'How does he think he can win the presidency?'

None of the challengers looked promising. İnce's face adorned bus shelters around my neighbourhood, and on one I saw that a woman wearing bright red lipstick had kissed the glass over his forehead. Doğu Perinçek's people pasted some scrappy posters on construction hoardings, showing the brush-moustached leader glaring beneath thick eyebrows. I caught a glimpse of Meral Akşener, regal and smiling, on posters pinned to the central reservation on the road out of Istanbul to Silivri prison, where I went in late April to watch a hearing of one of the terror cases against Selahattin Demirtaş. It would have been his first public appearance since he formally announced he was running for the presidency. Journalists, international observers and Kurdish activists jammed the building, hammering on the door of the prison's courtroom as nervous young gendarmerie officers stood guard. But as proceedings got underway, we realised that even this stage was to be denied him – Demirtaş did not appear in the court-room at his own trial. The judge said he was ill.

Almost everywhere else, from Taksim to the *gecekondu* districts, it was Tayyip's stern face that gazed down on you. His face was on billboards in bus stations and bunting fluttering over ancient alleys. Every day, millions of Istanbullus riding in taxis and buses along the raised highways that cut through suburban-sprawl Istanbul caught Erdoğan's eye countless times, as he watched them from storeys-high banners pasted onto the tower blocks.

Erdoğan's people were determined to keep a grip on us as we covered the election. On a Saturday afternoon in late May, halfway through campaigning, the foreign press corps was called to the Hilton Hotel in Istanbul for a meeting with Mehmet Akarca, the head of the press ministry. Over more than two hours Akarca, a former jour-nalist with state television, accused us of launching a 'perception operation' against Erdoğan, and begged us not to call him a dictator until after the elections. 'Would you call Angela Merkel an alcoholic if you saw her with one drink?' he said. 'Then why are you calling our president a dictator!'

Things weren't always like this. Not so long ago, you could talk about almost anything with almost anyone in Turkey. Interviewees would proudly tell a journalist their full name, occupation and where they lived as they cascaded their opinions, and make sure you noted them all down correctly. Of course there were limits, Atatürk being one and the Kurdish issue another – it was always easy to slip up when discussing both subjects. But on the whole I had found Turkey refreshing at first, after the smog of noms-de-guerre, pseudonyms and suspicion I'd had to deal with in Syria, by-products of forty years under dictatorship and an inherited fear of the system. But then Turkey changed, starting around the time Erdoğan first became presi-dent in 2014, accelerating through the breakdown of the PKK peace process and becoming entrenched right after the coup attempt. Now most Turks will only talk anonymously, giving their first name but not their last, or else refusing to speak at all. Those who support Erdoğan might be happy to say so, but their suspicion of foreigners – and particularly of foreign journalists – mirrors the deepening paranoia of their leader. At some point an epiphany hit me. I had come to Turkey in 2013 thinking I would bear witness to the fall of one dictatorship. Now I was watching the rise of another.

No matter the shift in Erdoğan's demeanour or the depth of his political descent, those who were once close to him still speak with overtones of loyalty.

'If you lived his life for twenty-four hours a day, in three days you would be a dictator – all these people around you treating you like a god and saying yes to everything,' one of his closest former advisers, an ally of his since the late 1980s, told me during the 2018 election campaign. 'I see that the illness of power has now reached him. I'm often angry with him – there is not a week goes by when I don't try to help him. If I see him in a good mood, he is the same guy as he has always been. Then it falls apart. This is the curse of being too successful – I also see it with CEOs. They start to make mistakes because they think they know better. Now Erdoğan is surrounded by these young guys who had no successes in life before, and therefore they look at him like a god. They never dare to say no to him. The main question is whether he realises that he does not have good people around him.'

The charismatic rebel had started to look old and out of touch. It was not only the shrinking of his inner circle that had shifted the gears of his politicking: without Erol Olçok's polish, his shine had come off. Olçok's spin agency Arter was dropped by the AKP just before the 2018 elections and the new team had none of Olçok's old magic. There were plenty of slogans – 'A big Turkey needs a strong leader!' 'It's Turkey's time!' – but nothing about the future. At his rallies Erdoğan simply talked about all he had done, and blamed Turkey's mounting problems on shadowy foreign lobbies.

'There is no strategy. No perspective about the future. In political campaigns, you should enrich the policies with fresh perspectives and content. I couldn't find that in their latest campaign,' Atılgan Bayar, the AKP's strategic adviser between 2010 and 2015, told me. 'The Turkish nation needs to tend to its wounds. The campaign needed to assert a more positive and peaceful discourse. They didn't under-stand that. Surely this amateur campaign will affect the results. Political campaigns are like organic bodies. They evolve as you are working on them. And all the elements – films, slogans and music – harmoniously come together around a predefined strategy; there's no room for discord or wild cards. In a sense, campaigns are like sentences. Their campaign has elements of a sentence but with no syntax or coherence, and therefore no tangible meaning.'

As Erdoğan stumbled, Muharrem İnce, the man who couldn't even win control of the CHP, seized the bait. İnce ran a storming campaign, outstripping everyone's expectations including mine. After six years of watching them flail and bumble, I had written the opposition off as irrelevant and irredeemable, a fading snapshot of old Turkey. But three days before the election, a millions-strong crowd filled a rally ground to see İnce speak, the mass of fluttering Turkish flags turning the huge area into a blanket of red. In the heat and humidity of an İzmir summer evening, the mass sang and shouted slogans, roaring in glee each time the MC mentioned the main act's name.

This was İnce's 105th rally in forty-nine days, each one bigger and more enthusiastic than the last. He had been virtually blacked out from state television network TRT, Erdoğan getting 181 hours of coverage during the campaign, İnce just 15. Most of the other channels, owned by Erdoğan's allies, ignored him altogether. But on social media İnce was a hit. His witty put-downs of the president won him respect and adoration. Erdoğan's media army tried to hit back by unearthing some poetry that İnce had published decades ago, cringeworthy soft-erotica that they claimed indecent. İnce merely laughed. 'What can I do if you have never fallen in love?' he replied.

Professionals, students and families gathered in İzmir to hear İnce speak as the campaigning reached its climax. 'He is going to win it! If the other guys don't fake it, of course . . .' said Nuran Oğuz, a schoolteacher who had come along with her two colleagues.

The stage had been set up in a park that runs along the seafront, and an estimated two million people flooded the areas before and behind it as well as all the streets and alleyways around. Every balcony over-looking the stage was crammed with people waving Turkish flags, and the special forces cops on the rooftops were joined by crowds of İnce's supporters. In the bay, boats hoisted sails decorated with images of Atatürk, and from the speakers the İzmir March boomed out on repeat.

İnce arrived on his bus in the sticky heat of the late afternoon, just as the sun was setting and the crowd worked up to fever pitch. He strode on stage hand-in-hand with his glamorous blonde wife, Ülkü, and launched into a blazing hour-long speech. 'Erdoğan is tired, arro-gant and lonely. He is a man without dreams!' he laughed. The crowd roared in hysterics along with him.

Anyone who does not know the Turkish language might have thought from their onstage voices that Erdoğan and İnce were the same man. This rival adopted the president's oratory style exactly — the shouting, the key words drawn out for emphasis, the laughs at the expense of his opponent. His media team sliced clips of Erdoğan with performances by the classic Turkish comedy actor Kemal Sunal, whose best-known character is an Ottoman idiot, and beamed them onto the big screens. In the crowd people held aloft witty signs: TEACHER, TAYYIP IS TALKING TOO MUCH!

At last, the opposition had a living candidate whose face they could slap onto their merchandise. The hawkers said they had never seen such demand. 'I can't find İnce stuff from the producers any more, I have to go to the black market!' a trader called Serdar told me as he showed off his scarves, printed with İnce's picture at one end, Atatürk's at the other, and EVERYBODY'S PRESIDENT written in between the two.

*

It was easy to get swept up in this tide of hope – after all, it had been sixteen years since the opposition last seemed in the ascendant. İnce looked to have seized the political narrative. When he pledged to lift the state of emergency if he won, Erdoğan was backed into a corner and responded that he, too, would review the emergency law. Pollsters predicted that Erdoğan would fall below 50 per cent in the first round of the elections and be forced into a second-round run-off against İnce. And many Turks believed that if that happened, İnce could build enough momentum to take the presidency.

Meral Akşener and Temel Karamollaoğlu said that they would throw their weight behind İnce should the vote go to a second round. There was a chance that followers of Selahattin Demirtaş, the Kurdish HDP leader, would do the same – İnce visited him in prison, breaking the decades-old animosity between the Kemalists and the Kurds, and held a rally in Diyarbakır. Finally, after sixteen years, the opposition found something that they could agree on – that whatever their differences, Erdoğan must go.

But there were warning signs in İzmir on that midsummer night, even if the opposition did not want to see them. The crowd – like the ones in Ankara and Istanbul that would gather over the following two days – was millions strong but showed only one side of Turkey. I counted just a handful of women wearing headscarves, and the crowd's slogans and the way they packed into İzmir's seafront bars for beers once the rally was over left little doubt as to whose tribe they belonged.

I asked Serdar the street hawker when he would be getting in some more İnce merchandise. He told me the producers were hedging their bets. 'If the election goes to a second round then they will make a lot more,' he said. 'But they have to produce in big quantities, and there are only two days left, you know . . .'

## Defeat

At the CHP's Istanbul headquarters, election night began with high promise. İnce, having witnessed some of the first counts, tweeted that the news looked good. But when preliminary results started coming in the optimism withered like a punctured balloon. İnce, meanwhile, had disappeared. He had pledged to stay at the higher board of elections all evening to make sure the count was fair, but after casting his vote in his home province of Yalova he flew to Ankara and holed up in his hotel, presumably watching his defeat unfold.

It was Bülent Tezcan, the CHP's spokesman, who stood in front of the television cameras as Erdoğan declared early victory and his supporters thronged to the streets. As the sound of car horns and chanting filled the city centres, Tezcan tried to hold back the tide. 'We are following the count step by step and at no time did Mr Erdoğan's vote go above forty-eight per cent,' he said. 'This is open manipulation but the result is certain – Erdoğan will lose. We are asking people not to leave the ballot boxes. They want the election observers to stay at home so they can do their tricks.'

The state-controlled Anadolu Agency is the only news wire given access to the polling booths where the votes are first counted. It has a habit of announcing the figures from the staunchest pro-Erdoğan constituencies first, to make it seem as though he is storming to victory – on referendum night the results for *Evet* had started at 70 per cent before shrinking back to just over 51 per cent. Mehmet Akarca, the head of the press ministry, had implored us to go to a government-run press centre on election night, so we could take Anadolu's earliest results. The CHP was insisting that their own polling station tallies did not match with Anadolu's.

But Tezcan's words were lost in the racket – as far as the people waving flags were concerned, victory was already a done deal. Just after midnight, Fox News Turk, the last of six main Turkish television channels operating independently, reported that it had received a WhatsApp message from Muharrem İnce, who had still not been seen since counting started. İnce had admitted defeat, the Fox journalist, İsmail Küçükkaya, said. The atmosphere in the CHP's office became chill. On Twitter, the jokes started flying straight away. 'İnce literally just split up with his supporters by WhatsApp!' wrote one. Others insisted it must be a con on the part of the government, or that İnce must have been threatened. How could the man who had raised the hopes of half a nation and spoken in front of millions over the past three days have ended it all like this?

Within minutes Bülent Tezcan was back in front of the cameras, his demeanour flattened and distress clear. 'The turnout was very high. We are thanking all the voters,' he stated. 'We said that we will defend the law and ensure that what goes into the ballot box is the same as the result that comes out. Our friends are still waiting and the counting continues. But our figures are matching with those of Anadolu Agency. Be peaceful, be careful of provocations. Democracy is working and whatever the result, we will continue with our democratic fight.'

It was over, and everyone knew it. Erdoğan had won, and there would be no second round. Turkey would continue on Tayyip's path, reshaped to his liking and with a resounding restatement of his people's will. The nation had spoken, and they had said they wanted more of the same – no matter how authoritarian their leader, no matter how unfairly he had run his campaign, and no matter the 47 per cent who did not vote for this. Everyone started filing out of the CHP's offices.

Me too. I walked out into the deserted street and started searching for a taxi to take me back across the Bosphorus to Kadıköy. I knew no protests would take place there this time, as there were after Erdoğan's referendum victory. This time the defeat was too crushing, too final. Erdoğan had apparently increased his share of the vote since the last presidential elections in 2014. The opposition had bowed out with a disgraceful whimper. Over the coming days, international election monitors would raise serious questions over the fairness of the campaigning period and reports would emerge of ballot box tampering in the east. None slowed Erdoğan even for a minute as he soared on his self-declared victory.

My street was silent and empty as I buzzed open the heavy front door of my apartment building. But, looking out across the road from my window, I saw all my neighbours still awake, gathered around their television sets and smoking as they had on the night of the coup. All the channels were showing the scenes outside the AKP's Ankara headquarters, where huge crowds had gathered to see Erdoğan speak. From the balcony he delivered the speech of his political life-time, scorning his enemies at home and abroad and vowing to speed up Turkey's transformation.

'The winner of this election is democracy,' he boomed. 'The winner is the superiority of the national will. The winner is Turkey and the Turkish nation. The winner is all the oppressed in our region and across the world!'

The crowd thundered its approval. Flags waved for the television cameras swooping overhead. Erdoğan promised to keep on fighting all who stood against him and his people.

'We will not stop! We will not stop! We will never stop!'

Outside, I heard a distant din of car horns, growing louder as they came closer. As I peered out the window the convoy swung into my street, a long chain of cars flying Erdoğan flags and star and crescent banners from their roofs. His anthem blared from their stereos, and a young woman in a colourful modern headscarf hung out of a window and wailed at this Turkey, the old Turkey, the heartland of the 47 per cent. I saw her face as the convoy passed beneath my window; it was caught between ecstasy and fury.

'RECEP TAYYIP ERDOĞANNNNNNNN!' she screamed.

*June 2018*
*Travelling the Eastern Express*

A week after Erdoğan's election win I take a train ride across the breadth of Turkey. The Eastern Express runs from Ankara to Kars, the last city before the Armenian border. It takes twenty-four hours to cover the 700 miles between the two cities.

The route has recently become a hit with Turkish hipsters. The winter journeys through snow-locked Anatolia are picture perfect, like Narnia; the glistening vistas through windows branded with a kitsch star and crescent custom-made for Instagram. Thousands of young Turks from the wealthy and liberal west used the train to travel to the other end of their country for the first time over the most recent winter, hanging out of the open carriage doors to smoke cigarettes and feel the cold air slap their faces. But now, in the humid dog days of late June, the train has sunk back into its old unglamorous role – the workhorse carting Turks who can't afford plane travel from one end of the country to the other.

The towns the train stops in are the least alluring parts of Turkey, even though the scenery in between is stunning. Kayseri . . . Elazig . . . Erzincan . . . Erzurum . . . The carriages pull into one identikit city after another, shanty-houses next to the train tracks and dingy new apartment blocks behind them. Old women in shawls haul huge bags onto the train. Ragged children hurl rocks at it as it pulls out of the station again. Litter blankets the ground on either side of the tracks, and I can see little evidence here of the huge investment and modernisation that has swept across Istanbul and other cities to the west, or even the cities on the border with Syria, with their cosmopolitan new populations of refugees, diplomats and aid workers. The way young mothers line up with their small children to watch the train go past suggests there is little else new or exciting here – they have so far gained the least out of the New Turkey. But these are the places where Erdoğan's support is unshakeable: in the ramshackle villages the train line cuts through, huge posters of him are hoisted on the houses closest to the tracks.

I travelled to Kayseri two months ago, to see Erdoğan's first rally of the election campaign. That time I, like him, travelled there through the city's airport – a far more glamorous entrance than the railway station. I had happened to time my journey just right: my low-cost flight back to Istanbul left at almost exactly the same time as Erdoğan's private jet, and my taxi home from the airport at the other end trailed just behind his motorcade for a short stretch. He had been whisked to his jet from the town square rally on blacked-out buses with special forces soldiers balanced on the top, down roads closed to allow the convoy to pass through speedily.

'With love and respect, Kayseri!' boomed the bus's loudspeaker as it tore down the main street away from the rally, the soldiers training their assault rifles across pavements packed with Saturday shoppers.

'Have you ever read 1984?' I asked my Turkish friend, as we sipped coffee and watched the spectacle roll past.

'Dear, I'm *living* in 1984,' he replied, spluttering with laughter.

Erdoğan had tagged his Kayseri rally on to the opening of a new, PPP-funded state hospital – one of his tried and tested tactics to show just how much he is doing for his country. Days earlier he had promised to raise the state pension – a sure winner for the men with heavy moustaches who gathered around me as I pulled out my notebook in the crowd. Mostly, though, they wanted to talk about Europe.

'I like his tough stance against the foreign enemies – Greece, Armenia, France,' said one. 'They all support terrorism. And we don't trust the EU! They don't keep their promises.'

The others talked over one another, each wanting their quotes to be the ones I scribbled down. Each of them echoed the last.

'None of our other leaders defended our rights in the international community,' said another. 'That is why the world doesn't want Erdoğan to lead us – because he's against their colonialism.'

'Tell me,' said his friend, 'which European city has new hospitals opening? I lived in Germany for forty years and they don't!'

I felt like pointing to the figures that could show him exactly how many billions in grants and investments the EU has poured into Erdoğan's Turkey over the years. I had added it up; nearly four billion euros to bridges, tunnels, rail links – and hospitals. But a rally is no place to argue reasonably. The familiar music started and the MC came on stage to warm up the crowd. The speakers were turned up so loud I could feel each word hitting my eardrums. My interviews came to an abrupt end – it was almost impossible to hear anyone over the racket. But one of the men leant over to give me a final thought, holding up his index finger and striking it through the air to emphasise each word like a conductor leading an orchestra.

'*Tek millet! Tek bayrak! Tek Vatan! Tek lider!*' he shouted over the din – a twist on one of Erdoğan's campaign slogans: 'One nation, one flag, one Motherland, one state'.

My interviewee had added his own ending: 'one leader'.

Erdoğan's about-face on Europe is the most startling aspect of his metamorphosis. Back in 2003 he promised to be the man who would take Turkey into the European Union. Now, he often appears to be trying to get Turkey kicked out before it has joined.

'After [Erdoğan] became prime minister he did more to seriously move forward the EU process than any other government. When I think about Turkey today and how it got there . . . Erdoğan is the best politician in Turkey,' says one diplomat based in the country during the 1990s and early 2000s. But when Erdoğan began his snarling slide into real populist authoritarianism after 2016, the EU made an easy fall guy. Turks were already fatigued with the endless accession process – both Germany's Angela Merkel and France's Nicolas Sarkozy had said that the country would never become a full member, even back in the days when Ankara was playing nice. The final insult came when the Schengen visas Turks were promised under Davutoğlu's 2016 deal to stop refugees flocking to Europe failed to materialise in Erdoğan's Euro-Hate era. Brussels said the sticking point was the same as always – Turkey's refusal to liberalise its anti-terror laws, a condition for Schengen access. Erdoğan, then in the opening throes of his new war with the PKK, was never going to make concessions on that – and after the coup attempt in July that year the human rights outlook worsened. Soon the two sides were trapped in a spiral of mutual abuse – Europe criticising Turkey's latest human rights breaches, and Erdoğan picking up on their words to spit back to the adoring crowds at his rallies, with asides about hypocrisy and Turkey-phobia in Brussels.

'From my perspective, when Sarkozy and Merkel said never to the

EU membership, Erdoğan was liberated from having that as a national aspiration and he was able to substitute it with his own aspiration,' the diplomat says. 'And I think that is one of the reasons why we are where we are today . . . But I also think that people will look back and say that the secularists did not fight for their country. In 2003, the big business people were thinking that Erdoğan was great. They tried to ride the tiger but things did not work out the way they wanted them to. Secondly, there are secularists like the CHP party that never organised themselves to provide an alternative vision of what Turkey could become instead of no to Erdoğan. They provided nothing to the larger group of people.

'When this history gets written, we will see that Erdoğan holds the most responsibility for Turkey today, but some of it also belongs to the opposition and to Europeans who made a strategic error.'

Erdoğan's personal views on Brussels have always been far muddier than those of his AKP co-founders. He fits more naturally with the leaders of Muslim countries, who tend to look up to and flatter him, while among the leaders of Europe he appears awkward and surly. Turks' views on the EU have also shifted, so that now most say they do not want to join compared to the two-thirds who were in favour in 2002. Doubtless that is partly down to the endless agitations of Turkey's pro-Erdoğan media (one tabloid newspaper published a front page of Angela Merkel mocked-up as Hitler during the height of the row between the two countries in 2017). But as the EU bloc is engulfed by economic woes, squabbling over refugees, and its own rising swell of populism, it no longer looks the good bet it was at the start of the AKP's tenure. Turks believe they have other relationships they can turn to, in Russia, the Balkans – and post-Brexit Britain.

Back in Ankara there are few people left in Erdoğan's inner circle who can either speak truth to power, or who are sufficiently Europhile to push for a reconciliation with Brussels. Hours after Erdoğan was re-inaugurated following his election win – an event billed in the Turkish press as 'the first day of the New Turkey' – he announced his new, hand-picked cabinet. Twenty-six ministries had been stream-lined down to sixteen. One of those culled was the ministry for EU affairs, now absorbed by the foreign ministry. It is a clear sign of how far any thoughts of joining the bloc have slipped down Erdoğan's agenda. When I met with former president Abdullah Gül six weeks before the elections, it was the crumbling of the prospects for EU membership that disappointed him the most. 'I am not happy with the current situation. In the first five years [of the AKP's rule], all of us embraced the people, the different and we focused on the future. We did this. The soft power is the democracy. It is the separation of power. The transparency. The accountability. We proved this. If devoted politicians prove that they are on this line, it would be a wonderful gift to world peace,' Gül told me.

'We became the model for many surrounding countries. We became a source of inspiration. We were trying to be good Muslims but at the same time we were democratic. These were the soft policies. It created influence in our neighbourhood. I have always defended soft power . . . In my last years of presidency I was telling our friends in Europe that they should not block our progress [to join the European Union], that they should help us complete the negotiation process. I asked why they were opposed to all these things. I asked to finish the process, and maybe Turkey will be like Norway in the end. Maybe we would not be a full member [but] what is important is to reach that level and to adopt those [European] standards . . . We are in a very different position now [regarding] the EU, foreign affairs, the region.'

The void left by men like Abdullah Gül, Ahmet Davutoğlu and Bülent Arinc as they have drifted from the party or been shunted aside has been filled with ultra-loyalists, sycophants and yes men. Several ministers stayed in their posts following the election, but Erdoğan's appointment of his son-in-law Berat Albayrak to the treasury, his childhood friend Mustafa Varank to the industry and technology ministry, and Hulusi Akar, the army chief who stayed loyal on the night of the coup, to the defence ministry, showed he has little concern for diversity of opinion in his cabinet. Gone is the man who was once willing to learn, to hear outside voices and listen to criticism.

'Read Gabriel Garcia Marquez's *Autumn of the Patriarch*: the classic closing-in and narrowing of a circle of advisers around a . . . highly successful leadership personality,' said one diplomat based in Turkey at the time it all fell apart. 'One by one, founding members of the AKP were purged or simply fell away.'

The guest list for the official celebration of Erdoğan's inauguration in July 2018 is a good place to start if you are searching for hints of where the country might stand in the world in the years to come. His win met with a lukewarm reception from Western countries. Monitors from the OSCE observed that the vote was 'free but not fair'; although they had not witnessed any significant tampering with the ballots, the skewing of media coverage in Erdoğan's favour during campaigning had left the opposition at a crushing disadvantage. His early victory call squashed any debate about the results or the fairness. Once the crowds were on the streets it was all over.

No one from Washington or London flew in to sit among the crowd in the gardens of Aksaray, his presidential palace, though both had offered congratulations on his win. The only heads of state from the European Union were Hungary's Viktor Orbán and Bulgaria's Rumen Radev – both of whom face charges of undermining the bloc's democratic norms. Brussels sent its representative for migration, clearly keen to keep the refugee deal on track. Silvio Berlusconi, the corrupt and frisky former Italian prime minister was there, as was Venezuela's Nicolás Maduro, a fan of both Erdoğan and Turkey's neo-Ottoman TV series. North Cyprus, Azerbaijan, Bosnia, Sudan, Pakistan, Equatorial Guinea, Somalia, Qatar, Kuwait . . . all were represented as Erdoğan did a slow walk of honour through the crowd with Emine, to applause and the boom of cannon fire.

It didn't take Erdoğan long to start exercising his new powers. He had announced the cabinet within six hours of being sworn in. By the next morning he had issued his first presidential decree, appointing Hulusi Akar as the new head of the armed forces and changing the chain of command. The military's higher appointments council, once a group of generals who decided who would fill the top positions, was abolished. Now, the commanders of the navy, air force and army are all under the direct command of the president, and all officers down to the level of colonel are appointed by him.

Meanwhile, Erdoğan's crackdown widened. The day after the election, the nationalist leader Devlet Bahçeli, whose party went into the parliamentary polls in alliance with the AKP, took out full-page adverts in two national newspapers, listing the names of seventy journalists who had criticised or mocked him and using the headline: A THANK-YOU MESSAGE. Bahçeli's MHP had looked set to be the election's big losers, with everyone expecting them to haemorrhage their vote to Meral Akşener's rival-nationalist Iyi Party. Bahçeli had barely even campaigned – but the MHP increased its share of the vote, taking 11 per cent. It is now the kingmaker in the parliament – Erdoğan's AKP needs the support of Bahçeli's nationalists in order to keep its majority of seats. That means that any hopes for a new Kurdish peace process have died – and that Bahçeli now wields a dark new kind of power. Erdoğan did not grant him any formal cabinet position, and the newspaper stunt may look petulant. But the MHP preserves strong ties with the underworld, right-wing mob bosses who were only too happy to wipe out troublesome journalists and other opponents back in the 1990s and would not hesitate to do so again. 'It's as good as a target on their backs,' an outraged contact told me.

The day before Erdoğan is officially sworn in comes the largest single round-up of suspected Gülenists, almost two years on from the coup attempt. Eighteen thousand people, including soldiers, policemen and judges, are either sacked or arrested. The website of the Official Gazette crashes as Turks rush to check whether their names are on the list. The number of those dismissed now tops more than 180,000. The judiciary has lost more than a third of its manpower since the purge began – and under the new system, the top judges will be appointed jointly by Erdoğan and by the parliament that Erdoğan controls. The state of emergency has been lifted – almost two years to the day since it was first brought in – but that will make little difference now that Erdoğan has hollowed out the state and filled it with his loyalists, and rules by presidential decree anyway. Amendments to the anti-terror laws pushed through just before emergency rule ended allow the police to detain suspects without charge, for up to twelve days in some cases. Local governors, directly appointed by the government, can continue to restrict access to public areas on security grounds, and demonstrations can be banned on an even broader set of pretexts than under the emergency law.

Meanwhile, the foreign press corps is informed that the agency that issues our press cards – our tickets to stay in the country – is to be taken under the direct control of the presidency. Separately I receive a message from my oldest contact within the government.

'I am afraid we are no longer cooperating with you, Hannah,' it reads. 'People are unhappy.'

## Immortal Atatürk

My train journey had really been a means to an end – the very end of Turkey, and an event a friend and I had been vowing to see since we first heard of it years before. Bradley, a British photographer, was one of the first people I met in Turkey. Like me, he had lived in Antakya during the early stages of the Syrian war, covered the conflict, and then moved up to Istanbul at the same time as I did – when the odds of survival for Western journalists in Syria started lengthening. Over six years we had lived, travelled and worked together, and talked endlessly about whether it might be better to leave Turkey for an easier place. Like him, I always thought of what it might be like to live in another city, where I didn't have to hustle through hordes on the pavements or swear at people to get jobs done. But then I would catch one of the perfect sunsets over the Bosphorus, or a busker's melancholic tune on the ferry will hit exactly the right note for my mood, and would realise that I could never leave this place without leaving a huge chunk of my heart behind.

We arrived in the city of Kars, 620 miles east of Ankara, late on a Saturday night. It looked more like a post-Soviet town than one in Turkey, full of dark grey stone buildings and odd statues – and free of the huge posters hung by the loquaciously ambitious local mayors celebrating Erdoğan's election victory back in Istanbul and Ankara. The next morning, we found a driver to take us the final sixty-five miles to Damal.

The tiny town sits in huge folds of grasslands next to the Georgian border. In the last days of spring the velvet green was daubed in purple and white wildflowers, and the rippling grasses caught the sunlight in gentle waves. Our driver, Ali, was determined that we do a language swap on the hour-and-a-half journey along the smooth, newly built road, so we pointed to the things we passed and shouted out their names, like toddlers.

'İnek!' Ali cried.

'Cow!' we screamed back.

In my imperfect Turkish I tried to explain to Ali what I love about his country – still, despite everything. 'It's so different, everywhere you go,' I told him. 'Every province, every town there is something different.'

'No!' he batted back. 'Turks are one. After the coup we all came together, you saw!'

I explained that I was talking about the geography, not the people – the dusty deserts of the southern borders, the seaside party-towns of the western coasts, the luscious mountains of the Black Sea, the pounding metropolis of Istanbul . . . I wanted to tell him too that he was wrong, the people are also different. Erdoğan had once recognised that, with his old brand of neo-Ottoman pluralism. His nationalist-tinged rebrand had now put paid to that – and six years in this country had taught me when it was best to keep my mouth shut.

We stopped in a village to ask our way up to the viewing point. Everyone knew which way we should go. We followed their fingers up a winding track and there we found it — a small children's playground, a couple of shaded seating areas, and rows of benches laid out down the natural slope of the hill. At the top there was a concrete shelter like a bus stop, covered in Atatürk-themed graffiti.

Three young men sat chatting and smoking in one of the seating areas. In the other, three generations of one family — a tiny girl sucking on a carton of juice, flanked by her father and a well-preserved old lady with bleached-blonde hair, leopard-print trousers and a gold necklace in the shape of Atatürk's signature.

We looked across at the mountain opposite, and the shadows that were beginning to creep across it. Bradley thought he could see the shape of two eyes and a nose appearing. I squinted to make it out.

'No, not yet,' the woman, whose name was Nesilhan Akcan, told us. 'Fifteen minutes more, and you'll see him.'

It turned out that Nesilhan was the best person to ask, because it was her brother, Adıgüzel Kırmızıgül, who had first seen the image of Mustafa Kemal Atatürk appearing in the shadows on the mountain. 'He came home and told us, and we all thought he was crazy!' she said, laughing to show the two gold caps on her front canines. 'But then we came and saw it for ourselves.'

It was 1954, sixteen years after Atatürk's death and when Turkey was in the full throes of Adnan Menderes's reforms. The shadow, a perfect replica of that famous profile, is cast when the sun sets just right over the plains. Fleeting and impermanent, it appears for only half an hour each evening for one month of the year. Slowly the news of it spread and in 1975 the Turkish army sent a photographer to capture the image. The nearest hamlet renamed itself Atatürkköy (Atatürk Village). And, eventually, the local council built the viewing platform and pilgrims started thronging to watch the spectacle.

A wedding party arrived as the sun started its descent, the bride holding up huge layers of satin and tulle as she picked her way through the benches. Then some families pulled up in their cars, and a gendarmerie patrol, too. Food hawkers turned up with ready-bagged popcorn and a portable kettle, and started boiling up strong tea.

The shadow was taking shape, stretching from right to left in a series of curves that sharpened before my eyes. The wedding band, a clarinet player and drummer, began belting out Balkan music and the guests arranged themselves into a circle. More people arrived and the benches filled up. One young couple had dressed their tiny sons in miniature soldiers' outfits. And with the huge shadow face watching over them all, the wedding group started to dance.

I had been ready to scoff, mentally preparing my piece about how Atatürk's devotees sneer at the superstitions of the religious Turks and then rush to take part in their own crazy rituals. But the likeness, as it developed, was stunning. The straight nose, the heavy eyebrows, the jutting chin – all of them were there, perfectly aligned, looming over the wedding party as the bride and groom embraced in the middle of the circle. There was no chanting, no slogans, no merchandise and no power-play, just a happy crowd of people watching a mountain in the warmth of the evening sunshine.

I bought a bag of popcorn from the hawker's young daughter, and went to take my place on the benches as Bradley scooted around taking photos of the wedding crowd. Ali picked wildflowers from the grasses, looking up occasionally to watch the spectacle, and Nesilhan came and sat by my side. Arm in arm, we watched in silence as this vision of Atatürk came, and then melted away again into the shadows.

# ACKNOWLEDGEMENTS

My first thanks go to my agent, Kelly Falconer, who saw the potential in a half-baked idea and then guided me through two years of writing with total patience, wisdom and good humour. Also to my editors at William Collins, Arabella Pike and Jo Thompson, for their enthusiasm for this subject and belief in a first-time author.

To my colleagues at *The Times* for allowing me to travel widely, indulge my obsessions, and for their patience as I have been writing this book – I promise I won't take on any more projects! – and particular thanks to Anthony Loyd for his mentorship, friendship and encouragement.

To Bradley Secker, Yusuf Sayman and Marine Olivesi – the best travel and reporting buddies I could have wished for, and whose spirits are ever-present in these pages. I would not have been able to do any of the reporting without the help and guidance of Burhan Yüksekkaş, Onur Çakır, Ceren Kenar, Aymann Akkad, and all the other fixers, translators, local journalists and whisperers who have asked not to be named – you know who you are.

To Anthony and Jane Franks, Nathan Freeman and Glenn Middleditch for reading early versions of the manuscript and offering excellent and unflinching feedback – your free copies of what, thanks to you, is a much improved book are in the post.

And finally, and not least, thank you to Kadıköy, always a haven of hope and sanity, and without whose *meyhaneler*, tea gardens, clothes-wearing dogs, street musicians, graffiti artists, seafront, Fenerbahçe fans and protests, I probably would have gone home by now.

# LIST OF ILLUSTRATIONS

Rebels with the Free Syrian Army announce the formation of their brigade, Idlib province, 2012 (Bradley Secker)

A protester in Istanbul walks through tear gas clouds (Orlok/ Shutterstock)

A man recovers from the water cannons and tear gas used by Turkish police (Thomas Koch/Shutterstock)

Kurds wave a flag of Abdullah Öcalan as they wait for the announcement of a PKK ceasefire in Diyarbakır, March 2013 (Hannah Lucinda Smith)

Demonstrators in Istanbul use slings and improvised barricades against the riot police (cemT/Shutterstock)

Erdoğan supporters celebrate his victory in presidential elections, June 2018 (Bradley Secker)

Erdoğan supporters attack surrendering soldiers on Istanbul's Bosphorus Bridge as the coup attempt of 15 July 2016 crumbles (Stringer/Getty Images), and flock onto the bridge, 16 July 2016 (deepspace/ Shutterstock)

Erdoğan cries during the funeral of Erol Olçok (BULENT KILIC/AFP/ Getty Images)

Erdoğan and former president Abdullah Gül carry Olçok's coffin, 17 July 2016 (Kayhan Ozer/Anadolu Agency/Getty Images)

Opposition supporters join CHP leader Kemal Kılıçdaroğlu's Justice March from Ankara to Istanbul, July 2017 (Tolga Sezgin/Shutterstock)

Kılıçdaroğlu walks from Ankara to Istanbul in protest at the arrest of a party deputy, July 2017 (GURCAN OZTURK/AFP/Getty Images)

Erdoğan attends the Mausoleum of Mustafa Kemal Atatürk flanked by former Prime Minister Binali Yıldırım (ADEM ALTAN/AFP/Getty Images)

Post-coup 'Unity Rally' in Istanbul's Yenikapı parade ground, August 2016 (quetions123/Shutterstock)

Erdoğan emerges from the voting booth after calling a snap parliamentary and presidential election, 24 June 2018 (Chris McGrath/Getty Images)

Pictures of Erdoğan and Mustafa Kemal Atatürk hang side by side in Istanbul (Alexandros Michailidis/Shutterstock)

# SELECT BIBLIOGRAPHY

**Newspaper and Magazine Archives**
*Agence France Presse*
*Anadolu Agency*
*Associated Press*
*Bloomberg*
*Cumhuriyet*
*Economist*
*Globe and Mail*
*Hürriyet*
*New York Times*
*Newsweek*
*Reuters*
*Sabah*
*The Times*
*Turkish Policy Quarterly*

**Online Sources**
Abdullah Öcalan defence statement: ekurd.net/mismas/articles/
   misc2011/2/turkey3139.htm
Bellingcat.com
Curriculum of Imam Hatip schools:

dogm.meb.gov.tr/www/haftalik-ders-cizelgeleri/icerik/11
Reza Zarrab indictment:
    justice.gov/usao-sdny/press-release/file/994976/download
Turkeypurge.com
Turkish legal archive: mevzuat.gov.tr
Turkish newspaper circulation figures: medyatava.com
*Turkish Official Gazette*: resmigazete.gov.tr
Turkish Statistical Institute: turkstat.gov.tr
UK parliamentary records (Hansard): publications.parliament.uk
WikiLeaks.org

## Academic Papers

Seven Ağir and Cihan Artunc, 'The Wealth Tax of 1942 and the Disappearance of Non-Muslim Enterprises in Turkey', *Journal of Economic History*, vol. 79, no. 1 (March 2019)

Toni Alaranta, 'Mustafa Kemal Atatürk's Six-Day Speech of 1927: Defining the Official Historical View of the Foundation of the Turkish Republic', *Turkish Studies*, vol. 9, no. 1 (March 2008), pp. 115–29, University of Turku, Finland

Ceren Caner Berkman, 'Comparative Analyses for the Central Asian Contribution to Anatolian Gene Pool with Reference to Balkans', Thesis submitted to Graduate School of Natural and Applied Sciences, Middle Eastern Technical University, September 2006

William Joseph Bullen III, 'The Dynamic Between National Identity and Foreign Policy in Turkey', Thesis submitted to the Naval Postgraduate School, Monterey, California, December 2009

Michael M. Gunter, 'Political Instability in Turkey during the 1970s', *Conflict Quarterly*, journals.lib.unb.ca/index.php/JCS/article/download/14835/15904

Mahfud Junaedi, 'Imam Hatip School: Islamic School in Contemporary Secular Turkey', *Analisa Journal of Social Science and Religion*, vol. 1, no. 1 (June 2016)

Aram Yardumian and Theodore G. Schurr, 'Who Are the Anatolian Turks? A Reappraisal of the Anthropological Genetic Evidence',

*Anthropology & Archeology of Eurasia*, vol. 50, no. 1 (Summer 2011), pp. 6–42

M. Hakan Yavuz, 'Political Islam and the Welfare (Refah) Party in Turkey', *Comparative Politics*, vol. 30, no. 1 (October 1997), pp. 63–82

Reyhan Zetler, 'Turkish Jews between 1923 and 1933 – What Did the Turkish Policy between 1923 and 1933 Mean for the Turkish Jews?' *Bulletin der Schweizerischen Gesellschaft für Judaistische Forschung*, nr 23 (2014)

Sinan Zeyneloğlu, Ibrahim Sirkeci, Yaprak Civelek, 'Language Shift Among Kurds in Turkey: A Spatial and Demographic Analysis', *Kurdish Studies*, vol. 4, no. 1 (2016)

## Books

S. A. Arjomand (ed.), *From Nationalism to Revolutionary Islam* (London: Palgrave Macmillan, 1984)

H. C. Armstrong, *Gray Wolf: Mustafa Kemal* (London: Penguin Books, 1937)

Mustafa Kemal Atatürk, K.F. Kohler (trans.), *Nutuk* (The Long Speech) (Kindle edition)

Bülent Batuman, *New Islamist Architecture and Urbanism* (London: Routledge, 2017)

Frank Bovenkerk and Yücel Yeşilgöz, *The Turkish Mafia: A History of the Heroin Godfathers* (Lancashire: Milo Books, 2007)

Soner Cagaptay, *The New Sultan: Erdogan and the Crisis of Modern Turkey* (London: IB Tauris, 2017)

İpek Çalişlar, *Madam Atatürk* (London: Saqi Books, 2014)

Ali Çarkoğlu and Barry Rubin (eds), *Religion and Politics in Turkey* (London: Routledge, 2006)

S. Conermann and G. Haig (eds.) *Die Kurden: Studien zu ihrer Sprache, Geschichte und Kultur* (Schenefeld: EB-Verlag, 2003)

Umut Duyar-Kienast, *The Formation of Gecekondu Settlements in Turkey: The Case of Ankara* (Munich: LIT Verlag, 2005)

Andrew Finkel, *Turkey: What Everyone Needs to Know* (New York: Oxford University Press, 2012)

Zsa Zsa Gabor, *One Lifetime Is Not Enough* (New York: Delacorte Press, 1991)

Michael L. Galaty and Charles Watkinson (eds), *Archaeology Under Dictatorship* (Berlin: Springer, 2004)

George W. Gawrych, *The Young Atatürk: From Ottoman Soldier to Statesman of Turkey* (London: IB Tauris, 2015)

O. R. Gurney, *The Hittites* (London: Penguin Books, 1952)

M. Şükrü Hanioğlu, *Atatürk: An Intellectual Biography* (Princeton & Oxford: Princeton University Press, 2011)

Joshua D. Hendrick, *Gülen: The Ambiguous Politics of Market Islam in Turkey and the World* (New York: NYU Press, 2013)

Edward Hoare, *Rome, Turkey and Jerusalem* (London: Hatchards, 1876)

Bettany Hughes, *Istanbul: A Tale of Three Cities* (London: Weidenfeld and Nicolson, 2017)

Ali Kazancigil and Ergun Özbudun (eds), *Atatürk: Founder of a Modern State* (London: C. Hurst & Co., 1981)

Sylvia Kedourie (ed.), *Turkey Before and After Atatürk: Internal and External Affairs* (London: Routledge, 1999)

Charles King, *Midnight at the Pera Palace: The Birth of Modern Istanbul* (New York: W. W. Norton & Company, 2015)

Patrick Kinross, *Atatürk: The Rebirth of a Nation* (London: Weidenfeld and Nicolson, 1964)

Stephen Kinzer, *Crescent and Star: Turkey Between Two Worlds* (New York: Farrar, Straus and Giroux, 2001)

Jacob Landau, *Exploring Ottoman and Turkish History* (London: C. Hurst & Co., 2004)

T. E. Lawrence, *The Seven Pillars of Wisdom* (London: Jonathan Cape, 1935)

Sean McMeekin, *The Ottoman Endgame* (London: Penguin, 2015)

Andrew Mango, *Atatürk* (New York: Harry N. Abrams, 2002)

Andrew Mango, *Turkey and the War on Terror: 'For Forty Years We Fought Alone'* (London: Routledge, 2005)

Aliza Marcus, *Blood and Belief: The PKK and the Kurdish Fight for Independence* (New York: NYU Press, 2007)

Chris Morris, *The New Turkey: The Quiet Revolution on the Edge of Europe* (London: Granta, 2005)

Abdullahi Ahmed An-Na'im, *Islam and the Secular State: Negotiating the Future of Sharia* (Cambridge, MA, and London: Harvard University Press, 2008)

Kerem Öktem, *Angry Nation: Turkey since 1989* (London: Zed Books, 2011)

Şemsa Özar, Nesrin Uçarlar and Osman Aytar, *From Past to Present: A Paramilitary Organisation in Turkey* (Diyarbakır: DİSA Publications, 2013)

Ezra Özyürek, *Nostalgia for the Modern: State Secularism and Everyday Politics in Turkey* (Durham: Duke University Press, 2006)

George Perkovich and Sinan Ülgen, *Turkey's Nuclear Future* (Washington DC: Carnegie Endowment for International Peace, 2015)

David L. Phillips, *An Uncertain Ally: Turkey under Erdogan's Dictatorship* (London: Routledge, 2017)

Hugh Pope, *Dining with Al Qaeda* (New York: Thomas Dunne Books, 2010)

Eugene Rogan, *The Fall of the Ottomans* (New York: Basic Books, 2016)

Raja M. Ali Saleem, *State, Nationalism, and Islamization: Historical Analysis of Turkey and Pakistan* (London: Palgrave, 2017)

Alev Scott, *Turkish Awakening: A Personal Discovery of Modern Turkey* (London: Faber and Faber, 2014)

Jeremy Seal, *A Fez of the Heart* (New York: Mariner Books, 1996)

Aaron Stein, *Turkey's New Foreign Policy: Davutoglu, the AKP and the Pursuit of Regional Order* (London: Routledge, 2014)

Norman Stone, *Turkey* (London: Thames and Hudson, 2014)

Witold Szablowski, *The Assassin from Apricot City* (London: Stork Press, 2013)

Kabir Tambar, *The Reckoning of Pluralism* (Stanford: Stanford University Press, 2014)

Paul Theroux, *The Pillars of Hercules* (New York: Ballantine Books, 1996)

Nesrin Uçarlar, *Nothing in Its Right Place* (Diyarbakır: DİSA
   Publications, 2013)

Carla de la Vega, *Honour, Heels and Headscarves: Real-Life Stories of
   Women from Istanbul* (Ebook: self-published, 2014)

Jenny White, *Muslim Nationalism and the New Turks* (Princeton:
   Princeton University Press, 2012)

Christopher S. Wilson, *Beyond Anitkabir: The Funerary Architecture of
   Atatürk* (London: Routledge, 2013)

# INDEX